Association Football and English Society

1863–1915

Association Football and English Society

1863–1915

TONY MASON
Senior Lecturer in Social History, Centre for the Study of
Social History, University of Warwick

THE HARVESTER PRESS . SUSSEX
HUMANITIES PRESS . NEW JERSEY

First published in Great Britain in 1980 by
THE HARVESTER PRESS LIMITED
Publisher: John Spiers
16 Ship Street, Brighton, Sussex
and in the USA by
HUMANITIES PRESS INC.,
Atlantic Highlands, New Jersey 07716

© Tony Mason, 1980

British Library Cataloguing in Publication Data
Mason, Tony
  Association football and English society,
  1863–1915.
  1. Soccer—Social aspects—England
  I. Title
  301.5'7   GV944.G7
  ISBN 0–85527–797–1

Humanities Press Inc.
ISBN 0–391–01718–7

Printed and bound in Great Britain by
Redwood Burn Limited, Trowbridge and Esher and
Photoset by Thomson Press (India) Limited, New Delhi

If you would like to receive regular news on Harvester Press publications, please
send your name and address to our Publicity Department, The Harvester
Press Ltd., 16 Ship Street, Brighton, Sussex. We will then send you our new
announcements and catalogues and special notices of publications in your fields
of interest.

Contents

List of Illustrations

Figures

Appendices

List of Tables

'Because if we happened, just happened, to discover, or even suspect, that our spontaneity was part of their order, we'd know that we were lost.'

Tom Stoppard *Rosencrantz and Guildenstern are Dead* (1967) Act 2 pp. 42–43.

The English were 'a nation of footballers, stock exchangers, public-house and music-hall frequenters.' Mr. D. Lloyd George M.P. from his presidential speech to the annual music festival of Welsh nonconformist choirs at Cardiff, February 5 1896.

John Grigg *Young Lloyd George* (1973) p. 202.

ACKNOWLEDGEMENTS

No historian finishes any piece of work without owing something to other scholars, libraries and those organisations who allowed him access to their records. I am especially grateful to the Secretaries of the Football Association, Football League, Professional Footballers' Association, Birmingham and District Football Association and Lancashire Football Association who permitted me to look at their archives. Aston Villa Football Club and Derby County Football Club also let me look at minute books and although retaining no records to speak of I would like to thank Bolton Wanderers, Leicester City, Liverpool, Manchester City, Nottingham Forest and Preston North End for their friendly interest.

Many libraries have been helpful but in particular I would like to thank the staffs of the public libraries in Birmingham, Blackburn, Bolton and Sheffield. Many happy hours have been spent at the newspaper branch of the British Library at Colindale where, if the staff were not always cheerful, they usually brought you your papers in the end. Finally I must mention the support provided by the staff of the University Library at Warwick, in particular the ladies on inter-library loans and Mr Jolyon Hall.

This book would have been written long ago if it had not been for the staff and students at the Centre for the Study of Social History, but it has to be admitted that it would have been worse than it is without exposure to their athletic intellects. Many individuals have provided references but Margaret Elsworth, David Englander, Laurence Marlow and Michael Shepherd were particularly energetic in this respect.

Harry Dickinson, John Field, Chris Fisher, Simon Frith, Royden Harrison, David Martin, Valerie Mason and Jay Winter all read the manuscript and they will know what the final version owes to them although of course it is not their fault. Jean Oswin typed it splendidly and Mary Merrell drew the maps.

Last, but not least, I would like to thank Daniel and Elizabeth Fine of Ealing whose hospitality made my visits to London so much more enjoyable.

INTRODUCTION

ONE thing that mattered to most working men in late Victorian England was how they spent the time when they were not at work. It is a history still largely to be written.[1] By 1900, a considerable minority of the male population spent at least some of their leisure time either playing or watching sport. The game which attracted them most strongly during the months from September to April each year was association football.[2] Any history of the English working class in this period ought not to neglect the growth of interest in sport in general and football in particular. Such an analysis will not provide an explanation of why late Victorian and Edwardian England did not undergo a revolution. Nor will it account for the fact that the Socialist movement remained the province of a small number of more or less dedicated activists. But what it will do is add to the store of knowledge about the quality of working-class life and of what the possibilities were in an area where an element of choice existed.

The attractions of football are easy to list but difficult to arrange in any explanatory order. It was, and is, a simple game, easy to play and follow. Relatively little equipment was required to join in. It was inexpensive to play and could be played almost anywhere, even in the streets of towns. The player did not need to be possessed of extraordinary physical characteristics. The game could be enjoyed with less than eleven-a-side or more. Football has, and had, that combination of spontaneity and order which allowed scope for individuality and unpredictability within an organised, disciplined context.

Most historians are agreed that it was in the Victorian period that the separation between work and leisure first became clearly established. Industrial work rhythms, especially in the factory, led to a much clearer demarcation between time that was work and time that was not. Moreover, this change was accompanied by the rapid growth of towns which provoked the diminution of customary forms of behaviour and opened the way for new choices. Finally both economic expansion and town development helped to stimulate a demand for leisure by 'eroding traditional constraints on the utilization of non-work time'.[3] The suppliers who met this new demand varied from capitalist entrepreneurs

I

and voluntary associations to local authorities. By the end of the nineteenth century these organisations and individuals were in some sense competing against each other in what might be termed a mass leisure market. Certainly, as some voluntary associations, churches for example, came to realise, the individual male member of all classes had more choice as to what he did with his spare time in the 1890s than ever before.[4]

Members of the professional and commercial middle classes were the first to obtain the Saturday half holiday. Nonetheless it should not be forgotten that many groups of skilled workers took Saint Mondays off.[5] The Royal Commission on the Employment of Children in 1843 concluded that it was common practice in many districts to finish work at an early hour on Saturday afternoon although it seems that only in Lancashire and western Scotland was it very widespread.[6] It is no coincidence that both were textile districts and it was the concern over the long hours of 'dependent' female and child labour in textile factories which produced the Factory Act of 1850 and a cessation of work in textile mills on Saturdays at 2 p.m. As Bienefeld points out it is hardly surprising that Manchester, the centre of the cotton trade, should be the first major British city in which the shorter Saturday was obtained by all trades.[7]

The first working men in England to stop at 1 p.m. on Saturdays may well have been the engineers who were employed by Worsdells of Birmingham in 1853. Richard Tangye, later to become a powerful industrialist in the city, also worked at Worsdells. He read an article advocating the closing of works from one o'clock on Saturdays and the paying of the wages of the workmen on Fridays. At that time Worsdells' men stopped work at 4.30 p.m. on Saturdays and then had to wait, sometimes for up to two hours, while the correct amount to pay them was worked out. As Tangye's biographer so neatly understated it, it was 'a fruitful cause of ill-humour'.[8] Tangye suggested the adoption of the new scheme as an experiment and both management and men acknowledged its success.

Working men in the second half of the nineteenth century gained the Saturday half-holiday at different times, depending on job, employer and geographical location. In Liverpool, for example, stonemasons, coachmakers, building workers, some cabinet makers, railway, canal and carrying company employees all achieved an early Saturday, finishing work between 12 noon and 2 p.m. during the years 1857–62. By the early 1870s, most skilled workers in the city had Saturday afternoon off but it was the late 1880s or early 1890s before most of the unskilled labour force, dockers and carters for example, had a similar privilege. In fact, the dockworkers did not win it until April 1890.[9] It is interesting to compare Liverpool with Birmingham where most workers did not work on Saturday afternoons from the early 1870s.[10]

There were still large groups of workers who did not have Saturday afternoon off in the 1870s: shift workers of various kinds, most notably in transport, and shop assistants were obvious exceptions to an increasingly general rule, certainly so far as the bulk of skilled workers was concerned. Saturday afternoon became the great time for football playing and watching in winter and cricket playing and watching in summer. That the expansion of those two games from the 1870s in particular is connected with the coming of the Saturday half-day can hardly be in doubt. Organised sport could only be played on an English Sunday with difficulty. Certainly money could not be taken at the gate. The period from 1870–1915 is punctuated by complaints that unorganised games of football were being played on the Sabbath. As Shaftesbury had said in 1856 when supporting the idea of an early finish to work on Saturday, 'if Saturday were reduced to the condition of an ordinary working day' Sunday worship might be impaired.[11] As Lowerson and Myerscough point out (p. 30) the annual holiday, the shorter working week and the weekly half-day off were a unique experience in nineteenth-century Europe and go far to explain Britain's dominant influence in the development of new forms of recreation. It is the emergence of one of these new forms, association football, with which this book is concerned.

A preoccupation with two main issues first prompted me to begin work on this book. First, how far was football in this period a working-class game? What might be meant by so calling it? Did it mean that it was a game devised by working men to be played and watched by them? Was it a game developed by other social formations and in some way taken over by working men? Or was it a game which was originated by working men but later dominated by other social formations? These considerations led directly to the second major issue. How far was the game of association football professionalised and staged by a new breed of tertiary sector entrepreneurs who saw mass leisure and especially professional sport as a medium for getting rich quickly? Was the soul of the game perverted by the need to create a spectacle which would attract the largest number of paying customers?

Concern with these two issues recurs throughout the text. But they could hardly be examined in a satisfactory way without asking the more prosaic, detailed, but essential questions such as who played and who watched, who bought shares in football clubs and why, who sat on club committees and, later, boards of directors, and how far a specific middle-class response to the game and a specific working-class response can be identified.

The structure of the book is a straightforward one. The first chapter looks at the origins of the organised game and considers the role of public school and university educated, young men in devising a body of rules and persuading large numbers of players to accept them. In order to provide an essential minimum of background knowledge for the more detailed chapters to follow, the chapter ends with a sketch of the game's main structural and organisational developments from the founding of the Football Association in 1863.

Chapter two looks more closely at football clubs, how they were formed, who were the members and who were the responsible officials. An attempt is made to estimate the growth in club numbers in the half century from 1863. The adoption of limited liability by a majority of professional clubs has made it possible to sample the records of companies in order to discover the occupational background of club shareholders and directors and the chapter ends with a discussion of their motives for becoming financially involved with the clubs.

The third chapter describes the advent of professionalism and the conflict which surrounded its coming. It is difficult to characterise simply those who were in favour of professionalism and those who were against. In any event the second group were certainly divided into those who were unhappy but resigned to the change and a number of more diehard opponents. The differences of opinion on the subject were overlaid by rivalries of north and south or perhaps, more accurately, London against the provinces and these were probably just as important in determining attitudes as whether a man had attended a public school or not. The split over professionalism did not produce a clear conflict between public school and university men on the one hand and self-made traders and manufacturers from the midlands and north of England on the other; some of the truth lies here but certainly not the whole of it.

Chapter four examines, in as much detail as the sources will allow, the players, both those who were paid and those, the vast majority, who were not. Much more is known about the first group and the major part of the chapter concentrates on the professional player, his wages, conditions and later prospects.

The football spectator is the subject of the fifth chapter. An attempt will be made to answer the question, what sort of people went to football matches in the last three decades of the nineteenth century and the years before the First World War? Crowd behaviour will be analysed. The increasingly large assembly of spectators was one of the most distinctive features of the professional game and it may be that where association football is called a working-class game then it is the crowd phenomenon that commentators had in mind. If rugby football was a hooligan's game played by gentlemen, then association was a gentlemen's game not only played by hooligans but also watched by them.

An important accompaniment to the growth of association football was those activities which both stimulated its development and profited from it. Football gave rise to a new kind of newspaper, the Saturday evening sports special, and the expansion of the game was mirrored by the extension of the coverage offered by all classes of newspaper, daily and weekly, local and national, as well as specialist sporting. Football results and match reports, like racing tips and results, sold papers, particularly from the 1890s onwards. Nor was it only the professional elite on which the press concentrated although it was the matches in which members of that elite took part which were given the most space. Organised local amateur football was featured in most local newspapers from an early date and a further if unquantifiable dimension was thus added to the attraction of the game as a social event. Chapter six also examines the relationship between drink and gambling, and football. The evidence is not conclusive as to how far both of these activities were part and parcel of the football experience of both players and spectators although drinking appears to have been more common than betting.

Chapter seven concentrates on activities on the field of play itself. An attempt is made in this chapter to describe the kind of game that might have been seen in the 1870s, 1880s and around the turn of the century. It was also felt that the leading professional clubs and players of the period ought to be identified and this is done here.

Finally chapter eight confronts the issue of the meaning of football both for the propertied elites of society on the one hand and the working classes on the other. It will be argued that these two groups did see the game in different ways and the discussion will hopefully bring us fruitfully back to that earlier question of how far association football could be considered to be a working-class game.

Most of the sources used for this study were published sources. The vast majority of football clubs of the period 1863–1915 have disappeared without trace and particularly without leaving behind them such things as written records. Some lasted for only a short period: others formed and reformed continually over time but most left little behind them for the historian save a few match results and the names of a handful of players in an old newspaper. Many have not left even that modest spoor. Even those semi-professional and professional clubs which have had a more or less continuous existence for one hundred years or so cannot be relied upon for exemplary record keeping. Although most of them currently employ a good many ancillary staff whose tasks and salaries would come as a surprise to Victorian and Edwardian club committees, no club has yet got round to appointing an archivist.[12] Most clubs do not have records for this period and those which do are extremely reluctant to let anyone look at them unless he is a club 'trusty'. The author asked to see the records of thirty-three current league clubs who were in existence before 1914. Of those thirty-three, eighteen claimed to have no records, seven had records but refused access, four clubs had a very small number of items which they were willing to show and only two clubs, Aston Villa and Derby County, had incomplete but interesting collections of materials, mainly the minutes of directors' meetings, which were open to examination. Two clubs could not be persuaded to reply.

Outside the clubs, the Football Association, the Football League and the Professional Footballers' Association were all as helpful as they could be but none of them possessed the detailed records which might have illuminated, for example, the occupations and age groups from which the Victorian and Edwardian professional player was recruited. This thinness of organisational or manuscript material, together with a relatively weak secondary literature[13] meant that considerable use had to be made of contemporary newspapers. Concentration has been on newspapers in Lancashire, Birmingham and Sheffield because those were the areas where the game grew fastest in the post-1870 period. Contemporary attitudes to the game were occasionally revealed in leading articles or editorials. Sports reporters sometimes strayed outside their immediate brief by describing something of the context in which particular matches took place but much searching of newspapers often produced very little in terms of hard data or opinion. The *Athletic News* has been relied upon rather heavily for two main reasons. First, because it had a continuous existence from 1875 to 1915—few other sports papers could boast such prosperity. Second, because of its increasing emphasis on association football from the early 1880s, together with its northern and midland orientation. Without this source it would have been even more difficult than it was to write this book. Other contemporary periodicals and newspapers were used less systematically but extensively as the footnotes indicate. The other, previously unexploited, major source which has been used in this book is the records of companies kept at Companies House. They provided the details of both directors' and shareholders' occupations which feature prominently in the analysis and description in chapter two.

Notes

1 The historiography of late Victorian leisure is growing. Asa Briggs was a pioneer with his essay 'Mass Entertainment: The Origin of a Modern Industry', 29th Joseph Fisher Lecture in Commerce, University of Adelaide, 1960. Helen Meller has examined the attempt of the middle class in Bristol between 1870 and 1914 to provide working people with improving things with which to fill their spare time. Stedman Jones's attempt to link the growing commercialism and conservatism of the London Music Hall with a remaking of the London working class has stimulated some work in that area as the 1975 Brighton conference of the Society for the Study of Labour History demonstrated. See the report in the *Bulletin* of the Society, no. 32, Spring 1976 pp. 5–18, and for the Stedman Jones article 'Working Class Culture and Working Class Politics in London 1870–1900: Notes on the remaking of a Working Class' see *Journal of Social History*, vol. 7, no. 4, Summer 1974. John Lowerson and John Myerscough have recently published *Time to Spare in Victorian England* (Brighton, 1977) which looked at some general problems through the local example of Sussex and in the autumn of 1977 *Victorian Studies*, vol. 21, no. 1, devoted a whole issue to the subject of leisure in Victorian Britain although only one article really represented the later years.

2 Historians have been reluctant to write about the rise of organised sport in the late nineteenth century. H.J. Dyos and M. Wolff (eds), *The Victorian City, Images and Realities*, 2 vols. (1973) contained no essays on Victorian sport, for example, and apart from Wray Vamplew's book on horse-racing, *The Turf: A Social and Economic History of Horse Racing* (1976), no work based on an examination of primary historical materials has appeared. James Walvin in *The People's Game* (1975) devoted only three chapters to football's origin and early history and did not really take his readers much beyond M. Marples, *History of Football* (1954) and P. M. Young, *A History of British Football* (1968).

3 M.R. Marrus (ed.), *The Emergence of Leisure* (New York, 1974) p. 9.

4   Of course, he probably often chose just to stay in. See R. Hoggart, *Uses of Literacy* (1976 edn) p. 35.

5   See D.A. Reid, 'The Decline of Saint Monday 1766–1876', *Past and Present*, 71, May 1976. It is possible that the occasional league football matches held on some Monday afternoons in Sheffield in the 1890s were a recognition of the fact that this practice still lived in some of the trades there.

6   M.A. Bienefeld, *Working Hours in British Industry* (1972) p. 71.

7   Although work seems to have stopped at 4 p.m. rather than 2 p.m. in most trades in the 1850s there, M.A. Bienefeld, pp. 79, 87, 94.

8   S.J. Reid, *Sir Richard Tangye* (1908) p. 41.

9   R. Rees, 'The Development of Physical Recreation in Liverpool During the Nineteenth Century', University of Liverpool, M.A. 1968, pp. 49–57.

10 Ibid. pp. 324–5. It is instructive that from October 1879 to March 1880, local newspapers in Birmingham listed 811 district football matches whereas the Liverpool press, in the same period, noted only two.

11 Letter to *The Times* quoted by Bienefeld, p. 85. For a typical complaint about Sunday football see *Glasgow Herald* 12 November 1891, *The Times* 31 January 1898.

12 Nor do archivists seem to be very interested in attempting the, admittedly Sisyphean, task of persuading football clubs to deposit what records they do have with them. A few local Football Association minute books have surfaced in county record offices.

13 Compare the much larger number of books on cricket, especially for this period.

CHAPTER ONE
ORIGINS AND DEVELOPMENT

THIS book is an attempt to write a social history of association football in the late Victorian and Edwardian periods. A variety of games of football had existed long before those years.[1] Before the coming of the railways, communications in Britain were far from good. Individual hamlets and villages, indeed whole regions, existed in an isolation difficult for us to appreciate. One result was the growth of essentially local customs and traditions in all areas of social life. So far as football was concerned, this isolation produced an infinite number of forms. Some games, for example, contained a lot of kicking, some a large amount of handling, and others various mixtures of the two. Similarly the nature of the ball varied from place to place: inflated animal bladders encased with leather in one locality; smaller and harder balls in another. The scene of the game also varied. The field of play might comprise a whole village or a large area of countryside. The goals might be well known local landmarks several miles apart. On the other hand the game might take place in a large field with wooden posts to mark the goals. Some games were subject to fairly detailed sets of rules and regulations designed in part to curb the activities of the more aggressive participants whereas others had few rules. Moreover, those which they did have were often in the form of customary practices and traditions handed down from one generation to the next. A large proportion of the male population of a community might take part in these games at the same time. On the other hand many games had fixed and relatively small numbers of players.

The main matches were played on holidays and festivals. Shrove Tuesday, a traditional holiday for apprentices in many parts of the country, was an especially popular day for football but Christmas and Easter also had their adherents. By the early nineteenth century different games of football were still being played at Alnwick and Chester-le-Street in the north, Derby and Ashbourne in the midlands, and Kingston-on-Thames in the south. There were almost certainly others.

Apart from the enjoyment of a traditional open air activity, such games had more important functions in the towns and villages of a still largely rural society. Especially in those places where the

9

matches amounted to community confrontations between village and village or parish and parish they contributed to community solidarity and to the clarification of social identity for players and spectators alike. A similar function can be attributed to games between members of different crafts and occupations. Apart from all the obvious social benefits accruing from a shared experience, such as the occasion to talk about it long afterwards, a skilled football player might receive an accession of status which, though not permanent, would be sweet enough while it lasted. It will be seen below that the standardised game which developed after 1860 fulfilled similar functions.

There is little doubt that most of the football played before the last four decades of the nineteenth century was rough. All games were not equally violent but those which were characterised by few restrictions on personal behaviour and involved large numbers of players and spectators often led to personal injury and damage to property. It is not surprising that local and national authorities often attempted to prevent football from being played. Every schoolboy knows, for example, that for two hundred years during the Middle Ages football was disliked because it was thought to distract young men from archery. Moreover, during the eighteenth century there is evidence that demonstrations against enclosures were organised by crowds which had ostensibly gathered to play or watch football. In one instance such a crowd initiated a food riot.[2] Further, as towns grew in size and became busier, the idea of playing football through the streets was not enthusiastically embraced by property holders or businessmen who disliked both the public disorder that such occasions often brought and the disruption of everyday commercial activities. The Highways Act of 1835 specifically prohibited the playing of football on the highway and fines of up to forty shillings could be levied on those who were caught. Industrial expansion and the growth of towns did much to bury old customs and traditions even among an urban population whose origins were largely rural. Moreover, in many country districts, enclosures took away those areas traditionally used for common sports and pastimes. The final nail in the coffin of rough football probably lay in the attitude of so many of the evangelicals towards games. 'Ethical values were more vigorously injected into play activities and it came to be assumed that if recreation was permissible at all, it must be "rational" and must prepare the mind and body for work, instead of being an end in itself.'[3] It is not without some irony that this attitude to games was to be taken up by the middle classes in the

public schools, transfused into the working classes by the mission-
aries of muscular Christianity and distorted, via professionalisa-
tion, into the mass spectator sports of the late Victorian and
Edwardian periods.

A kind of rough football not dissimilar to that played in many
places up and down the country was also played in the leading
public schools in the eighteenth century.[4] It was like its more
popular contemporary in that it did not have a fixed, written body
of rules and both its form and nature were dependent in part on
the configurations of the playing area and in part on oral tradition.
Any number of boys could usually play and matches might last
all afternoon or for just a few hours. The determination of senior
boys might be sufficient to modify customary practice.[5] The
public school game was also like the popular game in that each
public school played a game which was unique to itself with its
own special characteristics however similar to games at other
schools it might be in general.

But the public school version of rough football differed from
the more popular one in several important respects. In the first
place it had a clearly marked season and within that season was
regularly played either once or twice a week. Second, it was
played, not by the common people, but by the sons of the landed
aristocracy and the prosperous middle classes. Finally the development of the game was closely bound up with the prefect-fagging
system in the schools.[6]

By the end of the eighteenth century public school pupils
were mainly drawn from the upper classes. Unfortunately not all
the masters were and this fact seems to have placed something of
a strain on the relationships between the two groups. The public
schools at this time were inclined to be very disorderly institutions. Rebellions by the boys against the staff were by no means
uncommon; Winchester had six between 1770 and 1818 and
following one at Rugby in 1797 troops were called and the Riot
Act read.[7] Playing football was one of the ways in which the
senior boys dominated the other boys in the schools. It was usually
compulsory and the fags were generally forced to keep goal for the
bigger boys. Only the senior boys could play 'out'.[8]

During the 1830s and 1840s, the public schools, like several
other important institutions, and for largely the same reasons,.
underwent reform.[9] It was mainly middle-class pressure which
brought about the change. Not only did this aspiring class desire
easier access for their sons to the schools; they were also in favour
of a somewhat improved attitude to work among the pupils

and even more important, a raising of the standards of behaviour. This inevitably involved reestablishing the authority of the teachers. The prefect-fagging system was not abolished, however, partly because it was thought to stimulate a desirable independence among the senior boys, partly because it proved capable of adaptation to the new goals.

Rugby under Thomas Arnold, headmaster from 1828–42, was the classic reformed institution. Arnold aimed to produce an enlightened ruling class imbued with Christian principles and values. His priorities for the boys were, first, to inculcate religious and moral principles; second, to foster gentlemanly conduct; and finally to encourage the development of intellectual ability.[10] Arnold built up the sixth form to be his men, a moral elite who would set an example to the rest of the school. He appointed the prefects, controlled their activities and clarified both their duties and those of the fags.

What was the role of games in this new educational institution? It was clear that playing games did have certain advantages, both in keeping boys out of mischief on free afternoons, and in providing an experience in which masters and boys might share to the ultimate benefit of both.[11] But mid-Victorian schoolmasters of the Arnold stamp had a 'passion for knowledge ... inspired by the hope and conviction that knowledge was supremely worth while, that in the possession of wisdom lay the promise of a better world as well as the certainty of a better understanding of God's revelation and His purpose in creating men'.[12] If leisure was to have true educational value each boy must be given the opportunity to pursue his own interests. It was no part of the Arnoldian scheme to have all pupils compulsorily playing organised team games.[13] David Newsome has shown that before 1860 a wide variety of out-of-school-hours activities, of which games was one, took place in the schools. *Tom Brown's Schooldays*, published in 1857, was not a description of school life as it was, but more as it was to become. How did organised team games come to occupy such a dominant role in public school life and ideology in the period 1860–80?

Clearly the process was a complex one. Organised games already existed in the schools, as we have seen, and inter-school as opposed to intra-school matches had begun.[14] But the cult of athleticism appears to have had its origins in conflict within the established Church about both the nature of that Church and its relationship to the wider society. One product of this conflict was the 'muscular Christians' who embraced views about the nature of games which were to become widely accepted both in the public schools and outside.

The two men whose names are usually most closely associated with muscular Christianity are Thomas Hughes and Charles Kingsley. In fact, Kingsley was not a great lover of games but a man who enjoyed the robustness and vigour of all that nature had to offer. What he helped to do was to revise an older notion of what constituted manliness, changing it from, for him, an overly subtle, quasi-intellectual concern with maturity and the need for man to elevate his moral character to an emphasis on muscle and masculinity and enjoying life in all its splendid variety. Kingsley saw the introversion of the Tractarians and their concentration on other-worldliness as undermining the Anglican Church in the face of the serious problems posed by modern society.[15] Kingsley believed that the priesthood should tend their flocks, not merely by ministration and living among them, but in a language and by the adoption of ideals which ordinary people could comprehend and to which they could aspire.

Thomas Hughes believed that too, but he also believed that playing games did much to bring out manly qualities; not only assisting the development of co-operative ideas, but, even more important, leading to individual independence and self-reliance. Games provided the companionship of a shared experience and helped cultivate manly self-restraint. People could be taught, via games and in particular boxing, of which Hughes was very fond and a keen practitioner, how to keep their tempers.[16] Moreover, Hughes was able to put these values and beliefs between the covers of one of the most popular stories of the nineteenth century, *Tom Brown's Schooldays*, the prototype for a long series of muscular tales.

But of course the crisis of the Church was also a crisis of religion. Increasingly, as the third quarter of the nineteenth century wore on, the discoveries of science, encapsulated to some extent in the work of Darwin but by no means limited to it, together with the development of new attitudes towards intellectual inquiry brought about a crisis of belief, especially among intellectuals. Such a complex subject can hardly be done justice to here. Suffice it to say that more and more thinking men found themselves unable to enter the priesthood and the balance among the clergy began to tip away from the more intellectual and towards the heartier, games playing recruit. The balance was on the move in the public schools also. It was facilitated there by the abolition, in 1877, of the rule that resident Oxbridge college fellows must remain unmarried. Not surprisingly, moreover, men who had enjoyed their games at school saw in schoolmastering a way of prolonging that enjoyment.

Furthermore, by the 1860s a growth of publicly expressed patriotism, an increased consciousness of Britain's exalted position in the world, coupled with the first suspicion of serious threat to that position in the expansion of Prussia and the emergence after the Civil War of a properly United States, contributed to an increasing concern with achievement and physical fitness. It was a concern articulated at the Public Schools Commission. It was to be returned to frequently as the century progressed and international competition and rivalries stiffened.[17]

With the reform of the public schools went the reform of the rough football which had previously been played there. Between 1845 and 1862 pupils and staff between them had written down the rules of the football games played at the seven leading public schools. The games were still on the physical side of robust.[18] After all, manliness in its new guise consisted very largely of being able to give and take hard knocks without malice. But a process of reconciliation was in train between spontaneity and vigour on the one hand and control and moderation on the other. There was now less chance of serious physical injury, an important factor for young men hoping to make their way in the world and even more crucial if football was to be accepted as a proper game for young gentlemen after their schooldays were over.[19] Of course, some of them wished to go on playing at university and it was at Cambridge, first in 1848 and then in the 1860s, that formal and informal experiments finally produced a body of rules that appeared to have a fairly wide acceptance.[20] It was not until 1882 that all football players in the United Kingdom outside the public schools accepted what came to be known as association or rugby rules, although a spectacular expansion in the numbers playing both games had taken place some time before.[21]

In the 1860s there was the first of several middle-class missions to the people which were to be such a feature of the remainder of the nineteenth century. This increasing concern by one social group about the problems of another was hardly disinterested. It was stimulated by the mid-1860s trade depression and the apparent increase in pauperism that accompanied it; and by the activities of trade unionists both industrially and politically, especially their co-operation with middle-class radicals in the Reform League which pressurised Parliament into giving a million working men the vote in 1867. 'A healthy mind in a healthy body' was a slogan manifested in the growth of the new working men's clubs as well as in games like football.[22] It was the call sign of the muscular Christians and it was to beam out strongly over the next two decades as the most popular justification for the expansion, amounting to almost manic proportions, of games in general, and football in particular.

The Football Association was formed by the representatives of a small number of mainly southern clubs in 1863. It was basically an agreement between them to play each other under the same set of rules. Thirty clubs had joined by 1868.[23] By that year, another association of football clubs had come into being in Sheffield. As we shall see below in chapter two the Sheffield Football Club had been going since the late 1850s and in 1866 had visited London where a match against a Football Association eleven had been played. Moreover, there had already been some discussion between the two bodies about the differences in their respective rule books.[24] Although agreement on a single code of laws could not at first be reached, the new Secretary of the Football Association, Charles Alcock, took a team from London to Sheffield at the beginning of December 1871.[25]

The fact that London could play Sheffield in 1871 suggests that the two associations were moving towards a compromise over their different rules and in April 1877 one set of laws was finally achieved with some of the Sheffield ideas, notably relating to the corner-kick, for example, being adopted by the London organisation.[26] This arrangement with the Sheffield F.A. did much to strengthen the position of the Football Association in London as the game's leading authority. Moreover, by the mid-1870s, other associations were growing and affiliating. The Birmingham F.A. was set up in 1875–6 and Lancashire in 1878. Further local football associations claiming jurisdiction in their areas were organised in London, Norfolk, Oxfordshire, Essex and Sussex in 1882 and Berkshire and Buckingham (Berks and Bucks), Walsall and District, Kent, Nottinghamshire (Notts.), Middlesex, Liverpool and District, Cheshire, Staffordshire, Derbyshire and Scarborough and the East Riding in 1883. After the speed of this expansion the other most significant fact to notice was that all these local associations looked to the F.A. itself and wished to affiliate with it.

It was also in 1882 that the International Board, comprising the English, Irish, Scottish and Welsh Football Associations was established and an agreement reached on such knotty problems as the size of the ball and the way it should be thrown in from touch. Fixed crossbars as opposed to tapes were also deemed essential as were clearly marked touchlines. From 1882, one set of rules for the playing of association football was accepted nationwide.[27]

Alcock's importance in this early period of the game's growth is well known. Almost from the time he first collected the minute book in 1870 he initiated the England against Scotland matches and it was he who introduced the idea of a knock-out cup competition between member clubs, the F.A. Cup, which was first competed for in 1871-2. It was apparently based on the cock house competition at Harrow where Alcock had been at school. The consolidation of the F.A. was obviously helped by his energy and the fact that he kept the job for twenty-five years.[28]

The Football Association, originally an association of clubs, was by the mid-1880s an association of county and district associations together with a limited number of clubs in direct membership. These clubs were in the main the larger and more powerful ones, professional and urban after 1885. Of the thousand or so clubs in England in the late 1880s only 200 were directly affiliated to the Football Association. The rest were connected by virtue of their membership with local football associations. At this period only twelve local F.A.'s qualified for a seat on the F.A.'s governing council by having at least fifty clubs in membership. Local football associations ran their own cup competitions and in general dealt with player discipline in their area. The Football Association was the ultimate authority for all football, both amateur and professional. It oversaw the laws of the game. It organised the F.A. Cup and, in conjunction with the F.A.'s of Ireland, Scotland and Wales, the home international championship. It also dealt with any matters brought to it by member clubs and associations. It is not surprising that it had to seek a permanent office in 1880 nor that six years later the Secretary became a salaried official.[29]

The Football League was a quite separate organisation of initially twelve clubs which recognised the F.A.'s overall responsibility for all football while largely running its own internal affairs. It arose out of the plethora of cup competitions of the 1880s which disrupted the previously arranged friendly fixtures between more or less equally matched sides and produced, especially in the early rounds of the cups, games between sides of unequal ability which were unattractive to spectators.[30] Occasionally major clubs, although drawn at home, were prepared to play on the ground of a lesser club where they would be a bigger attraction at the gate and in theory have an easy passage into the next round.

Needless to say the desired result was not always obtained. In 1885 Aston Villa agreed to transfer their cup-tie with the young, unfashionable and apparently weak Derby County from Birmingham to Derby. The gate was good but Villa lost 2–0.[31]

The league idea was probably taken over from American baseball. Clubs would contract to play 'home and home' matches with each other on fixed dates through the season. Based on the notion of two points for a win and one for a drawn match, an eventual champion would emerge. It was hoped that such a competition between the leading teams would maintain spectator interest and limit the financially damaging disruptions of cup-ties.

Notes

1 What follows is largely based on R.W. Malcolmson, 'Popular Recreations in English Society 1700–1850', University of Warwick, unpublished Ph.D. thesis, 1970.

2 The food riot was in 1740 at Kettering. Northamptonshire was also the scene of protests against enclosure by a football crowd in 1765. Malcolmson, op. cit. pp. 89–91.

3 Malcolmson, op. cit. p. 362.

4 What follows is based largely on the work of D. Newsome, *Godliness and Good Learning* (1961) and E. Dunning, 'The Development of Modern Football', in E. Dunning (ed.) *The Sociology of Sport: A Selection of Readings* (1971) pp. 133–51. The seven leading public schools in this period were: Charterhouse, Eton, Harrow, Rugby, Shrewsbury, Westminster and Winchester. See also J.R. de S. Honey, *Tom Brown's Universe* (1977).

5 Dunning, op. cit. pp. 137–8.

6 Ibid. p. 135.

7 For more details of these activities see E.C. Mack, *Public Schools and British Opinion 1760–1860* (1938) pp. 79–82.

8 In relatively unorganised scratch games between groups of boys today it is noteworthy that rarely does anyone volunteer to play in goal. The weakest, that is to say the fattest or most junior in terms of years, or the least accomplished of the players, is invariably placed in that position.

9 See T.W. Bamford, 'Public Schools and Social Class 1801–1850', *British Journal of Sociology*, XII no. 3, September 1961. Reform was probably easier to initiate at Rugby than at Eton or Harrow because there were few sons of aristocrats at Rugby.

10 Newsome, op. cit. p. 34.

11 Edward Thring, headmaster of Uppingham 1853–87, believed that games allowed mixing between staff and boys, trained character and provided a healthy competitive environment especially in so far as it helped those boys not so good in class to restore self-respect and win praise. But games were to be only part of a coherent programme of physical education which was also to include country pursuits, gymnastics and athletics. M. Tozer

'The Development and Role of Physical Education at Uppingham School 1850–1914' University of Leicester M.Ed. 1974, pp. 82–5.

12 Ibid. p. 80.

13 Marlborough was probably more of a pioneer in the use of games and sports in education. See P.C. McIntosh, *Sport in Society* (1968) p. 6. See J.R. de S. Honey, op.cit. pp. 104–10, on the way headmasters Cotton and Bradley used organised games to combat indiscipline at Marlborough in the 1850s and 1860s.

14 Eton and Harrow first played each other at cricket in 1818 and regularly from 1822. Rugby first played Marlborough at cricket in 1855. Inter-school football matches started rather later, as would be expected given the variety of different forms of the game. Some writers felt that a compromise between the schools would be impossible to achieve. See F. Wood in *Beaton's Football Book* (1865) pp. 6–7. Wood was, *inter alia*, editor of *Every Boy's Magazine*. For a suggestion that public schools should cast aside 'prejudice and sentiment' and abolish their own games in favour of rugby or association football see the editorial in *Football*, 29 December 1882. Even then some schools were reluctant. Uppingham did not relinquish its own football game in favour of rugby until 1889 and did not begin playing other schools until ten years later. M. Tozer, op.cit. pp. 219–20. Athleticism was also on the march at Oxbridge, with colleges purchasing playing fields and putting back the hour of dinner from 3 p.m. to 4 or 5 p.m. and eventually later. J.R. de S. Honey, op.cit. p. 110. See also *The Field* 23 October 1875.

15 On the way in which the content of manliness was changed see N. Vance, 'The Ideal of Manliness', in B. Simon and I. Bradley (eds) *The Victorian Public School* (1975) pp. 115–28. On muscular Christianity see H.R. Harrington, 'Muscular Christianity: the study of the Development of a Victorian Idea', unpublished Ph.D. Thesis, Stanford University, 1971. Also Newsome, op.cit. pp. 196–9. 'It is this second stage of Tractarianism— when the Oxford Movement went out of Oxford, when 'Puseyite' became the chief form in which its impact was felt by the country at large—that provided the greatest stimulus to the doctrine which represented its complete antithesis—muscular christianity.' Ibid. p. 208.

16 Though he did not like being punched on the nose. See E.C. Mack and W.H.G. Armytage, *The Life of Thomas Hughes* (1952) p. 80. Newsome, op.cit. pp. 212, 214–15.

17 Note the importance of the war scare in 1859 which, *inter alia*, produced the Volunteer Movement, for which see Hugh Cunningham, *The Volunteer Force* (1975).

Bodily training ... is imparted at the English schools, not by the gymnastic exercises ... employed on the continent but by athletic games, which, while they serve their purpose well, serve other purposes besides. ... The cricket and football fields ... are not merely places of exercise and amusement: they help to form some of the most valuable social qualities and manly virtues. ... They hold ... a distinct and important place in public school education.

Royal Commission on the Public Schools XX, 1864, vol. I, p. 56.

18 Indeed Frederick Wood in 1865 criticised 'the indisputably dangerous nature of the modes of play generally in vogue in our great schools—too rough, indeed, for the more brittle bones and less reckless temperaments of adult players'. *Beaton's Football Book*, op.cit. p. 6.

19 The argument that businessmen did not want to be injured and therefore unable to work, and that they would not play if remnants of the old violence such as deliberate hacking were not made illegal by the laws, was a feature of the split in the group of ex-public school men who met to form the Football Association in the autumn of 1863. Darwen Football Club was supposed to have played both Harrow and Rugby rules until 1875 and changed to association following an accident to one of their founder members. J.A.H. Catton, *The Real Football* (1900) p. 44. See also a letter to the *Athletic News* 23 October 1875 in which association was labelled science and rugby as brute force. A.H. Fabian and G. Green (eds), *Association Football*, 4 vols. (1960) vol. I, p. 52. For the interesting idea that the 1863 differences sprang from earlier status rivalry between the public schools of Eton and Rugby see E.E. Dunning, 'Industrialisation and the Incipient Modernisation of Football', *Stadion*, vol. I, no. 1, 1975, pp. 103–39.

20 This is a well known story and a good account of it may be found in P.M. Young, *A History of British Football* (1968) pp. 89–101. Though the possibility that there may have been a more generally accepted form of the game before this is suggested by a description of football in the *Boy's Own Book* for 1859.

A match is made between two sets of players of equal numbers; a large ball made of light materials—a blown bladder, or an india-rubber ball, cased with leather is the best—is placed within them and the object of each party is to kick the ball across the goal of the other, and to prevent it from passing their own ... the two goals ... are generally about a hundred yards asunder. The rustic boys use a sow's bladder, without the covering of leather, for a foot-ball, putting peas and horse-beans inside, which occasion a rattling sound as it is kicked about.

Boy's Own Book (1859) pp. 22–3. On the other hand their description of the game is suspiciously like that in J. Strutt, *The Sports and Pastimes of the People of England* (1903 edn, first published 1801) p. 94.

21 See A. Gibson and W. Pickford, *Association Football and the Men Who Made It* (1906) 4 vols., vol. I, p. 72. For the early years of rugby football see K.G. Sheard, 'Rugby Football: A Study in Developmental Sociology', unpublished M. Phil. thesis, University of Leicester, 1972.

22 On the growth of admiration for the healthy mind in a healthy body ideal see Vance, op.cit. p. 125 and below, especially chapter eight. For examples of contemporary comment see W.H. Davenport, *Secret of Success* (1879) p. xiii and the editorial in the *Athletic News* 28 September 1881.

23 Of the 39 clubs affiliated by 1870, only 4 were still in existence in 1900. N.L. Jackson, *Association Football* (1900 edn) pp. 86–7.

24 For more detail see P.M. Young, *Football in Sheffield* (1962) chapters 1 and 2.

25 Sheffield won the match 3–1.

26 P.M. Young (1962) op.cit. pp. 31–2. The Sheffield Association contained 26 member clubs in 1877.

27 For more detailed comments on rule changes see chapter seven below.

28 He resigned in 1895 having been salaried Secretary at £200 per year since 1886–7. Born in 1842, he had helped to form the Wanderers F.C. in 1864. He was a journalist, specialising in cricket and football on *The Sportsman* and *The Field*. He was first elected to the F.A. committee in 1866 and became honorary Secretary in 1870. Two years later he became Secretary of the

Surrey County Cricket Club at a salary of £250 p.a. In 1868 he initiated the *Football Annual* and was later associated with several other annuals and periodicals including *Football*, begun with N.L. Jackson in 1882 and the small handbook explaining the rules of the game entitled the *National Football Calendar* which first appeared in 1881. He died in 1907. See N.L. Jackson (1900 edn) op.cit. pp. 143–5. W.G. Grace, *'W.G.': Cricket Reminiscences and Personal Recollections* (1899) p. 124.

29   The most detailed account of the administrative development of the F.A. is in G. Green, *History of the Football Association* (1953) esp. pp. 83–91, 119–23 and 179–80.

30   The Football Association recognised this problem by reorganising its own competition in 1888–9. The previously monolithic competition was divided into two parts, a qualifying competition and a competition proper with the previous season's four semi-finalists plus the eighteen best clubs, in effect the leading professional sides, excused the first part. All the other entrants were divided into ten groups on a geographical basis with the winner of each group joining the other twenty-two in the first round proper. For N.L. Jackson this was another triumph for business over sport. N.L. Jackson (1900 edn) op.cit. p. 118.

31   *Derby Daily Telegraph* 1 February 1896.

CHAPTER TWO
THE CLUBS

THIS chapter explores the nature of the late nineteenth-century football club. In particular, it looks at the varied origins of the clubs and, after a brief attempt to measure the growth in the number of clubs, emphasis will be placed on the coming of the professional club, how it was run and by whom, both before the widespread adoption of limited liability and after. This section will concentrate on two types of question. First, what was the socio-occupational background of club shareholders and directors? Second, why did directors become involved in football clubs and in particular how far was the pursuit of money-making a leading motive?

The formation of clubs is not necessary in order to play football. It is obvious that relatively unorganised games between groups of friends and acquaintances, or people casually coming together on a park or patch of waste ground with a ball and the inclination to play with it, will form the bulk of active football at any given time. That must have been true in the 1860s, the 1920s and the 1960s. But if you want to play an organised game regularly then you probably need a more permanent kind of organisation. Otherwise you have to rely on the man with the ball turning up. Moreover, clubbing together might be crucial in collecting the not especially extensive but nonetheless not completely inexpensive items required such as a place to play, for example, and goal posts. Football clubs, like most other voluntary organisations, depend for their success on people doing things. When they stop, the club stops. Finally in club forming, like any other organisational activity, it is useful to have a base from which to begin.

It looks as though a considerable proportion of football clubs, it is impossible to be more precise, came into existence via organisations which already existed for another purpose. The three major pre-existing institutions that spawned football clubs in our period were churches and chapels, public houses and places of employment. It is very likely that many of the earliest clubs, especially those formed in and around London in the late 1850s and 1860s, were formed by young men who had been to school together. They had played some kind of game at school, and perhaps university, and wanted to play on after formal education had ceased. Enough of them were already either professional men in London: lawyers, doctors, clergymen, teachers, or in the process of becoming such.[1] One of the best known examples of such a club was the Forest Club which was formed in 1859–60 and played near Epping Forest at Snaresbrook. The club was, according to one of its founders, 'the creation of a few enthusiastic Old Harrovians'.[2] It advertised in the sporting press for fixtures as the following extract from *Bell's Life*, dated 7 October, 1862, illustrates.

'FOOTBALL—The hon. Secretary of the FOREST FOOTBALL CLUB will be happy to make arrangements for MATCHES to be played during the coming season, on the rules of the University of Cambridge. Alfred W. Mackenzie, hon. Sec., F.F.C., Woodford, Essex.' The club seems to have survived for about four years and obviously played some role in stimulating the growth of the game in the London area.[3]

Old boy clubs were probably more numerous in the south but were not only to be found there. The Sheffield Club, for example, was put on a formal organised basis in the autumn of 1857. Most of its players were former pupils of the Sheffield Collegiate School where they had presumably been taught by ex-public school men and the rules which they produced were something of a mixture of the Cambridge rules of 1856 and those common to several of the leading schools.[4] The club was a very exclusive organisation and remained so at least into the 1880s. As the early minute books and membership lists have survived, it is possible to document its middle-class, and, in the context of mid-Victorian Sheffield society, largely upper-class membership. By using the membership lists in conjunction with local directories it was discovered that of 36 members in 1858, the occupations, or father's occupations of 29 could be traced. All 29 could be termed middle class. Similar tests for 1859 and 1870 produced the same general result. The details are set out in Table 2 : 1.

The *Sheffield Daily Telegraph* of 9 May 1865 was quite clear about the club's origins and social status when it commented, following the holding of the club's annual athletic sports, that 'the club enjoys a prestige not possessed by any of its now many rivals and numbers among its members and friends the elite of the town and neighbourhood'. Two years later the paper reiterated that 'a good deal of the prestige of the club is due to the character of the members . . . [who] are almost exclusively of the middle class and its patrons and supporters include most of the leading

TABLE 2.1 Known occupations of Sheffield FC members or their fathers
1858, 1859, 1870

Occupations	1858	1859	1870*
Doctors	2		
Surgeons	2	3	I
Dentists	2		
Solicitors	3	5	2
Manufacturers	II	18	2
Veterinary Surgeons	I		
Land Surveyors	2		
Land Agents	I		
Brewers	2	3	I
Architect & Surveyors	I	3	
Wine & Spirit Merchants	I	I	
Clergy	I	I	
Coal Company Secretaries			I
Licensed Victuallers		2	
Stationers		I	
Tailors		I	
Grocers		I	I
Academics		2	
Gentlemen			2
Bankers			2
Timber Merchants			I

*The 1870 figures relate to members enrolling for the first time. There were
18 of these for whom the occupations of 13 were found.

Sources: Records and Minutes of the Sheffield Football Club located in the
Sheffield Central Reference Library, Local History Section. Lists of members
FCR 1, FCR 2, FCR 5.

Directories used: Melville Commercial Directory of Sheffield, Rotherham and
the Neighbourhood (1859); E.R. Kelly (ed.), Post Office Directory of Sheffield with
the Neighbouring Towns and Villages (1865); W.M. White, General Directory
and Topography of the Borough of Sheffield and all the Towns, Townships, Parishes
and Villages within the distance of more than twelve miles round Sheffield (1864);
W.M. White, Directory of the Boroughs of Sheffield, Doncaster and Chesterfield
(1868); W.M. White, General Directory of the Town, Borough and Parish of
Sheffield (1860); F. White, General and Commercial Directory and Topography of
the Borough of Sheffield and Official Guide (1871-2).

men in the neighbourhood'.[5] The Sheffield Club originally played
matches with both sides drawn from the members but increasingly
with clubs outside the town in the 1860s notably Notts. County,
Nottingham Forest and Lincoln, all largely middle-class organisations.[6] They did play some matches with the growing number of
other local Sheffield sides but gave it up sometime during the
1860s because they claimed that local clubs always strengthened
their eleven by including the best players from several other

teams.[7] In spite of itself it is clear that the Sheffield Club helped to stimulate the formation of other local organisations of a much more socially heterogeneous nature than itself.

Of course, not all ex-public schoolboys who wanted to continue playing a game they had learned to enjoy at school lived and worked in communities large enough to support anything so tightly knit as an old boys' team. Two of football's earliest historians had a romantic notion of what was done in such cases. 'A younger son, with his school career behind him, was dumped down in a distant county, and as winter came along and he pined for the thrill of the beloved game, he would gather round him the village tenantry, the squire's boy, the blacksmith's 'prentice, and the schoolmaster, and in one of the Manor fields, there would be transplanted the old game under new conditions.'[8] Certainly two of the oldest clubs in Lancashire, Turton and Darwen, do not seem to have departed too far from this pattern. At Turton the son of the local landowner, James Kay, recently down from Harrow, together with the village schoolmaster, W.T. Dixon, called a public meeting early in 1872 to formalise what had clearly been an existing playing relationship and 48 members enrolled at 1/- each.[9] At Darwen three sons of Nathaniel Walsh, owner of the Orchard Mill, went to Harrow and played football with some of the workpeople during the school holidays. They appear to have been instrumental in grafting a football club onto a pre-existing cricket team.[10] At Wednesbury in Staffordshire it was a young teacher who had learned his football at teachers' training college who convened the meeting which produced Wednesbury Town F.C. in 1873. Again the players and members seem to have been recruited mainly from the local professional and manufacturing elites. At least half a dozen early members were former students at Saltley College. In the first ten years of the club's existence matches were played at places as far away as Blackburn, Oswestry, Sheffield and Newton and 'every member paid his own travelling and all other incidental expenses'.[11] But there were other ways in which ex-public and grammar school or college-trained boys, keen to enjoy the game and foster it in their own communities, could do so, largely by using institutions which brought young men into contact with each other although for other purposes.

It is impossible to know when the first football clubs were set up by churches and chapels. It is well known that two of the oldest English professional clubs began in this way as early as 1874. Aston Villa was formed 'by some of the young men' connected with the Aston Villa Wesleyan Chapel at Lozells in Birmingham.[12]

Unfortunately we do not have much more detail than that about who they were and how closely they were related to or backed by the minister. We do know that members of the chapel had formed a cricket club in 1872 and it seems that it was members of this club who decided to form a football club as well.[13] Meantime in Lancashire 'some of the scholars and teachers connected with Christ Church Schools Bolton' founded a club. The vicar was president for a time and one of the schoolmasters became captain. Membership was priced at one penny per week and matches were played on a public park. The club changed its name from Christ Church to Bolton Wanderers in August 1877 after the vicar had objected to the club holding meetings in Christ Church schools when he was not there. There is little doubt that Christ Church was in the process of becoming a football-only club and the breach with the vicar mirrored that fact. Similarly Aston Villa rapidly outgrew its religious origins.[14] Birmingham City, Everton, Fulham and Barnsley are among other clubs whose early years were closely bound up with religious institutions.

There can be no doubt, though the evidence for it is hard to come by, that many church and chapel clubs had long continuous existences and remained primarily a way of maintaining church solidarity, recruiting fresh adherents, and providing physical exercise and recreation for the members. Many young curates, vicars and ministers had not only enjoyed games at school and college but had been persuaded of their moral as well as physical value.[15] It must have been common enough, in both town and country, for 'sporting parsons' to encourage or organise games, teams, or both.[16] Certainly by the mid-1870s there were many church teams wherever football was played and particularly in the midlands and north west of England. Blackburn in 1876 had at least four church clubs playing regularly and the local paper was still publishing the results of their matches two years later. On a typical football Saturday in Sheffield in March 1879 a newspaper mentioned the following clubs which seem certain to have been church or chapel clubs. Pitsmoor Christ Church, Dronfield (U.M.), St. Judes, Ebenezer (Wesleyan), Crookes (Wesleyan), Fulton Road (Wesleyan), Upper Chapel (Unitarian), and All Saints. By the middle of the 1880s nineteen clubs connected with Nottingham churches formed their own competition.[17]

Perhaps the most interesting and certainly the most comprehensive survey of local club origins was conducted by D.D. Molyneux for Birmingham. After compiling lists of football and cricket clubs, the names of which he had obtained from the

Birmingham newspapers, for the years 1871, 1875 and 1880 in the case of the cricket clubs and seasons 1876–7, 1879–80 and 1883–4 in that of the football clubs, he used the local directories and estimated that almost 21 per cent of the total number of cricket clubs and just under 25 per cent of association football clubs had connections with religious organisations. Moreover, it is possible that these figures are on the conservative side because clearly many names which do not suggest a religious origin or affiliation may well conceal one.[18]

Clearly, the nature of the connection between the football club and the church or chapel from which it may have sprung varied enormously. It would be a mistake to imagine that all such clubs were controlled by the minister or his curate and none by the young working men in the congregation. It would be foolish to doubt that these young men could form and sustain a club themselves without paternal help or encouragement. We do not have enough case histories to begin to be very definite about it and it is most unlikely that we ever will have. We do know that many clergymen were interested in the physical and moral value of games and that the church was one institution which brought potential games players together. Of course the church or chapel might be producing something which in the end it could not control and which would become independent and take forms of which the church or chapel was unlikely to approve. Nevertheless, church and chapel teams, and Sunday school clubs (of which a little more later) flourished in our period and probably formed up to a quarter of all organised, regularly playing clubs.[19]

The second major pre-existing institution to play an important role in the origin of football clubs was the public house. Brian Harrison has shown how pubs had three main functions in the nineteenth century: as transport centres, although the railways gradually eliminated that role; as social centres where working people could meet for a whole variety of purposes; and as recreational centres where people went simply to enjoy themselves.[20] As one of the relatively few institutions largely designed to cater for working people it is hardly a surprise to find pubs and publicans playing a prominent role in the growth of football clubs. Apart from being places where working men could meet, pubs were traditionally associated with a whole variety of what might be freely labelled sporting activities from boxing and cricket to the less subtle ratting and the more conventional pub games. Pubs very often had material advantages attractive to the potential football club. They could, for example, provide facilities for changing before a match and dining after it. Finding a ground on which to play was a serious problem for a football club, especially one largely made up of working men, in the 1870s. Some pubs had paddocks or pieces of grassland which they could offer. The Grove Tavern in Handsworth, Birmingham, had a field attached on which football could be played. The Turton club in Lancashire played on a ground at the front of the Cheetham Arms.[21] Many clubs used public houses as their headquarters certainly into the early twentieth century. Heeley F.C. of Sheffield, for example, had their headquarters at the Wagon and Horses for fourteen years in the 1860s and 1870s: Everton's first few seasons were spent at the Queen's Head in Everton village and they were still using a pub as a pavilion in 1885. Newton Heath changed at the Three Crowns in Oldham Road, Manchester, in the 1880s, later removing to the Shears Hotel, while the Bay Horse Hotel was still the headquarters of Blackburn Rovers in 1895. Of nine clubs in the Bristol and District League in 1892–3, eight used public houses for changing.[22]

It is perhaps worth making a distinction here between the use of pubs by football clubs and the establishment of football clubs by groups of people frequenting the same pub and forming, literally, a pub team. It is obviously very difficult to find detailed information about the latter although the names of some clubs playing in places such as Blackburn, Bolton, Birmingham and Sheffield are suggestive. The Royal Oak and the Burton Star in Sheffield in the 1870s, for example, and perhaps Clarence Rangers also, were all pub teams.[23] In Birmingham the Unicorn, Victoria Cross, Marlborough, Holte, Alma, and The Grove look likely pub teams.[24] Publicans certainly seem to have encouraged the growth of the game. The landlord of the Anchor Inn at Darwen offered prizes of £5 and £2 to local clubs in an Easter knock-out competition in 1882.[25] Walsall Licensed Victuallers had their own challenge cup by 1880–1.[26] By 1908 there were allegedly public house leagues playing matches on a Sunday in London.[27] Moreover, publicans had been quick to capitalise on the growing interest in football by having the results of matches telegraphed to their establishments where they could be seen free and earlier than elsewhere. When Blackburn Olympic reached the F.A. Cup Final in 1883 telegrams giving the latest score were displayed every few minutes at the Cotton Tree Inn in the town.[28] The proprietor of the Cafe Royal in Peter Street, Manchester, 'respectfully requested' club secretaries and members to 'wire' the results of matches and post up lists of teams 'for the benefit and convenience of football players and the General Public'.[29] Harry Liston's Bar in Market Street was advertised as the 'Football Players' Resort' and the results of all matches played in Manchester and District were telegraphed there every Saturday afternoon. The Crown Inn in Booth Street had a results board and many other examples could doubtless be found.[30] Leading players were found places as publicans from the early 1880s.[31] Of course, much of this activity was hardly the result of disinterested philanthropy. If more people could be attracted into the pub more drink could hopefully be sold. We shall have cause to note the prominent role, as shareholders and directors, which the denizens of 'the trade' played in many professional football clubs. For the present suffice it to say that a sizeable minority of football clubs in our period were based on or originated from pubs.[32]

The third major institution playing some role in the lives of many people in the last three or four decades of the nineteenth century, and therefore likely to provide a focus for sporting activity, was the workplace. Works football teams are a commonplace of the twentieth century. The provision of playing pitches and changing rooms by employers for their employees has been a not inconsiderable part of modern welfare capitalism. Such provisions not only help to attach workers to the firm or company, providing the young worker in particular with an aid to identity, but may even attract some workers to join the firm in the first place. This kind of direct provision does not appear to have been very widespread before 1900 although the evidence is fairly thin. Again when discussing works' football clubs we ought to bear in mind the distinction between clubs originated and sponsored by management; those begun and continued by the workmen themselves but with managerial material support which retain their original character; those which, begun as working men's clubs, are later taken over by outsiders; and the workmen's clubs which are founded and run by workmen throughout whatever period of existence they have.

There were certainly works teams playing regularly in Sheffield and Birmingham from the 1870s. It would be tedious to list all the names, but an examination of the football fixtures in the *Sheffield Daily Telegraph* for the months of March and December in the years 1873, 1876, 1879, 1882 and 1885 revealed twenty-nine works teams. Molyneux suggested that there were at least twenty-five in Birmingham for the years 1871, 1875 and 1880.[33] Unfortunately, we do not know very much more than that. The best known works club in Sheffield in this period was Lockwood

Brothers, the file steel and cutlery manufacturers. The firm had had a football club since about 1870 and by 1882 it had 140 members. Two years later the local newspaper could say that 'the eminent firm have taken great interest in the club, and done all in their power to encourage and develop it'. But we do not know what that was.[34] Whatever it was it probably owed a good deal to the fact that George Francis Lockwood, the grandson of the firm's founder, who learned his football at the Sheffield Collegiate School and according to his obituary notice, had been keen on football and cricket all his life, took an active interest.[35] Jardines F.C. of Nottingham appear to have been supported by the management for a time, at least to the extent of providing jobs for good players previously with other clubs.[36] But this could be an expensive business and might not be pursued for long, especially if the club's results were not good. Mitchells, the Birmingham brewers, obviously felt they might make something out of the popularity of professional football in their area when they merged their own side with the shaky St George team to produce Mitchell St Georges in the mid-1880s. But they decided to call it a day by the end of the decade because support at the gate was so poor. Most of the Derby Midland eleven in the 1880s were employed by the Midland Railway Company. The club collapsed when the Company refused to support the continuance of a professional team in 1891.[37] Church F.C. in Lancashire was formed by employees at Steiner's dye works around 1878 but it is unclear how closely the firm itself supervised the club, or how far the workers themselves were responsible for its organisation and day to day administration.[38] Nor is it clear who founded Wills A.F.C. at the W.D. and H.O. Wills plant at Bristol in 1893 but the company apparently provided facilities for play as did another leading Bristol firm, E.S. and A. Robinson, although their works football club had been in existence twenty years before they did so.[39] Perhaps the most famous professional clubs to have had their origins at the workplace were Arsenal and West Ham United. Arsenal was formed by a group of workmen at the Woolwich Arsenal in 1886. They certainly did not receive any help from the management![40] West Ham United was much more the product of one man one firm paternalism. The club was originally known as Thames Ironworks and it had been set up in 1895 as one of several works societies which aimed to cater for the leisure needs of the firm's employees. It was a part of the overall strategy for securing peaceful industrial relations which the owner of the largest surviving Thames shipyard, A.F. Hills, had adopted after serious disputes between management and workforce earlier in the 1890s. Hills continued to support the club after its elevation to the Southern League and open avowal of professionalism in 1900, although with apparently diminishing enthusiasm.[41]

There is insufficient evidence to say whether any particular industries or occupational groups were more likely to form football clubs than others. However, it does seem that clerks and railwaymen, and especially railway clerks, often used their places of work around which to organise their games playing. Both the Stoke and Crewe clubs (the latter hardly a surprise given its function as a railway town) were originally set in motion by clerks working in the offices of the Staffordshire Railway Company and the London and North Western Railway Company respectively. Newton Heath F.C. was formed and run, around 1880, by the Dining Room Committee of the Carriage and Wagon Works of the Lancashire and Yorkshire Railway in Manchester.[42] Molyneux has shown that in Birmingham, both the Midland Railway Clerks and the North Western Railway Clerks had football teams in 1880.[43] But in that city, clerks were not only prominent in the clubs of railway companies. Enjoying the Saturday half holiday for the first time in the 1870s, clerks from Van Worts warehouse were playing the game by 1873. By November of the following year, the Birmingham Clerks' Association had a football section which later took the name of Calthorpe F.C. after the public park in which it played. Calthorpe was probably the leading club in the city during the mid-1870s and several of its members were instrumental in establishing the Birmingham Football Association in 1877.[44] Aston Villa was put on its footballing feet by a young clerk from Scotland, George Ramsay. He joined the club when it played in Aston Park in 1875, quickly became its captain and best player and was secretary from 1886–1926. The life and culture of the late nineteenth-century clerk, especially in the provinces, still awaits investigation.[45]

Few genuine works teams became active professional organisations, financially supported by a particular company and bearing its name. However, many individual manufacturers and businessmen became involved with professional and semi-professional football clubs in their home districts and, as we shall see, were willing to put money into the game. However, on a lower level of performance and with the main aim recreation for the workforce, with whatever beneficial by-products for the employer which that might bring, or which individual employers thought it might bring, works teams were a feature of most local football scenes by 1900.[46]

Of course not all football clubs had their origins in religious institutions, pubs or workplaces. Many football teams in many places must have been set up by groups of young men who just lived close to each other. Some club names certainly seem to bear this out. On a Saturday in January 1879, for example, the following clubs took part in matches in Blackburn: George Street West Rovers, Red Row Star, Gibraltar Street Rovers, Cleaver Street Rovers, Hilton Street Star, Heys Lane Rovers (from Darwen).[47] We do not know anything about these clubs: who the members were, how they were organised, how long they survived. It is doubtful if many of them even kept any records. Perhaps a few very old Blackburnians can remember them. But there can be no doubt that neighbourhood clubs were prominent especially in those early days before the coming of cups and leagues.

Cricket clubs often gave birth to football clubs. Again it is a commonplace. It would be otiose to list all the clubs which are known to have begun as continuations of cricket clubs through the winter months and the following group of what later became well established and independent football clubs will have to suffice: Sheffield F.C., Sheffield Wednesday, Accrington F.C., Darwen, Everton, Preston North End and Sheffield United.[48]

The number of clubs grew very rapidly from the late 1870s, especially in the midlands and the north of England. It is difficult to be very precise about this expansion. In 1867 the Football Association had ten clubs affiliated to it; by 1871 it had fifty, by 1888 one thousand and by 1905 ten thousand.[49] The Lancashire Football Association was formed by thirty clubs in 1878: four years later it had sixty-two clubs and four years after that, in 1886, one hundred and fourteen. There were fifty-two clubs in the Birmingham Football Association in 1882.[50] In 1880–1 the Northumberland and Durham Football Association had twenty-five clubs affiliated to it whereas it had had only three in 1879.[51] Thirty seven clubs were playing regularly in the Sheffield district in 1873: by the end of the decade the Sheffield Football Association had forty clubs affiliated with five thousand players.[52] In 1883 it was estimated that twenty-four first teams and fifteen second teams, comprising over four hundred players, were to be found in Burnley. The Nottinghamshire F.A. claimed 1630 registered players and thirty-six clubs in 1885 with up to fifty games being played each Saturday afternoon in the season. By 1889, ninety matches a week were taking place in Sunderland and district with over two hundred clubs and two thousand players involved.[53] In a sense such incomplete figures are very superficial. Much more football playing and club forming went on than any historian can hope to know about.

Who were all these new football players? It is generally thought that the majority of them were working people of one sort or another. Were the bulk of these new clubs formed by working people, run by working people and joined by them? Unfortunately no club records with membership lists, addresses and occupations appear to have survived. The *Sheffield Daily Telegraph* in 1889, just prior to the start of the football season, published a list of the names and addresses of one hundred and ten local football club secretaries. An examination of the local directories made it possible to trace the occupations of an insignificant handful of these.[54] Now as local directories tend to concern themselves with the industrial and commercial elite of the district, or at the very least, those in business for themselves, this might be useful negative evidence. Most of the secretaries will have had working-class jobs. But until the census enumerators' returns can be used it will not be known for certain.

Certainly there are no major reasons why the bulk of these teams should not have been working class in origin and run by working men for working men, like the Elswick leather works team in Newcastle-upon-Tyne in 1881. Writing to the local paper their secretary said that the club had been started by the men in the previous season to play association rules.

At first it was feared there would be a difficulty in getting active members, but after a few games the good points were seen, and at the present time there are nearly ninety members, almost all taking an active part in the play. As a further proof of the popularity of the game, I may state that when our team goes away to play a match it is accompanied by a considerable proportion of our members. Many works in the town employ more men than the leather works and therefore it should not be a hard matter for many more working men's clubs to be formed.[55]

Moreover, the *Preston Herald* noted in 1888 'the requisites of the game are so few and cheap that with very little outside help the poorest may take part in it'.[56] Lewis's of Manchester were selling men's football jerseys for 3/11 in the autumn of 1880 with knickerbockers at 6/9 a pair and stockings at 1/9. Hand-sewn footballs could be had for 10/6. New balls could be bought in Birmingham from 6/- to 9/6 in 1885 and waterproof boots from 8/6 to 10/6.[57] But new items were not necessary in order to play. Football boots were almost certainly optional for many players and teams clearly turned out in a variety of costumes. Most teams would be unlikely to play matches far outside their own home territory and if they did walking would probably be the way they would get there. Difficulties might multiply for teams of working

men when they began to achieve a success which tempted them
out of their local and cheap milieu. The cost of travel over long
distances could hardly be met by working men 'clubbing' together. The Darwen club may have had its origins in the desire
of ex-public schoolboys to play games they had begun at school,
as we noted above. Moreover, it is clear that as a club, it was a
combined cricket and football club with only one committee
until 1884, which contained some middle-class members. Indeed,
in 1884 the committee appears to have included two local cotton
manufacturers, two bank managers, two solicitors, an accountant
and the manager of the local gas and water company.[58] Nevertheless, by the end of the 1870s the first eleven football team was
composed largely of operatives in the local cotton mills.[59] When
the team entered for the F.A. Cup in 1878–9 and found itself
drawn to play the Old Etonians in London it had to ask for public
assistance to 'enable the working lads of our town to compete
against government inspectors, university professors, noblemen's
sons etc'.[60] Collections were taken in the mills and workshops of
the town and something like £175 were raised.[61]

A similar situation faced Blackburn Olympic during their
successful F.A. Cup run in 1883. Much has been made of the
fact that the Olympic was a team of northern working men who
came south with factory muck still on their brows and conquered
the leisure-sated sybarites of Eton whom Darwen had so narrowly
failed to overcome four years before.[62] They were undoubtedly a
team of working men. But they had spent the week before the
semi-final undergoing special training at Blackpool and the exercise was repeated before the final. The *Blackburn Times* knew
who to thank for it.

Much of the success of the club this season has been due to the interest which
Mr Sydney Yates, of the firm of W. & J. Yates, iron founders, has manifested
in it. Not long ago, when he heard that some subscription books had been issued
for the purpose of obtaining contributions towards defraying the heavy cost
of preparation for the closing ties of the competition, he sent word that they must
not be used, and last week generously forwarded a cheque for £100 as a donation
to the fund from which the expenditure will be met.[63]

In fact, Mr Yates had been interested in the Olympic since their
victory in the East Lancashire Charity Cup in the previous season.
He provided a treat for the club's playing members and told
them, *inter alia* 'that although they were merely working lads
they might, if they could stick together in the future, *and with
the assistance of people of influence*, soon be able to reach the top of
the tree' (my italics).[64] The point I wish to emphasise is that public

subscriptions were all right for special occasions. But if a club, largely composed of working men, expected to meet other clubs from outside its own immediate area regularly in 'friendlies' or cup-ties, then it required the support of 'influential people'. The takings through the gate, at least initially, were never enough, or might not be.

Moreover, some spare time was necessary to administer the day-to-day business of a growing club. Blackburn Rovers, for example, held fifty-seven committee meetings in season 1881–2 plus numerous sub-committee meetings. Running a large and expanding football association might present even greater problems. In 1882–3, there were almost four thousand communications passing through the Post Office from the secretary of the Lancashire F.A. on association business.[65] Of course what we are talking about here are the elite clubs, the ones which became the most successful in their districts, regularly challenged the best clubs from other areas and whose growth tended to outgrow their origins. An interesting example of a team of working men run by working men who achieved elite status but could not remain unsullied by middle-class expertise and money was the Woolwich Arsenal and it is worth looking at that club's rise and rise in some detail.

As we noted earlier, the club was formed in 1886 by workers at the Arsenal and although it did not openly turn professional until 1891 it was widely believed that some foremen in the Arsenal took on good football players and made sure that they got skilled men's rates. They also received expenses for playing. But so far as we know the club was run by a committee of working men elected by the membership.[66] The club publicly embraced professionalism in 1891, but rejected the idea that it should become a limited company. John Humble, an engineer in the Arsenal by trade, club committeeman and later director, said that the club's membership and democratic way of going about its business were unique. 'It had been worked by working men and his ambition was to see it carried on by them.' If it adopted limited liability, it would degenerate 'into a proprietary or capitalist club'.[67] Limited liability was turned down in 1891 but embarked upon two years later after the owner of the ground on which the club played had demanded a rent increase of £150 per year, the transfer of rate payments from him to the club, and a nominee on the committee.[68] Although these demands were rejected, it was decided to form the club into a limited liability company in order to raise enough money to buy a ground of their own. The company had a nominal capital of four thousand £1 shares of which 1,552 were allotted to 860 shareholders. The vast majority of the shareholders were manual workers living in the Plumstead and Woolwich districts and almost certainly employed at the Arsenal. Their holdings were in units of one or two with only three individual holdings of more than twenty shares, one of fifty by a local coffee house proprietor, one of twenty-five by a surgeon and one of twenty by a local builder. The first board of directors included the surgeon and the builder, plus six engineers.

Theoretically the club could have continued to be run in this way providing it won most of its matches (it played in the Second Division of the Football League from 1893) and a sufficiently large number of people turned up regularly to watch. Unfortunately neither of those conditions was met although it did obtain promotion to the First Division in 1904. Before that, however, it had lost money regularly, partly due to the large annual mortgage repayments to which it was committed, partly to its inability to attract large enough crowds to an area of London not well blessed by public transport. The Boer War made the club's position almost impossible because although it led to a large increase in the workforce at the Arsenal, it also produced massive overtime working, notably on Saturday afternoons.[69] The result was a loss of £3400 in 1900 and a request to a local clothier to put some money into the club. Control of the club passed into the hands of interested local business and professional men and an interesting experiment in the running of a professional football club by working men was over.[70]

So if a club became successful, ambitious and, from 1885 openly professional, then time and money in some plenitude were going to be required in order to run it and neither of these was a commodity with which working men were much blessed. The Bolton Wanderers balance sheet (Table 2.2) for the last season before professionalism was legalised, 1884–5, gives some idea of the growing complexity of football club finance and administration as well as the actual amounts involved. It is worth noting that players' wages do not appear on the balance sheet although it was well known that they were paid.[71]

Before the coming of limited liability most leading clubs were run by a committee of the membership, usually elected at the annual meeting. Aston Villa, for example, had 382 members by 1889 with a management committee of nine plus the secretary. A new committee was elected at each annual general meeting.[72] Qualification for membership of most clubs was the purchase of

TABLE 2.2 Bolton Wanderers F.C. Balance Sheet 1884–5

Receipts		Expenditure	
Balance in Hand	£83.12.4	Teams' travelling expenses, entertainment of visiting clubs etc.	£481.13.3
Gate Receipts	1630.6.9		
Subscriptions	167.8.9	Opponents' share of gate receipts	698.3.5
Rent of Refreshment Tents, Proceeds from Special Trains etc.	68.5.6	Outlay on Ground, New Stands etc.	108.6.10
		Rent, rates, ground and gate keeping, police, accounts etc.	278.2.9½
		Footballs, Jerseys, shoes, etc.	54.5.8
		Printing, Posting, Advertising	131.16.0½
		Representatives' expenses attending meetings etc.	31.13.0
		Medical Attendance on Players	16.18.9
		Players' Insurance	9.2.0
		Postage, Telegrams, etc.	17.4.6
		Petty Cash	7.17.11
		Association Subscriptions	2.6.6
		Salaries	10.0.0
		Balance in Hand at Bank	102.2.8
	1949.13.4		1949.13.4

Source : Athletic News 23 June 1885

a season ticket, the cost usually amounting to the total entrance money of all the club's proposed home matches although discounts for paying in advance were common practice. The committee usually looked after all the club's affairs both on the field and off, selecting the team or teams, arranging travel, buying kit and attending to all the other incidental matters that accompanied running a football club on an enclosed ground with money taken at the gate.[73]

Increasingly one of the most important tasks of the club committee through the 1880s was finding ways to boost club finances. Some clubs, like Stoke and Nottingham Forest, had fairly well established annual athletic sports meetings which brought in healthy sums. Others had recourse to bazaars and prize draws.[74] Before they fell foul of the betting and gaming laws football club lotteries were important local events making big sums for the local club and arousing a good deal of interest. Blackburn Olympic sold over 30,000 tickets in 1886. Accrington's draw in the same year offered a first prize of a dwelling house worth £150, and all for sixpence. The top prize in the Blackburn Rovers draw was also a newly-built cottage which would entitle the owner to a parliamentary vote. The winner was a meter inspector in the Corporation Gas Department earning 22/- a week.[75]

But an easier way of raising money was via incorporation and limited liability. We saw earlier that some of the committee of Woolwich Arsenal disliked this idea although they were forced to accept it in the end. Similarly a sub-committee set up by Aston Villa to consider a limited liability scheme in 1889 emphasised that the club was not to be conducted as a source of profit to the members because that would be 'against true sport'.[76] Several clubs did form themselves into limited companies under the Companies Acts in the 1880s but the rush was to come in the 1890s and beyond. The *Athletic News* strongly urged all clubs with an annual turnover of £1000 or more to take advantage of the legislation. It would mean that they could sue and be sued; it would limit the individual responsibility of directors and reassure creditors, of whom some clubs had already accumulated a good many.[77] The paper also seemed to think that shareholders 'would be the more intelligent' supporters of the club.

They would not be influenced by any private motives in the election of a board of management, and would not allow any pique to upset their discretion in a purely business transaction, as they would in the case of a club on the present lines, in which they have no monetary interest and in the financial results have no responsibility whatever.

They do not sound quite human.

Who were the people who bought shares in football clubs? What kinds of people became the directors of those elite clubs which became incorporated in our period? Why did they do it and what did they get out of it? In order to try to answer the first question a rough sample was taken of forty-seven professional football clubs incorporated between 1886 and 1913 and an examination made of the lists of shareholders which they were obliged to return annually to the Registrar of Companies. It should be said at once that not all clubs complied with the law and that several clubs were in receipt of frequent reminders of their failure to do so. Moreover, although the majority of shareholders had an occupation listed in the returns there were some gaps. The list of shareholders in the initial year of incorporation was examined and again in a year towards the end of the period where that was possible.[78] The following description is largely based on the earlier, mainly because no significant changes appear to have taken place in either the occupational composition of shareholdings or in their quantitative distribution, although there were several exceptions to the last of those two generalisations. I started out with the assumption that most shareholders would be middle class and that their occupations would mirror the general economic and industrial structure of the community and the evidence does seem to support that notion. Nevertheless, I was surprised that the sprinkling of working-class shareholders was as large as it was; statistically insignificant for many clubs, but large in numbers, if not in impact, for others, notably Darwen, Dartford and Woolwich Arsenal.[79] Of course, most working-class shareholders had only one or two shares and it surely must have been club identification and support which prompted the outlay rather than hope of financial return.

It is clear that some clubs did not expect working people to buy their shares. The cost of a Sheffield United Ordinary share in 1899, for example, was £20. Preference shares were £10. This issue came in the summer after United had won the F.A. Cup and was clearly an attempt to consolidate a period of considerable playing success in the 1890s.[80] Sheffield Wednesday too, in the same year, floated a new share issue pricing their original shares at £5 and Ordinary ones at £10.[81] The leading professional club of the 1890s was Aston Villa. They won the League championship in 1894, 1896, 1897, 1899 and 1900 and the F.A. Cup in 1895 and 1897. Their shares were £5 each when issued in 1896. Although they had over 700 individual shareholders there were no exceptionally large individual holdings although a Birmingham butcher had a block of 70 by 1914. In 1896 the largest individual shareholding was that of the Birmingham and Aston Tramway Company with 50.[82] Glossop also valued their shares at £5 but as 194 out of a total of 200 were in the hands of Samuel Hill-Wood it had obviously never been the intention to pull in money from the wider community.[83]

At the other extreme three clubs fixed the price of their shares as low as 5/-. Croydon Common, Dartford and Southport Central were all spectacularly unsuccessful. The first named was part of an ambitious scheme in 1908, apparently for making money, in an expanding area to the south of Greater London. In spite of the low price of the shares the vast majority was held by builders, including over 2,000 by the club chairman. The company was wound up after eight years.[84] Dartford only lasted four years and they numbered 25 labourers among their 119 shareholders in 1896. There were also a good many other working-class shareholders although the largest individual holdings were in the portfolios of a licensed victualler, a stationer, an engineer, a land agent, draper, physician, carpenter, warehouseman and timekeeper.[85] Southport Central survived for twelve months as a 5/- share club before being reformed as a 10/- share club and limping along for a further five years. It had no working-class shareholders in 1912.[86]

There were four clubs in our sample, in addition to Southport Central's second attempt, whose shares were 10/- each: Accrington, Clapton Orient, Gateshead and South Shields. Accrington could not persuade enough local people to take up their shares and the company had ceased to trade within three years.[87] Clapton Orient was a product of the mini-mania for setting up professional football clubs in London which was a feature of the first few years of Edward VII's reign. Again it had a short and not particularly gay five-year existence. It had a small number of apparently working-class shareholders, but the largest shareholder was Horatio Bottomley with £50 worth.[88] The other two 'ten bob' (10/-) clubs were both on the south Tyneside. Gateshead was not incorporated until 1911 and it survived eight years before dissolution and a fresh start. In 1912 the club had 128 shares in the hands of 25 clerks: 184 in the pouches of 15 licensed victuallers and 100 owned by the Newcastle Brewery. 849 shares were issued altogether.[89] The other shareholders included two coal miners, four gas workers, two forgemen, three moulders, a grocer's assistant, a turner, two enginemen and twelve fitters. South Shields had only 37 shareholders in 1898 and the club was defunct by 1902. There were four platers, a caulker, a rivetter and a hammerman, as befitted a shipbuilding community, but the leading shareholders were three solicitors, an estate agent, a brewer, builder, wine merchant and land agent.[90]

The vast majority of the clubs whose shareholder lists were examined, 34 in all, had shares priced at £1, but this seems to be their only common characteristic. Some had a large number of

shareholders, some small; some were among the elite of professional clubs, others suffered a wretched lack of success and in
consequence a short life; some were dominated by directors with
large shareholdings, others had no especially large shareholders
and their directors had the same quantity of shares as many other
holders. Woolwich Arsenal, whom we earlier characterised as
a working-class club, had over 900 shareholders possessing 1500
shares in 1893, with the occupations of engineer, turner, fitter,
machinist and labourer appearing most frequently.[91] Darwen's
shareholders were also largely working class. The shares were
divided between 108 occupations.[92] The club went into liquidation
after two years, finding the competition of its near neighbour,
Blackburn Rovers, particularly severe. The Rovers, of course,
had never been a working-class club in the sense of being founded
by working men and run by them. The club had been established
in 1874 by the ex-grammar and public school educated sons of
local business and professional families. It provides an interesting
contrast with Darwen. The Rovers had only 93 shareholders in
1897 with cotton manufacturers, mill managers and publicans
the most frequently listed occupations. Holdings of 20 or more
shares were common. By 1914 the club had 241 shareholders
with one brewer possessing 150 and two cotton manufacturers
150 between them.[93] Bolton Wanderers also had a thin scattering
of working-men shareholders but it was journalists and jewellers,
publicans and innkeepers, brewers and bleachers who dominated
the holdings in 1895.[94] By 1914, with the number of shares taken
up almost doubled, one brewer and his two sons had four hundred
between them. There were two other batches of one hundred
each and the rest were largely in the hands of local business and
professional people. Remaining in Lancashire, Preston North
End had a lot of small shareholders in the total of 390 in 1893.
But 'the trade' was again prominent with 26 publicans and licensed
victuallers, and six brewers, two of whom had 50 shares each.
There seems to have been very little change in either individual
shareholders or the size of their holdings by 1914.[95] It is interesting
to compare the share structure of the two Manchester clubs.
Apart from two breweries with 50 and 100 each respectively,
an innkeeper and a secretary with 20 each, and a publican and
another brewer with 10 each, the other 209 shareholders of
Manchester City in 1894 had only one or two shares against their
names. Moreover, there was a wide cross section of working-
class occupations among them, from brick layers, carters and
labourers to checkers, finishers, lampmen and makers up.[96]

Manchester United, on the other hand, had risen from the ashes of Newton Heath which had been officially received in 1902. That club's shares had also been mainly distributed in small numbers to a variety of working-class occupations together with the familiar collection of local trades and professional men, decorators, reporters, painters, pawnbrokers, hotel-keepers, teachers, grocers and the like, although Rothwell the brewer did have 150 shares.[97] By 1908, Manchester United was being run by a brewery managing director, J.H. Davies, whose 100 shares exceeded by 40 the holdings of all the other six directors put together. Moreover, three of them were his employees and two others connected with the brewery. There were still only 68 shareholders in 1913 and apart from one foreman, one warehouseman, a compositor and a groundsman, the remainder were solidly middle class. The club had opened a fine new ground at Old Trafford and was well on the way to becoming one of the country's leading clubs.[98] Finally, half of Sunderland Albion's two thousand shares in 1890 were in the hands of an accountant, a corn miller, Fenwick's Brewery (600) and the glass manufacturer, James Hartley (200). But the club could never attract the crowds that Sunderland did and successive seasonal losses of £748 in 1891 and £643 in 1892 led to it being voluntarily wound up in that year.[99] Sunderland F.C. did not go limited until 1896 and there was some local criticism that at £1 at a time the shares had been priced out of the reach of those working men who made up the bulk of the club's support.[100] In fact, the club had only eleven people holding single shares in 1896. The old committee, consisting of two members of a family of wine merchants, two members of a family of shipbuilders, a timber merchant and a gentleman took 350 shares between them, one hundred for the gentleman and fifty each for the others. Other blocks of 25 and 50 were owned by the local newspaper proprietor, a cabinet maker, the Vaux and Newcastle breweries, one of the local M.P.s, another timber merchant and a whiskey merchant. Three joiners, two coal fitters, a foreman and a barman may have been working men.[101]

Apart from documenting what was probably common enough knowledge anyway, that most football club shareholders in the period 1886–1915 were middle class, it is not clear what the above description amounts to. Perhaps it is surprising that there were as many working men, and in the one case women, shareholders. Perhaps more detailed local studies will be more penetrative especially in the area of what kind of business or professional man bought shares, big or small. Common sense would suggest that the amount of shares purchased bore some direct relation to the size and prosperity of the business. But common sense can, occasionally, be an untrustworthy guide. Again, local studies might illuminate the connection between shareholders of football clubs and individuals active in other areas of community life such as politics or religion.

The above survey also emphasises the prominence of the drink trade. Only one of our clubs had no shareholders from the trade and Blackburn Rovers in 1897, for example, had as much as 15 per cent of its shares in the hands of members of the trade. West Bromwich Albion relied so heavily on local breweries for financial support that, by 1909, Mitchells and Butlers held £700 worth of debentures, two other breweries £500 worth each and another £100 worth.[102] When Wolverhampton Wanderers moved from their ground at Dudley Road to Molyneux, the new grounds were laid out by the Northampton Brewery Company. The facilities included dressing rooms, offices and a covered shelter round almost half of the area, and all for £50 per annum.[103] We shall return to the connections between drink and football, the old form of working-class leisure and the new.[104] Suffice it to say here that publicans and brewers were unlikely to have become involved in the clubs with hope of direct financial gain since profits were by no means assured and dividends limited by the Football Association to 5 per cent. Of course, by the beginning of the twentieth century a sizeable minority of current players and former professionals were publicans; it is impossible to know precisely how many. It would not be surprising if they invested a little in the game via shares in their local and perhaps former or current club. On the other hand investment in an institution responsible for regularly bringing large numbers of people together who might drink before and after the match might seem a sensible and ultimately indirectly profitable speculation. We do not know. Brewers and publicans might also have bought shares because, like most shareholders, they enjoyed the game, wished to support their team, and perhaps liked the admission privileges which accompanied the shares. Of course, becoming a director might be another matter.

What kind of people became directors? On one level that is an easy question to answer. Once again using the returns made by registered companies to the registrar, an examination was made of the occupations of 740 directors of 46 professional football clubs between 1888 and 1915. The results are summarised in Table 2.3. Most of the categories are clearly self-explanatory but

TABLE 2.3 Football club directors 1888–1915: summary of occupations

Occupational Category		No.	%
Gentlemen		32	4.3
Professional		90	12.2
Schoolmasters		20	2.7
Manufacturers		79	10.7
Managers		35	4.7
Builders and Contractors		41	5.5
Wholesale and Retail	(a) Employers	159	21.5
	(b) Assistants	7	0.9
	(c) Travellers	15	2
Financial and Commercial		70	9.5
Food and Drink Trade		89	12
(a) Brewers		(19)	(2.6)
(b) Publicans, Licensed Victuallers Hotel Keepers, Beer Retailers, etc.		(66)	(8.9)
(c) Refreshment House Proprietors, Cafe Managers etc.		(4)	(0.5)
Skilled Manual		42	5.7
Engineers		14	1.9
Unskilled Manual		4	0.5
Others		43	5.8
Total		740	99.90

It is interesting to compare these proportions with the occupational composition of the membership of the F.A. Council in 1903 (Table 2.4). There were a total of 46 members of whom probably at least eleven were also directors of league clubs.

perhaps it should be pointed out that under wholesale and retail employers are included, for example, gentleman's outfitter, tobacconist, coal merchant, grocer, butcher, pawnbroker, furniture dealer, china and glass merchant, baker and confectioner, and wholesale fruit merchant, and under financial and commercial estate agents, land agents, agents and clerks. What the table tells us about the background of the directors of football clubs in this period will hardly come as a surprise to anyone possessing a modest knowledge of the subject. Wholesale and retail is the largest single group followed by the professions, the drink trade and manufacturers. Such a crude table leaves many interesting questions unanswered. For example, can we say that it was relatively small, rather than relatively big, businessmen who became football club directors? Was there a tendency for them to get bigger as time went on? Or was it relatively non-political members of the middle classes as opposed to the politically active

TABLE 2.4 Membership of the F.A. Council 1903: summary of occupations

Occupational Category	No.	%
Banker	I	—
Divisional Chief Clerk	I	—
Solicitor	3	6.5
Journalist	5	10.9
Auctioneer and Valuer	I	—
Clerk to the Commissioners of Taxes for the Hundred of Blackburn	I	—
Accountant	5	10.9
Builder and Contractor	I	—
Gentleman	2	—
Plumber's Brassfounder	I	—
Clerk	2	—
Commission Agent	I	—
Schoolmaster	7	15.2
Army Captain	I	—
Draper	I	—
Fuel Agent	I	—
Licensed Victualler	I	—
Managing Director	2	—
Secretary	2	—
Photographer	I	—
Cashier	I	—
Chief Clerk	I	—
Engineer and Surveyor	I	—
Lace Draughtsman	I	—
Colliery Agent	I	—
Clerk in Holy Orders	I	—

The details were taken from G. Green (1953) op.cit. pp. 194–5 but Banker and Journalist have been substituted for Peer of the Realm and Justice of the Peace for the Country of Surrey against the names of Lord Kinnaird and C.W. Alcock respectively.

who became directors? It may well be both of course but, again, only detailed local studies are likely to furnish convincing answers. As we will see below, some large manufacturers, traders and financiers were heavily involved with some football clubs by the outbreak of war in 1914. Why did they put some of their money into football clubs? Why did football directors want to become directors?

It is not very likely that many of them were in it for the money which could be made directly out of it. We saw earlier how Aston Villa had initially fought shy of limited liability and were opposed to running the club as a source of profit to the members because that would be 'against true sport'.[105] When the club did eventually become a limited company in 1896, the chairman emphasised that 'he would not like to see the club become purely a money-making machine. While the gates must be more or less attractive as finding the wherewithal to carry on the sport, he hoped they would have the truest exposition of football to be found and the finest development of athletes to be seen.'[106] Similarly the *Athletic News*, commenting on the 30,000 crowd which turned up to watch Sheffield United play Sheffield Wednesday in December 1896 pointed out that 'there is no question of any private individual making a profit. The proceeds go to the advancement of football in Sheffield.'[107] More crucially perhaps the Football Association limited the payment of dividends to shareholders to 5 per cent. No one could wax very fat on that.[108] Nor was it permissible to receive directors' fees.[109]

Of course not everyone put money into football merely for the love of the game. John Houlding, brewer, leading local Conservative and president of Everton F.C., not only owned part of the land on which the club's ground lay but acted as agent for the landlord of the other half. He also loaned the club money at a price and had the sole right of providing refreshments inside the ground. He also owned the Sandon Hotel which was situated next to the entrance of the Anfield ground and past which match-goers had to walk twice every alternate Saturday. After Everton won the League championship in 1890–1, and made a profit of over £1700 in the process, Houlding demanded more rent and interest. There was no written contract specifying the amount of rent to be paid nor had the club any form of lease. Houlding was opposed by a large majority of the club membership and an extremely acrimonious if somewhat complex dispute followed. It ended in 1892 when the Everton club moved to a new ground at Goodison Park and Houlding, after the Football Association had refused to allow him to use the Everton name, built from scratch a rival professional football team, Liverpool F.C.[110]

H.A. Mears, a London builder and contractor, bought the London Athletic Club's ground at Stamford Bridge in 1896.[111] After failing to sell it to the Great Western Railway and St. George's Hospital he decided to build a professional football club there. Although it is not entirely clear what his motives were there is no doubt that it proved a profitable venture. The club paid a high rental, over £2000 per annum and catering for the big crowds attracted to the ground in the years 1905–15 was provided by the Chelsea F.C. Catering Company of which Mears was also chairman.[112]

Sir Henry Norris[113] actually removed the Arsenal Football Club from its original home at Woolwich to Highbury in North London because he believed that it was more likely to draw big crowds there and make, rather than lose, money.[114]

Bradford City was formed out of an existing rugby league club, Manningham R.F.C., in 1903. The Committee of the Manningham club claimed that the professional rugby code was losing support. Frequent changes in the laws had damaged the game's integrity. The Manningham club had regularly lost money—£1000 in the last three years—and only the proceeds of a recent carnival had got the club out of debt. The West Riding had no league soccer club at this time north of Sheffield yet the game was popular in the schools. Officials of the Bradford and District F.A. were also heavily involved. It is clear that a promise of second division status had been given by the Football League. It was hoped to take advantage of an opportunity to at least avoid losing money before the city of Leeds came forward with a scheme. In spite of some vocal opposition, especially at the Manningham club's annual general meeting, a resolution that the club abandon rugby and adopt soccer for the next twelve months was carried by 75 votes to 34.[115]

Of course there was money to be made by successful league clubs. Everton, for example, only failed to make a profit in one year between 1891 and 1914 and Liverpool made a surplus in every year from 1900. Chelsea had a surplus of income over expenditure regularly between 1908 and 1915 and received the highest annual receipts of any league club, £22826 in 1908.[116] Reliable figures are difficult to acquire and the dearth of club records means that the local press or the *Athletic News* are the main sources. Clearly successful big-city clubs, indeed successful small-town ones, could produce sufficient surpluses to keep the club functioning smoothly.

But if there was money to be made in football there was money to be lost too. We noticed earlier the difficulties which beset the running of Woolwich Arsenal and the losses made there. It was by no means an isolated example. The Official Receiver's report on Newton Heath in 1902 showed that in ten years the club had largely been carried on by means of loans and had never paid a dividend. £2670 was owing to a variety of creditors.[117] Most league clubs had a poor season in 1892–3. Sheffield Wednesday and Wolverhampton Wanderers showed surpluses—Wolves won the F.A. Cup that year—but Newton Heath, Middlesbrough, Aston Villa, Blackburn Rovers, Nottingham Forest, Small Heath, Newcastle United, Darlington, Bootle, Middlesbrough Ironopolis and West Bromwich Albion all made losses ranging from £94 to £645.[118] West Bromwich Albion, Cup finalists in 1886, 1887, 1888, 1892 and 1895 and winners in 1888 and 1892 were continually in financial difficulties. In the summer of 1893 they held a grand fête and military tournament in an effort to raise funds.[119] Six years later they were still hard up and were holding a prize draw with tickets at 4d each and the top prize a £25 piano.[120] A shareholders' meeting decided to appeal to the people of West Bromwich to contribute £500 or £1000 in order that the team might be strengthened while the directors paid the summer wages of the players out of their own pockets.[121] In 1900 it was decided to find a new ground 'between the densely populated districts of Handsworth (Birmingham) and Smethwick and within comparatively easy reach of the north west side of Birmingham'.[122] But problems remained and the *Birmingham Evening Despatch* launched a shilling fund to help the club in 1904–5.[123]

The 1898–9 season was another bad year, so much so that the Football League felt it necessary to issue a circular asking clubs to contribute to a common fund which would be used for the purpose of assisting clubs in a poor financial position.[124] We saw earlier how Woolwich Arsenal's attendances suffered during the Boer War because so many of the workmen at the Arsenal were working Saturday overtime. Bad weather may also have been a cause of poor crowds and related financial losses. Most grounds had very little shelter for the sixpenny customers and a succession of wet Saturdays could dampen the wildest enthusiasm.

It is very likely that some of the losses could be placed at the feet of eccentric management. Before the 1901–2 season there was no maximum wage for football players and, although it is impossible to document it is certain that some clubs paid more than they could realistically afford.[125] The suggestion is obvious that many football directors did not always run the clubs on the strict business lines which they were wont to apply to their personal commercial activities. Had they done so, many more clubs would have gone out of business. A strong whiff of Micawberism permeated football club boardrooms: indeed it has never entirely disappeared in the twentieth century.[126]

Summing up, it seems some people may have become football club directors for the money which they could make directly out of it. However, they must have been few and far between and even fewer those who actually did make much. It is difficult not to agree with the *Athletic News* of 6 September 1909 which asserted

that the vast majority of gentlemen who are pecuniarily interested in clubs look upon their financial obligations as of secondary importance to the sport they get. Hundreds of them have for years maintained guarantees at banks, and thousands have helped to create clubs by taking shares without hope of seeing their money back or any return for it.

We look in vain in the financial papers for quotations in shares of football companies. . . . No one who is out for a business return would look at football shares. Directors have to do all the work freely. Not one club in fifty has paid interest on shares, year in and year out.

The paper went on to claim that in the season just finished, 1908–9, only 6 of the leading 62 clubs paid a dividend of 5%.[127]

Of course there might well be secondary profits as we have seen; such as catering contracts, stand and terrace building agreements, provision of kit, free advertising in the programme. Moreover, if the president of the Football League was correct when he wrote in 1905 that 'in most towns it is considered a distinct privilege to be on the board of the local club directorate, and the position is as eagerly sought after as a seat in the council chamber' then we must expect other motives to get mixed up with love of the game.[128] Samuel Hill-Wood clearly ran the Glossop side as part of his political struggle with the local Liberal family, the Partingtons. No town with a population of only 20,000 could have supported a first division football team through the turnstiles alone. According to his obituary in the *Glossop Chronicle and Advertiser* of 7 January 1949, Hill-Wood put over £33000 into this generally very unsuccessful football club in sixteen years, 1898–1914.[129]

Again A.F. Hills of Thames Ironworks, later West Ham United, also thought that providing a football team for his workmen's pleasure was a contribution to sound industrial relations and it would be surprising if he was a solitary case. Moreover, association with a successful side, a place to meet other local business and professional men, the privileges of the directors' box, all these were doubtless attractive to many men who wished to become or actually did become directors of professional football clubs. Perhaps the social attractions were not quite as great as in the days when club committees entertained the visitors and the visiting committee to dinner after the match but they were nonetheless important for all that.[130] Indeed members of the Aston Villa club met every Monday evening during the season in the late

1870s at a coffee house in Aston High Street. By 1883 they had their own club room with its practice nights and musical evenings; 'as pleasant premises at which to spend a quiet social evening as can be found in many places devoted alone to social intercourse'.[131]

It is clear that professional football clubs were not primarily profit-making institutions and what profits were made were usually ploughed back. They were, by the end of our period, mostly limited liability companies with a largely middle-class body of shareholders and a directorate whose occupational composition would almost certainly reflect the economic structure of the town. As long as affairs did not go too disastrously the directors had more or less complete control. In some ways the football club can be looked upon as a family firm with both shares and directorships being passed down the generations. The Mears family, for example, who formed the Chelsea club in 1905 are still prominent members of the Board today and many similar examples could be cited. In spite of professionalism, transfer fees and a whole series of questions which can be summed up in the fashionable contemporary cliché, 'business or sport', the consensus, both at Preston, where the Football League had its head office, and the headquarters of the Football Association, was against the one man club, the dominating individual capitalist, the money-bags United. Manchester United, for example were stigmatized as a 'private monopoly' which did not issue balance sheets like other clubs.[132] The vast majority of clubs, the largely amateur clubs which we discussed at the beginning of this chapter, probably did not issue balance sheets either. But few can have remained completely untouched by the activities of the professional elite, certainly by 1915. In the next chapter I want to examine how professionalism in association football was accepted and to see what the controversy surrounding its legalisation tells us about the state of the game and the state of the society in which it was played.

Notes

1 Note the backgrounds of the individuals who drew up the Cambridge rules in 1863, see P.M. Young (1968) op.cit. pp. 86–8. Although it need not necessarily have been public schools that the young men had attended. Darlington, for example, was formed by players who had been to local grammar schools. A. Appleton, *Hotbed of Soccer* (1961 edn) p. 51.

2 See C.W. Alcock's article on association football in *English Illustrated Magazine* (1890–1) pp. 282–3.

3 According to Alcock the players became dispersed after about four years and the club was reformed as the Wanderers F.C. This club drew its players from old boys of all the leading public schools and dominated the early years of the F.A. Cup in the 1870s.

4 See P.M. Young, *Football in Sheffield* (1962) pp. 16–18.

5 *Sheffield Daily Telegraph* 7 May 1867. 'Care is taken to ensure perfect respectability in the attendance (at the sports) and perfect order and decorum follows as a natural consequence. Money is not taken at the doors for admission and parties have to provide themselves with tickets beforehand.' Members were elected to the club after being proposed and seconded by existing members, two blackballs to exclude. See FCR 1, Minutes of Club A.G.M., October 1858.

6 Most of Notts. County's players in the 1860s were 'men of position' with one a leading banker. See *Famous Football Clubs* (Boots, Nottingham, 1898).

7 FCR 10 Misc., and FCR 13 October 1887. This practice was not reversed until 1887 when the club merged with the Sheffield Collegiate F.C. By this time, of course, local football had grown enormously in terms of the number of clubs and the standard of play achieved.

8 A. Gibson and W. Pickford op.cit. vol. I, p. 32. See also N.L. Jackson, *Sporting Days and Sporting Ways* (1932) pp. 21–2. Sometimes a letter to the press might set the process in motion. See for example the letter suggesting that an association club be formed in Manchester, *Athletic News* 2 October 1875.

9 On the Kay family see B. Scholes, *Notes on Turton Tower its successive owners* (Bolton, 1880) pp. 43–7. W.T. Dixon, *History of Turton Football Club and Carnival Sports Handbook* (Bolton, 1909). P.M. Young, *Bolton Wanderers* (1961) pp. 14–15. J.A.H. Catton (1900) op.cit. pp. 43–4. It would be interesting to have had the occupational backgrounds of all those members. How many labourers' sons, either in the mill or in the fields, could afford a 1/- for such a thing as football in 1872? We do know that among the club committee, one member was the son of the local grocer and one the son of a local innkeeper.

10 See J.A.H. Catton (1900) op.cit. pp. 43–4.

11 *Ryder's Annual*, The Wednesbury Red Book and Directory (1910) pp. 145–59. *Athletic News* 2 June 1880. Wednesbury Old Athletic was formed in the following year by the headmaster and some of the ex-pupils of the St John's Night School. Most of their players were working men hence the local nicknames for the two clubs, the 'Hand Leathers' and the 'Kid Gloves'.

12 See 'Tityrus' (J.A.H. Catton), *The Rise of the Leaguers from 1863–1897: A History of the Football League* (Manchester, 1897) pp. 18–19.

13 *Saturday Night* 29 April 1893.

14 See 'Tityrus' op.cit. pp. 32–3. Anon, *Bolton in 1926: its trade, sport, history* (Bolton, 1926) p. 2 and P.M. Young (1961) op.cit. pp. 12–19. The early records of the club were destroyed in a fire. Blackpool St Johns wished to change their name to Blackpool in 1887 as there was no club bearing the town's name at that time. However, the vicar of St John's and club chairman refused to allow the change. The result was that 'a

large number left the meeting and went to the Stanley Arms Hotel next door'. Blackpool F.C. was the outcome. *Blackpool Gazette* 29 July 1887. I owe this reference to Miss M.H. Elsworth.

15 Even organists helped organise football. See E. Ambrose, *Melford Memories* (Sudbury, 1972) p. 107.

16 N.L. Jackson remembered the mid-1860s when

Saturday afternoons off were as yet a thing unknown. . . . However, by the aid of a sporting parson it was at last arranged that we might play games on Sunday afternoons—cricket in summer, football in winter—on condition that the participants should have duly attended Church in the morning. Further difficulties then arose from the opposition of the village's two dissenting ministers but one was won over and the other disregarded.

Jackson (1932) op.cit pp. 21–2. They eventually had to give up cricket in summer because the agricultural labourers had to work in the fields on Sunday afternoons. In rural England unorganised football had often been a part of harvest festival celebrations. See for example L.E. Denison (ed.), *Fifty Years at East Brent, The Letters of George Anthony Denison* (1902) p. 278, quoted by John Kent in 'Feelings and Festivals: an interpretation of some working-class religious attitudes' in H.J. Dyos and M. Wolff (eds), *The Victorian City* (1973) vol. 2 pp. 855–71 and W. Plomer (ed.), *Kilvert's Diary 1870–79* (1967) p. 149

17 Sheffield Sunday Schools also formed their own football union in part to 'remove the present objections connected with playing ordinary cupties, stripping at public houses, and playing on public-house grounds'. *Blackburn Times* October, November, December 1876, 5 January 1878, 2 March 1878. *Sheffield Daily Telegraph* 4 March 1879, 24 March 1887. *Athletic News* 29 September 1885.

18 See D.D. Molyneux, 'The Development of Physical Recreation in the Birmingham District from 1871 to 1892', Unpublished M.A. thesis, University of Birmingham 1957, pp. 39–40 and Appendices A and B.

19 The churches and chapels were inclined to grow more critical as 1900 approached because they saw themselves competing with the institutions of the burgeoning leisure industry for support. 'If working-class men and women patronised public-houses, bet on horses . . . and went to football matches they were unlikely to support financially the parish churches and mission chapels which middle-class religious institutions erected in working-class areas.' J.H.S. Kent, 'The Role of Religion in the Cultural Structure of the Late Victorian City' Royal Historical Society, *Transactions* 5th series 23 (1973) p. 164.

20 See B. Harrison, *Drink and the Victorians* (1971) esp. chapters 14 and 15 and his article 'Pubs' in H.J. Dyos and M. Wolff, *The Victorian City*, vol. I (1977 edn) pp. 161–90.

21 Molyneux, op.cit. p. 41. *Blackburn Standard* 15 January 1881.

22 *Athletic News* 17 March 1877, 22 September 1885, 9 May 1892; T. Keates, *History of the Everton Football Club 1878–9—1928–9* (Liverpool, 1929) p. 3; P.M. Young, *Manchester United* (1960) p. 9; Blackburn Rovers *Bazaar Handbook* (Blackburn, 1895) p. 74. *Bristol and District Football League Handbook* (Bristol, 1892). In 1865 the Post Office local directory for Sheffield listed thirteen football clubs and all save two had public house addresses. West Bromwich Albion used the White Hart Inn and

the Roebuck as dressing rooms between 1879–81 and, as late as 1894, three well known professional clubs, Gainsborough Trinity, Nottingham Forest and Manchester City, still changed before matches in pubs and walked to the ground; in the Gainsborough case, for example, a distance of some 150 yards through busy streets. P. Morris, *West Bromwich Albion* (1965) p. 6; *Athletic News Football Annual* (1894).

23 See *Sheffield Daily Telegraph* 4 March, 2 December 1879.
24 See Molyneux, op.cit. Appendix B.
25 *Darwen News* 13 May 1882.
26 *Cricket and Football Times* 6 January 1881.
27 *Athletic News* 28 December 1908.
28 *Blackburn Standard* 31 March 1883.
29 *Athletic News* 28 September 1881.
30 Ibid, 28 September 1881, 6 October 1885.
31 See below pp. 118–19.
32 For the role of the drink trade in the professional club see below p. 42. For the relationship between the growth of professional football and the consumption of drink see chapter six.
33 See his Appendix B.
34 *Sheffield Daily Telegraph* 25 March 1884.
35 See volumes of obituaries at the Sheffield City Library, Local History Section. The club appears to have faded after the legalisation of professionalism in 1885. *Sheffield Daily Telegraph* 16 April 1888.
36 *Athletic News* 6 July, 7 September 1886.
37 *Athletic News* 2 September 1889, 8 June 1891.
38 *Preston Herald* 1 October 1887.
39 For Bristol see H.E. Meller, *Leisure and the Changing City, 1870–1914* (1976) p. 275, n. 77. For more general employer attitudes in this area and other examples see B. Meakin, *Model Factories and Villages* (1905) pp. 203–48.
40 Though no hindrance either as far as is known. For a sketch of their early history see B. Joy, *Forward Arsenal!* (1952) pp. 2–4, and for the impact of professionalism on the club and its organisation see below pp. 34–5.
41 On Thames Ironworks see J. Booker, *Essex and the Industrial Revolution* (Chelmsford, 1974) p. 199 and P. Banburn, *Shipbuilders of the Thames and Medway* (1971) pp. 268–77. On Hills and the football club see R. Day, 'The Motivation of Some Football Club Directors: An Aspect of the Social History of Association Football 1890–1914'. Unpublished M.A. thesis University of Warwick 1976, pp. 39–49, A. Gibson and W. Pickford op.cit. vol. III, pp. 87–9 and C.P. Korr 'West Ham United Football Club and the Beginnings of Professional Football in East London 1895–1914', *Journal of Contemporary History*, vol. 13, no. 2, April 1978, pp. 211–32.
42 They were, of course, eventually taken over by a brewer and formed into Manchester United. See P.M. Young (1960) op.cit. p. 5. For Stoke see 'Tityrus' op.cit. pp. 122–23. P.M. Young (1968) op.cit. p. 98 casts doubt on the founders being old boys of Charterhouse. For Crewe Alexandra see *Crewe Chronicle* 22 October 1887.
43 D.D. Molyneux, op.cit. Appendix B.
44 On the early history of Calthorpe and its pioneer work in Birmingham see *Athletic News* 21 October 1876. The first secretary of the Birmingham

F.A. who served from 1877–86 was a commercial clerk and the next secretary and treasurer, who remained in office for over forty years, had been a founder of the Birmingham Clerks' Association F.C. Similarly the President from 1875–1923, Mr Charles Crump, began work as a clerk in the Stafford Road Works of the Great Western Railway at Wolverhampton. He became chief clerk in 1868. The skills of clerks would be essential to any football club with aspirations, and useful even to those with few. See D.D. Molyneux, op.cit. pp. 21–4, J.A.H. Catton, (1900) op.cit. pp. 42–3 and *Birmingham Daily Post* 16 April 1923.

45 As late as 1871 there were only 100,000 commercial and bank clerks in the country but numbers had doubled in the 1860s and doubled again in the 1870s. S.G. Checkland, *The Rise of Industrial Society in England* (1964) p. 218. Even G. Anderson in his *Victorian Clerks* (Manchester, 1976) does not look at their lives outside the office but he does point out that clerks made up about 0.8 per cent of the labour force in 1851 and 4 per cent by 1901 (p. 2). For Ramsay see his obituary *Birmingham Mail* 10 October 1935.

46 Some works were probably stimulated into forming teams after the coming of professionalism. Preston North End, for example, wishing to tap local talent, presented a challenge shied to be competed for by teams from local mills and workshops, in 1887. See *Preston Herald* 17 August 1887.

47 *Blackburn Times* 4 January 1879. Blackburn Olympic, the F.A. Cup Winners of 1883, were formed by an amalgamation of the John Street and Black Star clubs. *Blackburn Standard* 16 February 1878.

48 P.M. Young (1962) op.cit. pp. 16, 37: 'Tityrus', op.cit. pp. 104–5 and 93–5: T. Keates, op.cit. p. 2: *Athletic News* 9 December 1876: *Sheffield Independent* 6 September 1867: *Sheffield Daily Telegraph* 23 March 1889: *Preston Herald* 3 May 1884, 20 May 1885. It was clearly a way of keeping the cricketers together during the winter as the Sheffield Wednesday minutes underlined.

49 W. Pickford in the introduction to C.E. Sutcliffe, J.A. Brierley and F.Howarth, *The Story of the Football League 1888–1938* (Preston, 1938).

50 *Athletic News* 2 October 1878, 31 May, 21 June 1882, 25 May 1886.

51 *Football* 4 October 1882.

52 *Sheffield Daily Telegraph* 22 December 1873; *Athletic News* 29 January 1879.

53 *Preston Herald* 24 October 1883, 14 October 1885: *Nottingham Daily Guardian* 26 January 1885: *Athletic News* 18 November 1889.

54 In most cases the surname was the same but the christian names different which suggests the secretaries were the sons. The occupations were the fathers' with the exception of the dressmaker. The occupations were farmer, greengrocer and beer retailer, provision dealer, dressmaker, builder, insurance agent and foreman tailor.

55 *Newcastle Daily Chronicle* 11 October 1881.

56 24 March 1888. It went on to say that the game therefore deserved support from all classes.

57 *Athletic News* 29 September, 20 October 1880, 6 October 1885.

58 *Darwen News* 15 March 1884; *Preston Herald* 19 March 1884.

59 See for example *Darwen News* 9 March 1878, 22 February 1879.

60 *Darwen News* 22 February 1879.

61 G. Green, *The Official History of the F.A. Cup* (1949) p. 25: *Darwen News*

8 March 1879. At this period the club, making an admission charge of 3d per head, had gates of £40 and £25 for matches against Blackburn Olympic and Blackburn Rovers respectively. *Darwen News* 19 April 1883. The Old Etonians finally won the match 6–2 after two drawn games of 5–5 and 2–2, all in London.

62   G. Green op.cit. p. 32. J. Walvin, *The People's Game* (1975) p. 74. The *Blackburn Times* 7 April 1883 listed the occupations of the Olympic team as three weavers, a loomer, a gilder, a labourer in an iron foundry, a dresser in an iron foundry, a clerk, a master plumber, a licensed victualler and a dentist. The editorial in the *Athletic News* had characterised the Blackburn Olympic—Old Carthusian semi-final as being between 'patricians and plebians'. The Old Boys were all 'educated gentlemen, and undoubted "swells" when compared with their rough and ready opponents, every man of whom has inherited the primeval curse, and has to earn his bread by the sweat of his brow'. The paper went on to say that the Old Carthusians were stronger physically but that the Olympic were more skilful and secured 'an easy, and we are happy to say, bloodless victory'. *Athletic News* 21 March 1883. Six months earlier a southern football journal had characterised Olympic as 'matured and accomplished professionals'. *Football* 22 November 1882.

63   *Blackburn Times* 7 April 1883.

64   *Preston Herald* 30 August 1882. Unfortunately for the Olympic, Yates died in 1886 and the club was unable to replace him. It collapsed in 1889 after a brief and unsuccessful flirtation with professionalism. It was, of course, involved in stiff competition with Blackburn Rovers. See *Athletic News* 16 February 1886, 18 January 1887, 28 January 1889. *Blackburn Standard* 30 October, 4 December 1886, 18 June 1887, 31 August 1889. *Blackburn Times* 31 August 1889. *Bolton Daily Chronicle* 12 January 1887.

65   *Blackburn Standard* 13 May 1882.

66   Most of this section is based on R. Day, op.cit. pp. 87–107. As one member said during the crisis of 1893, Arsenal F.C. 'had worked on independent lines as a working men's club, and he only hoped that they would work it out successfully to the end'. *Woolwich Gazette and Plumstead Times* 10 February 1893.

67   Ibid. 15 May 1891: Public Record Office (PRO) Board of Trade (BT) 31/5563, 38703. Humble remained a director when the club was moved to North London for the 1913–14 season by which time it was certainly a 'capitalist club'. See Arsenal F.C. programmes for that season. On similar opposition to limited liability at Reading see S. Yeo, *Religion and Voluntary Organisations in Crisis* (1976) p. 193.

68   The club estimated that the cost of their landlord's proposal would be between £500 and £600 a year and that the highest rent paid by a football league team was Nottingham Forest's £200 per year. Day, op.cit. p. 92. When Everton were involved in arguments with their landlord in 1891 they published the following ground rental annual figures for thirteen leading clubs: Aston Villa £175, Notts. County £135, Bootle £80, Burnley £75, Stoke £75, Blackburn Rovers £60, Darwen £50, Wolverhampton Wanderers £50, Sunderland £45, Accrington £40, Bolton Wanderers £35, West Bromwich Albion £35, Preston North End £30. *Athletic News* 12 October 1891.

69 *Athletic News* 22 January 1900.

70 With the ending of the Boer War the Arsenal was run down by the government and the subsequent trade depression in the district produced further losses for the club. It went into liquidation in 1910 by which time it was in the hands of a rich London property developer and estate agent, Henry Norris. See below p. 46.

71 *Athletic News* 23 June 1885 from which the details were taken. Aston Villa paid £479.6.6 to their players in the same season. *Athletic News* 7 July 1885.

72 *Birmingham Daily Mail* 30 January 1889. Derby County did it rather differently when they reorganised in 1891. The club was to consist of persons willing to guarantee £5 or more. They would control and manage the club through appropriate officers and committees which they elected from among themselves. Derby County F.C. Minutes of Committee Meetings, 11, 21 May, 1, 8, 15, 22, 29 June 1891.

73 It is safe to assume that several clubs were dividing the work among various specialist committees by the end of the 1880s. By that time Aston Villa was proposing a match committee, a finance and ground committee and a second team committee with a general committee to meet monthly and oversee the work. *Athletic News* 2 June 1890.

74 Blackburn Rovers were still holding a bazaar in 1895.

75 But Woolwich Arsenal was successfully prosecuted following a lottery they had organised in 1902. See the report in the *Bradford Daily Telegraph* 10 January 1903. *Blackburn Standard* 13, 20 March 30 October 1886; *Football Field* 20 March 1886. The winner's ticket had been one of many apparently purchased by penny contributions from half a dozen people who then raffled the ticket off among themselves. Unfortunately the winner did not long enjoy his good fortune, dying of smallpox in 1892. J. Baron, *Blackburn Rovers: The Blackburn Weekly Telegraph's Handy History* (Blackburn, 1906) p. 39. The first prize in the Blackburn Olympic draw went to a local stationer and the announcement was greeted with cries of 'be hanged' and 'he's enoo' 'bout 'em' and, as the *Blackburn Standard* had it, 'to him that hath shall be given but not so piously expressed'.

76 *Athletic News* 18 March 1889. The scheme was shelved.

77 See the two editorials in the paper dated 5 and 12 June 1888. The *Birmingham Daily Mail* claimed that without limited liability, no club's rules could be enforced in a court of law. See *Birmingham Daily Mail* 30 January 1889.

78 Seventeen of the companies ceased to do business before 1914.

79 All three of these clubs eventually went into liquidation although the socio-occupational character of the shareholding was obviously not the most important factor.

80 PRO BT 31/61564. There were only 87 shareholders in 1899.

81 PRO BT 31/62478.

82 PRO BT 31/46572.

83 PRO BT 31/16048/58704. On Hill-Wood see below p. 48.

84 PRO BT 31/18499/98951. The prospectus observed:

In addition to the revenue to be derived from the gates taken at Football Matches, which the Company anticipate will be sufficient to cover all the expenses of carrying on the Club and paying a Dividend to the Shareholders, the Company anticipate a large income by letting the Ground during the summer months for Cricket and Athletic Sports, Lawn Tennis and Other Games, Horse and Flower Shows, Fetes, etc., for which there will be ample accommodation.

85 PRO BT 31/6930/48754.
86 PRO BT 31/2076/122899 BT 31/13580/115306. There was a letterpress printer and a signwriter among the shareholders but these were almost certainly independent operators although, of course, they may have begun as employees.
87 PRO BT 31/5927/41707.
88 PRO BT 31/11072/84244. Bottomley was a company promoter, journalist, racehorse owner and high liver. He founded and edited the weekly *John Bull* 1906–21, and was Liberal M.P. for South Hackney, 1906–10, and the Independent member for the same constituency, 1910–12 and 1918–22. It is doubtful whether he took much interest in the club. In 1922 Bottomley was charged with fraudulent conversion under the Larceny Act, 1916, and on conviction sentenced to seven years' penal servitude. For more details of his life see Julian Symons, *Horatio Bottomley* (1955).
89 PRO BT 31/20140/116965.
90 PRO BT 31/7853/56220.
91 PRO BT 31/5563/38703. There were 65 engineers, 68 turners, 76 fitters, 46 machinists and 53 labourers in 1893. There were also 54 married women, most holding one share each, whose names and addresses indicated that they were the spouses of the engineers, turners, fitters and machinists. As women rarely appeared as club shareholders this is an intriguing piece of information although what it signifies I do not know.
92 PRO BT 31/6729/47303. See Appendix 1 to this chapter.
93 PRO BT 31/53482.
94 PRO BT 31/43026.
95 PRO BT 31/39494.
96 PRO BT 31/40946.
97 PRO BT 31/5336/36563.
98 PRO BT 31/95489. Its fortunes did flag somewhat after 1918 and did not recover until after 1945.
99 PRO BT 31/4716/31109. *Athletic News* 16 May, 25 July, 15 August 1892.
100 *Sunderland Herald* 10 July 1896.
101 PRO BT 31/49116.
102 PRO BT 31/34292.
103 *Athletic News* 23 December 1889.
104 See below pp. 175–9.
105 *Athletic News* 18 March 1889.
106 *Birmingham Daily. Gazette* 30 June 1896.
107 *Athletic News* 28 December 1896. Or at least the advancement of the city's two leading professional sides.
108 It went up to $7\frac{1}{2}$ per cent after the 1914–18 war. Sir F. Wall, *Fifty Years of Football* (1935) p. 125. There was no limitation on dividends in Scotland. Glasgow Celtic paid 25 per cent in 1909. *Athletic News* 17 May 1909.
109 Was 'Tityrus' implying that some did when he wrote that the directors of Sheffield Wednesday were always gentlemen and gave their services free? See 'Tityrus', op.cit. p. 112.

110 For the quarrel in more detail see R. Day, op.cit. pp. 55–69. T. Keates, op.cit. pp. 37–9 and 'Tityrus' op.cit. pp. 77–9. The new club remained very much Houlding's creature until he died and his brother sold all the family's shares.

111 He did not, however, have freehold possession until 1903.

112 See R. Day, op.cit. pp. 69–80.

113 Norris was a south London estate agent and property developer who built over 2000 houses in the Fulham and Wimbledon districts. He was a member of Fulham Borough Council for many years and Mayor from 1909–19. He was Coalition Unionist M.P. for East Fulham, 1918–22, and was knighted in 1917. Before becoming Chairman of Arsenal F.C. he had been a director of Fulham F.C. He was suspended from football management by the F.A. in 1927 after an inquiry into the financial affairs of the Arsenal club. When he died in 1935 he left an estate worth £71,733 gross. See *The Times* 12 April 1913, 9 December 1919, 31 July 1934, 15 January 1935.

114 This seems to be the only instance of a professional club that had grown up in a particular place being moved to another place completely unconnected with it. American baseball, of course, is littered with such traumatic moves which suggests that the profit motive was much more a part of American professional sport almost from the start than it has ever been in England. If a team could not make money in Cleveland, for example, then the franchise, controlled by the League, would be sold to the highest bidder and the team would go and play elsewhere. Considerable ruthlessness was shown in ejecting clubs from the National League if they could not attract enough support to make healthy profits. See for examples, D.Q. Voigt, *American Baseball: From Gentleman's Sport to the Commissioner System* vol. I (Norman, 1966).

115 For a more detailed account see the *Bradford Daily Telegraph* 14, 16, 23, 29 January, 12, 26, 28 February, 27, 28 March, 30 April, 4, 28, 30 May 1903 and the *Bradford Weekly Telegraph* 30 May 1903. Apparently it cost £917 to get the team together. Gate receipts and members' subscriptions totalled almost £4000 in the club's first season and by 1906–7 exceeded £7000. *Athletic News* 27 April 1908.

116 *Athletic News* 27 July 1908.

117 P.M. Young (1960) op.cit. p. 38.

118 *Athletic News* 29 May, 5 June, 3, 17, 31 July, 21 August, 4 December 1893: *Globe* 1 February 1893. The same season saw Bootle resign from the second division for financial reasons, Gorton Villa expired and Ardwick were compelled to auction some of their players in a public house.

119 *Athletic News* 21 August 1893.

120 *Athletic News* 11 September 1899.

121 P. Morris (1965) op.cit. p. 42. Public meetings were not uncommon means of rejuvenating an ailing football club. Walsall held a town meeting when in severe financial trouble in 1895 and Wolverhampton Wanderers had recourse to a similar method in the same season. *Wolverhampton Express and Star* 14–15 February 1895. Stoke went through a similar experience in 1908. *Birmingham Gazette and Express* 19 June 1908.

122 *Athletic News* 5 February 1900.

123 P. Morris (1965) op.cit. p. 52. Aston Villa contributed 100 guineas to the appeal. Aston Villa F.C. Directors' Meetings Minutes 2 February 1905.

124 Blackpool had been unable to travel to London for their match with Arsenal

because they had no money to pay the rail fares. The *Athletic News* felt that the only solution was the pooling of gate receipts although it agreed, apologetically, that such a proposal sounded like socialism. *Athletic News* 6 February, 4, 18 September 1899.

125 The *Athletic News Football Annual* was fond of making this charge. See for example the years 1894 and 1895. In the latter year 'Rob Roy' claimed that 'the adroit use of figures in many of the published balance sheets is quite transparent, and must be set down to a strong desire to make the assets remove the big margin of debt on the current income'. The article went on to claim that professional auditors were by no means always employed on club accounts. See also chapter four.

126 Sir F. Wall, op.cit. p. 113. 'A man who gives himself up to football, body and soul . . . will take risks and get himself entangled in such a way as he would never dream of in the conduct of his own business.'

127 *Athletic News* 27 September 1909. See another article on similar lines in the issue of 18 October 1909. These pieces did appear after the abortive players' 'strike' for which see below pp. 111–14.

128 See the article by J.J. Bentley in *C.B. Fry's Magazine*, vol. IV, October 1905–March 1906, p. 146.

129 On the history of Glossop see the chapter by H.J. Perkin in A.H. Birch (ed.) *Small Town Politics* (1959). On the use a politician might make of football see Arnold Bennett's story, *The Card* (1911). We saw earlier that no profit was ever made, nor did Hill-Wood expect to make any. See R. Day, op.cit. pp. 26–38.

130 Some of these early dinners were grand affairs. When Sheffield played Manchester in 1877, players and officials dined afterwards at the Imperial Hotel. There were speeches, champagne and popular songs including one rather recondite number called 'Kafoozlem'. The proceedings were completed by an entertainer. *Athletic News* 3 March 1877. Blackburn Rovers were entertained to a 'knife and fork tea' at the Royal Hotel following their match at Sunderland in 1880. Toasts were drunk and songs rendered before they caught the 6.40 p.m. train home. *Sunderland Daily Herald* 14 November 1880. See also *The Sportsman* 28 January 1889 for an account of the festivities after the Corinthians match with Preston at Leyton.

131 *Birmingham Daily Mail* 24 October 1883. It is not clear that English football clubs generally had the same importance as centres of sociability built around drinking and talk, especially for those too old to play, as R.J. Holt claims French sports clubs had. R.J. Holt, 'Aspects of the Social History of Sports in France 1870–1914', University of Oxford D. Phil. 1977, pp. 150–64.

132 *Athletic News* 4 October 1909. We saw earlier that they had been supported by a brewer since their origin out of the ashes of Newton Heath in 1902. The F.A. was unhappy with the way in which the club was run and set up an inquiry into its affairs in 1910. The inquiry found, among other things, that the club was 'extravagantly run', was paying the Chairman's brewery £740 rent for fourteen acres of land which they were not using and in general had violated agreements reached with the F.A. in 1904. See *The Times* 31 March 1910; *Athletic News* April 4 1910.

APPENDIX I

Darwen F.C. Occupations of shareholders 1896
The numbers of individual shareholders are in brackets.

Overlooker	(28)	Collier	(3)	Saddler	(1)
Publican	(21)	Beerseller	(3)	Draper	(2)
Carter	(8)	Printer	(5)	Iron founder	(1)
Oil Dealer	(1)	Paper Merchant	(1)	Back Tenter	(2)
Packer	(2)	Fitter	(1)	Shuttlemaker	(2)
Gardener	(1)	Coal Dealer	(1)	Commercial Traveller	(1)
Quarryman	(6)	Presser	(1)	Salesman	(2)
Barber	(2)	Gentleman	(1)	Drysalter	(1)
Hairdresser	(1)	Dealer	(1)	Designer	(3)
Cab Proprietor	(1)	Fruiterer	(1)	Cloth Broker	(2)
Labourer	(19)	Newspaper Proprietor	(1)	Bricklayer	(1)
Restaurant Proprietor	(2)	Shopkeeper	(1)	Winder	(1)
Paper Maker	(14)	Porter	(1)	Farmer	(3)
Moulder	(3)	Bottler	(1)	Chimney Sweep	(1)
Taper	(5)	Paper Stainer	(1)	Reelerman	(1)
Tape Sizer	(6)	Drawer-In	(4)	Contractor	(2)
Tailor	(3)	Insurance Agent	(3)	Rope maker	(1)
Weaver	(28)	Grocer	(11)	Jeweller	(2)
Mechanic	(5)	Journalist	(2)	Pattern Maker	(1)
Manager	(3)	Painter	(6)	Waste Dealer	(1)
Mineral Water Manufacturer	(1)	Schoolmaster	(2)	Engine Tenter	(3)
Cashier	(1)	Key Maker	(1)	Slater	(1)
Spinner	(7)	Cloth maker	(1)	Manufacturer	(1)
Newsagent	(4)	Brass founder	(1)	Agent	(2)
Loomer	(10)	Bill Poster	(2)	Postman	(1)
Mason	(2)	Butcher	(6)	Brickmaker	(1)
Clerk	(15)	Colour Mixer	(2)	Grinder	(3)
Engineer	(6)	Mill-Hand	(1)	Tripe Dresser	(3)
Machine Joiner	(7)	Herb beer Maker	(1)	Confectioner	(1)
Book-keeper	(1)	Fireman	(1)	Photographer	(1)
Plumber	(2)	Pawnbroker	(1)	Size Mixer	(1)
Chemist	(1)	Tea Merchant	(1)	Machinist	(1)
Tobacconist	(2)	Tackler	(1)	Block Cutter	(1)
Stoker	(2)	Wheelwright	(1)	Baker	(2)
Shoemaker	(1)	Shopman	(1)	Architect	(1)
		Water Inspector	(1)	Fireheater	(1)
		Stationmaster	(1)		

Source: PRO BT 31/6729/47303

APPENDIX II

MAP 1   F.A. Cup Entrants 1871–72

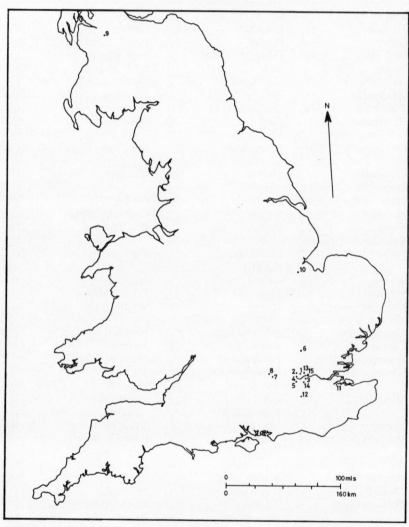

1. Wanderers
2. Harrow Chequers
3. Clapham Rovers
4. Upton Park
5. Crystal Palace

6. Hitchin
7. Maidenhead
8. Great Marlow
9. Queens Park Glasgow
10. Donington School
(Spalding)

11. Royal Engineers
12. Reigate Priory
13. Hampstead Heathens
14. Barnes
15. Civil Service

MAP 2   F.A. Cup Entrants 1883–84 (2nd round draw 14th April 1883) 100 Clubs

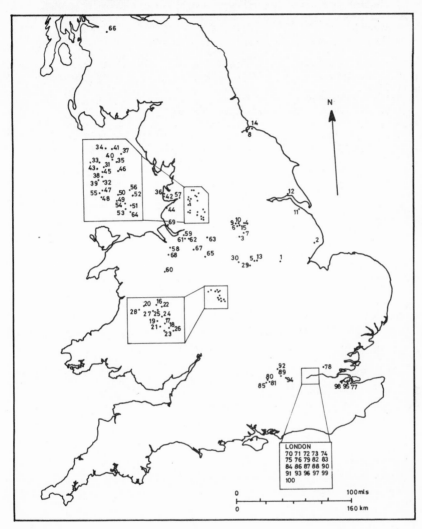

1. Grantham
2. Spilsby
3. Spital (Chesterfield)
4. Rotherham
5. Notts County
6. Heeley (Sheffield)
7. Staveley
8. Middlesbrough
9. Lockwood Bros (Sheffield)
10. Sheffield Club
11. Grimsby
12. Hull Town
13. Nottingham Forest
14. Redcar and Coatham
15. Sheffield Wednesday
16. Walsall Town
17. Calthorpe (Birmingham)
18. Birmingham Excelsior
19. Small Heath Alliance (Birmingham)
20. Stafford Road (Wolverhampton)
21. Aston United (Birmingham)
22. Wednesbury Old Athletic
23. St. Georges Birmingham

24. West Bromwich
    Albion
25. Wednesbury Town
26. Aston Villa
27. Walsall
28. Wolverhampton
    Wanderers
29. Long Eaton Rangers
30. Derby Midland
31. Blackburn Olympic
32. Darwen Ramblers
33. Blackburn Park Road
34. Low Moor
35. Accrington
36. Blackpool
37. Padiham
38. Lower Darwen
39. Darwen
40. Church
41. Clitheroe
42. South Shore
    (Blackpool)
43. Blackburn Rovers
44. Southport
45. Eagley
46. Hallwell
47. Bolton Wanderers
48. Bolton Olympic
49. Great Lever

50. Astley Bridge
51. Hurst
52. Turton
53. Rossendale
54. Irwell Springs
55. Bolton
56. Bradshaw
57. Preston North End
58. Druids (Ruabon)
59. Northwich Victoria
60. Oswestry
61. Hartford St. Johns
62. Davenham
63. Macclesfield
64. Manchester
65. Stoke-on-Trent
66. Queens Park Glasgow
67. Crewe Alexandra
68. Wrexham
69. Liverpool Ramblers
70. Brentwood
71. Hanover United
72. Hendon
73. Old Etonians (London)
74. Mosquitoes
75. Pilgrims (London)
76. Old Westminsters
77. Cheltenham
78. Romford

79. Woodford Bridge
80. Reading
81. South Reading
82. Upton Park (London)
83. Acton
84. Old Carthusians
    (London)
85. Reading Minster
86. Old Foresters
    (London)
87. Dreadnought
    (London)
88. West End
89. Maidenhead
90. Clapham Rovers
    (London)
91. Kildare
92. Great Marlow
93. Hornchurch
94. Windsor Home Park
95. Royal Engineers
96. Old Wykehamists
    (London)
97. Upton Rangers
    (London)
98. Rochester
99. Uxbridge
100. Swifts (London)

MAP 3 F.A. Cup Entrants 1913–14

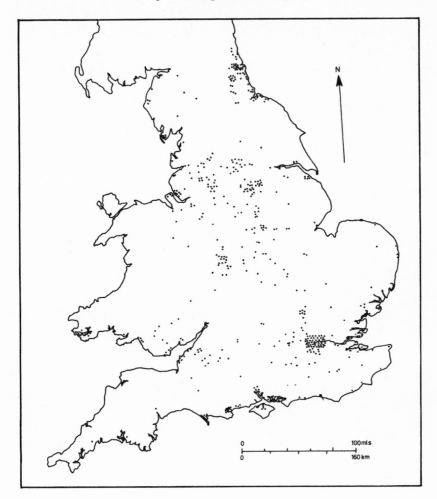

MAP 4   FOOTBALL LEAGUE 1888–89

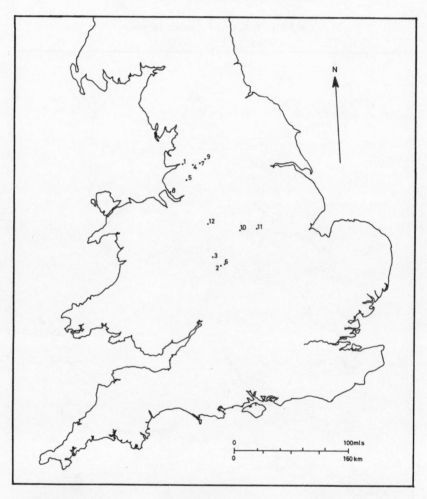

1. Preston North End	5. Bolton Wanderers	9. Burnley
2. Aston Villa	6. West Bromwich	10. Derby County
3. Wolverhampton	Albion	11. Notts County
Wanderers	7. Accrington	12. Stoke
4. Blackburn Rovers	8. Everton	

MAP 5   FOOTBALL LEAGUE 1892–93

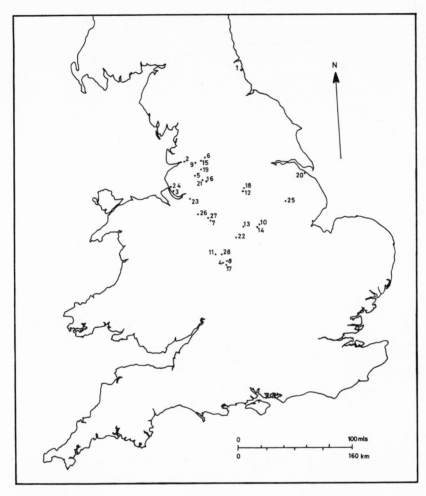

1. Sunderland
2. Preston North End
3. Everton
4. Aston Villa
5. Bolton Wanderers
6. Burnley
7. Stoke
8. West Bromwich Albion
9. Blackburn Rovers
10. Nottingham Forest
11. Wolverhampton Wanderers
12. Sheffield Wednesday
13. Derby County
14. Notts County
15. Accrington
16. Newton Heath
17. Small Heath
18. Sheffield United
19. Darwen
20. Grimsby Town
21. Ardwick
22. Burton Swifts
23. Northwich Victoria
24. Bootle
25. Lincoln City
26. Crewe Alexandra
27. Burslem Port Vale
28. Walsall Town Swifts

MAP 6   FOOTBALL LEAGUE 1913–14

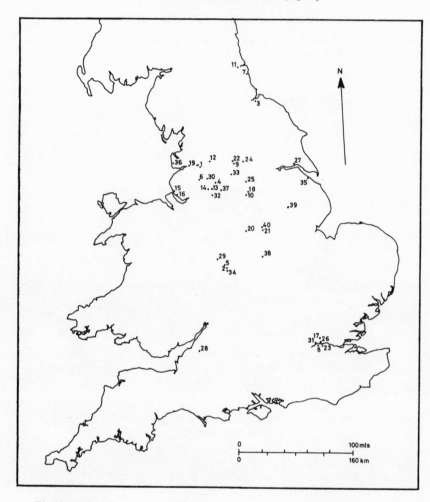

1. Blackburn Rovers	15. Everton	28. Bristol City
2. Aston Villa	16. Liverpool	29. Wolverhampton
3. Middlesbrough	17. Tottenham Hotspur	Wanderers
4. Oldham Athletic	18. Sheffield Wednesday	30. Bury
5. West Bromwich	19. Preston North End	31. Fulham
Albion	20. Derby County	32. Stockport County
6. Bolton Wanderers	21. Notts County	33. Huddersfield
7. Sunderland	22. Bradford Park	34. Birmingham
8. Chelsea	Avenue	35. Grimsby Town
9. Bradford City	23. Woolwich Arsenal	36. Blackpool
10. Sheffield United	24. Leeds City	37. Glossop
11. Newcastle United	25. Barnsley	38. Leicester Fosse
12. Burnley	26. Clapton Orient	39. Lincoln City
13. Manchester City	27. Hull City	40. Nottingham Forest
14. Manchester United		

MAP 7   SOUTHERN LEAGUE 1894–95

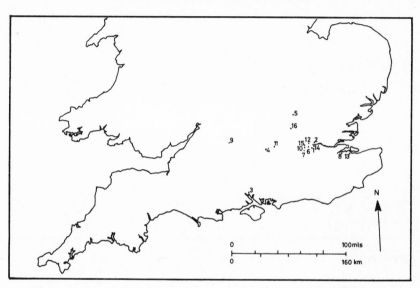

DIVISION I

1. Millwall Athletic
2. Ilford
3. Southampton St. Mary
4. Reading
5. Luton Town

6. Clapton
7. Royal Ordnance (Woolwich-London)
8. Chatham
9. Swindon Town

DIVISION II

10. New Brompton

11. Maidenhead
12. Old St. Stephen's (London)
13. Sheppey United
14. Bromley
15. Uxbridge
16. Chesham

MAP 8   SOUTHERN LEAGUE 1913–14

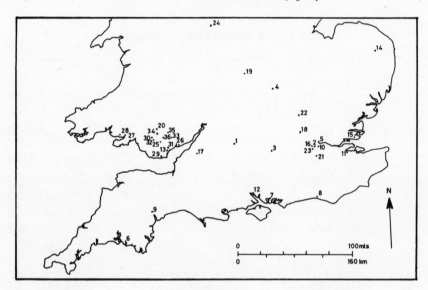

DIVISION I

1. Swindon Town
2. Crystal Palace
3. Reading
4. Northampton
5. West Ham United
6. Plymouth Argyle
7. Portsmouth
8. Brighton & Hove Albion
9. Exeter City
10. Queens Park Rangers (London)
11. Gillingham

12. Southampton
13. Cardiff City
14. Norwich City
15. Southend United
16. Millwall
17. Bristol Rovers
18. Watford
19. Coventry City
20. Merthyr

DIVISION II

21. Croydon Common
22. Luton Town
23. Brentford

24. Stoke
25. Pontypridd
26. Newport County
27. Swansea Town
28. Llanelly
29. Barry Town
30. Mid-Rhondda
31. Caerphilly
32. Mardy
33. Ton Pentre
34. Abertillery
35. Aberdare
36. Treharris

CHAPTER THREE
AMATEURS AND PROFESSIONALS

WE have seen that organised football, based on a widespread acceptance of a more or less uniform code of laws, expanded quite quickly through the 1870s, with areas of particularly rapid growth being located in Greater London, Birmingham and Staffordshire, Lancashire, the West Riding of Yorkshire and the Eastern Midlands. When London clubs met clubs from the regions, which they were doing more often as the 1870s drew to a close, they usually won. Members of all social classes played although the majority of players were increasingly working men. But in and around London both the Football Association and the leading clubs were dominated by either leisured gentlemen or by professionally or commercially employed products of the public and grammar schools. Most of these men almost certainly subscribed to some variant of the healthy mind in the healthy body syndrome. Play was good for you but it was also done for fun. Indeed, that was why it was good for you. It was not to be confused with work which was also good for you. Playing for money was something gentlemen did not do.

It is difficult to be exact about when football players were first paid for playing. As early as 1876 Peter Andrews and James J. Lang had left Scotland to play for the Heeley club in Sheffield, but although they were often said to have been the first professionals no satisfactory evidence has ever been uncovered.[1] In the spring of 1879 Darwen played a match with Turton 'for the benefit of two Scotch gentlemen who have played with Darwen during the past season'. The two gentlemen were Love and Suter. There is not much doubt that Suter was paid for playing and Love was probably giving his services for a consideration. Even before that, Suter had played for Turton in the final of their own challenge cup in 1878 and 'the Second Prize money, £3 won by the Turton First Team, be handed over to C. Tootill, that he pay Suter out of it (he not being elected to play by the committee)'.[2] A few weeks earlier, following a defeat by Blackburn Rovers, the Darwen paper had commented that the Rovers had been 'well marshalled by McIntyre, who, we believe is engaged as professional to the Rovers'.[3] McIntyre was an upholsterer by trade who had allegedly left Glasgow, where he had played for the Glasgow

Rangers football club and where work was slack, to look for a job in Lancashire.[4]

Whoever the first professional was, rumours of professionalism were widespread in the early 1880s. The *Midland Athlete*, for example, noted in 1881 that

at present we know of no GLARING case wherein men have been paid to play football ... we do know of cases where men have received more than their legitimate expenses to play for a club. But though men are not often paid in cash they are in other ways; it is no uncommon thing for influential members of a club to obtain situations for good players as an inducement for them to play with certain clubs. Then it is not improbable that club funds may or have been used to find a small business for popular players who pose as 'mine host' before their admiring clubmates. ... Men who can afford to give up business for football, who can travel here, there and everywhere at all times and seasons, men who receive payment for playing in certain matches, men who make a profit out of the game they play, are professionals.[5]

Similarly the *Football Annual*, in the same year, felt that it was a mistake 'to disguise the speedy approach of a time when the subject of professional players will require the earnest attention of those on whom devolves the management of Association Football'.[6]

Of course, professionalism existed in other sports, notably pedestrianism, prize fighting and, even more relevantly, cricket. More relevantly because the first two activities had apparently permanent bad names, largely as a consequence of dishonest betting and the fixing of contests. The experience of professionalism in cricket was much more interesting and one with which leading members of the Football Association, such as its secretary, C.W. Alcock, who was also secretary to the Surrey County Cricket Club, were familiar. In the middle years of the nineteenth century it had looked as though first-class cricket was going to be in the hands of touring elevens of professionals playing each other and local clubs and hopefully making a living out of it. But the formation of the county club and the coming of touring teams from overseas put an end to that prospect. By the 1880s the county clubs and the M.C.C., both acmes of aristocratic patronage and middle-class exclusiveness, clearly ran the game and kept the professionals firmly in their place. Cricket was a model for the football administrator faced with the issue of professionalism.[7]

The first stage of the problem of professionalism in association football manifested itself in the crisis surrounding importation. Importation was the playing of men brought into the town, district or team from outside. The borrowing of players from other clubs for important matches, particularly knock-out cup-ties, began to grow with the increase in number of those competitions at the end of the 1870s.[8] Some particularly sought-after players might appear for several different clubs in the same cup competition during one season.[9] Such activities were considered by many leading football officials to be outside the spirit of the game, particularly when the imported 'professors' came from north of the border. Local clubs, it was argued, should consist of local players.

I understood when I gave my mite towards purchasing the handsome cup (the Lancashire Football Association's trophy) that it was for Lancashire lads, and they alone. If the richer clubs can afford to pay professionals, let them do so, but when they compete for our grand trophy, let the true Lancashire lads have equal chance of winning it.[10]

Importation undoubtedly caused ill feeling and some clubs apparently went to a good deal of trouble to seek it out and expose it. According to a letter to the magazine *Football*, in early 1883, Nottingham Forest had several placards put up in the streets of Sheffield offering a reward of £20 to any person who would bring them evidence to establish that three players who had recently appeared for Sheffield Wednesday in a cup-tie against Forest had not been members of the Wednesday club until just before the game.[11] The Albion club of Sheffield tried to obtain a suspension of the local F.A.'s cup competition in 1882.[12] Some people were even prepared to rank importation above professionalism in the hierarchy of sins and an argument advanced more than once was that if professionalism was legalised then importation would cease to matter. The footloose 'amateur' would be replaced by the contract professional.[13]

But as we noted above importation was really the first stage of the struggle over professionalism and local football associations responded to the problem in different ways in accordance with their interpretation of their own local situation. In Lancashire, for example, which by the 1880s clearly had more than just a few imported players, not to mention actual paid men, the football association tried to ban imported players from cup-ties in 1882, but the clubs threw out the recommendation of the committee.[14] Most people at the meeting said they did not like importation but that fairness could not be neglected when considering how to deal with it. As the Bolton Wanderers representative said 'the Scotch players in their team had put them in a position that they would not otherwise have attained ... in the football world'.[15] The compromise reached at the A.G.M. in May 1882 was to insist on two years of continued residence before players born outside the county could play in cup-ties. Nor would players be allowed to play for more than one club in the various cup competitions in the same season.[16] The Sheffield F.A. went somewhat further in 1883 when they decided to require any footballer, who was objected to on the grounds of professionalism, to prove to the satisfaction of the committee that he had not received more than travelling and hotel expenses. They also insisted on the one club per player per season rule for all cup-ties.[17] The Birmingham F.A. refused to believe the problem existed much locally but threatened to deal firmly with any local players accepting inducements from outside.[18]

But it was professionalism, rather than importation, that was the subject of a good deal of public and, one suspects, private discussion in the game from about 1883 onwards, with Lancashire being the focus of most of the comment. Looking forward to the new season of 1883–4, the *Athletic News* indicated the changes which it thought had taken place over the preceding three or four years. Football, which was played and enjoyed almost free of expense, 'has developed into a vast business institution. A club now needs as much managing as a big shop, whilst there are many concerns which do not enjoy the turnover of which some of our leading clubs can boast.' The paper went on to note that Bolton Wanderers had expended £1082 in the previous season and their balance in hand was only £11. With most matches played at home, where had the money gone? The answer was clear enough: into the players' pockets.[19]

What was wrong with that? The opponents of professionalism replied with two major arguments. First, to accept professionalism would mean accepting that what up until then had been a voluntary leisure activity run by the participants for the participants would in future become a business. It would then be run like any other business and that would mean maximising profits by playing to win, if not at all costs, then with not too much attention to sporting scruples. Second, in such a situation, the larger, wealthier clubs, by paying the most money, would secure the best players and the smaller clubs, with relatively meagre financial resources, would have to do the best they could. Many would not survive in the best company. The effect of this would be to damage irreparably the old structure of the game based, as it was, on essentially local rivalries. In addition to these two major arguments there was a subsidiary one: that the football professional stood by himself because in nearly all other cases the professional is looked upon as a teacher of the game or sport by means of which he gains a livelihood, while at football the paid man is simply one who is called upon to give as good a display of his powers as he can, in order that the club which engages him may make its matches as attractive as possible, and so draw together large attendances. When he can't do this, he is replaced by others, hence the concentration on winning by fair means or foul.[20]

Those in favour of making the professional a legal part of the structure of association football were divided, although not necessarily equally, into two groups by virtue of the reasons with which they defended their views. The first group felt that the whole issue was inflated and the remedy very simple. As the *Sporting Life* succinctly put it,

there can be no possible objection to the recognised payment of men who cannot afford to pay for amusement, and we can see no reason why the principle which exists in almost every sport should be considered detrimental to football. The sooner the Football Association opens its eyes to the fact that the recognition of professionalism is a certainty in time, the better it will be for the consolidation of the game.[21]

The second, and perhaps more influential, group agreed that professionalism existed and that although stamping it out might still be possible it would also be very difficult. Even obtaining proof that a player had been paid was far from easy.[22] Professionalism should be allowed, therefore, but vigorously controlled so that the spirit of true sportsmanship should not be lost to the game. This group went on to make another shrewd point. It was fairly widely recognised that under the current system, those players who *were* receiving money for playing were in a strong position *vis à vis* the clubs. Not only were they independent agents who could shop around for the best price for their football skill, but if need be they could threaten recalcitrant clubs with exposure of their illegal activities. The *Athletic News* was very clear about the advantages which strict legislation would give to clubs in their relationship with players.

It is quite possible to bind a man to a particular club for an entire season, and otherwise bring the professionals under much stricter discipline than at present exists . . . in the new order of things [the players] must be impressed with the reality of the fact that they are only servants to those from whom they receive wages. Those, therefore, who have been hostile to the admission of the professional have the means, if they like to use them, of holding a stern and controlling hand over the class it is proposed to call into being . . . . The clubs who employ the paid men will only be too glad to possess a strong authority over them.[23]

The timing of the final, if somewhat protracted, discussions at the Football Association was determined by the disqualification of Preston North End from the F.A. Cup in January 1884 and the subsequent threat on the part of thirty-six prominent northern clubs to leave the Association and form their own British Football Association in the autumn of the same year.[24] At the Annual General Meeting of the F.A. in February 1884, the committee recommended that professionalism should be made legal but an amendment in favour of setting up a sub-committee to investigate the subject and to suggest ways in which 'these abuses' might be suppressed was carried by a substantial majority. Before the end of the year, the powerful local football associations of Birmingham and Sheffield, together with those at Nottingham and Walsall, had all passed resolutions opposing any ideas that professionalism should be legalised.[25] A further special meeting of the Football Association was held in January 1885. This time, the committee's proposal to make professionalism legal was carried by a narrow majority but not by the two-thirds vote which was required. Moreover, the confusion of the delegates was shown when a second resolution aiming at repression was passed by almost two to one.[26] Finally the committee's proposals in favour of legalisation were accepted at a special general meeting on 20 July 1885.[27]

No player was to be termed an amateur who received any remuneration or consideration above his necessary hotel or travelling expenses. Eligibility for cup matches would depend on birth or residence for the past two years within six miles of the ground or headquarters of the club for whom the professional wished to turn out. Professionals were not to sit on any F.A. committees, nor to represent their own or any other club at any meeting of the Football Association. Professionals would not be allowed to play for more than one club in any one season without the special permission of the F.A. committee. Infringements of the rules would be punished by suspensions.

Was it simple class prejudice which underlay the opposition to professionals? There were undoubtedly many who shared the view of W.H. Jope, a leading member of the Birmingham Football Association, that 'it was degrading for respectable men to play with professionals'. The *Sporting Mirror* alleged that there had been no such thing as amateur-professional distinctions in the middle of the nineteenth century. 'A crack performer, whether at athletics or anything else, if desirous of earning laurels in the arena, had to contend with anyone who would throw down the gauntlet.' It was only when gentlemen 'found that they were unable to hold their own in leading events that exception was taken to leading performers on account of their social status and a clique established'.[28] C.W. Alcock, on the other hand, told the meeting of the Football Association in February 1884 that 'he had sounded the greater number of amateurs, and he found very few of them objected to play with professionals, but they did object to play with them as amateurs'.[29] Moreover, we have already noted the important role which young professional men and businessmen in general, and ex-public school and university men in particular, had played in introducing association rules to their districts and recruiting working men for the teams.

We do not have a detailed socio-occupational breakdown of the delegates to those meetings of the Football Association in 1884–5 nor do we know in any detail who voted for what. We would expect most representatives of Lancashire clubs, irrespective of whether they were solicitors or manufacturers, to want to preserve a system which had enabled their teams to improve their game. Similarly it would not surprise us to find the bastions of southern amateurism in the opposite camp. London against the provinces or North v. South differences may be important here. Pre-existing rivalry had been sharpened by the north's successes in the F.A. Cup since Blackburn Rovers had been the first northern club to reach the final in 1882. Olympic won the next year and Rovers in 1884 and 1885.[30] When it began to look as though Preston North End might be accused of professionalism the local paper was quick to defend them. 'Even if some of the North End team are professionals, why should the London team have the right of interference? If the Preston public is satisfied, and the Executive of the North End is satisfied, what matters it?'[31] As *The Field* had noted in 1882 'in the North of England . . . the game is often played in a very different spirit, and at times the anxiety to win leads to much unpleasantness.'[32]

Clearly there is no simple gentlemen v. the rest dichotomy here. There were undoubtedly ex-public school men on both sides of this controversy. Obviously there were extremists who did not want to play with working men and especially 'do-nothing-but-play-football men'. As a letter from a Scot to the *Athletic News* put it in 1884, it would be 'monstrous' to allow such a team to play a cup-tie 'against a body of gentlemen and amateurs, who play football for sport and not for money—such as The Queen's Park or Oxford University'.[33] But the division among the gentlemen was really in essence a tactical one. Did you fight the monster and refuse to recognise its existence or did you accept that it had grown too large to fight but might be tamed by a controlled environment? All would have agreed with the *Athletic News*

Football Annual of 1895 which noted that 'there is no instance in the whole history of English sport of any single branch thriving apart from the intervention of amateurs'.[34] Only amateurs could be objective, free, and able to run a game for the benefit of the game itself. Only amateurs were not tainted by pecuniary interest. Professionals would, if allowed, run it for themselves and not necessarily fairly at that.

We shall have to return to these issues when we look more closely at changing attitudes to the game in chapter eight. The conflict surrounding the amateur-professional issue in football went simmering on throughout our period, shot through as it was with North-South rivalries and punctuated by accusations of class prejudice. The selection of teams to represent England in matches against the other home counties was a particular area in which ill-feeling was generated. They were chosen, of course, by a committee of the Football Association and prior to the end of the 1870s, were usually composed of London-based amateur players. The first professional to play in the major fixture, England against Scotland, did so in 1886. The Scots, who as we saw earlier, had not recognised professionalism, objected and although their objection was rejected, the player in question was made to wear a different shirt from the rest of the eleven.[35] In the same year the *Athletic News* complained that the F.A. 'did their level best to make the pros look like pros' in the Gentlemen v. Players match. 'Dark blue jerseys savour more of the collier than anything else, and the Gentlemen were clad in spotless white shirts. The difference was marked as doubtless it was intended to be.' In spite of their increasing lack of success against professionals, amateurs continued to find it relatively easy to get into England teams right up to 1900.[36] And an amateur would always be appointed captain. In 1894–5, for example, the Professionals played the Amateurs in an international trial at Nottingham and won 9–0. Consequently only one amateur was chosen for the England side but he was appointed captain.[37] When this phenomenon had first occurred, in 1892, it had raised ticklish questions of protocol. How should the amateur who was to lead the professionals on the field, relate to them off it? N.L. Jackson wrote in *Pastime*, the magazine which he edited, that 'paid football players are supposed to be inferior in manners and breeding to the average run of cricket professionals; and it might be supposed that the solitary amateur in the English team, who, as captain, was called upon to associate to some extent with his men, would have found his position more or less irksome. As it happened, however, these particular professionals turned out to be men of easy and gentlemanly demeanour, and they found their captain a very sociable companion.'[38] The *Athletic News* by this time rarely allowed a slur to be cast on the professional game save by itself. Least of all would the paper stand idly by and see the professional patronised by one of the high priests of southern amateurism. Its reply, the truth of which does not appear to have been contested, throws interesting light on the relationship between amateur and professional at the highest level of the game.

We have very little doubt that well behaved English pros would have 'found their captain a very sociable companion' had their captain given them a chance, but it hardly seems the right thing to our unsophisticated mind for a captain of an international team not to recognize his men on a long railway journey, not to speak to them in any way, to travel in a separate compartment, to dine away from them at the hotel, to leave them severely alone until driving off to the match, and generally to behave as if he were a superior sort of being. . . . Sport levels all classes. It is a rare good text, Mr. Jackson.[39]

Jackson, sound fellow, was unrepentant and in his autobiography published in 1932 he claimed that class prejudice or snobbishness were irrelevant to the issue. For example, amateurs and professionals preferred to dine separately and for two good reasons, namely that the professionals liked to dine earlier in order to be able to attend a music-hall or theatre and that they 'all felt a little constrained when with the amateurs, thinking that they could not talk among themselves so freely as they might wish'.[40] Moreover, he had returned to the attack in 1900 when arguing that amateurs should not be compelled to mix with pros if they desired to play for England but should be at liberty to choose. Servants did not dine with their masters in the dining room, nor did they come and go through the front door and professional footballers were paid servants. 'The amateurs, if they are *bona fide*, must be at some expense to play the game, and as such are as much the masters of the game as *bona fide* amateurs are at cricket'.[41]

Masters and servants. In a sense that goes to the root of what Alcock and those who supported him were aiming at when they proposed in 1884–5 that professionalism should be legalised. In the next chapter we shall try to assess how servile the servants were; to discover what sort of career opportunities were presented by professional football to what type of young working man; to see whether having been a professional player was a handicap in social circles outside the game and the working class: and to see how the professionals' circumstances changed over the period 1885 to 1914.

Notes

1 See Gibson and Pickford, vol. I, op.cit. p. 59, 'Tityrus', op.cit. pp. 105–6; and an article by C.E. Hughes in *C.B. Fry's Magazine* vol. III 13 April 1905, p. 41. Wednesday brought Lang down from Scotland to play in a Sheffield cup match in 1878. *Sheffield Independent* 28 January 1878. On Lang see R.A. Sparling and *The Romance of The Wednesday* (Sheffield, 1926) pp. 35–6.

2 W.T. Dixon, *History of Turton Football Club and Carnival Sports Handbook* (Turton 1909), p. 27. *Darwen News* 3 May 1879. Love was later killed during the bombardment of Alexandria in 1882. J.A.H. Catton, in his book *The Real Football*, told a probably apocryphal but nonetheless delightful story of how Suter became a professional, pp. 54–5. Suter was a stone-mason by trade in Scotland but he said that the English stone was so hard that it produced swelling of the arms and hands so he had to give it up and turn to football for a living. *Saturday Night* also alleged that Suter was the first professional in 1882. *Blackburn Standard* 16 December 1882. See also Gibson and Pickford, op.cit. vol. I p. 59 and chapter four below.

3 *Darwen News* 19 April 1879. The *Athletic News* noted in November that McIntyre was playing for the Rovers again and was to remain in Blackburn for the Cup-ties. 'It looks as if the Blackburn men were afraid to fight out their own battles in a fair and honest manner, and if allowed it would justify other clubs in bringing down the best Scottish players to help them in important encounters.' *Athletic News* 12 November 1879.

4 *Football Field* 18 October 1884. By 1884 he was mine host at the Castle Inn, Blackburn.

5 *Midland Athlete* 12 October, 29 December 1881.

6 The *Football Annual* 1881, p. 91. The 1882 *Annual*, referring to the failure of Blackburn Rovers to win the F.A. Cup in that year, said that it would have been good for the sport if a northern club had won it at last but 'the presence of so many Scotchmen among the Rovers and the air of profes-sionalism which pervades the team militate considerably against their popularity outside Lancashire.' Rovers' defeat by the Old Etonians in the final was their first defeat of that season in 36 matches. *Athletic News* 29 March 1882. For further examples of the rumours see *Football* November 1882, *Cricket* 17 May 1882, *Athletic News* 12, 19, 26 October 1881, 25 January, 29 November 1882. It may not mean much but the *Athletic News* dropped its subtitle, 'a weekly journal of amateur sports' in May 1881.

7 On the growth of cricket see R. Bowen, *Cricket: A History of Its Growth and Development Throughout the World* (1970) especially pp. 111–14 and W.F. Mandle, 'The Professional Cricketer in England in the nineteenth century,' in *Labour History*, 23, November 1972.

8 The first F.A. Cup competition was in 1871–72; both the Sheffield and Birmingham F.A.'s had knock-out competitions from 1876–7, Stafford-

shire's senior Cup was first competed for in 1877–8, Blackburn's began in 1878–9, as did that of Berks and Bucks, and Lancashire's in 1879–80.

9 *Athletic News* 14 January 1880, *Sheffield Daily Telegraph* 27 February 1883.
10 'Fair Play' in *Athletic News* 25 January 1882. See also 8 February 1882.
11 *Football* 24 January 1883. The letter writer was contemplating putting up a similar sum for proof that the Forest officer who authorised the reward offer was of sound mind at the time.
12 *Sheffield Daily Telegraph* 21 February 1882.
13 See for example the letter from A.T. Bye in the *Sheffield Daily Telegraph* 25 November 1884 and Alcock's remarks at the January 1885 meeting of the Football Association as reported in the *Preston Herald*, 21 January 1885.
14 See Minutes of the Lancashire Football Association 25 January, 6 February 1882.
15 *Blackburn Standard* 11 February 1882.
16 Minutes Lancashire Football Association A.G.M. 27 May 1882. The Lancashire F.A. also ruled that 'a man actually undertaking an engagement for his livelihood out of the county, and thereby residing beyond its limits for any protracted period shall not be eligible'. *Athletic News* 8 February, 31 May 1882. Blackburn Olympic were disqualified from taking any further part in the Lancashire Cup competition of 1882–3 for importing a player from Sheffield. *Preston Herald* 4 November 1882. Players today who have appeared for one club in the F.A. or Football League Cups may not appear for another in the same season.
17 *Sheffield Daily Telegraph* 27 February 1883. *Athletic News* 26 December 1883.
18 *Athletic News* 24 October, 14 November 1883.
19 Ibid. 1 August 1883.
20 *The Field* 27 June 1891. Cricket professionals were nearly always bowlers (although many of them could bat as well.) In many club and county sides it was their job to bowl to the gentlemen, who were nearly always batsmen, thus providing them with practice. For further comparisons between the football and cricket professional see below chapter four.
21 *Sporting Life* 15 September 1884.
22 There were several attempts by clubs to charge other clubs with playing professionals in the early 1880s, usually after they had lost cup-ties. In March 1884, for example, Notts. County objected to Blackburn Rovers having played Inglis, formerly of Glasgow Rangers, against them in their F.A. Cup Semi-Final. County argued that 'as a resident of Glasgow, Inglis, by playing for a club so distant as Blackburn, breaks what ought to be the fundamental principle of the cup competition, viz. a healthy and patriotic rivalry between the various localities—that the fact (fully established) of Inglis having been expelled from the Glasgow Rangers Club, and travelling so great a distance to play for the Rovers, is in itself sufficient to justify the committee of the Association in declaring him ineligible.' Inglis was alleged to be a mechanic earning 25/- a week and it was hardly likely that his visits to Blackburn to play in the cup-ties were due to love of sport alone. But no positive evidence of payment could be obtained and the case was dismissed. *Preston Herald* 15 March 1884.
23 *Athletic News* 7 April 1885, 11 January 1887. A. Gibson and W. Pickford, vol. I op.cit. pp. 81–9.

24   For a list of the clubs see Appendix I, p. 81. Upton Park, a team of London amateur players, objected to North End on the grounds that their eleven had included professionals although they did not return the money received as their share of a large attendance at the match at Preston which was drawn 1–1. The charge of professionalism against North End was not proven but the club was found guilty of importing men from other towns and finding them what were thought to be excessively well paid jobs in order that they might play football for Preston. See *Athletic News* 23 January 30, 5 November 1884, *Blackburn Standard* 2 February 1884. The *Preston Herald* claimed that North End's players were 'following their respective employments' in the latter part of the 1883–4 season. *Preston Herald* 9 April 1884.

25   *Athletic News* 10 December 1884.

26   Ibid. 27 January 1885.

27   Ibid. 7 July 1885. As late as May 1885 the Committee of the Birmingham and District F.A. had voted 13–5 against legalising professionalism. Birmingham and District F.A. Committee Minister 7 May 1885.

28   *Sporting Mirror* vol. II August 1881-January 1882, p. 165.

29   *Preston Herald* 1 March 1884. There was also the notion that it was more manly to become a professional than to remain a paid amateur. *Athletic News* 9 October 1899.

30   That football in the South had lost prestige in the eyes of Northerners is indicated by a satirical headline in the *Athletic News* of 14 November 1883 over a report of a match between the Old Etonians and Hendon: 'The Bitter Cry of Outcast London'!

31   *Preston Herald* 23 January 1884. The previous month the paper had suggested that it might be necessary to form a Northern Football Association for the area from Warwickshire north 'where football is no doubt best understood and most enthusiastically followed'. Ibid. 5 December 1883.

32   The article was reproduced in *Cricket* 17 May 1882. In his autobiography, Sir Frederick Wall, the second secretary of the F.A., related how Charles Clegg (a former President) did not enjoy his first game for England in 1872 because 'the great majority of the players were snobs from the south who had no use for a lawyer from Sheffield. The ball was never passed to him and nobody ever spoke to him. . . . They did not understand him and he resented their air of superiority.' Sir F. Wall, op.cit. p. 31.

33   *Athletic News* 17 September 1884. The Scottish Football Association refused to accept professionalism in 1885, but failed to eliminate it although it was not openly allowed until 1893. In the first year fifty clubs registered 560 professional players. F. Johnston (ed.), *The Football Encyclopaedia* (1934), p. 25.

34   See also A. Gibson and W. Pickford, vol. III, op.cit. p. 201.

35   C. Francis, *A History of the Blackburn Rovers Football Club 1875–1925*, (Blackburn, 1925) op.cit. p. 198, A. Gibson and W. Pickford, vol. IV, op.cit. pp. 108–12. It was J.H. Forrest's first 'cap'. See below chapter four, p.12, *Athletic News* 21 December 1886.

36   The Corinthians did win many matches against professional sides but they were themselves a representative eleven made up of the best amateur players of the day, mostly ex-public school and university footballers based in London and district. However, there were exceptional years. See chapter seven below. In 1892, for example, only one amateur played for England against Scotland.

37 E. Needham, *Association Football* (1900), p. 75. The first professional to captain England was Robert Crompton in 1900.
38 *Pastime* 6 April 1892. Jackson went on to say that 'the only members of the English Party who manifested any constraint were certain officials, who seemed to be painfully conscious of their inferiority in social qualities. It is a pity that the present commercial organization of football should bring such men to the front.'
39 *Athletic News* 11 April 1892. The idea that 'sport levels all classes' will be returned to in chapter eight below. In county cricket, of course, this was the golden age of the amateur player. He not only enjoyed separate changing facilities from the professionals and the title of Mr but he also entered the field of play by a separate gate.
40 N.L. Jackson, *Sporting Days and Sporting Ways*, op.cit. pp. 175–6.
41 *Athletic News* 15 January 1900.

APPENDIX I

List of clubs represented at a meeting to discuss the formation of a British Football Association 1884

Accrington	Hurst
Accrington Grasshoppers	Kersley
Astley Bridge	Little Hulton
Barnes Rovers	Loneclough
Bell's Temperance	Manchester and District
Bolton Wanderers	Nelson
Bolton Association	Newton Heath
Bolton and District Charity Cup	Padiham
Association	Park Road (Blackburn)
Bradshaw	Preston North End
Burnley	Peel Bank Rovers (Accrington)
Burnley Ramblers	Preston Swifts
Burnley Trinity	Rawtenstall
Burnley Union Star	Rossendale
Burnley Wanderers	Sunderland
Clitheroe	Turton
Darcy Lever	Walmersley
Great Lever	Walsall Swifts
Halliwell	Wigan

This total of 36 clubs plus the Bolton and District Charity Cup Association contained at least eight major clubs. Moreover, the possibility that other clubs would join could not be ruled out.

Source : Athletic News 5 November 1884.

CHAPTER FOUR
THE PLAYERS

Sir—will you allow me, through the medium of the public press, to call the attention of our Chief Constable to a rapidly spreading nuisance in the shape of football. Almost in any street or open space, such as the crossing from the Orchard to Lord Street, may be seen daily groups of boys, and even young men, kicking at anything in the shape of a ball, regardless of passers-by, and especially dangerous to young children going to and from the different schools. The nuisance does not end here. On a Sunday the parks are visited by numerous gangs of young lads, who seem to vie with each other in the use of obscene language whilst indulging in their wonderful game. There is one place in particular visited weekly—to the east of the tramway bridge, on the Preston side of the river. I should almost imagine there is a match arranged for at this place each Sabbath afternoon, the contestants are so eager and noisy. Surely the police would not be exceeding their duty in trying to put down all football playing in the public streets and parks. In its proper place I should be one of the last to discourage the healthy recreation of football; but played in the streets, it becomes, as I have before described it, a public nuisance.[1]

THIS chapter will concentrate on the elite of football players: the professionals. It will try to discover their socio-occupational background, to discuss how they were paid, to say something about their working conditions and in particular to note the controversies surrounding the players' relationship with the clubs. It will look at the origins and early years of the Players' Union, attempt an evaluation of what sort of job was open to a professional footballer once his playing days were over and finally try to say something about the attitudes of the professional player to the game and to wider issues.

But before we go on to do that it is essential to look briefly at two levels of football of which all the professionals of the twentieth century have had some experience: unorganised football and schoolboy football. Of the former there is little to say save to remind the reader of its widespread occurrence. Preston was by no means the only place where boys and youths played football in the street and a combing of local newspapers would produce a plethora of similar examples. Suffice it to say that as late as 1911, of the 605 children brought before the Birmingham Juvenile Court for non-indictable offences, 132, easily the largest number, were accused of playing football in the streets.[2] Spontaneous kickabouts or serious matches between sides (usually with less than eleven players in each) on waste ground and convenient fields or parks were almost certainly common enough. By the end of our period, many of the boys who took part in such games would also be playing or have played at their elementary school; they were much less likely to have done so in the 1880s and 1890s.

We saw in chapter one that, certainly by the 1870s, physical recreation in the public schools was an important part of the education offered by those schools. It was built into the curriculum and, especially in the form of team games, was widely praised for its character building qualities as well as its importance in aiding the individual to attain physical fitness. However, when the state intervened to plug the gaps in the system of voluntary elementary schools by the Education Act of 1870, no provision was made for games playing nor indeed for any form of physical education. It is difficult to know exactly why this was. Certainly the education provided for the working classes had to be done as cheaply as possible. Moreover, shortage of space for playing fields, especially in the industrial towns of the north and midlands, was a perennial problem. Again, what was being provided was an absolute minimum. Individual districts might do more if they wished but the state was concerned only with the bare essentials in 1870. Finally, there seems to have been a belief among influential politicians and educationalists that games were unsuitable for the elementary school child. Drill, a kind of austere physical jerks, with military associations, was preferred because it was thought to inculcate habits of obedience.[3]

Of course some voluntary schools did include games and probably allowed for them in their timetables. Children at St Luke's School in Wolverhampton, for example, were apparently playing football from the mid-1870s. The log book of the school for 15 March 1877 notes: 'let boys out earlier on Friday afternoon and they had a football match'.[4] Several well known Blackburn footballers of the 1880s had previously attended St John's School where the headmaster approved of a 'sound body' and encouraged outdoor games.[5] It is difficult to know how regular and widespread such provision was. Cost, together with a strict adherence to reading, writing and religion, certainly must have obstructed the growth of games playing in most voluntary elementary schools just as it did in the post-1870 Board Schools.[6]

Nevertheless, with the expansion of the number of such schools in the twenty-five years following the Act, the growth in numbers of the children who went to them and, crucially, the rising numbers of staff employed to teach them, a movement in favour of team games for the pupils did emerge. Where there had been 6,395 qualified male teachers in elementary schools in 1870, in 1893 there were 21,223. The numbers of assistant male teachers had also been increased. Many of these teachers were concerned by the physical condition in which some of their pupils came to school, and had themselves enjoyed games in their own schools or colleges. Teacher training colleges may have been especially important here. St Peter's College at Saltley, Birmingham, for example, probably took up the association game early in the 1870s. As we saw in chapter two, T. Bryan and F. Hackwood, graduates of the college, organised one of the leading football clubs in Wednesbury. Another product of the college, T. Slaney, was a prominent member of the Stoke club and two others, G. Copley and C. S. Johnstone, both played for Aston Villa, Johnstone later becoming a committee member and a director. He was headmaster of several Birmingham schools. J. Adams, captain of the College team in 1875, became treasurer of the Birmingham F.A. in 1883 and a well-known referee. He, too, took a headmaster's post in Birmingham. Jack Brodie and John Addenbroke were ex-'Salts' who did much to establish Wolverhampton Wanderers.[7] The first breakthrough appears to have come in Birmingham where the School Board was in receipt of several donations from local people, including one from the Board's Chairman of £100, which enabled it to equip schools with both cricket and football clubs so that sixteen schools had football clubs for the 1880–1 season.[8] Organised games were still not actually timetabled. They were played outside normal school hours and this brought extra work and ate into the leisure time of the masters who were responsible for organisation and supervision. The advantages were not merely to be seen in improvements in the boys' wind and limb. The headmaster of Brookfields School found that 'it has induced more regular attendance in the upper standards, tended to attach the children to the school, and formed a bond of sympathy between the teachers and the boys'.[9]

In May 1881 the Birmingham School Board set up a Physical Exercises Committee to 'stimulate and supervise the workings of the clubs'. Separate sub-committees concerned themselves with cricket, football, gymnastics and swimming. The Committee said that it hoped to raise the level of individual performance as well as stimulate team competition. For the 1883–4 season the Committee offered prizes for dribbling against time, 'punt-kicking' and place kicking. There was to be a challenge shield and schools could compete with teams of six. Individual medals were to go to the winners.[10] The following year the Birmingham and District Football Association presented a challenge shield for competition by all the elementary schools in the city.[11] By the beginning of the 1890s, when the Birmingham Athletic Institute took over the work of the Physical Exercises Committee, there was already a schools league in the south of the city, Aston and Birmingham schools were playing representative fixtures against each other and in 1893 Birmingham schools entertained a team selected from London schools at the Aston Lower Grounds.[12]

It is difficult to know how far Birmingham was ahead of other places. Certainly it seems to have been the most active Board, as a Board. A South London Schools Football Association was formed in 1885, Sheffield had one by 1887, Manchester by 1890, Liverpool and Nottingham by 1891, Brighton by 1892, Sunderland and Leicester by 1893, Leeds by 1896 and Blackburn by 1897. Most of these associations were the work of teachers.[13] Sheffield schools were playing for the Clegg Shield for the first time in 1889–90 and 6,000 spectators saw a team drawn from the town's elementary schools beaten by a bigger and heavier eleven from London in the spring of 1890.[14] When the Manchester, Salford and District Elementary Schools Football Association was formed in the summer of that year it was the London and Sheffield examples to which they specifically referred.[15] Bolton and District Elementary Schools Athletic Association met for the first time in 1898. Its main object was to organise a football competition. The Chairman of Bolton Wanderers became President, Lord Stanley gave a shield and 28 clubs competed in 1898–9.[16] The 1890s certainly seems to be the decade when organised schoolboy football really kicked off although it was not until 1904 that the English Schools Football Association was finally formed with 21 towns affiliated, including six from Lancashire.

While all this grass roots activity was going on the Board of Education remained hesitant about officially sanctioning organised games in elementary schools in spite of the Department's own Special Reports of 1897, 1898 and 1900. The 1898 Report described games and, especially football as a 'simple, ready, and pleasant means of physical education'.[17]

McIntosh says that the main reason for the department's delay was its firmly held belief that the purpose of physical education was primarily disciplinary. He may be correct but even in their own terms it seems a remarkably short-sighted view.[18] It was not until 1900 that the new Board of Education instructed Her Majesty's

Inspectors that games were a suitable alternative to Swedish drill or physical exercises. They were to be supervised by members of staff 'who should teach the most skilful method of play, and should encourage orderly behaviour and stop quarrelling'.[19] Four years later Robert Morant, the ex-Winchester boy, now Permanent Secretary to the Board of Education, prefaced the New Code of Regulations for Elementary Schools by observing that the

school must afford them [the children] every opportunity for the development of their bodies, not only by training them in appropriate physical exercises and in encouraging them in organised games, but also by instructing them in the working of some of the simple laws of health. . . . The corporate life of the school, especially in the playground, should develop that instinct for fair play and for loyalty to one another which is the germ of a wider sense of honour in later life.[20]

It is slightly ironic that organised games for the children of the working classes should be given the official seal of approval just at the time when their social and physical benefits were being seriously called into question in some educational, political and religious quarters and the public schools in particular were being accused of an unnatural concentration on athletics.[21]

Clearly with so many schoolboys playing football the reservoir from which the professional and semi-professional elite clubs might draw players and spectators was growing rapidly through the 1880s and 1890s. Senior clubs occasionally gave some help to schoolboy football but never consistently. Nevertheless, it might have been important in Preston, for example, where the committee of the North End club offered a challenge shield for inter-school competition in 1884–5. It was agreed that 'half-timers' were eligible to play in school teams but some schools were accused of playing 'full-timers'! Similarly, Aston Villa, having won the Birmingham and District F.A. Challenge Cup outright, presented it to the Children's Hospital for competition among all the public elementary schools of Birmingham and district. It attracted 37 entries in 1891. Leicester Fosse allowed the use of their ground for schoolboy matches and gave 100 free season tickets for the boys who played for school teams.[22]

Of course facilities for games playing among elementary schoolboys (or indeed the new secondary schoolboys brought into being by the 1902 Education Act) were still very poor in many places. Molyneux was probably right when he claimed that it was 'more than co-incidental that those Board Schools in Aston and Birmingham which achieved success on the games field were invariably situated near to public parks'. The availability of Preston Park from late 1883 probably stimulated the growth of organised schoolboy football in Brighton.[23] But places to play on did increase in numbers if only slowly. Birmingham in 1886 had only ten open spaces comprising 222 acres; by 1913 it had 63 open spaces covering 1,298 acres.[24] Obviously some places continued to do better than others and London probably worst of all. Clearly the spread of association football to the elementary schools was an important element in maintaining its impetus and extending its capacity for growth. A good many boys now learned the game at school, played it regularly and developed a considerable interest in it. They may also have been able to watch some level of senior football. Unfortunately none of that was any guarantee that they would have an opportunity to play once they had left school, especially if they lived in one of the great cities.

Part of this problem was the old one of lack of open space and a consequent inadequate supply of decent pitches. One voluntary response was the London Playing Fields Association formed around 1891. Its aims were to 'encourage and develop the playing of cricket, football and other like games by the clerks, working men, and boys of London'. To this end the Association sought to discover how many grounds were needed and to represent the working classes in negotiations with 'the public authorities as to parks, commons, and other open spaces, and with railway companies in regard to reduction of fares and facility of access'. Moreover, the Association was to 'acquire land ... to let pitches for the season to clubs which, though not able to give the high rent necessarily demanded by persons who let for profit, can yet pay a moderate charge' thus reducing the competition for the limited space available in the parks and public open spaces leaving them free for the less well off.[25] By 1907 at least two similar bodies had appeared. The Birmingham Playgrounds Open Spaces and Playing Fields Association had been set up in the previous year by J.S. Nettlefold. This was followed in 1907 by the Manchester and Salford Playing Fields Society. By the outbreak of war this Society administered 94 acres of freehold and $13\frac{1}{2}$ acres of leasehold land which provided about one hundred cricket and football pitches. In addition 30 football pitches had been prepared and were reserved without any charge in four of the major Manchester parks. Manchester Parks Committee was itself providing about 200 football grounds by 1914 and Salford 60.[26] Not all the pitches provided were either conveniently situated nor in very good condition. W.J. Braithwaite noted in 1904 that it was

heart-breaking to go over to Wanstead Flats or 'the Marshes' on a winter afternoon with a club football team that would be keen if it had a chance. The boys
get off work at irregular times from varying distances and it is good luck if both
teams have assembled by 3.30 to commence in winter a half hour's game in
semi-darkness on a dismal swamp miscalled a football pitch.[27]

If part of the problem of the young lad leaving school and
wishing to continue with football was having nowhere to play,
another part was having no one to play with. The lack of organised
facilities or of those clubs and institutions around which regularly
playing teams could group and grow worried many of society's
leaders. The Bishop of Manchester, for example, when opening
the Bolton Lads' Club in the middle of 1890 said that if youth
was not given the opportunity for 'healthy outdoor exercise'
then 'he would seek some substitute which was not a good one'.
He went on to explain that the substitute would almost certainly
include gathering at street corners to 'hurl scurrilous language'
at passers-by, playing pitch and toss in dark lanes or going to
public houses, music halls and cheap theatres.[28] A considerable
literature in the first decade of the new century is a monument to
the concern for the boy with a minimum of formal education,
no apprenticeship and a dead-end job which pointed the way
inexorably to the pool of casual labour before he was eighteen.[29]
Boys' clubs were one attempt to 'improve' him; mind and body,
and team games in general and football and cricket in particular
were considered to be ideal channels for communicating those
values of fair play, self reliance, endurance and how to take a
beating which were considered so vital to Britain's future. As
C.E.B. Russell said shortly before he was appointed Chief
Inspector of Reformatory and Industrial Schools, 'the years
between fourteen and twenty will decide whether each individual
is to become a valuable asset to his country, a negligible quantity
possessed at best of the value of a machine, or a worthless parasite
and drag on its prosperity'.[30]

We shall return to the question of attitudes to the game in
chapter eight. This present chapter is about players, at school and
after. It is impossible to be precise about how many players there
were, organised or unorganised, at school or out of school, junior
or senior, amateur or professional, at any particular time in our
period. But snatches of statistics can be presented which give
some idea, for different times and places, of how many males
were taking part in football playing. In 1875 for instance, the
Sheffield Football Players' Accident Society claimed 560
members.[31] It was in 1877 that the *Athletic News* suggested that

there were some 12,000 regular players in the United Kingdom as a whole of whom 9,000 were in the North of England and Scotland.[32] The following year the Scottish Football Association claimed to have 116 clubs affiliated to it with a total of 6,264 members but it is doubtful whether they would have been all playing members. Similarly, the Birmingham Football Association in 1879 published a strength of 29 clubs and 2,200 members.[33] By 1879 the Sheffield F.A. were claiming 5000 players although there were then several clubs in membership who were located outside the immediate vicinity of the town.[34] More scattered and fragmentary material suggests 400 playing every week in Burnley in 1883, about 1,500 in the Nottingham F.A. area in 1885 and some 2,000 weekly in Sunderland in 1889.[35] Clearly numbers were growing throughout our period, but even the Football Association was far from certain about the exact total. It was stimulated into doing some counting in 1909 when the Budget's Land Tax proposals appeared to threaten football grounds. In a letter of complaint to the Chancellor of the Exchequer the F.A. claimed jurisdiction over 12,000 amateur clubs and 300,000 amateur players. But the unreliable nature of these figures is suggested by the fact that only one year later, the number of players had risen to 500,000.[36] It is likely that between 300–500,000 is somewhere near the mark for Edwardian England.

The number of professionals, of course, was much less. In 1885 the Nottingham F.A. had only four professionals registered among its 1,500 players.[37] By 1891 the twelve clubs in the Football League had a total of 448 registered players, the bulk of whom were almost certainly part or full-time professionals and this number had increased to 675 in the sixteen clubs in 1896.[38] In 1908 the *Athletic News* reported that 5,000 professionals were registered with the Football Association who themselves said 6,800 in 1910. In 1914 the Players' Union reckoned that 158 clubs engaged 4,740 players.[39] It is on the professional player, as he evolved over the period 1885 to 1914, that the rest of this chapter will concentrate.

What was the social and occupational background of the first professional footballers? It is a commonplace that most of them were working class. But is it possible (or indeed worthwhile) to say more? Can the historian penetrate beyond this comfortable generalisation to say something about the kind of occupational background professional players had; in essence were they skilled or unskilled? Did most of them have trades or not? It will not surprise the reader to learn that evidence is on the thin side.

Nor will it cause too much disorientation to discover that even where there is some occupational data it is no easy matter to decide what it means. It has been possible to discover the occupations of 67 players who appeared for nine elite clubs between 1884 and 1900. Of these 67, 16 were amateurs and 51 professionals. (See Table 4.1) There are several difficulties with this material. The problem of categorising occupations is well known. If the definition of skill used is based on the fact of a recognised period of training or apprenticeship, then the name of the trade might be significant but we can never be certain. Nevertheless, the manual occupations listed all seem likely to have been skilled, save perhaps bone cutter, cotton mill worker, dyer, factory hand,

TABLE 4.1 Occupation of football players with elite clubs, 1884–1900

Articled to Solicitor	(A)	Pattern Maker	
Bone Cutter		Pickle Maker	
Bricklayer		Plumber	
Chemist		Preparatory School Teacher	(A)
Clerk	(4)	Publican	(A)
Coachbuilder	(2)	Professional Cricketer	(2)
Coalminer		Professional Cricketer and Publican	
Colliery Manager	(A)	Professional Cricketer and Tobacconist	
Corn Factor			
Cotton Mill Worker	(3, 1 A)	Professional Musician	
Dentist	(A)	Railway Worker	
Doctor		Sawmaker	
Dyer		Schoolmaster	(2, 1A)
E.T. Grinder		Silver Cutler	
Factory Hand		Slater	(3)
Felt Hatter		Solicitor	(2A)
Gentlemen's Outfitter	(2, 1A)	Solicitor's Clerk	(2A)
Hotel keeper		Steel Melter	
Iron founder		Stoker	
Iron Dresser	(A)	Tape Sizer	
Iron Turner	(2)	T.K. Hafter	(A)
Lace Maker	(2)	Turner	
Lawyer	(A)	Upholsterer	(2)
Master Baker		Warehouseman	
Moulder		Weaver	
Painter		Wholesale Tailor	

Sources : Athletic News : Sheffield Daily Telegraph : Blackburn Times : Football Field : Bolton Evening News : J.A.H. Catton, Wickets and Goals (1926)

Clubs : Blackburn Olympic, Blackburn Rovers, Bolton Wanderers, Everton, Manchester City, Notts. County, Preston North End, Sheffield Wednesday and Sunderland.

A = Amateur

painter, pickle maker, stoker and tape sizer. It may also be relevant that none of the players were described as labourers. If the designations of the occupations under the, admittedly crude, skilled-unskilled headings are correct, then leaving out the obvious professions, the self-employed and the clerks, 28 might be skilled manual workers.

The notion that most of the first generation of professional football players in England was drawn from the ranks of the skilled rather than the unskilled is buttressed from another interesting source. Between 1888 and 1896, the *Athletic News* published a series of advertisements from football clubs who were seeking new players. These advertisements often stated that certain types of work would be available to the right kind of football players. It is clear from a careful study of these advertisements that that meant a man, preferably with a trade, who had a record of steadiness, reliability and skill. The advertisements also indicate the widespread amount of part-time professionalism, even among the leading clubs of the Football League, in the 1880s and 1890s. The following sample of advertisements actually mentioned specific jobs.

To Footballers—Two good Brass Moulders may have constant employment. (piece work) State for what club now playing and particulars by letter [to an address in Newcastle-on-Tyne]. Situations found for good Football Players; iron turners preferred [Nottingham]. Association Football—Good Players Wanted. Amateurs or Professionals for a good club near Manchester; situations for good workmen in fitting, boiler-making, or general iron trade. . . . '
Football Players—Wanted, First Class Men, amateurs or professionals; immediate and constant employment found for suitable men. Trades:—Coppersmiths, brass finishers, blacksmiths, pattern makers; labourers of all classes; payment for playing in addition to employment. [Burton-on-Trent].
Wanted good Iron Turners and Engine Fitters; must be good Association Football players. [Leicester].
Wanted, a good Outside Right, Centre Forward and Left Full Back. Big men, and with trades, preferred.
Permanent Berths offered to First-Class Footballers who are competent workmen at Boring, Finishing, Pan or Bass Drawing. [Southampton].
Good Forwards Wanted for a rising Second League Club; steady men in building or kindred trades can be found good work. [Rotherham].[40]

By the mid-1890s the number of such advertisements had decreased which suggests that other methods of player recruitment were being adopted. But the implication is that steady men with a trade were the aim of the professional, industrial and commercial men who increasingly, as we saw in chapter two, ran the professional and semi-professional elite clubs.[41] How often they obtained what they sought is another matter. Clearly, as the major clubs built up their scouting arrangements, as the number of leagues grew and more 'competent men' were needed, the occupational net was cast wider. But it is perhaps not surprising to find the relatively skilled man in a majority in the early years, the product no doubt of his more regular work, better pay and increased opportunities for leisure.[42] Even in 1907–8 the skilled trades appear to dominate a list of the occupations of 114 football professionals published in H.R. Brown's *Football Who's Who*. The full list is reproduced in Table 4.2 together with the trades of a further ten players whose work before they joined a professional club has been obtained from articles about them in the *Athletic News*. Two reservations have to be made about this material. In the first place the skilled-unskilled category, as was noted above, is difficult to operate when the only information available is a brief and bald description. Moreover, there are individual problems; for example, in which section do you place coal miners, an apparently growing source for the recruitment of professionals? Secondly, it is not clear from the list in *Football Who's Who* whether the occupations were followed by the individuals up to the point of signing professional forms, or whether they continued to do these jobs afterwards. Moreover, the numbers in the sample are not large. Nevertheless, when all objections are assembled the material seems to suggest that the first generation of professional footballers was largely drawn from the ranks of skilled manual workers.

I now want to return, briefly, to the subject of recruitment. Most of the early professionals were probably recruited by club committeemen directly approaching players or being casually informed by supporters, friends or acquaintances of allegedly good players whose signing would benefit the club. The use of the press suggests a desire to enlarge the catchment area and a lack of well-organised recruiting networks on the part of clubs.[43] This idea is further supported by the apparent flourishing in the 1890s of the football agent.

It is not possible to discover how many of these agents there were but that some were doing good business is indisputable. At least one club, Middlesbrough Ironopolis, had its playing strength apparently built up solely by an agent in three days in 1893.[44] J.P. Campbell appears to have conducted a moderately thriving business from an address in Liverpool. In March 1891, for example, he required 'three good men to fill the position of centre-forward. One must be a champion', to whom he could give from £3 to £4 per week plus a large bonus and 'if he be a

TABLE 4.2 *Occupational background of professional football players 1907–10*

Skilled	Unskilled	Unclassified	Others
Mason (3)	Lace Hand (2)	Earthenware	Chemist
Steel Moulder	Brickburner	Printer	Publican (2)
French Polisher	Iron Worker (2)	Decorator (2)	Coal Miner (14)
Master Builder's	Gardener	Builder (3)	Schoolmaster (3)
Merchant &	Trimmer on a	Tailor	Clerk (11)
Monumental	liner	Painter	Traveller (2)
Mason	Button-Maker	Block Cutter	Assistant Coach
Blacksmith (5)	Army (2)	Warehouseman	Grocer
Striker	Engine & Dy-	Wagon Builder	Coal Merchant (2)
Coachsmith	namo Attendant	Maker of	Pupil Teacher
Master Plasterer (2)	Dyer	Chemicals	Cricket
Mill Overlooker	Shoe Operator		Professional
Engineer (2)	Coal Trimmer		Sports Outfitter
Carpenter (8)			Journalist
Moulder (3)			Pawnbroker
Machine File			Wood Merchant
Cutter			Coal Factor
Bedstead Mount			
Maker			
Bricklayer (5)			
Fitter (3)			
Plater (2)			
Upholsterer			
Lawyer			
Steel Fitter			
Steel Analyst			
Electrical			
Engineer			
Boilermaker			
Brass Dresser			
Pattern Maker			
Shipbuilder			
Gun Rifler			
Boilersmith			
Steeplejack			

Sources : H.R. Brown, *Football Who's Who, 1907–8 : Athletic News.*

clever musician, he will probably get an appointment worth two guineas weekly'. One wonders if he had anyone in mind with these fairly unusual qualities. He was offering from two to three guineas per week to the other two together with a bonus according to ability. He also had

a list of five young fellows waiting engagements, well known League and Associa-tion men, English, Scotch and Welshmen. Also soldiers from a crack team, fit for a place in any club, having height, weight, speed, ability and experience, just the class of men to draw big gates. He also has a few very good moderate men, suitable for small and second class clubs. Secretaries, now's your time to introduce new blood, drop out the weeds, and strike in your teams for next year. You will find it both cheap and safe to engage your men through me. My agent in Scotland is hard at work and I expect some tip-top men from him next week.[45]

By April he claimed to have on his books 'nine goalkeepers, seven right full-backs, six left full-backs, eleven right half-backs, six left half-backs, sixteen centre-half-backs, eight outside rights, eleven inside rights, four outside lefts, five inside lefts, eight centre-forwards'.[46] By 1896, however, Lucas and McGregor of Preston claimed to be the only 'recognised English firm' of football agents and the trade does not receive the attention of the sources after that.[47] It is not difficult to explain why the football agents' career was almost certainly a short one.[48] Before the clubs had organised their own scouting and recruiting methods, he could be useful, like the press, although sometimes things could go wrong. None of the Aston Villa committee had seen a group of Scots play, nevertheless the players signed for the club in the summer of 1893 with predictable results. Sometimes it was the agent who was at fault. One newspaper alleged that an agent had offered the same player to three different clubs as a fine back, a reliable half-back, and a dashing forward.[49] But even if the agent was efficient he could not do more than a reasonably well-set-up club. Moreover, he might prove expensive and was bound to be blamed for the failures which the nature of the game made inevitable. Finally, although it is not clear whether the players retained any contractual ties with the agent, the suspicion that agents might seek to interfere in the control which clubs exercised over their employees probably helped to damn them further in the eyes of club officials.

What did the first professionals earn? Obviously remuneration depended on the wealth and success of the club and the player's age, skill and experience, not least in the business of negotiating his own wage agreement. It is worth reiterating at this point that the source materials for this subject are far from ideal. It is clear that some clubs kept very inadequate records of their dealings with players and what accounts were kept have been lost or destroyed in many cases. Moreover, clubs have generally refused access to those records which they do have. Press reports may be of dubious veracity in these matters. Having said all that however, it is hardly the essence of entrepreneurial risk to suggest that the earnings of the early paid players showed a good deal of variation. This would be particularly true of those years immediately following the legislation of 1885 when it was more likely that the professional player would have a job outside the game. When West Bromwich Albion turned professional in August 1885 the players received 10/- per match. The club's total wage bill was reported to be still only £10 per week when it won the F.A. Cup in 1888.[50] In 1885–6 seven Stoke players received 2/6 per match which was probably little better than a broken time arrangement. In February 1886 Blackburn Olympic, in an attempt to solve their financial difficulties, reduced the wages of their professionals to 10/6 per week. [51] James Crabtree, who played for Burnley, Aston Villa and England claimed that he was paid 2/6 per week when he first turned out for Burnley as a young man in 1888. His wage was later raised to 4/- although, according to the *Athletic News*, Burnley were then generally paying 25/-, from 1 September to 30 April with a bonus for every match won and a 10/- per week retainer in the summer.[52] N.J. Ross, signed by Everton in 1888, apparently received £10 a month; Ardwick paid their first professional 5/- a week in 1889 and Hyde were offering 25/- a match in the same year; in the New Year of 1890, the Sunderland players took part in 'four first-class matches' in a week and were rewarded with 30/- each per match.[53] When Sheffield Wednesday embraced professionalism in 1887 they paid small retainers of 9/- for home matches and 11/- for away ones, players finding their own togs save the shirts.[54]

We noted earlier that part-time professionalism was always a feature of the game and was common among the clubs of the Football and Southern Leagues before 1915. It is probably true to say that few clubs were employing many full-time professionals before the mid-1890s. The idea that professional footballers did not require to be permanently employed at the game and that it would be much healthier if they also did a proper job of work crops up intermittently through the period.[55] Moreover, the 'semi-pro' could do well enough. For example, and as we saw above when discussing player recruitment, he often gained preferential treatment for jobs. As an 'Anglo-Scot' put it in a letter to the *Athletic News* in 1886 'Is a player (who may be an inferior artisan) not to a large extent benefitted [sic] by constant employment than if he was only working now and again? Certainly he is; and why? Because the reason of that player's constant employment is owing to his work as a football player.'[56] Clearly being able to offer a job was a considerable advantage when trying to find good players. The *Athletic News* thought it a big help to Sunderland that they are backed up by employers of labour who can always find work in their yards or offices for importations. One establishment, whose members are generous supporters of the club, literally swarms with them and as they earn the current rate of wages they are able largely each week to supplement their professional retainer by a good round sum.[57]

Without doubt the part-timer who, by virtue of his football expertise, could also attain regular work, that comparatively rare commodity in late nineteenth-century Britain, was doing quite well for himself.

The coming of the Football League in 1888–9 and the intensified competition between the elite clubs which this engendered in a context of an increasing willingness on the part of the public to pay to see the play, gradually undermined the role of the part-timer. Of course there was always to be a place for him: in 1905 for example, Sheffield United had 33 professionals on their books of whom 22 were full time. The rest were local lads who worked at a job and trained in the evenings.[58] But increasing competition led to a more severe struggle to obtain the best players. A direct result was an increase in players' earnings and a corollary of that was a desire on the part of the clubs to get the best out of their well-paid athletes: to ensure that they concentrated on the game and did not, for example, get injured at work. Some of Derby County's players were apparently still working on the Saturday morning before league matches in 1891.[59] Moreover, once wages went up some players doubtless felt less need for other work.

A writer in the *Athletic News Football Annual* of 1893 claimed that the *average* wage of the professional footballer was £3 per week in winter and £2 per week in summer. That was certainly what George Davie claimed that he had while a Woolwich Arsenal player in 1891, and in the same year two Derby players were offered immediate payments of £75 and £50 respectively plus £3 a week. Sunderland's players were allegedly receiving £3 a week all the year round by 1893. Tom Brandon, the Blackburn Rover and England international, was taking home £4 per week in 1896.[60] More direct evidence that these figures are not far off what players in the better-off or more ambitious clubs could earn is obtained from the minutes of the directors' meetings of Aston Villa, one of the most successful clubs of the late Victorian and Edwardian period. In the spring of 1896 the Board was busy discussing the next season's wages with individual players. Wilkes, for example, was to receive £2 a week in the close season and £3 during the football season, while Campbell and Athersmith were to get £3.10s per week in the summer and £4 during the football season. In addition Athersmith was guaranteed a benefit of £100 if he played for Villa during the next season. Crabtree, whom we encountered earlier, was offered £4 a week all year round and Spencer £3.10s per week throughout the year. In fact, Athersmith demanded and obtained £4 throughout the year plus a benefit match with a guarantee of £120.[61] Some reserve team players got £1 per week in summer and £1.10s or £1.15s in the football season, the latter wage to rise to £3 if they made the first team. Other second team players were guaranteed 10/-, 15/- or £1 per week to be increased to £2 if they played for the first eleven.[62] Bonuses might be paid for good performances. Villa were paying win bonuses of up to £2 for away matches in 1895–6, depending on the strength of the opposition and the importance of the matches. Derby County paid out £295 in bonuses during the 1897–8 season including £2.10s each extra to Bloomer and Methven for 'standing out' in games against Liverpool and Wolves respectively.[63] The players of Sheffield Wednesday in the 1890s received a bonus which grew by £1 for each round of the F.A. Cup which they won. By 1899 the players of Sheffield United, just across the city, were pocketing £5 for each cup win and £2.10s for away cup draws and a local tradesman had offered them £100 between them if they won the cup, which they did.[64] There were also bonuses for signing on, limited to £10 by the Football League from 1892.[65]

Of course, a relatively small number of professional players could supplement their earnings by playing for England in the three annual international matches against the other home countries, and increasingly, as the Edwardian period went on, against foreign nations.[66] Ten shillings was paid in 1886 and £1 from 1887 until 1907 when it went up to £4. They might also be chosen to represent the Football League. Those players who turned out for the League against the Football Alliance in 1891, for example, were paid 21/- and their third-class rail fare. By the end of the century a player had a choice of £3.3s or a gold medal if asked to play for the Football League against the Scottish League.[67] Yet another way of increasing earnings for the favoured minority involved allowing the players' names to be used in advertising. It is difficult to be very precise in this area but the impression comes through strongly that such opportunities for leading players were increasing in the immediate pre-war decade. In 1884, Archie Hunter, for example, 'had great pleasure in stating that the Aston Villa have used your Hygienic Football Boots for the past two years with the very best results. For speed and accuracy in kicking they are far superior to any make we have ever tried'. Mercer's football boots had been endorsed by Welsh international Albert Powell in 1886: 'I like your Boots immensely: I have never played in better.'[68] George Dobson, captain of Everton, was a Mercer agent. The players of Aston Villa and Mitchell St. Georges were advertising another special brand of football boots in 1891.[69] An advertisement in the *Athletic News* of 24 July 1893 ran: 'To FOOTBALLERS—A few AGENTS wanted by a firm of football shirtmakers; a good commission; whole or spare time.' Gratton's embrocation had been used by every side to win the Cup since 1893.[70] By 1905 the secretary and manager of the Manchester City team which had won the F.A. Cup in the previous season could say that they owed it all to Oxo and both Everton and Newcastle United were soon adopting this particular short cut to stamina and success.[71] Writing for the press began early and the Players' Union thought that at least 80 players were doing it in 1914. Billy Meredith, for example, had a column in the *Football Argus* of Bradford in 1908 which was probably syndicated to other sporting papers.[72]

It seems unlikely that many players received greater financial rewards than those of Aston Villa although rumours of excessive demands by players were rife in those circles interested in curbing costs in general and wages in particular.[73] But as we saw in chapter two many clubs in the 1890s were finding it difficult to break even consistently and this led to suggestions from some of them that as payments to players were such a high proportion of total costs, they would have to be curtailed. The first move to institute a maximum wage came in 1893 but a meeting of Football League clubs, although voting in favour by 14 to 10, failed to obtain the required three quarters majority.[74] The issue was subsequently revived on several occasions during the 1890s but the clubs could never quite agree. In general the richer clubs were suspicious of restrictions. The annual meeting of the League in 1899 provides a good illustration of the confusion and consequent indecision. The president that year advocated an upper limit of £5 per week but other speakers supported the idea of men being worth what they could get and emphasised the sacred laws of the market.[75] The Football Association finally broke the deadlock by passing a resolution at their annual general meeting in 1900 that the maximum wages which might be paid to any player should be £4 per week.[76] Twelve months later, two of the wealthiest clubs, Aston Villa and Liverpool, moved an amendment to the £4 maximum regulation. Again all they could manage was a simple majority which was not enough; two-thirds of those present and voting was needed at a Football Association A.G.M. The result was that the new maximum wage came into effect from the 1901–2 season. Rule 32 of the F.A. set out the details.

Clubs shall not pay any player a bonus of more than Ten Pounds as a consideration for his signing a professional form. A bonus cannot be paid to a player on his resigning from his old club. The maximum wages which may be paid to any player shall be Four Pounds per week or £208 per annum, and the payment of bonuses dependent on the result of any match shall not be allowed. A player may be allowed a benefit after five years service with a club, in case of accident or when he is giving up playing. A player shall not be allowed more than one benefit. The consent of the Council of this Association must be obtained before a player is promised or receives a benefit.[77]

If there had been some differences of opinion among clubs before the maximum wage it was as a whisper compared to the cacophony which broke out after the restrictions came into force. There is not much doubt that it was honoured more in the breach than in the observance, especially by clubs in the First Division and particularly where signing on fees and match bonuses were concerned. The chairman of Aston Villa had been called before the Management Committee of the League in 1900 and asked to substantiate an allegation which he had made that it was a 'matter of common knowledge' that the £10 bonus rule of the League was continually broken. He was not prepared to give details but there is little doubt that he was right.[78] Sunderland, for example, were definitely paying bonuses and in 1904 the F.A. fined the club £250, suspended three of their directors for three years and severely censured the players.[79] Glossop were also fined £250 for paying re-signing bonuses, match bonuses and broken time payments to amateurs. Four members of their committee were suspended until May 1907.[80] Middlesbrough were fined by the Football League for paying match bonuses in 1905 and Manchester City suffered a similar fate in the following season.[81] The most sensational case also involved Manchester City. In 1906 the club was fined £250, their secretary and chairman suspended *sine die* from all football and football management and two other directors suspended until May 1907. The remaining directors were ordered to resign. Seventeen players were suspended until the first day of 1907, fined sums ranging from £25 to £100 and forbidden to play for City ever again. It was clear that leading City players, notably Billy Meredith and Livingstone, had been receiving as much as £6.10s per week plus bonuses for wins and draws. The infringements were discovered after Meredith, on the instigation of the

Manchester City secretary, had offered an inducement to an Aston Villa player to allow Manchester City to win a match between the two clubs in April 1905. The City team had been promised a bonus of £100 if they won the championship or finished level on points with Newcastle United, who were the eventual champions. Meredith was found guilty and suspended, demanded wages and bonuses while under suspension for which a much confused Manchester City management reported him to the F.A. Other clubs were either not found out or bent the laws more subtly. Liverpool, for example, were alleged to have appointed their captain as a bill inspector. It was his job to go round and check all the club's posters, for an additional consideration, of course.[82]

The Football Association Council had their Rules Revision Committee investigate the whole issue of the maximum wage in 1903-4. The committee recommended an incremental scale of wages relating to seniority in order to encourage players to show loyalty to their clubs but no action was taken.[83] The view of perhaps a majority of the clubs, and certainly most of the big city clubs, was clearly put by a director of Aston Villa in 1908. The wage limit

had been the cause of all the scandals in connection with football, and was a direct inducement to unjust and unfair—he would not say dishonest—practices. They were compelled to pay players for the whole year, whether these men played well or badly, and they were restricted from rewarding those members of the team who showed special skill and displayed enthusiasm on behalf of the club. The directors wished to have complete control over their players and they did not consider that this wage limit restriction was in the interest of the good government of the game.[84]

The view of the F.A. Council, meanwhile, was probably more in line with William Pickford's: 'there are bound to be professional players of small moral fibre who might not be expected to possess a very high standard of the ethics of the game, but no excuse whatever can be found for those who are presumed to be their "betters"'.[85] By 1910 573 players, mainly in the Football and Southern Leagues, were receiving the maximum wage of £4 per week.[86] How did this compare with the wages working men could expect in a range of other occupations?

Clearly this cannot be recovered in any systematic way because the material for such an exercise does not exist. What can be offered is merely a rough guide. From the story so far it will be apparent that before the maximum wage legislation took effect in the 1901-2 season full-time professional footballers might earn anything from about £1 per week to at least £5 per week, depending on the usual variables of age, experience, skill and club. It is interesting to compare that with the wages of the professional cricketer. The county professionals were paid by the match. Surrey professionals in the 1860s, for example, received £3 per match plus £1 bonus if they won. They were unlikely to have played more than ten or a dozen matches in a summer. By the 1870s matches were usually three day affairs and the rate of pay had gone up to £5. £80 might be made from a five month season, although a really good player might double that. If chosen for the Players against the Gentlemen a man might receive as much as £10.[87] By the 1890s the Yorkshire players were receiving £5 for home matches and £6 for away ones out of which the cost of food and travel had to be found although the 1890s was the last decade in which this was the case. The Test Match fee was £10.[88] In place of the old talent money system, whereby a player received a sovereign for every 50 runs or 5 wickets and a new bat for every century, the Yorkshire captain, Lord Hawke, first appointed in 1883, gave marks for good batting, bowling, fielding, catching and wicket-keeping. Each mark was worth 5/-. Every September at the end of the season he would entertain the players for a day at his home and hand the money over to each player in an envelope. He also put the proceeds of players' benefit matches into a trust fund in order to prevent its being squandered.[89] A player who went on an overseas tour could earn up to £300 in six months at the turn of the century.[90] Mandle has estimated that a good man might make £275 per annum in 1900 although much might depend on who he played for. There were fifteen so-called first-class counties but they did not all play the same number of matches. In the championship of 1901, for example, Yorkshire played 25 and Sussex 24 but Hampshire and Derbyshire played only 16 each. It is doubtful whether cricket club professionals made anything like as much as the 180 professionals with the counties in 1896.[91] Both professional cricketers and footballers had the opportunity to add to their income either by allowing their names to be used for advertising purposes, opening athletic outfitters or other shops, or moving into the ubiquitous public house. But in general only the really successful could hope to benefit in this way, the top 200 or so professionals in association football and the top 75 or 50 in cricket.

How does this compare with the earnings of industrial workers? The crude answer is pretty favourably. Foremen's average earnings in a wide range of industries in 1906 can be seen in Table 4.3.

TABLE 4.3 Foremen's average yearly earnings in 1906

	£s
Textiles	100
Clothing	105
Metals & Engineering	134
Paper and Printing	127
Pottery, Chemicals, etc.	111
Food and Drink	104
Other Manufacturing Industry	105
Building, Woodworking	118
Public Utilities & Railways	86

Source : G. Routh, *Occupations and Pay in Great Britain 1906–60.* (Cambridge 1965), p. 82.

Many individual foremen's earnings would exceed the average. Foremen at the Swindon Works of the Great Western Railway, for example, received £3.10s per week of 54 hours in the summer of 1914. Provided they worked for 52 weeks a year that would produce an annual sum of £182, more than any of the average figures in the table but less than the 600 or so best paid footballers.[92] Foremen probably had more job security than the vast majority of both football professionals and other industrial workers, but the figures are instructive nonetheless.

A further comparison may be attempted by using some of the wage data collected by E.H. Hunt in his book *Regional Wage Variations in Britain, 1850–1914* (1973). In Table 4.4 the average weekly earnings of agricultural labourers in four regions are given for the years 1898 and 1907.

Table 4.5 gives the average weekly earnings of carpenters and their labourers for the years 1886 and 1906. I have taken the liberty of multiplying Hunt's daily figures by 6 to obtain a weekly average.

TABLE 4.4 Agricultural labourers : weekly average earnings by regions in shillings and pence 1898 and 1907

	1898	*1907*
Northumberland and Durham	20/5½	21/5½
Lancashire, Cheshire, West Riding	18/8	19/7
South West	15/7	16/10
Midlands	17/10	18/4½

Source : E.H. Hunt, p. 64.

TABLE 4.5 *Carpenters and labourers: average weekly wages in shillings and pence 1886 and 1906*

	Carpenters		Labourers	
	1886	1906	1886	1906
Northumberland & Durham	35/–	42/–	21/6	28/–
Lancashire, Cheshire, West Riding	33/6	40/6	23/6	27/–
South West	24/6	33/–	16/6	21/6
Midlands	35/6	41/6	23/6	29/6

Source : E.H. Hunt, p. 70.

The third table in this group (Table 4.6) shows the average weekly earnings for coal hewers and labourers in eight coalfield districts for the years 1888 and 1914. Once again as Hunt calculated the earnings per shift, I have multiplied by six to simplify the comparison.

There were a good many men in 1901 who would have welcomed the professional footballers' maximum wage. Indeed there were probably a good many footballers who would! But promotion must always have seemed a possibility even to the players on 30/- per week. An injury to a regular first-team player might result in his moving up towards £4 per week. Of course, money was not the only thing which tempted men into professional football: hope of glory, status, a more flexible work routine, a more generally attractive life must all have been important. But certainly not many skilled workmen could command £4 a week regularly throughout the years before the Great War.

If it is difficult to make meaningful comparisons between the

TABLE 4.6 *Coal hewers and labourers: average weekly wages, in shillings and pence 1888 and 1914*

	Coal Hewers		Labourers	
	1888	1914	1888	1914
Northumberland	30/6	54/6	20/–	30/–
Durham	30/–	53/6	22/6	34/6
Lancashire	31/–	51/6	20/–	35/–
Notts. and Derby	32/–	59/–	20/6	34/–
North Staffs.	29/–	54/6	18/–	33/6
South Staffs.	27/–	42/6	20/–	35/–
Warwickshire	30/–	60/6	18/–	37/–
South Yorkshire	—	61/6	—	40/–

Based on E.H. Hunt, p. 72.[93]

wages of professional footballers and other workmen, it is almost impossible to compare the working conditions of paid footballers with those of other occupational groups, save in the most general terms. But the professional footballer did experience one unique restraint upon his freedom of movement: the retain and transfer system. In theory at least, any workman could leave his employer after giving the appropriate notice and go where he liked. If he had a contract, he was free to find another job when it ran out. Professional footballers did not have that freedom. We saw in the previous chapter how, even before the official recognition of professionalism, clubs were not above trying to persuade the best men in rival teams to change their allegiance. After 1885 it was a continuing source of ill-feeling between clubs and it took the Football League several seasons to eliminate the worst of the practice, in which time several clubs were fined for offering inducements to the players of other clubs.[94] It was the mechanism of the retain and transfer system which at least made the poaching of players a hazardous affair. It also gave the clubs a firm grip on their footballing employees. Players of Football League clubs could not be signed on for more than one football season.[95] Transfers of players between clubs during the season required the permission of the League Management Committee and the secretary of the local football association in whose area the transfer took place. At the end of each season, clubs issued a list of those players they intended to retain and those who were available for transfer. By the 1890s the latter usually had a price put on their heads which interested clubs would be expected to pay. The Football League was publishing and circulating such lists from 1892.[96] The less well-off clubs apparently saw the retain and transfer system as an important obstacle to their richer and greedier comrades. Without such a barrier, promising players reared by small clubs would be whisked away without any form of compensation. It was an important but necessary curb on free competition. Football was not just a business in which the failures went to the wall. 'To argue that a rich club should be able to go into the market and buy up as many men as it might like, without regard to the poor and struggling organisations, is to set up a creed which would soon bring disaster among its apostles.'[97]

But it did mean that club control over the players was very tight indeed. True, if a player did not wish to be transferred from Aston Villa to Plymouth Argyle, he need not go. But if he wanted a move, and his club refused, then he could not go unless he could persuade the Football League to listen to his case. No player could leave if offered the maximum wage. Moreover, if he rejected the terms offered by his club for the following season and the Management Committee of the League turned down his appeal, there was nothing he could do. The options open to him were basically two: accept the club's wage offer or give up professional football and do something else. Transfer fees were often reduced by the League but the number of appeals by players against clubs grew to such an extent that a special sub-committee of the Management Committee had to be set up to deal with them.[98] Moreover, in 1911 the Management Committee had to ask clubs to fix more reasonable transfer fees and to exclude from their retained lists all those players who, it was common knowledge, had long since given up playing.[99] Particularly obnoxious to some players was the widespread practice of placing a transfer fee on players who had not been offered an engagement for the next season.[100] From the players' point of view, of course, many of them did get a contract for the season. As their opponents were wont to remind them, especially during the period of the threatened strike of 1909, 'the footballer claims to be a workman. Let him be treated as such and placed on the same level—no work, no pay, and subject to the usual notice'.[101]

The main opposition to the retain and transfer system in our period came, at first, not from the players but from the Football Association and, in particular, from the influential F.A. councillor from Sheffield, solicitor J.C. Clegg. As early as 1894 he had proposed a package, part of which aimed at the abolition of the transfer fee.[102] Nothing came of this initiative but five years later he tried again.

When . . . clubs require payments of sums of money before they will consent to the players entering into agreements with other clubs, it is submitted that there is an interference with the rights of the players, contrary to the rules of the Football Association, and also the terms of the agreement into which the players have entered.

In the opinion of your committee the practice of buying and selling players is unsportsmanlike and most objectionable in itself, and ought not to be entertained by those who desire to see the game played under proper conditions.

During the enquiries it was stated that some clubs derived considerable pecuniary advantages from training young players and then selling them to the more prominent clubs. We think the practice in such cases, when applied to human beings, altogether discreditable to any system bearing the name of sport.

The only money which should change hands when a player moved from one club to another was 'legitimate expenses'. But it was all to no avail.[103] Clegg and the F.A. made one last effort in the spring of 1905 after the shock of the willingness, nay eagerness, of Middlesbrough to pay £1000 to Sunderland for the transfer of their centre-forward, Alf Common. The F.A. actually made a rule, to come into effect from New Year's Day 1908, that no club should be entitled to pay or receive any transfer fee, or other payment exceeding £350 'upon or in respect of the transfer of any player'. It lasted three months. It was so obviously being ignored by the clubs that it had to be withdrawn. As we saw earlier, by *that* time, the Football Association had decided that handling the money was too unsavoury a business, best left to the clubs and the tradesmen who ran them. So far as the players themselves were concerned their union resolved to 'petition' in favour of longer contracts and the greater security they would bring. 'Give him [the player] some security of tenure . . . he will get married, make a home, become a citizen, stand by the club as long as it stands by him.'[104] Treat him like a human being and, who knows, under those long shorts, hairy legs and big boots, you might find one. The clubs were reluctant to get off the good thing which they knew themselves to be on. After the reorganisation of the Players' Union in 1907–8, the retain and transfer system was a frequent target of their reform proposals although these were generally contained in a package aimed at instituting free *individual* bargaining between player and club. But with the League adamant and the Union a little short on members and sanctions it was a hard game to win.

What of other working conditions? Much depended on the individual club. If a player played for a leading First Division or Southern League side, or even a Second Division club in the Edwardian period, he was probably not doing too badly. Other clubs, perhaps trying to cut their coat according to their cloth, were sometimes harsh and unsympathetic in their dealings with players. In 1899, for example, a player of Crewe Alexandra was suspended without pay for refusing to pay the fare from the Manchester district, where he lived, to Crewe for training each week. He said that had he done so he would have had only 5/- per week left from his wages as a professional.[105] But if the players were sometimes treated with severity, they were also valuable club assets and this was realised by most of the more successful sides very early on. The manifestation of this realisation was a strange kind of paternalism in which the players were treated rather like some Victorian middle-class wives; stifling their independence perhaps, but cushioning them from some of the natural contingencies of life which most working people could rarely face with equanimity. Sick or injured players usually remained on full wages until they were back to normal. Aston Villa had insured 26 of their players against accidents under a collective policy with the Cyclists' Accident Assurance Corporation Ltd.—a real creature of its time—as early as 1883. The Football League had its own comprehensive insurance scheme by 1908.[106] Leading clubs could be quite generous to a player who received a serious injury in their service and so might other local sources. When Joyce, the Bolton Wanderers centre-forward, broke his leg in 1896 he received about £100; made up from a match collection and the proceeds of a performance at the Bolton Grand Theatre.[107] It would be wrong, of course, to say that a professional footballer's life did not have its precarious side. Loss of form or fitness could lead fairly quickly to loss of earnings, especially if a relatively poor club became the player's employer in place of a relatively affluent one.[108] It may be that many young players who failed to make the grade as professionals were turned out on to the labour market without trades and with no better prospects than if they had never tried to take up a career in football. On the other hand if we are correct in suggesting that the majority of professional players in this period did have a background of skilled work, then, when they dropped out of professional football, they might have returned to their old trade. But it is all very speculative. We shall return to the post-playing careers of professional footballers later. But in general for those players who were successful, the prospects were good with the hope of a decent benefit after five years to help prepare for the inevitable day when the playing had to stop.

If the leading clubs in particular were inclined towards paternalism, part of the explanation for their attitude was the feeling that professional footballers did not really have enough to do. Training, travelling and playing was the programme and, as that left the players with rather a lot of time on their hands, keeping them out of mischief, and especially out of pubs, seems to have been a perennial problem for club committees and boards of directors. Aston Villa went so far as to project a scheme for a club house which would have the dual purpose of bringing the players under better control and keeping them out of 'public house taprooms'. The club was to have reading and writing rooms; billiard tables and smoking concerts were to be held there. Meals and refreshments would be served. Unfortunately it is not clear whether the idea ever materialised.[109] We do not know a great deal about the form and content of training. We saw earlier that special training for cup matches certainly began as early as 1883 but of the regular, daily work done by the professional and how this may have changed through the period we know relatively little.[110] Some of the Derby County professionals and directors had a discussion about the best methods of obtaining proper training shortly after the start of the 1892–3 season. It was agreed that all players who had not regular employment should meet every morning at 10.00 a.m. and take such exercise and practice as the trainer directed.

Certainly by the Edwardian period, mornings only appears to have been the rule with a civilised starting time of ten a.m. to increase the envy of the mass of the male working population. George Davie claimed that training was on only two days a week when he first went to Woolwich Arsenal in 1891.[111] Billy Meredith who played for both Manchester clubs and was still turning out for Wales after the First World War, explained that it was an error to think that a professional's life was not extremely busy. 'At most headquarters he is required to present himself for training not later than ten o'clock in the morning.' Training itself varied from 'the use of heavy clubs and dumb-bells to twenty minutes skipping, ball-punching, sprinting, and alternating with an eight or nine mile walk at a brisk pace'.[112] At Tottenham in 1904 it was also a ten o'clock start. 'Then they have an hour or an hour and a half of sprinting and ball practice, with turns at skipping. . . . A bath and a rub down complete the morning's work. After dinner the men can go for a stroll if they like—there is no organised walk. . . .'[113] A week's training at Derby at the start of the 1900–1 season comprised:

	Morning	Afternoon	Evening
Mon. 20 August	walking		baseball match
Tues. 21 August	sprinting and running	ball kicking	
Wed. 22 August	sprinting and running	cricket match	
Thurs. 23 August	walking	sprinting	
Frid. 24 August	sprinting		practice match
Mon. 27 August	walking		practice match[114]

The best contemporary descriptions of training generally relate to special training before particular matches. Teams usually went away to some seaside resort or watering place and the local press sent back reports designed to show the club supporters that the players were not on holiday. What follows is an account, allegedly by one of the players of Preston North End, when the

club went to the Palace Hotel at Southport in order to prepare
for their F.A. Cup match with Aston Villa in January 1888.

We came down here on Friday afternoon .... On Saturday morning we were
all up at seven o'clock for a walk on the sands; back at half past eight for breakfast (white fish, chops, ham and eggs); at ten o'clock proceeded to practise on
the ground of the Southport Wanderers ... until twelve; in the afternoon, had
a walk on the sands, and in the evening a few went to the circus, and others to
the theatre in the Winter Gardens, all being back in the hotel and in bed by
ten o'clock. And Saturday Night was New Year's Eve! Seven o'clock on Sunday
morning found the men astir but no practice was indulged in, though Turkish
baths were taken during the afternoon, and strolling along the promenade
filled up the remainder of the day until nine o'clock. On Monday, a similar
programme was gone through to that of Saturday .... In the evenings the team
attended, by invitation, Mr Cookson's concert, in the Cambridge Hall, where
they met with a flattering reception, but the rule as to 'early to bed' was strictly
observed. Yesterday morning the walk on the sands was indulged in as usual
before breakfast, with the usual practice on the Wanderers' ground .... The
afternoon and evening was by some spent at the Glaciarium. The dinner is only
plain, and consists of roastbeef, with a glass of bitter beer for those who prefer
it, rice, sago or tapioca pudding. Tea similar to breakfast. Supper consists of
gruel, with syrup or milk. Every afternoon each man has a salt-water plunge
bath, and night and morning, as well as after the practice, each gets a brisk
rub down.[115]

There was some criticism that not enough training was done
with the ball. 'Tityrus' complained in 1908 that it was the

lack of real skill with the ball which makes even the highest class of League football
so often uninteresting. ... Ball practice is too often neglected ... training is
too often on old-fashioned and stereotyped lines. It should be the object of
every trainer coach to make the men interested in their training.[116]

A famous English international, although at the end of his career,
largely agreed.

At present the players stand about six yards away from the goalkeeper and
shoot, which any navvy could do. There is no running about or dribbling,
feinting, passing with the inside or outside of the foot, trapping or heading the
ball and placing it with the head like you do with your feet, judging distances
etc; indulged in at all. Players should, in my opinion, try to do the things with the
ball they have to do on a Saturday.

In 1904 the Aston Villa directors decided that their players should
train more with the ball, practising dribbling, passing and shooting
on the run.[117]

Apart from the players already quoted we do not know what
players generally thought about training. Perhaps it was boring,
unimaginative and regular. At least it does not seem to have lasted

long. Travelling was another matter. Professional footballers with League clubs had to do a lot of it, mostly by train. In the 1880s, when Anglo-Scottish club fixtures were common, some of their travelling was done in conditions which today would seem rather uncomfortable. On the other hand it was all arranged and paid for and, if the lack of contemporary comment by players is any guide, largely taken for granted by the 1890s.

Did the professional player enjoy playing? Was the play element removed by the entry of the Cash Nexus Monster? It is not easy to discover evidence one way or the other. It has not been possible to discover any examples of players saying publicly that they did not enjoy playing any more. What evidence there is, and it is certainly very thin, suggests the opposite. At the eve of season conference between the representatives of the Football Association and the players in 1909, Harold Fleming, Swindon Town and England, said that 'he played for money, but he also played for the love of sport in the true sense of the word'.[118] Although it seems hardly sensible to use the behaviour of professional players on the field of play as illustrations of whether or not they liked playing, when we are told that, after scoring for Wolves against Blackburn Rovers in the F.A. Cup Semi-Final in 1889, Wykes was so elated that he rushed about like 'a bear on a hot plate, and finally wound up by turning a Catherine-wheel in true gutter-arab style', we suspect that it was a spontaneously joyful act and that he enjoyed *that* bit anyway.[119] Even allowing for the sense in which the play of professional footballers was work, it seems unlikely that the Saturday release was not welcomed and enjoyed, especially if the side won.

Enjoyment, however, did not mean lack of grievance. We noted earlier the obvious irritants of the wages question and the retain and transfer system. In an age when trade unionism was slowly gaining ground, with another spurt just around the corner, it was not altogether surprising that an attempt was made to organise footballers. In fact, one of the major problems for the Players' Union was that it hoped to win a big victory in order that it might take off in terms of membership and general strength. A more prudent, although perhaps more impractical, strategy would have been to build up its muscle first. However that may be, the origins and growth of the Professional Football Players' Union is interesting enough in itself and throws a little more light on players' attitudes to their position in the game if not to wider issues.

Many organisations have obscure origins and the Players'

Union is in a long, if not especially honourable, tradition. The idea was first floated seriously in 1893 when the Wolverhampton Wanderers goalkeeper, W.C. Rose, called a meeting of League club captains in October of that year.[120] The threat of a maximum wage, or even no wages in summer, was in the air and it was those two possibilities which probably prompted Rose's initiative. An advertisement in the *Athletic News* on 23 October hinted at difficulties. 'The clubs who have not replied to my letter will oblige by doing so at once, that a Meeting may be arranged at an early date. If we are to have a successful Association, every league players must be a member.' In the event, as we noted earlier, nothing came of the proposals to limit players' wages and apparently nothing came of the proposed union either.[121]

The players made another attempt at forming a union during the 1897–8 season.[122] Once again the actual beginnings are far from well-documented but the issues which prompted the attempt were similar to those of four years before, with freedom of contract now the most important. The *Athletic News* commented that the players were 'resolved to petition in favour of professionals signing on for more than a season at a time. The present system means that a player is uncertain as to whether he will be re-engaged or not at the season's end'.[123] The president of the union was R. Holmes of Preston North End and the secretary, a Scotsman, John Cameron, who had recently been appointed manager of Tottenham Hotspur.[124] The *Athletic News* reported that there was some 'unlooked for and inexplicable opposition . . . from certain players who have never taken to the Union scheme'.[125] The paper itself was generally favourably disposed towards the union and optimistic about its chances of success. An England-Scotland match was held in March 1899 to help boost union funds.[126] Despite all this activity however, the union appears to have collapsed again. It did not revive until 1907–8 when a match between Manchester United and Newcastle United was held to raise money to support a provident fund. We shall see below that it was the players of these two clubs who were the strongest supporters of the union in the pre-1915 period.[127]

Once more we are not in danger of being overwhelmed by the richness of the sources, but we do know that the ubiquitous *Athletic News* reported a claim by the union to have 700 members in January 1908 and 900 out of an estimated five thousand professional players in April of the same year. By the first A.G.M. the membership claimed had risen to 1300.[128] At that meeting several resolutions were unanimously adopted. The conviction of every prominent professional football player that the only solution of the wages problem clubs are faced with annually is to be found in the abolition of all restrictions on the financial relations of players with their clubs, for the policy of limitation and restriction has failed after a trial of seven seasons.

The Players' Union beg leave to offer the policy of mutual arrangement, based on free bargaining on all matters affecting the services of players and their clubs, as a substitute for the present unsatisfactory practice of allowing clubs to retain players who had been offered the limit wage.

The Players' Union suggest that clubs and players should be encouraged to enter into engagements for periods of two seasons and upwards.

A policy of mutual arrangement in all financial matters between clubs and players would naturally permit players to share in transfer transactions, and thus eliminate the abuses of the present transfer system. Free bargaining . . . would cause the scandal of suspensions to cease, and save gentlemen of high social position the humiliations of being pilloried in the public Press.

This was obviously merely staking out a position: the details would come later. It provoked a mixed response. On the one hand, an article by C.E. Sutcliffe headlined 'Who shall be Masters? Players or Clubs?' appeared in the *Athletic News* on 11 January 1909. But the paper itself seemed to support the players when urging that the goal to be aimed at was 'the removal of all restrictions, save the right of retention of professionals'.[129] The conflict rumbled on throughout the spring and summer of 1909, particularly in the columns of the *Athletic News*, fuelled by pieces like the one from Sutcliffe and two articles from Billy Meredith. Meredith's first article, in an un-named weekly magazine, was entitled 'If the pros struck'. Sutcliffe's response was scornful.

What an optimist he is! He is only looking forward three or four seasons, so he tells us. When I read this wonderful dream I thought it was a rich joke, but I was solemnly and publicly assured on Wednesday last by a member of the Players' Union that they are laying all their plans for a strike three years hence.

Meredith's picture of inadequate payment and scurvy treatment, of empty trams and deserted trains, of public resentment and withdrawal of football editions is a cheery phantom from the professionals' point of view. I really grew alarmed until I got near the end, when I found the strike which commenced on Saturday had ended on Monday in a complete victory for the players.

The Players' Union is the foundation upon which this strike has to commence. In three or four years time I reckon the Players' Union will be worth sufficient to pay its members one week's wages. The discontents among the players are comparatively few. The number of players able to stand a strike of, say, a month, are much fewer. The number of clubs which would welcome a strike is legion. A month's rest would be a glorious relief.

Directors and club committees get no remuneration for their services. A strike would give a chance to hundreds of players craving an opportunity. If William Meredith thinks the public are with the Players' Union he is sadly mistaken.

I come across very few who do not think footballers are amply paid at £4 per week and a £250 benefit after five years' service.[130]

Matters were apparently brought to a head by the action of the union in going to the courts with the case of a player in dispute with his club. This was not allowed by the F.A. rules and when the club involved complained to the Football Association, that body asked the union why it had failed to request permission of the F.A. before seeking justice in the courts. The union replied that such permission did not need to be asked: every Englishman had recourse to the law. The F.A.'s response to that was to suspend the chairman and secretary of the union from all football and football management for life and to call on all players to resign from the union by July 1909 or their registrations with the F.A. would be cancelled.[131] Shortly before the deadline the *Athletic News* published a letter which, it was alleged, had been sent by the secretary of the union to all members. It was certainly combative.

The opportunity has now arrived for concerted action and in endeavouring to smash the Union the F.A. have overstepped the mark and placed us in a better position for striking a decisive blow for independence than ever we were before. . . . Now there are one or two of the best Teams in the Country who wish to stand out, this is glorious news and means success, for if we have a few Teams of class standing out the whole football world is at a standstill . . . we have waited our chance and we must decide once and for ever whether the professional player is to be a man or a puppet in the hands of the F.A. . . . '[132]

A further complicating factor was the decision of the Players' Union to seek membership of the General Federation of Trade Unions, rather feeble offshoot, as it turned out, of the T.U.C. which had been set up in 1899 to provide a central fund for the support of unions in conflict with their employers. To some club and Football Association officials this conjured up the interesting fantasy of professional footballers engaging in sympathetic strike action on behalf of other workers.[133] By the time the F.A. Council met at Oxford in early July it was claimed that over 800 players out of a union membership total of 1,200 had resigned in compliance with the Football Association's ultimatum.[134] The Manchester United, Newcastle United and Middlesbrough teams seem to be the ones who were most determined and were sticking to their membership.[135] The talk in the press was of a players' strike. Two meetings were held between representatives of the F.A., the G.F.T.U., and the P.U.[136] Finally, at almost the eleventh hour a compromise was reached at a conference between the Football Association and the players' representatives where it was agreed to remit the suspensions and pay the wages of those players who had not resigned from the union by July 1, to recognise the union and to get together to examine the grievances of the players, especially with regard to wages and the retain and transfer system.

In the negotiations which followed, the union made some interesting proposals. Players not offered a re-engagement should have a free transfer. After five years' continuous service with a club players should be allowed freedom of contract. After four years' continuous service players should receive an additional £1 per week, and 10/- after two successive years with the same club. Bonuses should be paid on the basis of £2 for a win and £1 for a draw. In Cup matches a cumulative scheme, the rewards increasing as each succeeding round was reached, was worked out. Finally, save in those cases where players had been guilty of misconduct, transfer fees were to be divided between club and player.[137] None of these proposals suited the Football League. But if the League was against change, and certainly the kind of change which the players had in mind, the clubs could hardly behave as if nothing had happened, particularly since, as we saw earlier, a considerable portion of the better-off clubs were disgruntled about the operation of the maximum wage.[138]

Early in 1910 the new arrangements were completed. They can be briefly summarised. Existing rights of the clubs to retain a player on offering a wage of £208 per annum were confirmed, but it was to be permissible for any league, by resolution of its A.G.M., to extend the maximum wage to £5 per week or £260 per year, the increase not to operate more quickly than a rise of 10/- per week after two years' service and a further 10/- per week after four years. The £10 signing on fee could only be paid when a player joined a new club. The top five clubs in Divisions One and Two, and in the Southern League could, at the end of a season, distribute talent money to their players, the sums not to exceed £275, to be shared by the players of the club finishing first, £220, to the runner up and then £115, £110 and £55 respectively for third, fourth and fifth. Similar merit payments could be made for progress in the F.A. Cup. Benefits were to be paid after five and ten years' service although agreements about benefits might be entered into after three years. Where players were transferred at the club's request a fixed percentage of the fee might be paid to compensate for loss of benefit. Clubs were to have the right to insert a clause in all players' agreements allowing the club, on giving fourteen days' notice to the player, to terminate such agreement (without prejudice to the club's right to transfer fees) where a player did not prove efficient or was guilty of serious misconduct or breach of disciplinary rules. Players were to have the right of appeal to the management committees of the respective leagues without payment of deposit, with a further right of appeal to the appeals committee on payment of a deposit of £5.[139]

The compromise settlement, if compromise it was, did at least provide the elite of paid players with the real possibility, indeed certainty, of increasing their earnings. But if the dispute had really been about control in general and freedom of contract in particular, as some of the rhetoric during the crisis had suggested, then the players had lost by a wide margin. The retain and transfer system remained untouched. Professionalism remained firmly in its place which was where both F.A. and League believed it had to be; that was the justification for 1885.

Under its [the F.A.'s] strong hand and its restrictions the professional game is reasonably sure of a sport that the public, ladies included, can enjoy. Let loose from control to what sordid lengths would the game be prostituted? But the F.A. does more. The professional side of the game gives it the money that enables it to keep in hand the enormous volume of football that if left to its own resources would speedily make the game a by word. ... [140]

The F.A. did permit the Players' Union to test the validity of the retain and transfer system in the courts in 1912, but again the players lost and were left with costs of £725 as well as some disappointment.[141] Just to emphasise who was really boss the League refused to allow Players' Union members to wear union badges on the field, in spite of their 'kindest and most sympathetic feelings towards the union'.[142]

Where did all this leave the union? During those late August days of 1909 when talk of strikes was in the air, the executive committee of the union contained the names of several well known players, including internationals such as Bob Crompton and Ernest Needham, Arthur Bridgett and Frank Bradshaw. But the most energetic union activists were undoubtedly the chairman, Colin Veitch and, later, Charlie Roberts. We have met Roberts before as a trenchant critic of training methods. He was an iron worker in Darlington, a mill furnace man in the late 1890s and he played for a local side, Bishop Auckland, and then Grimsby Town before moving to Manchester United for £600 in 1904.[143] Veitch had been educated at Rutherford College in Newcastle-on-Tyne and had played for United as an amateur before signing professional forms. He was a well-known socialist on Tyneside, an articulate, thinking man although rather optimistic about what might be achieved by the union.[144]

Sometime in 1911 the union started a journal, the *Football Players' Magazine*. It appeared monthly through the season and seems to have lasted until the close of the 1913–14 season. What was probably its last issue featured an interesting article by Charlie Roberts which illustrated very well the difficulties faced by anyone trying to organise professional footballers into a union. The article shows clearly the failure of the union to capture the support of more than a small minority of the players and to stimulate a more active interest in collective affairs. Roberts began by pointing out that out of 158 clubs employing professionals, only 45 had any connection with the union. After noting that the union had contributed to the increase in earnings and bonuses and that many more members were receiving these benefits he gave some account of where the membership was weakest.

Let me give you a few of the teams who have not a single member of the Union in the First Division and I hope the Trade Unionists of these towns where the clubs are will duly take note: Aston Villa, Blackburn Rovers, Chelsea, Everton, Middlesbrough, Sheffield Wednesday, Tottenham; and in the Second Division . . . Blackpool, Bradford, Bury, Glossop, Huddersfield, Hull City, Leeds City, Lincoln City and Wolverhampton Wanderers.[145]

I know of no class of workpeople who are less able to look after themselves than footballers; they are like a lot of sheep. A representative from the Union could go and speak to them on the why and wherefore they should join the Union, and they would immediately decide to join. Two minutes after a manager could go and say a few words to them, and then they would decide not to join. . . . Try and remember that union is strength.

Unions subs were 3d per week for those players earning less than £2.10s and 6d for those earning in excess of £2.10s. Roberts ended his piece with a plea heard in Labour halls and trade union branches everywhere.

You are for ever asking, What [sic] can the Union do for me? The Union stands for those in need of help. If you don't need it, don't you think you ought to support it in the interests of those who do. Has the player who is injured or wronged in any shape or form, to sit with bitter heart and think he has not a friend in the world? If his fellow players won't help him, who can he look to? . . . But I am telling you now that I have just about had enough of trying to raise the status of the professional footballer. It takes up time now that I cannot afford to spare, and unless the players next season take a greater interest in the Union, I, for one, am going to leave them to it, but not before we have paid our present debts. . . . He is a wretched, miserable fool who cannot see what is good for himself; and the working man of Great Britain has surely shown you during these last two years what can be done by Trade Unionism.[146]

It *was* difficult to organise the players. Many of them *were* doing well enough and while they retained their health and youthful strength and took home a regular £4 or £5 a week it was not surprising that they were slow to appreciate the need for a union at all, leave alone active support for one.[147] The professional footballers' relationship with his employer may not have been totally dissimilar from employer-worker relations elsewhere, but it was different enough to make the remedies of other workers seem irrelevant most of the time. With only two full-time officials and a reliance on volunteers to collect subscriptions, sell the magazine, organise meetings and in general do all those things which usually need at least a focus of permanent organisational skill, the fact that the union was weak can hardly astonish us. It was to be fifty years before, if a metaphor may be drawn from another sport, it gained the courage to threaten to punch its weight.[148]

So was the lot of the professional footballer enviable or not? Much might depend on where you were standing. Gibson and Pickford for example, in their famous book, were not impressed by the life.

Once registered . . . the player is considerably tied up, 'cribbed, cabined, and confined'. He makes the best terms he can with his employers, sometimes highly lucrative, often very moderate. He can only play for the club that registers him. If he leaves one club and joins another, he must be formally transferred and re-registered. His name is in an alphabetical index kept at headquarters, his movements from club to club are noted and published in official lists, and his misdeeds are black-marked against him. If he ceases his membership of his club, and does not join another in proper form as laid down by rule and schedule, he is debarred from playing at all, and he is at every turn subject to pains and penalties. An amateur may snap his fingers at a committee; but the professional, unless he is a very high prize indeed, dare not, and has instead to obey club regulations and do what he is told.[149]

Like most workmen everywhere, one might add, although one can appreciate that such an apparently regimented way of life would never do for the middle-class journalist which Pickford was. But Pickford received support from the professionals. John Cameron, for example, claimed to have spoken to many players 'and few would let their boys take football up as the serious business of life'. The career was short and might be made shorter by an accident and if you have no trade on which to fall back 'you are practically ruined'. Cameron went so far as to say that no club ought to be allowed to sign a player on until he has provided evidence of a 'marketable knowledge of some trade or profession'. Many are called, but only those with 'superlative talents' are chosen.[150] Billy Meredith pointed up some additional limitations.

Every hour of the day he lives in an atmosphere which reminds him of nothing else but football; and he finishes the week playing before a great crowd of people, who often expect him to perform more like a machine than a human being subject to pains, aches, and illnesses, to say nothing of some ugly wound which the stud of a boot has opened, but which his pluck and loyalty to his club causes him to forget in his whole-souled desire to secure a victory for his side. If he is married he has to say goodbye to many of the pleasures of home life, and at the festive time of the year, when everyone reckons to meet round the family circle, he is probably hundreds of miles away, perhaps shut up in a deserted seaside resort, undergoing 'special training' for the purpose of providing entertainment for the more favoured members of society. Add to all this the possible risk of having to stay for weeks in hospital nursing a broken ankle or a dislocated collar-bone, and it must surely be agreed that the life of the professional football player is not quite so gilded an occupation as it might appear.[151]

Perhaps not, although Meredith himself stayed in it for long enough: it was clearly better than coalmining in which he had worked earlier.[152] But however 'cramped and confined', the profession of footballer was never short of working-class aspirants who, although not necessarily believing that such a life was all beer and skittles, were convinced that it was a qualitative improvement on working for a living, with higher and hopefully more regular earnings, enhanced status in the community, especially among fellow workmen, and the possibility of glory as well. They were hardly to be blamed if they did not think too carefully about what they would do if they did not make it, nor what they would do after the room which they had had at the top had been filled by another.

What did professional footballers do after they finished playing? Did football provide a passport to better jobs? Did they experience upward social mobility as a result of their prowess in the game? It is obviously very difficult to make effective generalisations on these questions. All the historian can do is to show what was possible. So far as the first question is concerned what evidence there is suggests that the four employments most frequently mentioned are shopkeepers, public house licensees, football management, and whatever job the player held before he became a professional.

Several of the first generation of professionals in Lancashire kept pubs while still players. In Blackburn, for example, Douglas was behind the bar at the Cotton Tree Inn and Jack Hunter landlord of the Eagle and Child in 1883. Both houses were owned

(Manchester History Workshop)

A. J. Balfour looking for support: Manchester City v. Stoke City,
29 September 1900

(Radio Times Hulton Picture Library)

A face in the crowd: Tottenham Hotspur v. Sunderland,
20 January 1912

Four Faces of Professionalism. One:
Bob Crompton, Blackburn Rovers
and England, 1913

Four Faces of Professionalism. Two: Charlie Roberts,
Manchester United Captain, Manchester United v. Bristol City,
F.A. Cup Final, 24 April 1909

Four Faces of Professionalism. Three: Billy Meredith, Manchester City,
Manchester United and Wales, 1908. Here seen with the ball,
Manchester United v. Queen's Park Rangers, 1908

Four Faces of Professionalism. Four: A. Taylor,
Captain of Barnsley, 1912

Cup Final tie at Crystal Palace, Br

(*Radio Times Hulton Picture Library*)

v. Newcastle United, 22 April 1911

(Radio Times Hulton Picture Library)

Seeing the sights of London: Supporters up for the Cup Final,
25 April 1914, at the Changing of the Guard

(Radio Times Hulton Picture Library)

Soldiers at the F.A. Cup Final tie at Old Trafford, Manchester,
24 April 1915

(Local Studies Library, Nottinghamshire County Library)

A turnstile at Notts. County's new Meadow Lane Ground, September 1910

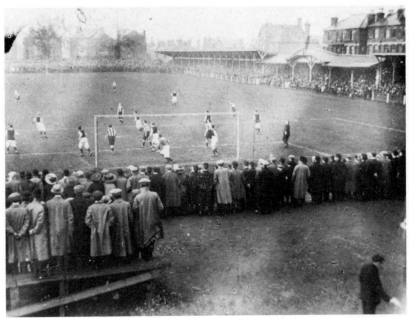

(Local Studies Library, Nottinghamshire County Library)

Behind the goal: Notts. County's last game on the Trent Bridge
Cricket Ground, 16 April 1910

(Radio Times Hulton Picture Library)

Latecomers or just socialising: the 1911 Cup Final

by the Little Harwood Brewery Company.[153] By 1885 Jim Ward was mine host at the Prince of Wales and Lofthouse in charge of the Black Horse. The next year saw another Rovers' player, Hugh McIntyre, landlord of the Castle. Another member of that team, Fergie Suter, was landlord of the County Arms in the town in 1896. Meanwhile Great Lever's captain, Jimmy M'Kernan was manager of the Market Hotel in Bolton in 1886 and Padiham's skipper the proprietor of the Cricketers' and Footballers' Arms in that place.[154] An advertisement for a 'first class forward' which appeared in the columns of the *Athletic News* in 1890 stipulated that the successful applicant would be 'required to act as manager of a fully licensed house, the headquarters of the club. . . .'[155] About half of the great Sunderland team of the 1890s were alleged to be public house landlords.[156] George, the Aston Villa goalkeeper, was given permission by the club to keep an outdoor beer house in 1903.[157] Similarly Harry Stafford, captain of Manchester United around the turn of the century, later became a licensee of one of the public houses owned by the brewery whose chairman was also chairman of the club.[158] Three internationals from Aston Villa, Denis Hodgetts, James Crabtree and Charlie Athersmith, all took pubs on giving up the game, as did Billy Meredith and Billy Bassett: it was clearly a common occurrence.[159]

In the summer of 1908, the *Athletic News* wondered what had happened to the players of the all-conquering Preston North End team of the late 1880s and the Sunderland 'team of all the talents' of the 1890s. Of the twelve former Preston players about whom the paper was able to discover some information, three had died, two were in football management, one was working as a coalminer in Scotland, one was a solicitor (he had worked in the office there before playing football) and one had emigrated to South Africa. The remaining four were simply described as living in Birmingham, Glasgow, Ayrshire and Preston.[160] Ten of the ex-Sunderland team were listed. Two were dead, two kept public houses, one had a 'large shop' in Newcastle-on-Tyne, one was farming, one an electrical engineer, one was employed at a printing works, one in football management and finally one was described as living 'on Tyneside'.[161]

The number of openings in football itself was not very large before the First World War. Most professional teams had trainers by then; some, indeed, had managers. But the trainers were still occasionally drawn from the ranks of ex-boxers or professional runners. Former professional cricketers were in steady demand for coaching both with clubs and the public schools, but apart from J. Ross being engaged by Ampleforth College for a few days in 1887 and T.D. Bradshaw obtaining a post as assistant coach at Harrow about 1907, the football professional was not required to teach his skills.[162] The growth of the game in Europe however, did provide opportunities for old players. Two famous English internationals, Fred Spikesly and Steve Bloomer were both interned in Germany during the war: they had been coaching there when hostilities commenced.

It is clear that even players with more or less distinguished careers did not have an automatic passport to better things. John Reynolds, who had played for Aston Villa, Ireland and England was described as a labourer in September 1899 when he was brought before the magistrates for being in arrears with an affiliation order. George Wall, of Manchester United and England, went to work on Manchester docks after leaving football and Abraham Hartley, who had spells at Dumbarton, Everton, Liverpool and Southampton, died of a heart attack on Southampton docks where he worked after his professional career was finished. Micky Bennett played for Sheffield United and England, but he was killed in the pit at the age of 33 whence he had returned after a premature end to his footballing life. Ted Brayshaw of Sheffield Wednesday and England died, aged only 44, in Wadsley Bridge Asylum, the later stages of his life marked by 'poverty, misery and despair'.[163]

If he played more or less regularly for ten years at least and earned close to the maximum wage for the whole of the period, if he saved what he could and prudently invested the results of any benefits, and if he was lucky with his friends and his club the professional football player could set himself up in some comfort, if not elegance and luxury. But there were so many important variables, many related to individual personality. Some players clearly found giving up the game difficult. After fifteen years they did not feel themselves fitted for anything else. Even if they had once had a trade, it was long since that they had practised it. Moreover, they had got used to the way of life, its rhythms and rituals, and adaptation to 'normality' was not easy. It is interesting to compare the post-playing careers of some members of the Aston Villa team which was so successful in the period 1895-1905. John Devey and Harry Hampton put some money into the new cinematograph industry. They formed the Winson Green Picture House Company and opened a 1500 seat cinema in 1915. Devey was by now a Villa director.[164] James Crabtree and Charlie Athersmith were also both internationals.

Both had long football careers at top wages. Crabtree died at the age of 37 following an attack of *delirium tremens* brought on by a scalding accident. Crabtree's doctor said at the inquest that the former Villa stalwart had not been in good health for two years due to 'intemperate use of liquor'. He had become a licensed victualler. Athersmith was similarly afflicted although his early death was thought to have been brought on by an injury received playing football.[165]

One clear indicator of social mobility among professional football players would be the number who later became directors of either the club for which they played or for some other leading side. This author has only discovered ten directors who had been professional players before 1915. We have already noted John Devey of Aston Villa and he was joined on the Villa Board by another former leading player of the club, Howard Spencer. The rest of the list comprises Jack Sharp and Dan Kirkwood, both players and directors of Everton, Richard Puden, Leicester City, Bob Crompton, James Forrest and John Forbes, Blackburn Rovers and A.C. Jephcott and W.I. Bassett of West Bromwich Albion.[166]

Kirkwood was born in Scotland but played for Sunderland. He worked in the shipyards there, later returning to Scotland before journeying south for a second time to spend four years with Everton.

James Forrest had been the first professional to appear for England against Scotland in 1886. He began life as a millworker and played for a junior team in Blackburn known as the King's Own before 'being induced' to join the Rovers. He played in five winning cup finals, scoring in three and when, late in his career he was transferred to Darwen, he was carried shoulder high around Blackburn. He later returned to help the Rovers fight off relegation. He was elected a director in 1906 about twelve years after he had finished playing. During the later years of his football career he had become licensee of the Audley Arms Hotel in Higher Audley Street, Blackburn. He was also interested in the firm of Messrs. Pickering, Brown and Company, shuttlepeg makers, joiners and mill furnishers and he eventually left the hotel to devote himself to that business in which he was a partner for over twenty years. When he died aged 62 in 1925 he left an estate which had a gross value of £5845.[167]

Crompton, who won a record 34 English international caps between 1902–14, was, like Forrest, in many respects the ideal of what respectable commentators on football thought a professional should be. He had played with Moss Street Board School in Blackburn in the 1880s, became an apprentice plumber and was spotted by Blackburn Rovers playing in a local Sunday School league. He played for Blackburn as an amateur for two years because he did not wish to jeopardise his amateur status in swimming and water-polo. He also kept up his plumbing and later set up a motor business as well. The gross value of his estate was £8871 when he died in 1941 although the net value of the personal estate only amounted to £63.6.4.[168]

Bassett played for West Bromwich Albion from 1886 until 1899. A popular international right winger, he was known locally as the People's William of Stoney Lane. He entered the licensed trade and was the landlord of several West Bromwich public houses. He joined the board in 1905 and was chairman for twenty-nine years from 1908.

If a few professional players became club directors, what can be said about the status of the professional player in general? For example how respectable was football as a profession by 1915? Were professional footballers welcome in middle-class circles? It is very difficult to even begin to answer such questions. We saw in the previous chapter that discrimination within the game against professionals took several forms and only slowly diminished. Billy Meredith went out of his way to defend the respectability of the paid player in 1904 in his contribution to Gibson and Pickford. He claimed that the previous twelve years had seen a great change in the character of the paid player.

Recognising the fact that the public eye was upon him . . . he willingly accepted the position and we now see him able to take his position in the best of company, and would have no hesitation in asking a lady to take a seat with him in his saloon. Why, it is a fact that Manchester City on our recent journey to London for the final for the English Cup, surprised the occupants of a station they were leaving by singing, and that too quite musically, 'Lead Kindly Light'. The days indeed when hotel proprietors absolutely refused to allow a football team on their premises . . . are now incidents of the past.[169]

What does one make of that?

John Cameron was also clear that rough play and rough manners were things of the past. To become a professional 'you must have exceptional qualities of a personal character' and brain as well as brawn. 'Education makes all the difference, and the incoming professionals will have to be men of considerable culture. . . .'[170] But there was a rather patronising tone to the story told by J.J. Bentley, the President of the Football League, about how he was out walking with some ladies and gentlemen one day when they encountered several young men 'well dressed and groomed' who raised their hats. 'Who are they?' came the question, and Bentley replied 'Only those disreputable football professionals you sometimes talk about.'[171] To be a professional footballer was not quite respectable in some eyes, basically because they did have rather more leisure than most other young occupied males and that was likely to lead to over-indulgence in wine, women and gaming. But in 1903 the Football Association Council accepted the idea that the F.A. should have the powers to allow ex-professionals to serve on club and F.A. committees. This was a recognition that some of them, at least, could be trusted to behave like gentlemen.

Notes

1 Letter signed J.W. in *Preston Herald* 29 March 1884. By-laws were made forbidding the playing of football in the streets but this led to complaints about the lack of public open spaces. 'It is supposed that one election cry next month is to be "Greenhouses for the working men". Let another be "Open spaces for the children". 'Ibid. 8 October, 1 November 1884.

2 M.G. Barnett, *Young Delinquents* (1913) p. 12. After the Mayor of Bolton had said football playing in the streets of the town was a great nuisance five boys were fined 2/6 each plus costs or seven days hard labour in March 1884. *Bolton Evening News* 24 March 1884.

3 There was some pressure put on the Education Department in an attempt to persuade them that games should be a vital part of the elementary curriculum. A pamphlet by M.D. Roth entitled 'A Plea for the Compulsory Teaching of the Elements of Physical Education in our National Elementary Schools' emphasised the poor physical quality of army and navy aspirants and underlined the link between Prussian military success and her system of physical training. Quoted in P.C. McIntosh, *Physical Education in England Since 1800* (1968 edn) pp. 107–8. On drill in elementary schools see J.S. Hurt, 'Drill, discipline and the elementary school ethos' in P. McCann (ed.), *Popular Education and Socialization in the Nineteenth Century* (1977) pp. 167–92.

4 Quoted by P.M. Young (1959) pp. 23–5. Old boys from this school formed their own football team in 1877 and later fused with a local cricket club and renamed themselves Wolverhampton Wanderers.

5 *Football Field* 3 January 1885.

6 The National Physical Recreation Society, founded in the mid-1880s to promote physical recreation among the working classes, was an active propagandist, particularly in the area of gymnastics. By 1891 this association, whose leading patrons included the Duke of Westminster, Earl Dalhousie, Lord Wolseley, Lord Brabazon and the Bishop of Liverpool and whose treasurer was A.F. Kinnaird, claimed to have established and furnished with honorary instructors over 200 classes 'composed of working

people who are unable to pay for professional gymnastic tuition'. *Pastime* 6 May 1891.

7   See the section on Sport and Sportsmen in J.Osborne (ed.), *Saltley College Centenary 1850–1950* (1950) pp. 135–41. On Johnstone see his obituary in the *Birmingham Post* 1 October 1941. By the 1890s the Borough Road College at Isleworth ran four soccer and rugby teams. F.H. Spencer, *An Inspector's Testament* (1938) p. 138.

8   D.D. Molyneux, op.cit. p. 222. By November 1882, 23 Birmingham Board schools had football clubs.

9   Quoted in Molyneux pp. 222–3. The Assistant Clerk to the Birmingham School Board enthused that

the practice of the game also takes the boys away for a time from the crowded and unhealthy districts in which they live, and prevents them from becoming obnoxious to the people residing in the streets in which they would otherwise play ... and not the least benefit ... is the business knowledge the conduct of the little club affairs (as managed in many of the schools) gives to the lads, a knowledge which cannot fail to be useful to them in after life.

10   *Birmingham Daily Mail* 19 November 1883.

11   In 1886 a group of Aston teachers arranged a similar knock-out competition for Aston schools. Molyneux, op.cit. pp. 224, 226. In February 1886 'three or four hundred' scholars from Birmingham Board schools were among the crowd who watched a Monday afternoon game between Aston Villa and Oxford University although it is not clear whether they were given time off in order to do so. When Notts. County invited the Nottingham School Board to allow children time off to watch them play Oxford University in 1891 the invitation was refused; apparently many went just the same! *Athletic News* 23 February 1886, 23 November 1891.

12   Molyneux, op.cit. pp. 241–2. At least two of Aston Villa's international players in the side which won both the F.A. Cup and the League Championship in 1897 first played the game in Birmingham Board schools. *Birmingham Daily Mail* 10, 17 September 1898. The Education Department special report on 'The Organisation of Games out of School for the children attending Public Elementary Schools in the large industrial centres as voluntarily undertaken by the Teachers' claimed that Associations were also known to exist in Barry, Bradford, Derby, Newcastle, Newport, Portsmouth, Rochdale, South Shields, Southampton and Southport with school football leagues in Bristol, Cardiff, Gateshead and Oldham, PP. XXIV (1898) pp. 169–70, 182, 184.

13   See P.C. McIntosh, op.cit. p. 122.

14   *Athletic News* 5 May 1890.

15   The Sheffield Schools F.A. caused such local interest that 'head and assistant teachers, and even parents, had taken a larger interest in the proper physical outdoor recreation of their children'. *Athletic News* 14 July 1890, *Manchester Guardian* 12 July 1890. By 1892, 50 schools were affiliated to the Manchester and Salford Elementary Schools F.A. *Manchester Guardian* 18 June 1892. 7000 people saw a match between Sheffield Boys and Manchester Boys in November 1891. *Athletic News* 16 November 1891. On the growth of physical education in elementary schools see the article by 'Rob Roy' in the *Athletic News Football Annual* 1893 pp. 11–12.

16 M.H. Elseworth, 'The Provision for Physical Recreation in Bolton in the nineteenth century', unpublished dissertation, Diploma in Advanced Study in Education, University of Manchester, 1971–2, pp. 67–8.

17 The 1898 Report talked of schools' football as having done more for 'the real physical well-being of the boys of this country than all the drill and callisthenic exercises yet introduced'. PP. XXIV (1898) p. 160. It recommended teaching games in school-hours 'or at least that the fixtures might be carried out at such a time, where it can be shown that the boys are under proper training, and supervised by teachers'. Ibid. p. 164.

18 McIntosh, op.cit. p. 118.

19 Ibid. p. 123. It was not until 1906 that games were *officially* allowed in school hours in elementary schools, although according to the 1898 report three quarters of an hour per week for games had taken the place of drill at the Halifax Higher Board School. PP. XXIV (1898) p. 170. Ibid. p. 147.

20 Quoted in McIntosh p. 145.

21 See chapter eight below. On the other hand organised games as a socialising agent still had a wide body of eulogistic support. For a contemporary example see A. Paterson, *Across the Bridges* (1911) esp. pp. 97–9. He was still prepared to say that 'in the organisation of games as a definite and regular part of school-work lies the hope of the future'. His book was based on his social work in proletarian south London.

22 *Preston Herald* 5, 26 November 1884, 27 June 1885. Molyneux, op.cit. p. 226. PP. XXIV (1898) p. 173.

23 For Birmingham see Molyneux, op.cit. p. 228; for Brighton D.G. Wilkinson, 'Association Football in Brighton Before 1920', University of Sussex M.A. 1971, p. 55.

24 N. Chamberlain, 'Public Open Spaces' in G.A. Auden (ed.), *Handbook for Birmingham* (1913) p. 228. In the same period the percentage increase in expenditure by the Baths and Parks Committee exceeded that of every other Corporation Department. C.A. Vince, *History of the Corporation of Birmingham*, vol. IV (1923) pp. 219–47.

25 C.E.B. Russell, *Manchester Boys: Sketches of Manchester Lads at Work and Play* (first published 1905, 1913 edn), pp. 62–3. Russell himself, though anonymously, invited junior clubs without grounds to apply to him at the start of the 1904–5 season, stating where they wanted to play and what they could afford. Some 60 teams representing about 1000 lads applied. Ibid. also C.E.B. Russell, *Lads' Clubs: Their History, Organisation and Management* (first published 1908; 1932 edn) p. xii.

26 C.E.B. Russell (1932 edn) op.cit. pp. 65–6, 92.

27 W.J. Braithwaite, 'Boys Clubs' in E.J. Urwick (ed.), *Studies of Boy Life in Our Cities* (1904) p. 197. For a similar description of the problems surrounding organised football for working lads in London's Victoria Park in 1891 see *St James's Gazette* 19 October 1891.

28 M.H. Elsworth 1971–2, op.cit. pp. 78–9. The progenitor of the club was the son of a local cotton manufacturer. By 1897 55 churches of all denominations had joined the Working Lads Competition Committee, by then known as the Bolton Sunday School Social League. Its aim was quite clearly to offer young lads counter-attractions to the street, pub and music hall. It is difficult to estimate how successful it was but by 1900 it had a football league consisting of two junior and one senior divisions and by 1908 the 13–17 age limit had been abolished, although members

must also be *bona fide* members of one of the federated Sunday Schools. Ibid. pp. 69–73.

29 See the books by C.E.B. Russell, E.J. Urwick and A. Paterson already mentioned. See also A. Freeman, *Boy Life and Labour* (1914), P. Newman, *The Boys' Club in theory and practice* (1900), Rev. C.F. Garbett (ed.), *The Work of a Great Parish* (1915) and Rev. H.S. Pelham, *The Training of a Working Boy* (1914).

30 C.E.B. Russell (1932 edn) op.cit. p. 3. 'He that encourages Whitechapel to play football comes near to doing something patriotic.' *St. James's Gazette* 19 October 1891.

31 *Athletic News* 2 October 1875. The following year the same paper reported that 700 players were taking part in matches 'in and about Sheffield' every Saturday, a number increased to 1500 by the following spring. *Athletic News* 9 December 1876, 17 March 1877.

32 Ibid. 10 March 1877.

33 Ibid. 11 September 1878, 30 April 1879.

34 Ibid. 29 January 1879.

35 60 junior teams entered for the Roker Cup in that year. *Athletic News* 28 October, 28 November 1889; *Preston Herald* 24 October 1883, 14 October 1885.

36 See G. Green (1953) op.cit. pp. 251–61. Around a million was being claimed by 1914–15 (Green, p. 289). See also *Birmingham Gazette* 19 June 1915. Gibson and Pickford in their four volume work on the game published in 1906 estimated that 50,000 played in London every week and 100,000 occasionally. A. Gibson and W. Pickford, vol. III, op.cit. p. 33. The Physical Education Committee of the British Medical Association suggested that 750,000 amateurs played football each Saturday in the season in 1936. They had probably obtained that figure from Sir F. Wall's autobiography, published the previous year which also gave 750,000. P.C. McIntosh (1968) op.cit. p. 239. Sir F. Wall, op.cit. p. 141.

37 *Preston Herald* 14 October 1885.

38 Football League Management Committee Minutes 29 May 1891. *Athletic News* 8 June 1896.

39 Ibid. 6 April 1908. G. Green (1953) op.cit. pp. 251, 415. *Football Players' Magazine*, vol. III no. 16, April 1914. For purposes of comparison there were 6980 professional players in 1949–50, (3192 with Football League clubs) and 7381 in 1951–2. There were about 2000 registered professionals with League clubs in 1978.

40 *Athletic News* 4 March, 17 June, 8 July 1889, 8 June 1890, 2, 16 March 1891, 15 May, 17 July 1893.

41 Walsall were still preferring men 'knowing a trade' in 1896. Ibid. 13 April 1896.

42 See Introduction.

43 As finding new players became better organised, promising boys would be taken on as apprentice professionals straight from school but it is unlikely that there were many instances of this before 1915. It is interesting that the earliest reference which the author has found to the old chestnut about going to the nearest pit shaft, shouting down for a couple of players, and two ready made articles immediately emerging was in 1899. See *Athletic News* 23 October 1899.

44 Ibid. 6 February 1893.

45   Ibid. 2 March 1891. I particularly liked the 'very good moderate men'
     suitable for second class clubs. The backbone of society and not only
     football society! One wonders also if the officers of the crack soldiers
     knew what was happening to their best men. If a player could persuade
     a club that he was good enough they might be prepared to buy him out
     of the Army. See, for example, G.R. Stead, *The Reds* (1899) p. 22.
46   *Athletic News* 13 April 1891.
47   Ibid. 23 March 1896. The firm of Lucas, Elithorn and McGregor held
     ten shares in Bolton Wanderers F.C. Ltd., in 1895. PRO BT 31/43026.
48   Nasty and brutish too if some of the tales about their Celtic experiences
     are to be believed. The Sheffield Wednesday Secretary for example, was
     badly knocked about when in pursuit of two Dumbarton players in Septem-
     ber 1891. R.A. Sparling op.cit. pp. 160–2.
49   *Birmingham Daily Gazette* 25 February 1893, *Birmingham Daily Mail*
     16 February 1893.
50   'Tityrus', op.cit. pp. 142, 146. Even in 1895 a local newspaper claimed that
     many of the club's players 'have been and are at the present time engaged
     at Messrs. Salter's Works but they have always been allowed to get off
     for practice, training, or to play matches'. *Birmingham Daily Gazette*
     20 April 1895.
51   'Tityrus', op.cit. p. 126. *Blackburn Standard* 13 February 1886. They
     immediately lost three players as a result. J.H. Forrest of Blackburn
     Rovers receiving £1 per week in 1886. C. Francis, op.cit. p. 198.
52   *Athletic News* 22 June 1908, 18 March 1889, Bolton Wanderers probably
     paid a similar retainer. See *Athletic News Football Annual* 1893.
53   T. Keates, op.cit. p. 25; Gibson and Pickford vol. III op.cit. p. 118;
     Athletic News 25 February 1889, 6 January 1890.
54   'Tityrus', op.cit. p. 110.
55   See chapter eight below. As one critic noted in 1886: '£1 per week should
     be ample remuneration for the services of the best professional footballer
     that ever existed'. *Football Field* 30 January 1886. See also an article
     entitled 'The Seamy Side of Professionalism' in the *Athletic News Football
     Annual* 1890 and also *Athletic News* 11 May 1908, 15 February 1909.
56   *Athletic News* 12 January 1886. It was implied that George Kynoch 'that
     enthusiastic sportsman' had given employment at his Birmingham am-
     munition works to a Queen's Park player so that he could play for Aston
     Villa. *Athletic News* 4 May 1886. Kynoch made a lot of money, became
     President of Aston Conservative Association in 1885 and was Aston
     Manor's M.P. from July 1886 until his death in February 1891. He did
     not appear in the Commons after his abrupt departure for South Africa
     in 1888 where he allegedly died a poor man. F. Boase, *Modern English
     Biography* (first published 1897, reprinted 1965) vol. III, p. 270. *Birming-
     ham Weekly Post* 7 March 1891, *Birmingham Daily Post* 22 November
     1889, 7 August 1909.
57   One Sunderland official was even quoted as saying that their players were
     actually taught trades. *Athletic News* 21 April 1890, 26 August 1889.
     Part-time players were obviously an attraction to small town teams. Dar-
     wen, for example, had an eleven made up of ten local cotton mill workers
     and a dentist and appropriately small wage bills in 1891. *Athletic News*
     20 April 1891.
58   *C.B. Fry's Magazine*, vol., III no. 13 April 1905, p. 47.

59   Derby County F.C. Minutes of Committee 2 November 1891.

60   *Blackburn Standard and Weekly Express* 11 February 1893. *Athletic News* 20 November 1893. *Blackburn Times* 6 June 1896. One Arsenal player received £3 a week in 1893 and twelve of Everton's players had been getting that since 1891–2. *Manchester Guardian* 26 January 1893. T. Keates, op.cit. p. 33. Derby County F.C. Minutes of Committee 2 November 1891.

61   He was an outside right with a famed turn of speed and several good years still to come. He was also a tough minded negotiator. On his less happy, post-Villa period see below, Aston Villa F.C. Directors' Meetings Minutes 15, 30 April, 2 June 1896.

62   Ibid. 27 August 1896. It is probable that not all teams paid summer wages to all players. In 1909, for example, Leicester Fosse, then in the Second Division, signed an agreement with George King to pay him £1.7.6 per week from September to April. Agreement in hands of Leicester City F.C.

63   A home victory over Stoke only merited 10/- while an away win at Sheffield Wednesday was only thought to be worth £1. But the bonus for winning two away matches at Easter was £5. It was agreed that bonuses for 1896–7 should be 10/- for home and £1 for away victories for the first team, and 2/6 for home and 5/- for away wins by the reserves. Ibid. 6, 13, 20 February, 31 March 1896. Derby County F.C. Minutes of Directors' Meeting 2 May 1898.

64   'Tityrus', op.cit. p. 108. *Athletic News* 20 February 1899. This sort of incentive was not unusual. G. Haywood, a Bolton M.P., added £5 per man to the £500 bonus offered to the players of Bolton Wanderers if they regained their First Division place in 1899–1900. As early as 1886 Leeds Murdock & Co., had said they would give a 5 guinea harmonium to the club which won most matches between the first Saturday in October and Christmas. Not all such offers could be taken up. A Leicester shop-keeper offered one of his guinea mackintoshes to any Leicester Fosse player scoring three goals in one match but for the previous three seasons no player had managed to do it! When Thames Ironworks first entered the Southern League in 1900–1 they worked out a system whereby a pool of £150 was made available to players for winning matches but it went down by £9 for each defeat and £4.10s for each draw. *Athletic News* 2 October 1899, 21 September 1886. *Half Time* 16 October 1907. Thames Ironworks Board of Directors' Minutes by permission of Chuck Korr of the University of Missouri.

65   The League came to an agreement with the Football Alliance and the Northern League. Football League Management Committee Minutes 11 December 1891, 21 January 1892.

66   England first played Germany in 1901 and Austria in 1903. Germany were convincingly beaten 12–0 at Tottenham but Austria forced a goalless draw in Vienna.

67   Football League Management Committee Minutes 20 April 1891, 10 March 1899. G. Green and A.H. Fabian (eds) vol. I, op.cit. p. 69.

68   The boots were made by G. Fitchett, a member of the Aston Villa committee. *Saturday Night* 14 February 1885, *Football Field* 30 October, 4 December 1886.

69   *Saturday Night* 17 January 1891.

70   *Famous Football Clubs* (1898–9) op.cit.

71 See *Athletic News Football Annual* 1904–5, 1906–7. 'I have much pleasure in testifying to the sustaining properties of OXO, the "City" team having used it regularly during the season.' See also the back cover of J.H. Jones, *Association Football* (1904).

72 *Football Players' Magazine*, vol. III no. 16 March 1914, *Football Argus* 12 September 1908. Some clubs played friendly matches at the end of a season for the benefit of the players. See report of Glossop *v.* Manchester City, *Manchester Guardian* 29 April 1899.

73 See for example *Athletic News* 30 November 1891 and *Birmingham Daily Gazette*, 28 June 1898. But see also the account of the Manchester City affair below pp. 99–100.

74 Football League Management Committee Minutes 23 October, 16 November, 18 December 1893. Another idea which was floating around at the same time was the abolition of all summer wages. *Birmingham Daily Mail* 23 October 1893.

75 *Athletic News* 22 May 1899.

76 The limits to the areas of responsibility of the two bodies was still being explored in 1900. The Football Association, as the ruling authority for all football, could still intervene in what would later come to be seen as Football League matters. It was 1904 before the F.A. agreed that matters concerning financial arrangements between clubs and players should be vested in the League. G. Green (1953) op.cit. pp. 401, 409. See chapter eight below.

77 Quoted in G. Green (1953) op.cit. pp. 408–9. One wonders what players like Steve Bloomer thought of the maximum wage. He was apparently earning £260 p.a. at Derby County in season 1900–1 when no other player there was earning more than £3.10s per week. For 1901–2 he was back to £4 per week all the year round. Derby County F.C. Minutes of Directors' Meetings 2 April 1900, 23 April 1901.

78 Football League Management Committee Minutes 9 October 1900.

79 G. Green (1953) op.cit. pp. 399–400, *Manchester Guardian* 8 October 1904, Football League Management Committee Minutes 6 January 1905. Three former directors were also suspended as were the financial secretary and the secretary.

80 *Manchester Guardian* 8 October 1904. Manchester City were deprived of their home matches between 11 October 1904 and 8 November for paying a sum of money to the father of a Glossop player whom they had signed.

81 Football League Management Committee Minutes 4 December 1905, 2 January 1906. When the F.A. inquired into the affairs of Manchester United in 1910 they were not satisfied that £598 paid to two players, Meredith and Millward, between January and April 1907 'were payments on account of the club'. *The Times* 31 March 1910; *Athletic News* 4 April 1910.

82 J.A.H. Catton (1926) op.cit. p. 186. See reports in *The Times* and *Manchester Guardian* 1 June 1906; *Athletic News* 4 June 1906.

83 A. Gibson and W. Pickford, vol. I op.cit. pp. 128–9.

84 *Birmingham Gazette and Express* 27 June 1908. *The Times* agreed although in the context of a mischievous article in which it told the Football Association that it had brought all its troubles on itself on the eve of the threatened players' strike in 1909.
No doubt £4 a week is a handsome wage for the average well-tempered cog

in the mechanism of a League. But players of superlative excellence—such as Meredith, Bloomer, and Crompton—are worth much more ... since they often win matches by the sheer force of that individual genius which ignores the rules of combination, and the attraction of their personality brings additional thousands of playing visitors to the arena.

    The Times 24 August 1909.

85   A. Gibson and W. Pickford, vol. I op.cit. p. 133.

86   G. Green, (1953) op.cit. p. 415.

87   W.F. Mandle, 'The Professional Cricketer in England in the Nineteenth Century', *Labour History* 23, 1972, pp. 6–7.

88   Sir Home Gordon, *Background of Cricket* (1939) p. 156. It was in 1896 that the Yorkshire players were voted £2 a week in winter. *Athletic News* 2 November 1896.

89   See Home Gordon, op.cit. pp. 116–17.

90   S. Rogerson, *Wilfred Rhodes* (1960), p. 79.

91   W.F. Mandle, op.cit. p. 3.

92   A. Williams, *Life in a Railway Factory* (First published 1915, 1969 edn), p. 309.

93   For more detailed work on nineteenth-century wages see in particular A.L. Bowley, *Wages in the United Kingdom in the nineteenth century* (Cambridge 1900).

94   See, for example, Football League Management Committee Minutes 10 January, 30 May 1890, 20 March, 4 May 1891.

95   Football League Management Committee Minutes 18 December 1891.

96   See, for example, Football League Management Committee Minutes 3 July 1891, 1 July 1892.

97   *Athletic News* 29 May 1899. For related arguments see also 6 September 1909.

98   Football League Management Committee Minutes 5 November 1906, 28 May 1908.

99   Football League Management Committee Minutes 3 April 1911.

100   *Football Players' Magazine* vol. II no. 7 February 1913.

101   *Athletic News* 30 August 1909.

102   See G. Green, (1953) op.cit. pp. 404–5.

103   The quotation is taken from G. Green, (1953) op.cit., pp. 407–8. The Management Committee of the League, on the other hand believed that 'some form of transfer is necessary otherwise the strong or wealthy clubs would have the power placed in their hands to injure the weaker or less wealthy clubs'. Football League Management Committee Minutes 7 April, 8 December 1899.

104   *Athletic News* 20 March 1899.

105   This case was apparently successfully fought by the Players' Union. *Athletic News* 20 February 1899.

106   *Athletic News* 19 December 1883. Football League Management Committee Minutes 2 August, 6 September 1907, 14 August 1908. In 1912 the National Health Insurance Commission ruled that a professional football player was employed by way of manual labour, and must accordingly be insured under the National Health Insurance Act. Ibid. 9 September 1912.

107 *Athletic News* 6, 20 January 1896. Aston Villa gave gold medals to long
service players when they ceased turning out for the club and James
Cowan was elected a life member, entitling him to free admission to all
matches, when he gave up the game in 1903. Aston Villa F.C. Directors'
Meetings Minutes 23 April, 25 June 1903.

108 Thomas Holland injured his knee while playing for Fulham against Chelsea
in 1913. He had to return to his old job as a 25/- a week cotton operative
and his attempt to obtain workmen's compensation under the Act of 1905
failed on a technicality. *The Times* 2 May 1914.

109 *Athletic News* 7 November 1892, although the Directors mentioned a
'clubhouse' in 1896. Aston Villa F.C. Directors' Meetings Minutes.

110 On early special training for Cup-ties see *Football* 4 April 1883, *Darwen
News* 7 April, 5 May 1883, *Athletic News*, 16 January 1884. Such training
was thought to be the essence of professionalism. At the F.A. A.G.M.
of 1884 N.L. Jackson asked, 'five years ago did they ever hear of a club
training for a week or more prior to an engagement?' (A Voice: 'What
about the Oxford and Cambridge Boat Race?') *Preston Herald* 1 March
1884.

111 *Blackburn Standard and Weekly Express* 11 February 1893, Derby County
F.C. Minutes of Committee 14 November 1892.

112 A. Gibson and W. Pickford, vol. II op.cit. pp. 10–11. For more on Meredith
see chapter seven.

113 *C.B. Fry's Magazine*, vol. II No. 8, November 1904, p. 178.

114 Derby County F.C. Minutes of Directors' Meeting 28 August 1900.

115 *Preston Herald* 4 January 1888. For other accounts of special training
see *Birmingham Daily Gazette* 18 March 1892. *Athletic News* 27 January
1896.

116 *Athletic News* 10 August 1908.

117 *Football Players' Magazine* vol. III no. 11 October 1913. Aston Villa
F.C. Directors' Meetings Minutes 8 September 1904. The player was
Charlie Roberts of Manchester United. The criticisms by both Roberts
and 'Tityrus' have resurfaced regularly through the years. Needless to
relate not all contemporaries in the game agreed. J.T. Robertson described
how, when he was a player at Southampton and Everton, 'all the training
we got was light sprinting exercises every Tuesday and Thursday'. Robertson believed that 'a man does not require to turn out and have football
practice every day of the week. . . . The player who has not seen a ball
from the one match to the other will be keener on the ball than one who
has indulged in practice games in the interval.' John Cameron, formerly
of Queens Park and Everton but currently player manager of Tottenham,
apparently agreed. 'During the season walking and some practice at
kicking, with an occasional sprint, are quite enough to keep the player
well.' Robertson's remarks appear in an essay entitled 'Advice to the Bud-
ding Left Half' in *Football: Described by Giants of the Game* (1904) p. 18.
For Cameron see J. Cameron, *Association Football* (1909) p. 33. For the
view by an old player that players were over trained in the 1890s see
J. Goodall, *Association Football* (1898) pp. 20–1.

118 *Athletic News* 6 September 1909.

119 *Athletic News* 18 March 1889.

120 *Athletic News* 9 October 1893.

121 Although the Chairman of the Football League Management Committee

was requested to meet representatives of the players to talk about wages in October 1893, Football League Management Committee Minutes 23 October 1893.

122 *Manchester Guardian* 13 January 1898 reported a meeting of the 'newly established' Association Football Players Union at which the Secretary was instructed to post a circular to the players explaining the purposes of the union.

123 *Athletic News* 20 March 1899.

124 *Athletic News* 20 February, 11 September, 20 November 1899. He was the same Cameron from whose book we quoted earlier. Strangely enough he makes no mention of his union activities in the book.

125 *Athletic News* 4 September 1899.

126 *Athletic News* 13 March 1899. About 6000 people saw the Scottish professionals win 2–1 at Crystal Palace. *Sheffield Daily Telegraph* 16 March 1899.

127 Professional Footballers' Association Minutes 21 January, 1 April 1908. C.E. Sutcliffe *et al.* op.cit. p. 118. Several of the Manchester United players had been among those Manchester City men suspended in 1906 for receiving illegal bonus payments. That experience may well have stimulated them to revive the idea of a players' union. H. Broomfield, the new union's secretary, had played goal for Manchester City (though he had not been suspended in 1906) and Billy Meredith, another former City man now with United after his conviction for receiving bonus payments was also prominent. See an interview Meredith gave to the *Clarion* 3 September 1909. For a note of an early meeting of the union see *The Times* 3 December 1907. Around 8–10,000 saw the Newcastle-Manchester United match which took place in the week following Newcastle's defeat in the cup final in April 1908. Manchester won 4–1. *Newcastle Daily Chronicle* 30 April 1908.

128 *Athletic News* 27 January, 6 April, 21 December 1908.

129 *Athletic News* 1 February 1909.

130 *Athletic News* 8 March 1909. For other reports and comments see *Athletic News* 22, 29 March, 5, 12, 19, 26 April 1909.

131 *Clarion* 3 September 1909, *Athletic News* 14 June 1909. P.F.A. Minutes 7 April 1909.

132 *Athletic News* 28 June 1909. This attitude is mirrored by an interview which Billy Meredith gave to the *Clarion* newspaper. In it, he was quoted as saying, *inter alia*, that

the Football Association is composed of autocrats who demand that we shall surrender our rights of citizenship. We must not go to law without first obtaining their permission, they themselves clinging like limpets to the privilege of suspending and punishing us—punishing us without allowing us to appear and plead our own cause before them.

What was the good of belonging to a union that is only recognised provided it observes the rules and practices of the F.A.? *Clarion* 3 September 1909.

133 See C.E. Sutcliffe, op.cit. pp. 15, 118 and *Athletic News* 18 October 1909. The P.F.A. was contemplating a change of rules so that it would be possible to pay members strike pay of £1 per week. P.F.A. Minutes 7 April, 9 September 1909. The *Railway Review*, journal of the Amalgamated Society of Railway Servants, did publish three articles supporting the P.F.A.,

suggesting in the third that other unions would come to the aid of the footballers, many of whom had been trade unionists before turning professional. 'These men are not novices in the art of organisation. . . . ' *Railway Review* 20 August 1909. See also the issues of 16, 30 July 1909.

134 See *Athletic News* 5, 12, 26 July 1909. The following teams were said to have left the union: Bradford City, West Ham, Liverpool, Everton, Manchester City, Oldham Athletic, Blackburn Rovers, Blackpool, Burnley, Birmingham, Notts. Forest, Notts. County and Hull City.

135 Football League Management Committee Minutes 16 August 1909.

136 Arthur Henderson suggested arbitration but as an F.A. Council member of long standing pointed out, where could they find men who knew more about football than they did? *Athletic News* 6 September 1909, *The Times* 31 August 1909.

137 C.E. Sutcliffe *et al.* op.cit. pp. 119–20.

138 *The Athletic News* 13 September 1909 listed 14 First and Second Division clubs which had voted in favour of keeping the maximum wage at the June meeting of the F.A. They were Blackburn Rovers, Blackpool, Burnley, Bury, Gainsborough Trinity, Glossop, Grimsby Town, Notts. County, Notts. Forest, Oldham Athletic, Preston North End, Stockport County, Tottenham Hotspur and Wolverhampton Wanderers. The 'big ten' of Aston Villa, Chelsea, the two Liverpool clubs, the two Manchester clubs, the two Sheffield clubs, Newcastle United and Sunderland were significantly absent. Early in 1910, 1725 voting papers were sent to the professional players by the Council of the Football Association asking whether they were in favour of the abolition of wage restriction. By 24 January, 795 said yes, 260 no. Circulars had also been sent to 74 clubs of whom 12 wished to abolish restrictions, 19 did not. *Athletic News* 24 January 1910.

139 Football League Management Committee Minutes 7 March 1910. C.E. Sutcliffe *et. al.* op.cit. pp. 118–19. After the war the maximum wage for players beginning their career was fixed at £5 per week rising by £1 per week per year to £9. Win and draw bonuses of £2 and £1 were also instituted. In 1922 the maximum wage was revised to £8 per week for the 37 week playing season and £6 per week for the 15 week summer break, a total of £386 per annum. Wages remained at those levels throughout the inter-war period.

140 *Athletic News* 23 August 1909. Even John Cameron believed that 'sports as a whole should be controlled by an Association of Amateurs in the proper sense of the word. . . . ' J. Cameron (1909) op.cit. p. 63. But he did want the transfer system abolished and he did not like the wage limit, pp. 65–7.

141 *Football Players' Magazine*, vol. III no. 10 September 1913. The case, Kingaby *v.* Aston Villa, was heard on 22 March. 'Plaintiff, a professional footballer in the employ of the defendants' was offered employment by another football club but the offer fell through owing to the transfer fee charged by defendants under the rules of the Football League. Plaintiff claimed damages for loss of employment and alleged that the defendants had maliciously charged an excessive transfer fee. The Judge found against Kingaby because, even if the fee was excessive, the course taken by the defendants was justified by the terms of employment and in any event there was no evidence of malice. For a more detailed account see the *Birmingham Gazette and Express* 27, 28 March 1912.

142   Football League Management Committee Minutes 5 September 1910.

143   After he finished playing he tried management for a time before turning
to shopkeeping. He was a failed Conservative candidate in local government. P.M. Young (1960) op.cit. pp. 47, 87, *Athletic News* 19 April 1909.

144   See for example his interview with a reporter from the *Clarion* 10 September 1909. Note also his article 'Football and Military Service' in
which he argued that in most cases it was economic necessity which compelled a man to join the Army. *Football Players' Magazine*, vol. II no. 7,
February 1913. Veitch, 1881–1938, became a football journalist in 1929
after a period of management with Bradford City. He was one of the
founders of the Newcastle People's Theatre. His father had been a Reliev-
ing Officer in Newcastle. *Newcastle Journal* 29 August 1938.

145   In the Southern League the clubs without a single member were Swindon,
Brighton and Hove, Portsmouth, Exeter City, Southampton, Millwall,
Bristol Rovers and Coventry City.

146   *Football Players' Magazine*, vol. III no. 16 April 1914. The last reference
relates to the increase in membership of trade unions, especially among
the less skilled, which was a feature of the 1911–13 period. On the continued difficulties of the union before 1915 see also P.F.A. Minutes 13 October,
1 December 1913.

147   On the issue of whether or not the Players' Union should withdraw from
the G.F.T.U. in 1909, 470 said yes, 172 no, many did not vote and 17
clubs failed to return a ballot paper. *Athletic News* 8 November 1909.

148   On the decline of the Players' Union in the 1920s when membership
apparently fell from 1900 in 1921 to 434 in 1929 see I. Sharpe (1952)
op.cit. p. 187.

149   A. Gibson and W. Pickford, vol. II op.cit. pp. 200–201.

150   J. Cameron, op.cit. pp. 54–58. Billy Meredith offered the same advice in
1908.

I believe that every player should be allowed to work, and I am convinced
that if it was so we should have better football and fewer begging letters
from old players. . . . If you are living the life you should lead you can put
in all the necessary training in spare time and you will play all the better
on Saturday for the fact that you have not lived on the ground all the week.
Football is like everything else in that you can have too much of it. . . .

Football Argus, Bradford, 12 September 1908.

151   A. Gibson and W. Pickford, vol. II op.cit. pp. 10–11.

152   But occasional voices from outside the immediate ranks of the profession
were raised in support of the idea that the footballer was under too much
pressure. See, for example, the article by John Lewis, founder member
of Blackburn Rovers, F.A. Councillor and well known referee in *Sport
and Play* 1 May 1899. If pressure had increased then the league system
with its enhanced level of competition was probably responsible. On the
other hand, in terms of actual numbers of matches played, the workload
of the professional player had probably decreased by 1900. Preston North
End, for example, played 64, 63 and 69 matches respectively in the consecutive seasons 1885–6 to 1887–8. Bolton Wanderers played in every month
of the year from July 1884 to June 1885 and Everton played 62 matches
and their reserves 57 in 1892–3. Luton played 65 in 1895–6 and Sunderland
played 68 in 1893–4, including 16 in April with only one at home, and

60 in 1895–6, a season in which Derby County played 58. Only 30 of all those matches were in the Football League. *Preston Herald* 6 February 1889, *Athletic News* 2 June 1885, 8 May 1893, 4 May, 22 June 1896.

153   *Athletic News* 4 July 1883.

154   *Athletic News* 20 January, 7 April 1885; 2 February, 25 May 1886. *Football Field* 27 February, 13 March 1886.

155   *Athletic News* 4 August 1890.

156   A. Gibson and W. Pickford, vol. II op.cit. p. 40.

157   Aston Villa F.C. Directors' Meetings Minutes 3 December 1903. Although according to William McGregor in 1910 Charles Athersmith left the club because they refused to change their rules and allow him to keep a public house.

158   P.M. Young (1960) op.cit. p. 42.

159   *Birmingham Gazette and Express* 22 June 1908. *Weekly Football Star* 15 September 1894. *Birmingham Mail* 8 April 1937. Note the advertisement which appeared in *Saturday Night* 19 January 1889.

TO FOOTBALLERS!
DENNIS HODGETTS
(left wing to the Aston Villa Football Club)
HAS TAKEN TO
'THE OLD PEACOCK', GOSTA GREEN
DON'T FORGET TO GIVE HIM A CALL.

160   *Athletic News* 28 June 1909.

161   *Athletic News* 13 July 1908.

162   *Preston Herald* 7 December 1887, H.R. Brown, op.cit. p. 19. James Lilly-white had been engaged as cricket professional at Marlborough as early as 1853. He was probably the first. F.A.M. Webster, *Our Great Public Schools* (1937) p. 185.

163   *Birmingham Daily Mail* 13 September 1899. Reynolds had been in the army in Belfast and had played for Ireland three times before his English birth qualification was discovered. P.M. Young (1960) op.cit. p. 91, *Athletic News* 23 November 1908, 11 October 1909, *Sheffield Daily Telegraph* 7, 9 April 1908. For some former professional cricketers who suffered poverty in later life see A.W. Pullin (Old Ebor), *Talks with Old English Cricketers* (1900). One observer claimed that he saw James Trainer and other famous players in a football circus after they had given up the game. B. Bennison, *Giants on Parade* (1936) p. 189.

164   *Kinematograph and Lantern Weekly* 25 March 1915. *Films* 30 September 1915. He left a gross estate of £2052 on his death in 1940. *Birmingham Post* 6 March 1941.

165   *Birmingham Gazette and Express* 19, 22 June 1908. *Birmingham Mail* 19 September 1910. Although not as physically dangerous as, say boxing, serious injuries could be suffered. Charlie Roberts died in 1939 following an operation on a skull injury which may have been a product of those days when he was frequently heading a wet, and therefore very heavy leather cased football. Illness had ended his playing career early. *Athletic News* 1, 19 April 1909. *Manchester Guardian* 8 August 1939. It is interesting to compare the post-playing careers of English professional footballers with those of French professional cyclists in these years. A survey of 15 ex-cycling professionals carried out by a French sporting paper in 1907

revealed that most ran cafes or cycle shops. There had been little social mobility although to have attained the status of *petit bourgeois* from nothing was an improvement. See R.J. Holt (1977) op.cit. p. 112.

166   Sir F. Wall, op.cit. p. 120, *Athletic News* 19 July 1909, *Football Players' Magazine*, vol. III no. 17 April 1914. Spencer finished playing in 1907 and became a coal merchant. He was managing director of Spencer, Abbott & Co., coal and coke contractors of Birmingham. *Birmingham Gazette* 15 January 1940. Permission was given by the F.A. in 1905 for two former professionals, J. Trainer and W.J. Joy, to act as directors for Preston North End. F.A. Council Minutes, 4 August 1905.

167   *Blackburn Standard* 4 April 1885, 15 March 1890, *Blackburn Times* 2 January 1926. It is interesting that in 1922 he signed his will with a mark.

168   He became a director in the 1920s. He was one of the first professional footballers to own his own motor car. A. Gibson and W. Pickford, vol. II op.cit. pp. 52–4, *Athletic News* 10 August 1908, *Football Players' Magazine* vol. III no. 11 October 1913.

169   A. Gibson and W. Pickford, vol. II op.cit. p. 10. He was probably referring to the kind of undergraduate style horseplay which apparently took place when Aston Villa stayed at the Crown Hotel, Newcastle, and caused damage costing £1.8.6. The Villa directors decided that if the offenders could not be found the money would be deducted from the players' bonuses. Aston Villa F.C. Directors' Meetings Minutes 28 April 1896. Apparently a leading hotel in Birmingham wanted assurances of good behaviour before agreeing to accommodate the ten professionals in the England team in 1899. E. Grayson (1955) op.cit. p. 102.

170   J. Cameron, op.cit. p. 57.

171   Sir F. Wall, op.cit. p. 41. See also the comment by the *Birmingham Daily Gazette* 12 February 1892.

APPENDIX I

PLAYER-CLUB AGREEMENT 1909 from a document in the files of Leicester City F.C. Ltd.

The Leicester Fosse Football Club Ltd., and James Donnelly. Agreement to play football as a professional player. Dated May 1st 1909.

An Agreement made the 1st day of May 1909 between GEORGE JOHNSON, of 48, Silver Arcade, in the County of Leicester, as Secretary for and on behalf of the LEICESTER FOSSE FOOTBALL CLUB Ltd., (hereinafter called the Employers) on the one part, and

James Donnelly hereinafter called the Player of the other part. Witnesseth that in consideration of the sum of –––––––––––– paid at or before the signing hereof and in consideration of the agreements and covenants hereinafter contained he the said James Donnelly agrees with the said Employers in manner following that is to say:

1. –That he the said Player will from the 1st day of May 1909, to the 30th day of April 1910, play football as a Professional Player for the said Employers at such times in such places and in such capacity as the Employers through their Secretary for the time being shall direct or require.

2. –That he the said Player will from the 1st day of May 1909 to the 30th day of April 1910, obey such instructions, perform such acts or abstain from per-

forming such acts as the Trainer appointed by the Employers for the time being shall in his absolute discretion from time to time direct and require the said Player to perform or abstain from performing for the purpose of rendering the said Player in the best possible physical condition to play as a Professional Football Player as aforesaid.

3. –That he the said Player will not during the continuance of this agreement play Football for any other Club or Clubs person or persons whatsoever without the consent in writing of the Employers or their Secretary for the time being first obtained and further the said player hereby undertakes to abstain from taking part in any private business or other undertaking without obtaining the consent in writing of the Employers.

3A. –That he the said Player does hereby undertake to observe the Rules, Regulations and Byelaws of the Football Association.

4. –And that he the said Player will in default of playing when required or directed or in case of playing for any other Club or person whatsoever without such consent in writing as aforesaid or if he neglects or refuses to obey the instructions of the trainer for the time being appointed by the Employers pay to the said Employers the sum of Five Pounds by way of liquidated damages and not by way of penalty for each and every such offence.

And in consideration of the Agreements and Covenants on behalf of the said player hereinbefore contained the Employers covenant and agree with the said Player that they will pay to the said Player the sum of £4 per week from the 1st May 1909 to the 30th of April 1910.

PROVIDED always that if the said Player neglects or refuses to perform any of the Covenants and Agreements on the part of the said Player hereinbefore contained it shall be lawful for the said Employers to cancel this Agreement or to suspend the said Player without pay for such length of time as they in their absolute discretion shall determine. AND IT IS HEREBY AGREED AND DECLARED by and between the parties hereto that if the said Player is at any time incapable of playing or obeying the instructions of the trainer by reason of illness he shall immediately forward to the Secretary a certificate stating the nature of his illness and his capacity to play signed by some respectable certificated Medical practitioner otherwise he shall be deemed to have committeed a breach of the Agreements and Covenants hereinbefore contained PROVIDED LASTLY that this Agreement shall be construed as a beneficial and personal one between the said George Johnson or other the Secretary for the time being of the Employers of the one part and the said Player of the other part and that in case of any breach hereof by the said Player it shall not be requisite to join the Employers as Plaintiffs but all such proceedings may be brought and proceeded in name of the said George Johnson or other the Secretary for the time being of the said Leicester Fosse Football Club Ltd., and no objection shall be taken by the said Player in consequence of the non-joinder of the Employers.

As WITNESS the hands of the parties the day and year first above written
– – – – – – – – – – – – – – – – – – – –

CHAPTER FIVE
THE CROWD

THIS chapter examines how crowds at football matches grew over time and the relationship between the improvement of facilities for spectators and their growth in numbers. It also looks at the cost of admission and the use of advertising to help mobilise support. It asks the question, who went to football matches in the years 1870 to 1915? Can the socio-occupational structure of the football crowd in this period be discovered? Moreover, how did those people who did go behave when they got there? What measures were taken by clubs in an attempt to keep that behaviour within fairly obvious limits?

There is no easy way of discovering exactly how many people watched football matches in our period, especially in the first thirty years from 1870. The records of surviving football clubs are, as has so often had to be said, of no help. Neither is the press, national daily, local, or sporting, of great assistance although it is possible that a painstaking survey of particular local papers might produce results. It is very doubtful. Papers did not always publish attendance figures and even where they did only provided estimates which it is almost certain were not distinguished by their accuracy.[1] Nevertheless newspaper prognostications are all that there are and we must make the best of them.

An examination of the *Athletic News*, the *Sporting Chronicle*, the *Sheffield Daily Telegraph*, the *Preston Herald*, and the *Blackburn Standard* (from 1876–9) produced 46 examples of estimated attendances at football matches. The number given ranged from 700 to 20,000; the latter for the Scotland-England match in Glasgow in 1878. Thirty-two fell within the range 2–5000. A more revealing indicator of change and growth may be found by compiling a list, from the same sources, of those crowds which exceeded 10,000 during the period 1875–85, the period when the association game had clearly taken off; the period culminating in the legalisation of professionalism in 1885. Table 5.1 makes the point clearly enough.

It is noteworthy that all save one of the 10,000 plus crowds traced for the period 1875–9, were in Glasgow.[2] By the 1880s, Lancashire and Birmingham were taking the lion's share of the 10,000 gates. Also by the mid-1880s, it was clear what kind of

TABLE 5.1 *Number of attendances in excess of 10,000 in Great Britain 1875, 1878–85*

Year	No of Attendances
1875	2
1878	3
1879	1
1880	3
1881	3
1882	10
1883	7
1884	18
1885	13

fixture attracted the best crowds: the additionally competitive element of the knock-out cup competition or the intense local rivalry of two clubs geographically adjacent were the occasions of the best attendances. Of those crowds in excess of 10,000 in England in the years 1882–5, 30 were recorded at matches which could be placed in these two categories.

Facilities for this ever increasing number of spectators grew only slowly. Save in those cases where grounds were also used for cricket, few early football grounds had even a pavilion in which the players could change let alone a grandstand or raised terracing from which spectators might watch. The ground was just a field although once it was clear people *wanted* to watch and that they would pay for the privilege efforts were made to make watching without paying more difficult.[3] Of course attempts to make watching inside grounds easier became a commonplace in the 1880s, in particular, by putting together earth mounds, occasionally with, but usually without, wooden terracing and by building small stands.

Descriptions of grounds in the 1870s and pre-professional era are few and far between, but the *Athletic News* did offer a few lines on Bramall Lane, Sheffield in 1877. In a sense Bramall Lane pointed the way to the football ground of the future: it was by no means typical of most other grounds in the 1870s. It had been used for cricket for many years, and not merely club cricket but Yorkshire county matches. Football matches had been played there since the 1860s. It was owned and run by the Bramall Lane Ground Company who rented it out to interested clubs.[4]

At the top or pavilion end there is a wooden stand that would seat on it about . . . 1500 spectators, whilst the side next to the lane is the place for the 6d 'pit', safely and securely railed off and made in a succession of terraces so giving everybody an opportunity of seeing what is going on . . . . The proprietors have been recently levelling one end of the ground, and I don't know how many thousand cartloads of earth have been put down to remove a dip which occurred at the bottom end of it.[5]

With the increase in the number of spectators in the later 1870s and early 1880s, most of the favoured clubs put up grandstands where people could sit, if not in comfort, at least protected from the wind and rain and, because of the small extra charge, protected from other spectators of a lesser social status. When Blackburn Rovers moved from the East Lancs cricket ground to Leamington Street in 1881 the erection of a grandstand with a seating capacity of between 700–800 was the second thing they did after draining the ground.[6] By 1882 Darwen had a grandstand capable of holding over a thousand people and even the more exclusive Sheffield Football Club had a covered four-tier stand for 216.[7] By the end of the 1882–3 season Preston North End had erected a covered stand to hold 600 and when Astley Bridge's ground was required for the laying out of a cemetery, the club was able to build a stand on their new ground for only £100.[8] In the same year Burnley put up a grandstand seating 800 and 'added to and re-arranged a natural earthwork making standing room for 2000 more'. An uncovered stand, covering two sides of the field and accommodating over 5000 was also in process of being erected.[9] By 1885 the Preston ground had much in common with twentieth-century English football stadiums. 'Staging [terracing?] has been erected all along the ground opposite the grandstand, and at the two ends which gives the place the appearance of a huge amphitheatre.'[10]

But Preston was very much a member of the football *avant garde* in the 1880s. Elsewhere, terracing was by no means universal. Wagonettes and other vehicles were often brought onto the grounds and used as stands.[11] On many grounds, the ordinary standing customer, especially if of modest height, must have found seeing the play a bit of a problem if the crowd was at all large.[12] Terracing was coming in, but slowly. Even in the 1890s, when it had become fairly obvious that a professional elite of clubs had emerged in the larger urban centres, and when Everton, with an annual turnover of £11,000, could move into a new ground at Goodison Park which had covered stands on three sides and a vast mound of ashes on the fourth, West Bromwich Albion's ground at Stoney Lane was still far from being a spectator's paradise.

There were no turnstiles and admission tickets to the ground were sold through openings in the walls. The Plough and Harrow on the opposite side of the road also retailed tickets. . . . There was little or no terracing on the ground nor was there any covering on the popular side.[13]

But in spite of this apparent tendency for accommodation to lag behind demand, demand itself in the shape of attendances at matches, reached new levels through the 1890s and into the Edwardian years. Nothing would be more tedious than to relate the steps by which the ground records of leading professional clubs were broken almost annually during this period. But growing attendance figures are an indication of the strength of the game's appeal and a brief sketch of some of the major quantitative landmarks, in so far as these can be established, cannot be left out.

At the close of the season which preceded the foundation of the Football League the *Athletic News* expressed some astonishment that Everton should have been watched by a total of 37,000 spectators at their last four games. By 1899, 20,000 would watch a pre-season practice match at Newcastle United and 15,000 turn out for a similar *hors d'oeuvre* at Villa Park.[14] Attendances rose rapidly for most clubs in the 1890s in both cup and league matches, especially for cup-ties. The size of the Oval kept the Cup Final crowd down to a ceiling of 32,810 for the 1892 match. But that in itself was a considerable expansion as the crowd had only exceeded 10,000 for the first time in 1884, although a steady increase can be traced from 1882 when the first team from the north reached the final. In 1893 the final was played at the Fallowfield athletics ground in Manchester: 45,000 paid to get in and a good many more got in without that irritant; the crowds broke through the barriers and although the game was played to a finish, many had the unpleasant experience of being part of a large and turbulent crowd unable to see events on the field at all. Everton's new Goodison Park ground was used for the Cup Final in 1894 but it was the move back to London and the Crystal Palace which really put the seal on the Cup Final as an annual national event. The first crowd to exceed 50,000 saw the Final of 1897 and the figure was reached and usually surpassed every year up to 1915.[15] Nor was it only the Final itself which was an indicator of the attractiveness of professional football in general and the knock-out cup in particular. It was estimated that 200,000 watched the 31 cup-ties in the competition proper in 1888–9. By 1905–6 63 matches attracted 1,200,000.[16] The range was considerable. In the first round in 1896, for example, while Derby County were enjoying a record crowd of 27,000 for their tie with Aston Villa, with receipts of £1254, Blackpool and Burton

Figure 5.1

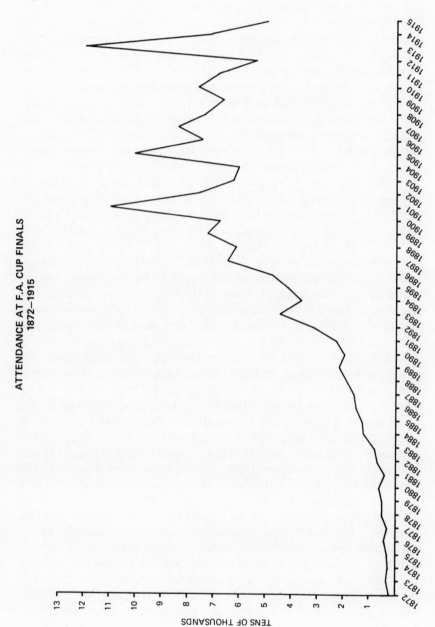

Swifts played in front of 3300. Similarly in the 1908 first round, only 3970 saw Hastings St. Leonards against Portsmouth whereas Newcastle United packed in 41,467 at St James's Park for the visit of Nottingham Forest.[17] According to the *Pall Mall Gazette* the average cup-tie attendance rose from 6000 in 1888–9 to 12,800 in 1895–6.[18] The 32 matches in the first round proper of the Cup in January 1913 drew 661,381 spectators paying £23154.[19]

Attendances at league matches showed similar tendencies to increase. In all 602,000 watched the matches played between the twelve league clubs in the first season of the competition, 1888–9. By 1895–6 this number had gone up to 1,900,000 although the number of clubs had also been increased from twelve to sixteen. Ten years later five million people watched the season's First Division matches, a division by then extended to twenty teams.[20] Obviously the clubs in the large urban areas did best. Birmingham, Manchester, Liverpool, Sheffield and Newcastle contained most of the clubs likely to attract the largest crowds, although, by 1914, London had in Fulham, Chelsea and Tottenham, three clubs which were certainly in the same bracket.

Averages, of course, conceal as well as reveal. A total of 558,266 spectators attended all matches at Villa Park in 1898–9.[21] Two final illustrations emphasise the strength of the game's appeal and although both have a 'fancy that' quality about them, they are very suggestive. A crowd of 23,000 saw Sheffield United and Sheffield Wednesday play a league match at Bramall Lane on a working Monday afternoon in October 1891. The local paper wrote: 'the day might almost be looked on as a general holiday, for although the shops kept open, a great many of the workshops were closed for the day, while others threw the band off at dinner time'.[22] Our second illustration amplifies the first. In January 1908, eight of the matches in the first round of the F.A. Cup were drawn. This meant that they had to be replayed on mid-week afternoons. Table 5.2 shows the size of the public's support.[23]

TABLE 5.2 Attendances at mid-week Cup replays January 1908

Birmingham City v West Bromwich Albion	24,896
Brentford v Carlisle	10,000
Grimsby Town v Bristol City	7,000
Hull City v Woolwich Arsenal	17,000
Manchester City v Glossop	20,000
Preston North End v Brighton	7,000
Sheffield United v Swindon Town	19,566
Wolverhampton Wanderers v Bradford City	13,800

It will never be known how many workmen risked the sack to attend: but the figures clearly show the extent to which popular support for the game had grown.

How did these crowds come together? In the 1870s, how did they find out that football matches were taking place, and how did they reach the venue? If we look first at how people discovered that football matches were to be played at a particular time and place then obviously those people living close to the ground had something of an advantage. They might see a match in progress, or the players going to the ground. They might be told about it by a player, a watcher, or some other branch of the local grapevine. In the early years of Newton Heath F.C. in the 1880s, matches 'were advertised largely by locally distributed "team sheets" which shopkeepers willingly placed in their windows'.[24] Such local community advertising must have been widespread. By the 1880s posters were common enough. Here is an example of one of 150 which were plastered on various Sheffield hoardings in December 1884 to provide advance notice of the Sheffield Club's forthcoming fixture with Hendon.[25]

SHEFFIELD CLUB

V

HENDON

This match will be played at the Old Forge Ground, Brightside Lane on Saturday next December 27 1884. Tramcars pass the door. Admission Threepence. Ladies free.

Word of mouth and posters remained important channels of intelligence. But the local press increasingly provided football clubs with free publicity and cheap advertising, particularly those local clubs which grew to dominate the football of the town and found their way into the professional or semi-professional elite. Blackburn Rovers were less than a year old when they had their first match reported in the *Blackburn Times* on 18 December 1875.[26] We saw earlier that the newspapers had been used by the better-class clubs to seek fresh matches. They had also been used to remind club members, as opposed to the general public, of matches to come although clearly interested parties might read the notices also.[27] Here are three examples of the genre, one from the 1870s in the pre-professional era, one from the mid-1880s, and a third dating from the second season of the league.

FOOTBALL
Royal Engineers (Chatham)
versus
SHEFFIELD
The above GRAND MATCH will be played at BRAMALL LANE
GROUND, on SATURDAY, December 20th, 1873.
Kick-off punctually at 2.30.
Players selected from the following:
ROYAL ENGINEERS

Major MARINDIN (Capt.)	Lt. H. RAWSON
Capt. MERRIMAN	” A.P. LEACH
Lt. A.G. GOODWIN	” OLIVER
” A. S. PYM	” WOOD
” P. G. VON DONOP	” RUCK
” S. BLACKBURN	” RENNY-TAILOUR
” T. DIGBY	

SHEFFIELD

JNO MARSH Capt.	J.R. BOWEN
J.C. CLEGG	R. GREGORY
W. E. CLEGG	A. WOOD
G. H. SAMPSON	E. SARSON
W.H. CARR	T.C. WILLEY
W.H. STACEY	T. BUTTERY
A. KIRKE-SMITH	

Umpire Richard W. Dickinson. The Match will be played in
Direct Contrast—Half Time Each London and Sheffield Rules
Admission 6d each. Ladies free.[28]

FOOTBALL—WREKIN CUP TIE
STAFFORD ROAD v WANDERERS
The Above Match will be played on the Dudley
Road Grounds To-morrow (Saturday) FEB. 16th
Kick-off at 3 o'clock
Admission 3d: Ladies and Members Free
BOARDED RESERVE 3d extra
Trams run from Snow Hill to Ground every few minutes.[29]

FOOTBALL AT STONEY LANE WEST BROMWICH
GREAT LEAGUE MATCH No 6
The Best in the District
WOLVERHAMPTON WANDERERS
V
WEST BROMWICH ALBION
On Saturday Next October 19, 1889
KICK OFF AT 3.30 SHARP
ADMISSION SIXPENCE   RESERVES EXTRA
Entrance for Vehicles—Stoney Lane.[30]

Having discovered, by whatever method, that a football match was being played, and having taken the decision to attend it, how did the potential spectator actually get there in the 1870s and 1880s? A good many certainly walked. But what undoubtedly extended the spectator catchment area was the provision of a cheap system of public transport inside many British towns after the mid-century. Two of the advertisements mentioned above, those at Sheffield and Wolverhampton, emphasised the availability of a tram service from the respective city centres to the grounds. Trams were first introduced in the 1860s and by the last year of Victoria's reign, 61 local authorities owned tramways and there were 89 in private hands. They have been described, not completely fancifully, as the 'gondolas of the people' and they certainly provided the opportunity for cheap mobility inside urban areas and widened the market for football in the process.[31] It should not be forgotten that the ubiquitous tram not only helped spectating to grow but also facilitated the transport of local amateur teams thus extending the scope of their fixtures.

Railways were equally important. It is a commonplace that they made possible sporting fixtures between teams from towns widely separated in miles. In 1879, for example, Queen's Park were able to leave Glasgow late on Friday night, arrive in Manchester at 4 a.m. and play a match that afternoon before returning to Glasgow the same Saturday evening. Such matches were crucial to the spread of the game's more advanced methods and techniques.[32] Railways also quickened and, just as vital, cheapened even short journeys thus making out-of-town fixtures a real possibility for the relatively well organised club. However, more central to the theme of this chapter, railways enabled spectators to travel to matches from quite a large hinterland. By the middle of the 1890s Aston Villa could count on solid support brought to Birmingham by the railway from many of the Black Country towns. Sunderland drew support from the mining districts of County Durham and the North Eastern Railway Company agreed with the club that cheap excursions should be run to Sunderland from many of the colliery settlements on match days.[33] Moreover, the railways meant that supporters could follow their team away from home, especially for the important matches, most notably the F.A. Cup-ties. Cheap excursions had been a feature of the railways certainly since the Great Exhibition of 1851. It is not easy to discover when the first football special was run but they were a regular feature by the early 1880s. Thus special trains were put on at different stations by the Lancashire and Yorkshire Railway Company in order to get people to Blackburn for the Rovers-Darwen third round cup-tie in 1882. When, in the same year, the Rovers reached the semi-final special trains were run from Accrington and intermediate stations via Blackburn and Darwen to Huddersfield, where the match was played, and as the fares were about half of what was normal, 2000 people travelled. The Manchester and Sheffield Railway provided similar facilities for the supporters of Sheffield Wednesday, the opposition that day.[34] Two special trains carried about 1200 Blackburnians to London for the F.A. Cup Final that same year and two years later three excursion trains took 2000 Aston Villa supporters to a cup match in Glasgow against Queen's Park.[35] The fares, though cheap, were not always cheap enough. Seven shillings return from West Bromwich to London was not thought to come within the range of the many working men who would want to see Albion in the Cup Final of 1886. George Salter, local manufacturer and club president, negotiated an agreement with the London and North Western Railway Company for a special 5/- return trip.[36] By the early twentieth century working men were saving up over the whole year for their Cup Final trips. In Sheffield, as many as 10,000 paid weekly subs to 'Final Clubs' and according to Gibson and Pickford it was a widespread practice.[37] In spite of the apparent boon of the railways, their monopoly often aroused criticism. The *Athletic News* was very disappointed when its attempts to persuade the railway companies to allow football clubs to travel at a single fare for the double journey failed. Its argument was based on the large amount of extra business which football brought to the railways.[38] The failure of the railway companies to offer cheap fares could sometimes have quite a bearing on the attendance. The replayed F.A. Cup Final of 1901 attracted only about 30,000 to the Bolton ground instead of the 60,000 expected. The Secretary of the Football League claimed responsibility lay with press comment expecting a crowd too large to be comfortably accommodated and controlled and the lack of cheap trips.[39] But only the railways could have transported the estimated 10,000 Aston Villa supporters who packed into thirteen special trains for a cup match at Derby in 1896.[40]

Who were these people who walked, trammed, trained, cabbed, or even travelled in their own coaches and, by the end of our period, motor-cars, to football matches? What can we say about the socio-occupational composition of the football crowd over the period 1870 to 1914?

Perhaps one ought to begin with a brief survey of admission charges. Is it possible that these were high enough to inhibit the attendance of some working people? It is difficult to imagine the late nineteenth-century unemployed, or the under-employed, being able to allocate even the smallest sums for non-essential leisure spending, apart, that is, from drink. On the other hand our knowledge and experience of the 1930s suggests that they might well have been prepared to spend a little money on recreation and relaxation even at the expense of necessities. Seebohm Rowntree noted in 1936 that people receiving low wages in York, being human and not satisfied with life on just a 'fodder basis', did spend small amounts on 'luxuries'. The football match might be one of them.[41] On the other hand the Pilgrim Trust found that in Liverpool in the 1930s the unemployed could not afford to watch football but had developed a rather bizarre alternative.

On a Saturday afternoon, when an important League match is on, the unemployed men in Liverpool turn out and gather along the streets where the crowds go up by foot, tram, bus or motor car to watch it. To watch a match is in itself a second-hand experience [an interesting if rather superior notion!] and the unemployed man . . . has to make do with this substitute for it.[42]

Other evidence from our period can be found to support Rowntree. The *Glasgow Herald*, for example, in an article on unemployment in Dundee in 1908, noted that attendances at Dundee's home games in the Scottish League were up on the same period of the previous season and observed that it was 'notorious that no matter how slender the finances of many households, the male must have his sixpence to witness the football' and although some women might complain it was equally likely that the family would cheerfully make a sacrifice 'in order that the head of the house . . . may have an hour or two's entertainment at the weekend'.[43] It is not easy to discover in any precise way how, in our period, attendances at football matches rose and fell as trade boomed and slumped. There is, as usual, a certain amount of impressionistic evidence. Sunderland's relatively poor support in 1892–3 was explained by one correspondent in terms of unemployment on Wearside.[44] Also in 1893 the coal strike in Yorkshire was alleged to have led to diminished attendances at Rotherham Town and in Sheffield.[45] Similarly falling attendances in Lancashire in 1886 were thought to be due to the depression.[46] But it is difficult to be sure. It may be that if loss of work appeared after regular match-going had begun then there would be an added reluctance to relinquish the Saturday afternoon outing. On the other hand it is difficult to imagine any members of Charles Booth's A and B classes scraping together even the relatively small sums required to pass through the turnstiles.[47]

There now follows a brief and unsystematic survey of those sums which were required to gain entry to a match. Unfortunately we do not have the detailed information to construct a clear and comprehensive table showing the minimum charges of a representative sample of football clubs in the 1870s and 1880s. All we can do is offer the kind of detail that nearly, but not quite, defies generalisation. In 1879 Blackburn Rovers appear to have charged 3d and 6d.[48] In the same year their near neighbours, Darwen, were charging 3d. This had gone up to 4d in 1880 and appears to have become fixed at 6d for the first team and 2d for the second by 1883.[49] Meanwhile, in Sheffield, two local teams, who seem to have primarily played against other local teams, Sharrow Rangers and Albion, charged 2d in 1879 and both Sheffield Wednesday and Heeley, who had more attractive fixture lists and fielded stronger teams, were doing the same in the 1880s, at least for 'ordinary matches'.[50] In 1883 Bolton Wanderers were asking 3d and 6d, Preston North End 3d, and Walsall Town 4d.[51] By 1884 you could not see Blackburn Rovers for less than 6d. It was 4d at Great Lever and Bolton Wanderers, 3d and 6d at Astley Bridge and 4d at Burnley. Halliwell, Preston Zingari and Wolverhampton Stafford Road, all charged 3d.[52] West Bromwich Albion asked a minimum of 4d in 1886 as did Blackburn Olympic while Newton Heath favoured 3d.[53] The following year saw Everton charging 3d, with boys 1d, Sheffield Wednesday 3d and Lockwood Brothers 2d.[54] In 1888 Derby Junction charged 6d for their cup-tie with Blackburn Rovers, a big attraction, while Derby Rangers generally asked 3d.[55] It must be stressed that these were minimum charges. Where grandstands existed it cost more for the privilege of sitting down and grounds rapidly developed the idea of having other areas set aside for those willing to pay a little more.[56] Moreover, matches which, for one reason or another, were deemed especially attractive, merited extra charges at the gate. By the 1880s the minimum price for admission to the F.A. Cup Final was 1/-. Similarly international matches between England and Scotland had a 1/- minimum admission by 1883.[57] Blackburn Rovers put up the cost of admission to their ground to 1/- and 2/- for their English cup-tie with Darwen in January 1882 and also charged ladies, normally admitted free, 1/-. The *Athletic News* thought that this 'handicapped' the working classes in their attendance but the ground was still full to overflowing. Preston North End raised the admission to their

Deepdale ground by 100 per cent, from 3d to 6d for the visits of Aston Villa and Queen's Park in 1887.[58] There is some evidence that charges were sometimes increased to keep out the rougher elements. When Renton, near Glasgow, were drawn at home to play Preston in the F.A. Cup in 1887 they decided to hire the Queen's Park ground at Hampden Park. The noble amateurs agreed but only on the condition that the minimum charge was placed at 1/-. 'This, it was thought, would keep out the rougher sections of the masses.'[59] The Football League decided in 1890 that for clubs in membership the minimum charge for admission should be 6d, ladies and boys under fourteen excepted.[60] This remained in force until 1920. The minimum for league matches was rarely increased by clubs in the 1890–1915 period. Even when Aston Villa decided to put up prices for the championship decider with Liverpool in 1899, the 6d entrance remained untouched. The cost of seats went up, applauded by the *Athletic News* because 'the gentry who can afford to patronise stands can generally pay for it'.[61]

To summarise, therefore, football of a good standard could be watched for anything between 3d and 6d throughout the late 1870s and 1880s. By the 1890s a league game could not be seen by adult males for less than 6d although obviously many local amateur and semi-professional sides would certainly be charging less. Special cup matches or internationals were always likely to have all prices, including the minimum, raised. It does not seem that the minimum charge was high enough to exclude anyone save the very poorest. Which brings us to the question with which we began this chapter: who went to football matches?

There is no doubt that by 1915 the majority of the spectators who went to watch professional football matches were working class in origin, occupation and life style. They paid 6d and stood on earth mounds or terracing, often made of cinders edged with wood. They might or might not be under cover. We know that most of them were working class because contemporaries said so. No Edwardian sociologist attempted a more accurate survey. No modern sociologist has bothered to attempt one either. But the working class in late Victorian, Edwardian, and early Georgian England were far from being a monolithic group. Is it possible to discover whether some members of that group were more likely to go to football than others? Is there any evidence to suggest that the occupational composition of the primarily working-class crowd changed over our period? And if I may be forgiven an historian's formulation, was the proportion of middle to working-

class people in the crowd the same in Blackburn in the 1870s
as it was in Portsmouth in 1910?

These are far from easy questions to even begin to attempt to
answer. Precision, of course, is quite impossible and all we can
do is to offer a speculation here or a tentative generalisation there.
But before that we must survey the evidence. Most of it is pleasantly interesting but far from conclusive. To begin with, it is what
some people in the trade call anecdotal. When one historian accuses
another of being anecdotal it is not meant as a compliment. It's
rather like wearing brown boots with a blue suit. In effect the
bulk of the evidence is made up of contemporary comment, often
by writers whose main interest lay in describing or analysing
something else, usually an actual football match. They were not
trained social observers (whatever they are). They were more
concerned to provide an account of the how and the why of
Preston's victory at Aston Villa than to pontificate sociologically
about the composition of the crowd. But historians have to use
what materials are available and it is churlish to complain that
Beatrice Webb failed to stand outside the Royal Arsenal ground in
1895 giving out questionnaires to those who went in. She did,
after all, have more pressing matters on hand. So, most of the
evidence is drawn from newspapers, usually sporting newspapers
or the sports pages of other newspapers.[62] It is provided by reporters who were probably largely middle class in origin, occupation
and culture. It is fragmentary, arbitrary, drawn from a variety of
places in a variety of years. But it is all there is.

In 1877, as we saw earlier, the *Athletic News* did a feature on the
Bramall Lane Ground in Sheffield. It noted that the 'immense
audiences' who turned up for a 'good match' at cricket or football
'are not drawn from one class of people. Each grade of society
sends its quota'.[63] Commenting on the huge crowd at the Preston
North End—Great Lever cup-tie in 1883 the *Preston Herald*
said it was composed of 'all sorts and conditions of men, rich and
poor, employers and employed'.[64] Another northern paper
emphasised the same point five years later. 'Next to the race
course a football field of the Midlands and North country presents
the most hetrogenious [sic] mass of humanity. Rags and tatters
and good old broadcloth awaited with equal impatience the
beginning of the contest, and in the struggle for places social
inequalities were totally forgotten'.[65] The same social mix was
allegedly a feature of crowds at Sunderland in 1890. At the league
match against Blackburn Rovers, 'all classes of Sunderland society
were represented, from a prominent M.P. and a coterie of town

councillors down to the humblest gutter-snipe'.[66] There is no doubt that in the 1880s at least, a significant proportion of a good many football crowds was made up of the better-off or middle classes. In 1880, for example, the thousand people who saw Middlesbrough play Redcar in the Sheffield Cup included 'many of the principal residents of the district'.[67] In 1883 the Birmingham *Saturday Night* noted the occupational varieties to be found on the stand at a football match, 'the tradesman who has afforded himself a holiday to witness the doings of his favourite club; the lawyer, always interested in a stiff fight ... ; the doctor ... ; the clergyman ... and the schoolboy.'[68] At the F.A. Cup semi-final at Nottingham in the following year 'the gentry of the district turned out in their carriages in large numbers'.[69] Similarly when the Sheffield Club played Aston Villa on Shrove Tuesday, a working day in 1884, it was mostly 'the well-to-do element of the town' who turned up.[70]

Moreover, this middle-class section of the crowd was not composed of men only. At the Darwen-Blackburn Rovers match of 1882 the *Blackburn Standard* noted that 'so lovely was the weather that the fair sex of all classes lent their charming presence to the extent of upwards of a thousand'.[71] Two years later, at Preston, admittedly a football-mad town by 1884 and at a match which was an F.A. Cup-tie with some southern amateur 'swells' from Upton Park, the *Herald* noted among the crowd 'slim-waisted girls as fresh as daisies, and sprightly and full of young life and vivacity ... adorned here and there with bright flowers, but, whether or not, exercising a wonderful effect wherever they turn in reviving seedy spirits'.[72] As we saw earlier, until the mid-1880s, ladies were usually admitted free but this privilege was abolished at Preston in 1885 after an Easter Monday game at which some two thousand were alleged to have been present.[73] We can imagine that with the legalisation of professionalism free admission did not survive long elsewhere. What impact this had on the attendance of females is hard to say. Everton were still being watched by enough ladies in 1887 to make it worthy of press comment and at a Second Division match at Leicester in 1899 'the fair sex' were present 'in every part of the ground'.[74] At Villa Park 'you will find no ladies on the unreserved side' but in the reserved stands 'there are almost as many ladies as men' and according to Gibson and Pickford, Newcastle United had a 'Ladies Outing Club' organised and run by the women themselves in 1906.[75] Many league clubs offered ladies' season tickets at half price. In spite of that, it seems likely that as crowds increased in size and watching became less comfortable through the 1890s, the proportion of women in the crowd would fall. This would certainly be true of the popular parts of grounds and, in spite of Aston Villa, probably true of the grandstand as well.

Of course, working-class married women might find few opportunities to go to matches, especially if they had children and even if they could afford it. In the depths of an English winter, from November until February, matches had to kick off early, at 2.00 p.m. or 2.15 p.m. in order to finish before dark. This meant that most working men who still worked Saturday mornings often until one o'clock had to go straight to the ground from work.[76] They would doubtless expect a meal to be ready for them after the match. If they were able to go home first then wives would be too busy to think of accompanying their menfolk to the ground. The *Preston Herald* correspondent who went to the North End— Upton Park Cup-tie in January 1884 noted that

workaday Preston, which only stops its looms at noon and has them to clean before leaving the shed on Saturdays, must have found it a rather difficult matter to get home and dine and dress and get to Deepdale so much before the time announced (2.30) for the commencement of the game. Yet workaday Preston performed the feat in downright good earnest.

Smooth chins were prominent 'proving that "the hot water" had been waiting for them when they got from the mill. How the wives must have grumbled and dratted all football matches.'[77] There were practical obstacles to the attendance of working-class wives.[78]

As the crowds grew larger from the mid-1880s on, the evidence suggests that they became increasingly working class in composition with the 'stand' a bourgeois island in a sea of working-class faces. At the West Bromwich Albion—Aston Villa match in 1886, the crowd of 7,000 was labelled that 'vast concourse of the British Artisan Class'.[79] Similarly in Lancashire and Yorkshire it was thought that it was 'the people in receipt of weekly wages who give to the game the warmest support'.[80] In Sunderland, although the crowd included all classes of the community, it was chiefly the 'horny-handed in the shipyards' who patronised the local club by 1890.[81] Again, at the Sheffield 'derby' of 1893, although all sorts were there 'the working element was undoubtedly in the ascendent'.[82] The paper alleged that in spite of the miners' strike, the colliers were there in force. 'The miner . . . may have tightened his waist-belt weeks ago, but want does not wither nor hunger stale his infinite passion to see Wednesday and United'. The *Athletic News* pointed up the change that had taken place by the second half of the 1880s when commenting on the crowd at the replayed F.A. Cup Final at Derby in 1886.

[It] was an entirely different one from that seen at a final tie at the Oval, and I could not help contrasting the appearance of the spectators with those who viewed the set-to between the Blackburn Olympic and Old Etonians in March 1883. On that occasion top hats predominated and it was awfully amusing to hear the 'chappies' ejaculate 'played Eton' or 'splendidly run Goodheart'. Today the working elements are in the majority.[83]

If, as the crowds grew bigger, they also became more working class in composition, what *kind* of working-class people were they? As in the case of our efforts to discover the socio-occupational background of the early professional players, such evidence as there is thin and difficult to evaluate. William McGregor wrote in 1907 that 'the football gate shows a tendency yearly to become more respectable, you do not see the class of people present at an Association football match that you see at a county cricket game . . . but the lowest class have never taken to football and are not likely to take to it either'.[84] He repeated his belief in the following year that the football crowd was becoming increasingly respectable, although he admitted that there was 'foul and obscene language' heard on football grounds but the class of people responsible did not 'constitute the bulk of the patrons of football'.[85] We do not know what he meant by 'lowest class'. Booth's A and B classes? We saw earlier that football crowds were often characterised as being of the 'British Artisan Class' but we cannot be sure what contemporaries meant when they used such a phrase. Does it mean the more skilled, regularly employed, higher-paid sections of the working classes as opposed to the unskilled, the labourers, the casual workers or the irregularly employed? As we will see below there was never sufficient in the way of crowd disturbances at football matches involving police intervention, arrests and charges to discover a meaningful occupational sample from that source. We do not know whether to attach any significance to the fact that it was a bricklayer's labourer who climbed a tree outside the Trent Bridge ground in March 1887 in an attempt to see the F.A. Cup semi-final, fell, broke his spine and died. We would not have known about him at all if he had not.[86]

But that does bring us to one interesting source which provides the only really 'hard data' about the socio-occupational composition of a football crowd in this or any other period. Although this book is primarily about England the example comes from Scotland. Early in April 1902, Scotland were due to meet England in what had been an annual football international since 1872.

The match was to be played on the Ibrox Park ground of the Glasgow Rangers club, a ground recently enlarged and modernised and capable, it was thought, of accommodating a crowd of 80,000. In the event the total attendance was 68,114 and part of the west terracing collapsed under the weight of spectators shortly before the game began, throwing some of them forty feet to the ground. Others were injured in the panic which followed.[87] Much of the brunt of the early rescue work was born by the staff of the nearby Govan police station and it was there that the details of those killed and injured were collected and published in the *Glasgow Herald* during the following week. There were about 550 casualties all told. The names and addresses of most of them were listed, the ages of about 160, and the occupations of 249. This is the most detailed material available on who went to football matches in early twentieth-century Britain. But before examining it one or two comments on its representativeness ought to be made. In the first place it was a special international match, in some respects a big attraction, especially in Scotland, but perhaps not drawing the same level or quality of support that the local team might expect for its home matches. Moreover, the minimum charge for admission was 1/- with boys under 14 charged 6d,[88] an increase of 100 per cent on the normal entrance fee levied by all English and most Scottish League clubs. The question is not whether this affected the kinds of people who went to Ibrox in April 1902 but how far such monetary considerations were important. Obviously the answer is unknowable but the key probably lies in the fact that football matches costing a shilling were fairly rare and special, and that those enthusiasts who paid out 6d a fortnight regularly could probably manage the occasional shilling even if it meant the sacrifice of something else. As can be seen from Table 5.3, 103 different occupations are listed for those hurt in the Ibrox accident. They range from a professor of hypnotism to a rivet beater in the shipyards and from an inspector of buildings to an office boy. In spite of the difficulties of occupational categorisation involved, it seems clear that the vast majority can be labelled skilled as against unskilled, that is to say, having received some formal training, often an apprenticeship (several were listed as apprenticed) as against no training at all in the formal sense. A corollory of this is that they were likely to be better paid and more often in work than the unskilled or casually employed workman. Of the 249 persons who had occupations ascribed to them, 166 had jobs which almost certainly fell into the skilled category and 59 could be classed as holding relatively unskilled

TABLE 5.3 Occupations of Casualties, Ibrox Disaster 1902

Skilled				Unskilled		Others	
Baker	3	Pastry Cook	1	Bag Maker	1	Chemist	1
Blacksmith	8	Patternmaker	6	Boot Top		Clerk	4
Boilermaker	3	Pipe Maker	1	Cutter	1	Colliery	
Book Binder	2	Plasterer	3	Buffer	1	Manager	1
Bootmaker	1	Plumber	5	Car Driver	1	Draper	1
Borer	1	Riveter	5	Carter	3	Grocer	2
Brass Finisher	4	Saddler	1	Cement Step		Housewife	1
Bricklayer	4	Sawmiller	2	Maker	1	Inspector	
Bridge Builder	1	Sawyer	1	Coach Painter	1	of	
Cabinet Maker	1	Ship Plater	5	Combmaker	1	Buildings	1
Carpenter	4	Sign Writer	1	Fireman	1	Miner	6
Caulker	5	Slater	3	Fitter's Boy	1	Professor	
Chairmaker	1	Stain Glass		Harness Tier	1	of	
Coachbuilder	2	Painter	1	Holder On	1	Hypnotism	1
Compositor	4	Steel Dresser	1	Horseshoer	1	Sculptor	1
Confectioner	2	Steeplejack	1	Ironworker	1	Shop	
Cooper	1	Tailor	3	Labourer	13	Salesman	1
Draughtsman	2	Ticket Printer	1	Machinist	3	Steward	1
Electrical		Tile Layer	2	Machineman	3	Teacher	3
Engineer	1	Timekeeper	2	Mechanic	1	Telephone	
Enameller	1	Tinsmith	1	Milkman	1	Worker	1
Engineer	13	Upholsterer	1	Office Boy	2	Traveller	4
Fancy Yarn Dyer	1	Yarn Twister	1	Pipe Weaver	1	Wine &	
Fitter	7			Porter	1	Spirit	
Glazier	1			Portman	1	Merchant	1
Gunmaker	1			Quarryman	1		
Hammerman	3			Rivet Beater	3		
Iron Moulder	1			Shoe Top			
Iron Roofer	1			Fitter	1		
Iron Turner	5			Soldier	1		
Jeweller	2			Steam			
Joiner	14			Craneman	1		
Mason	8			Stoveman	1		
Moulder	3			Tube Worker	1		
Painter	7			Warehouse-	1		
				man			
				Winchman	1		
			166		53		30

Source: Glasgow Herald 7, 8, 9, 10, 11, 12, 14, 15, 16, 17, 18 April 1902

positions including 13 labourers. As might be expected in Glasgow, the building trades, metal trades and shipbuilding provide the bulk of the occupations.

Now clearly it is prudent to be circumspect about what conclu-

sion is drawn from this but, when added to the more impressionistic contemporary evidence which we have been examining, it
does enable us to suggest what kind of people went to watch
professional football matches and how the composition of those
crowds might have changed over time. In the 1870s the proportion
of middle-class people in the crowd was greater than it was to be
later. This was especially true of matches in London and the south,
but not only there. Remember the descriptions of the crowds
who gathered to watch the matches of the more successful clubs
in Lancashire with their large numbers of 'ladies' and note also
the carriage trade and the speed with which grandstands were
put up. But as the popularity of the game increased, notably in
the north and midlands in the 1880s, and match crowds grew such
that the premier clubs in each area had to construct accommodation for spectators in the shape of earthmounds or banked terracing; so the proportion of middle-class spectators fell as the
proportion of working-class watchers increased. There may not
have been any absolute decline in the number of bourgeois spectators. But most watchers were now working people and the majority
of *them* were just those kind of men who had the misfortune to be
standing behind the western goal at Ibrox on that April afternoon
in 1902; skilled workers in the main, with relatively high wages
and relative security of employment. Of course, as crowds grew
to new record levels in the first decade or so of the twentieth
century, increasing numbers of the unskilled and semi-skilled
came to join their better-off comrades; especially in London,
although it can hardly be without significance that the best supported and most successful London professional sides were in
Tottenham, Chelsea and Fulham rather than Millwall or West
Ham which were closer to the classic East End. Although it is
impossible to document, it was probably only in the inter-war years
that association football in England was watched by representatives
of all sections of working men more or less in proportion, and of
course, by then, a changing economic and industrial structure
was producing a different balance to that which had existed
before the First World War.[89]

Contemporary observers in Victorian and Edwardian Britain
do not seem to have been able to agree on the most common
ages to be found among a football crowd. *Pastime* in 1886 thought
that the large number of 'elderly men present at the Cup Final'
was inexplicable. But Oval Cup Finals were probably special in
this respect.[90] F.E. Smith, in 1911, said that most spectators
were over 30 which seems rather doubtful.[91] On the other hand

it was alleged that in Dundee in 1908 the bulk of the support came from 'young and middle-aged tradesman and jute workers'.[92] Another Edwardian commentator in 1906 believed the gates to consist 'mostly of young men—with more than a sprinkling of boys'.[93] *The Times* thought the Cup Final crowd of 1913 largely composed of 'youths and young men'. If the Ibrox figures are an accurate reflection it would suggest that the 16–39 age group usually provided most of the crowd at a football match with a significant minority in their forties.

How did football crowds behave in our period? What did they do before, during and after the match? Once again contemporary comment on these matters is slight save in those cases where crowds got out of hand or exhibited what most observers consider- ed to be unnecessarily bad behaviour. So far as one can tell, spectators gathered fairly quietly before a game, but important cup-ties, with their additional quota of excitement, brought out a certain amount of prematch jollification. Before the F.A. Cup semi-final between Blackburn Olympic and Queens Park at Nottingham in 1884 'it was amusing to notice the display of cardboard badges. . . . About twelve o'clock troops of people were to be met, everyone with cards in the front of their hats, bearing the words "Play up Olympic", a football and two representations of the "coop".' Meanwhile over in Birmingham the supporters of Notts. County, preparing for their own semi-final with Black- burn Rovers, sported chocolate and blue cards with 'Play up Notts' written on them.[94] It does not sound madly gay or even particularly colourful. Nonetheless, the wearing of colours and cards with appropriate inscriptions was certainly common enough by the mid-1880s.[95] During Barnsley's run to the F.A. Cup Final in 1910, a local glassworker, dressed in a suit of red and white and accompanied by a donkey, fulfilled the role of club mascot.[96] *Pastime*, which tended to fear the worst when it came to the behav- iour of football crowds, especially northern ones, was pleasantly surprised on a Saturday in the early autumn of 1895 when

the Metropolitan Station at King's Cross was invaded by about a thousand gentlemen from Luton, on their way to the Southern League match between Luton and Millwall. Most of them had improved on the ordinary piece of paste board, which has "Play Up Luton" printed in large letters upon it, and wore a coloured and highly ornamental device, in the centre of which was a photograph of the wearers' favourite player.

Though they were all very excited they conducted themselves with as much decorum as if they had been millionaires, except that they showed more impati- ence over the slowness of the train.[97]

Before special matches, cup finals for example, singing and

other forms of co-operative cultural effort helped to pass the time before the kick-off. When rival groups of Barnsley and Newcastle supporters encountered each other before the Cup Final of 1910 'the occasion was one of chaff and hilarious merriment, each side quipping in turn and each wishing the other good luck before parting'.[98] On the other hand, prior to the kick-off of the 1891 Cup Final supporters of Blackburn Rovers sang a song with the refrain 'We've won the cup before—many a time' to which, we are told, the supporters of Notts. County responded with 'jeers and jibes'. The *Manchester Guardian* claimed that during the pre-match singing 'people could be heard—in a rude way it is true—to be taking parts, a thing quite beyond all South country folk.'[99]

During a match, the crowd doubtless responded to what was happening on the field and what descriptions of behaviour we have either involve outbursts of anger or the exultation that followed the scoring of a goal. For example, after West Bromwich Albion had scored their second and decisive goal against Preston North End in the F.A. Cup semi-final of 1887 'hats and sticks were thrown in the air: the cheering might have been heard a mile away; while many of the Albion supporters threw themselves on the grass in the enclosure, and rolled about in their delight'.[100] A similar scene had followed the last Sheffield goal against Glasgow in 1882 which 'almost sent the spectators frantic with delight and hats and caps were thrown up in clouds all round the ground, the excitement being intense'. At the end of this game 'the spectators burst through the boundaries and carried Mallinson, Mosforth and Marples bodily off the field'.[101] When Kitchen scored Sheffield United's second goal after 44 minutes of the Cup Final of 1915, 'a number of over-excited youths and men rushed on to the ground, wrung the hands of Kitchen and Utley with fine frenzy, and looked as though they meant to stay there'. They were quickly joined by others but the referee restarted the match and this led to the invaders returning in haste to the terraces.[102] Detail other than of this kind is hard to find, but one Sheffield reporter was so put out by the behaviour of some female supporters of Ecclesfield during the Sheffield Cup Final of 1888 that he did record a few of the epithets which they directed at the players of the opposing team, Sheffield Wednesday. These were 'Setpot', 'Fenian', 'Sunflower' and 'Sucking Duck'. The ladies also bestowed 'by-names on those of the spectators who applauded anything but Ecclesfield'.[103]

Bad crowd behaviour was, of course, much more interesting to the newspaperman than good crowd behaviour although match reporters did occasionally comment on the latter.[104] Disorders at football matches before 1915 can probably be placed into three main categories. The first, and almost certainly the largest number, was a result of anger at the decisions of the referee or at the attitude of the opposing team or of individual players within it. Friction between rival groups of supporters, especially during local 'derby' matches, seems to have almost always been sparked off by activity of this sort on the field although memories of past struggles cannot be ruled out as initiators of hostilities. The second most important cause of crowd disorder at football matches was the overcrowding of spectators on the ground. The third major cause was crowd dissatisfaction at some decision of the club or other authority about how to play the match or indeed whether to play it at all. Each of these will be looked at in turn.

Referees have never been exactly popular figures. As we mentioned in chapter three the game was often played without them in the 1860s and 1870s. The umpires, of whom one was provided by each side, were the ones to decide on knotty points and then only after appeal by the players. The referee was only brought in where the umpires failed to agree, an apparently increasing occurrence. With the growth of the game, and in particular its professional apex, the Football Association drew up a code of guidance for umpires and referees in the autumn of 1885. Clearly as the one neutral figure the referee was assuming increasing importance and in 1889–90 he was given increased powers, in particular the ability to award free kicks for foul play without waiting for an appeal by the players. Finally, in 1891, the referee became the sole judge to be assisted by two linesmen.[105] But from the 1880s dissatisfaction with the performance of referees was common enough and outbursts of anger spilling over into violence were regular if not frequent occurrences.

W. Pierce Dix was criticised for his refereeing of the Lancashire Cup Final in 1881. The letter which he wrote in reply illustrates the problems besetting referees in the early 1880s as well as providing an insight or two about how a relatively important match might be played. Dix wrote, in part, that

a considerable grievance to some gentlemen appears to be that I put up my umbrella. I quite admit that this is not the most convenient thing to do on a football field, and had I known that the weather would have turned out so unfavourably I should have prepared myself for it in a more effective manner; but seeing that I had only a very light overcoat to protect me from the drenching rain, and that I had to travel back to Sheffield the same night without any opportunity of changing my clothes, it does appear unreasonable to object to my taking to the friendly protection of my umbrella. As to the position upon the field which

I took up, this is a matter upon which I am certainly entitled to use my own judgement, although it is quite contrary to fact to say that I did not follow the play. ... Of course, as I have stated, when the heavy rain came on, I did not expose myself to it more than I could help, but for my own satisfaction I always kept such a position as would enable me to see the play, and as the ground was small and the play slow, and as I am fortunately possessed of good sight, this was not a matter of much difficulty for me. I do not find it needful, in order to follow the play, to be, as I have seen some umpires and referees, constantly in the way of the players, although on this particular day, much as it is said I kept out of the way, I think I accidentally got charged twice.'[106]

In the autumn of 1883 after the home team, Bolton Wanderers, had lost a cup-tie, the referee was 'hooted on the ground, followed by a large crowd from the enclosure, and in Pike's Lane was assaulted ... no steps were taken by the Bolton Wanderers Club for the protection of the referee on the way to the station'. Another official was assaulted on the ground at Padiham.[107] Not only did clubs not always take steps to protect referees but, as we noted earlier, changing facilities on many grounds were primitive or non-existent and the walk from pub or wherever to the ground, and certainly the walk in the reverse direction after the match, could be hazardous. Referees in minor matches, where the conditions sketched in above persist to this day in many places, were always likely hostages to fortune but even with the coming of purpose-built dressing rooms and regular policing on major grounds, referees could not always be saved from rough handling. Increasingly the Football Association inflicted heavy penalties on clubs whose spectators behaved aggressively towards the match official. Woolwich Arsenal had their ground closed for six weeks in 1895 after a referee had been mobbed and struck. They had to play their home matches outside a six-mile radius.[108]

Of course, some referees were a trifle irritating. During the Burnley-Blackburn Rovers league match in 1890, the referee disallowed what would have been Burnley's second goal and then allowed one for the Rovers which upset the Burnley players so much that they refused to play for five minutes. The crowd were beside themselves and the referee had to be smuggled out of the ground into a nearby house and then given a police escort to the station. Apparently what so outraged the home crowd's sense of fair play was the fact that the Blackburn Rovers' goalkeeper was the referee's brother![109] At Nottingham Forest in October 1893 the crowd broke in and stopped the game because the referee was thought to have played eight minutes overtime during which the visiting West Bromwich Albion turned a 1–2 deficit into a 3–2 lead.[110]

One referee has left us an interesting description of what it was like to be on the receiving end of one of these demonstrations. The match was played early in 1884 at Great Lever (Bolton) against Preston North End.

I cannot tell you why there was such a marked feeling of hostility against the visitors, but before they landed at the field there were several of the loafers in the streets who hoped they would get their . . . necks broken before the game was over, and immediately the game had started I could see very plainly that there was too much enmity all along the ranks of spectators for the contest to be played in an amiable spirit . . . when I found myself as referee being cursed and sworn at by a body of dirty low blackguards, who stood at the goal and touchline nearest the entrance gates, and who threatened to smash my (adjective) jaw when the game was over, I was vexed, as I did my best to give decisions fairly and honestly. . . . After the affair was over I was tackled by a flock of infuriated beings in petticoats supposed to be women, who without doubt were in some cases mothers, if I may judge from the innocent babes suckling at their breasts. They brandished their umbrellas and shook their fists in my face, voting me everything that was bad, and before I had got off the ground I was shied at by someone. Before I had got away from the mob another being—again a female—struck me on the back with her gingham and invited the dirty-nosed little rascals, who spoil every football match they go to, to crush me. I then was struck on the right shoulder by a clinker, when some gentlemen came to my rescue. I then got into a house to dress. Here my whereabouts was discovered and the rabble swore to wait until I came out. . . . I have reported the matter to the Lancashire Association, and if I can only get the names and addresses of one or two of my assailants I'll see what remedy I can gain in a court.[111]

Although such outbursts were not uncommon they do not appear to have been of weekly occurrence through the season, and in general they were relatively easily contained. Referees were sufficiently worried about it to form themselves into a union in 1908–9 although it is not clear how far this was a response to experiences in local amateur football rather than in the elite leagues.[112] We do not know much about referees. The Football League list for 1890 has a very middle-class look about it.[113] Cup Finals were referred by prominent Football Association officials until the late 1890s. Of 61 referees listed in the *Athletic News Football Annual* for 1892, 18 could act on Saturdays and holidays only which may be suggestive. The standard of refereeing was frequently criticised and the players' journal in 1913 suggested that this was due to the 'restricted class' from which referees were drawn, particularly those on the league list. They had to be free all day Saturday and able to get off work for an occasional mid-week game. Moreover the fees, a guinea up to 80 miles and £1.11.6 over 80 plus a third-class rail fare, were hardly tempting. The players' suggestion was for professional referees.[114] The material does not exist to do more than speculate on the sort of people who became referees in the professional game, but it does seem that the professional classes and the self-employed provided more than their fair share.

Visiting players were also likely to find themselves the victims of home crowd hostility and, as was indicated at the beginning of this section, clashes between groups of spectators, especially at local 'derby' matches, punctuate our period. It would be tedious to try to list these uproarious occasions but a few examples will illustrate the point and show the sorts of incidents which did take place. After Bolton Wanderers had won at Preston in 1884 orange peel and cinders were thrown at the Bolton goalkeeper and stones, kicks and blows were aimed at players and spectators at the end of the game. The *Athletic News* claimed that 'hardly a member of the Wanderers party got to the station unscathed'.[115] The same paper, in 1891, commenting on the Preston North End—Burnley game, said that it would be 'remembered for a long time to come, owing to the discreditable scenes that were witnessed. There was more than one free fight to be seen, ending up with destructive rowdyism in Fishergate and at the Police Station.'[116] Nor were these outbreaks confined to Lancashire. The disorder at the Birmingham Cup Final of 1885 between Aston Villa and Walsall Swifts led to the cup being withheld that year.[117] At the F.A. Cup semi-final between Small Heath and West Bromwich Albion, played on the Aston Lower Grounds in 1886,

[an] outbreak took place about five minutes before the termination of the match by a gang of the great unwashed element commencing to snowball a contingent of Black Country people who occupied one of the vehicles, and in a very short time a complete bombardment was going on, which resulted in the crowd breaking onto the field of play, and here hostilities were carried on with renewed vigour.[118]

One of the most notorious of football disturbances in England took place in Birmingham after Preston North End had defeated Aston Villa by five goals to one in 1885. The Preston players were attacked by the crowd and an eye-witness set down the following fascinating account of the proceedings.

Drummond (PNE), being one of the last to get over to the tent was assaulted by a young, well-dressed fellow [who] gave him a half hit and shove, saying 'Oh, here's one of them.' He was hemmed in and most unmercifully kicked, struck at, and poked surreptitiously in the ribs with sticks. . . . The distance from the tent to the field gate is about 80 yards. The driver started at a brisk trot to cover this distance, and earth, small stones, rubbish of all sorts, began flying about our heads. When about ten yards from the gates, a gang rushed up and closed them. We were thus brought to a standstill in the midst of 2000 howling roughs.

Thicker and faster came the stones, showers of spittle covered us; we were struck at over the side with sticks and umbrellas, and at last a big missile flew past my ear and caught Ross (PNE) on top of the head, smashing his hat and down he dropped.

They did manage to escape eventually but were followed by the crowd for half a mile.[119]

There is nobody so frustrated as a football spectator who cannot see and most of the occasions when crowds broke into the arena and got onto the playing area in the pre-1915 period were due to this combination of overcrowding and poor facilities. Football grounds have never been the most comfortable places, particularly for the standing spectator. But at least since the interwar period standing terraces of reasonable number and depth, providing most people with a decent view of the game, with plentiful crush barriers to break up the assembled crowds, have been the rule rather than the exception. Moreover, since 1945, the police have taken much more interest in the number of people who could safely be packed into any one ground and limits on attendances have been strictly imposed. It was a different story before 1915. Many grounds were simply too small to contain the increasing numbers of people clamouring to watch, especially for the most attractive matches. Clubs often did not know the capacity of their own grounds and the issue of whether the house was full or not was largely decided by trial and error with a dash of experience thrown in. We also noted earlier that the facilities inside the grounds were often inadequate; mounds of earth might not be steep enough to afford everyone an uninterrupted view but they were usually steep enough to cause people to slip and sway about. The surprise is not that there were crowd invasions and occasional accidents, but that there were not many more of both.

The best-known examples of crowd invasions were at an F.A. Cup match between Aston Villa and Preston North End in January 1888 and the Cup Final of 1893. This latter game was played for the first and only time on the Fallowfields athletic grounds in Manchester. The ground had never been used for football before. It was said that it could hold 68,000 in what late Victorians thought of as some comfort. However, the barriers were forced before the game began and the match was played with people at least six deep packed around the touchlines.[120] At the Villa-Preston game, one of the largest crowds to see a football match in England up to that time frequently broke through the fencing onto the ground. The first half lasted for 80 minutes instead of the normal 45. Although it had been clear that a large attendance would be present, the club were not very well prepared. Would-be spectators were queuing outside the Villa ground from half-past ten in the morning and it was very full over an hour before the scheduled start. An attempt was made to close the gates at half-past two when many people were still trying to obtain admission but ' . . . such threatening demonstrations were made that it would have been sheer madness to have carried the order into execution. The money-takers then continued the issue of tickets, intimating to everyone to whom they handed a ticket that he would not be able to see the game'. Although fifty constables were on duty at the ground there was little that they could do. When the crowd overflowed onto the pitch the club telegraphed for mounted policemen and the help of a troop of hussars stationed locally. Two mounted hussars eventually turned up but the mounted policemen did not arrive until ten minutes before the end of the game. 'The ground would not hold the number of people admitted, and once inside they must go somewhere. . . . I don't think one half of the spectators saw the match.'[121] On both of these occasions the spectators seem to have been reasonably well behaved although there were doubtless relatively minor incidents like throwing things at the people in front who were preventing others from seeing the game. Certainly over-crowding does not appear to have precipitated a major crowd disturbance.[122]

Football authorities, especially at club level, occasionally brought down the wrath of spectators upon their heads. These happenings usually involved a belief on the part of spectators that they were not getting their money's worth or were being presented with a spectacle which they did not want to see. For example, Blackburn Rovers were due to entertain local rivals Darwen on Christmas Day 1890. By this time, Darwen were not such a powerful club as in former years and the Rovers decided to field a second eleven augmented by three first team players, thus saving their best team for a League match with Wolves the next day. Needless to say they did not bother to tell anyone. Darwen did not discover it until they ran onto the pitch but, when they did, they offered to play their second team too! Some members of the crowd of about 3000 took exception to these proceedings and were sufficiently upset to pull and break up the goalposts, tear the carpets on the reserved seats, knock off the hat of a Rovers' official and break the dressing-room window.[123] Nor were dissatisfied spectators likely to receive a refund. A test case, Howard v Everton F.C. before Mr Justice Shand in 1896, finally decided that once a match had been begun, no money need be refunded to spectators if it should end prematurely due to bad weather or ground conditions. It was probably inevitable, however, that there should be some difference of opinion as to the fitness of the conditions between those who had paid to watch and those who had not.[124] But for the most notorious example of a football crowd rioting when it thought something should happen which was not going to happen a return visit has to be made to Glasgow. In April 1909 Rangers met Celtic in the Scottish Cup Final. The match was drawn and no extra time was played. The replay was drawn too. It is not entirely clear whether the crowd expected extra time or thought that it should be played whether scheduled or not. When it was not played, spectators invaded the pitch, destroyed the goal posts and nets, set pay boxes on fire, threw stones at policemen and firemen, who apparently threw them back, and did other 'wanton damage'. 130 men received medical treatment on the ground, 30 went to the Victoria Infirmary, but only one young man was arrested.[125]

The police had been used for the control of football crowds from the early 1880s. As we saw earlier, a force of 50 constables was present at the Aston Villa—Preston cup match in 1888. Two mounted policemen 'kept regularly parading just inside the ring' when Newton Heath met Grimsby Town in October 1890. Some 70 constables were present at the F.A. Cup semi-final of 1892 at Bramall Lane, Sheffield and 50 reinforcements, some mounted, were sent for when the crowd spilled onto the pitch.[126] At the Preston North End—Sunderland league match in 1893, over 50 policemen and 200 soldiers patrolled inside the ropes.[127] The 1893 Cup Final was policed by 192 constables but they could do little to stem the chaos that day. One eye-witness called them a 'helpless set of men' and they were stigmatised for roughness by one correspondent and for being over-polite by another. Both agreed, however, that they were ineffective.[128] At the Blackburn Rovers—Sunderland cup-tie, also in 1893, four mounted policeman had to be withdrawn when their horses took fright at the sight of the two teams.[129] Late Victorian professional footballers could be an awesome sight. Again the officers on duty at the F.A. Cup semi-final in Birmingham in 1896 were styled 'incompetent noonies'.[130] Clearly, the police were gaining in experience with each league season that passed. The examples, both of crowd turbulence and police difficulties which we have been discussing, were almost without exception at matches which, because of their importance, attracted extra large crowds. At the run-of-the-mill Saturday match crowd trouble does not seem to have been a serious problem. Where it did occur it was usually easily contained. It is stretching credibility to imagine that the football riot, itself a rather hyperbolic description of what usually happened, had any significance outside the context of the particular football occasion. The complacency of the *Athletic News* in 1899 seems totally justified and capable of application to the whole of our period: 'it is a striking proof of the peacefulness of football crowds that, as a rule, half a dozen flat-footed Robertos serve to keep both the members and ticket-holders and the casual sixpenny gentlemen as well in order'.[131]

In this chapter we have examined the growth in the number of people prepared to pay to watch professional football during our period. We have commented briefly on the intermittent improvement in facilities which this prompted. We have sketched in how people got to matches and what they paid to get in. We have tentatively suggested that the bulk of the crowd became the better-paid, more regularly employed, perhaps young skilled working men and that the middle-class element in the crowd, although by no means negligible, probably declined proportionately. We have looked very briefly at referees and only a little more fully at the behaviour of crowds. We shall have to return to crowd behaviour in chapter eight when we come to analyse the way in which different people saw the game and what they sought from it. Meantime we want to explore three activities which many football-watchers joined in on match days: drinking, betting and reading the paper.

Notes

1 Occasionally clubs complained to the press that published estimates were too high. It was embarrassing to find published estimates of the gate too far ahead of the actual receipts.

2 The only English one was a special novelty match under the new electric light at Bramall Lane, Sheffield in November 1878. Floodlit matches were staged on several occasions between 1878 and 1915. In October 1892, for example, Blackburn Rovers played a match with Darwen under Wells lights for the benefit of their centre-forward, Jack Southworth. White footballs were used in this match. *Lancashire Evening Express* 1 November 1892.

3 This presented problems for some clubs in Lancashire whose grounds were surrounded by hills from which a splendid and free view of the proceedings could be obtained. Between 4–5000 people stood in the fields on the hills above the Bolton Wanderers ground in 1884 for their cup

replay with Notts. County. Some entrepreneurially minded farmers charged half the entrance money to the ground. Blackburn Rovers lost revenue in the same way in the early 1880s. *Athletic News* 28 December 1881, 6 February 1884.

4   In the early 1880s the charge was 25 per cent of the gross receipts of the match: by August 1883 this had been increased to 33 per cent. Records and Minutes of the Sheffield Football Club FCR 7.

5   *Athletic News* 3 March 1877.

6   Ibid. 5, 12 October 1881.

7   *Darwen News*, 24 December 1881, 4 January 1882. The club issued £1 shares to raise the money for the stand, each share entitling the holder to a free admission ticket to all cricket and football matches until the money was repaid. The Sheffield Club's stand cost only £35 in 1884. Unfortunately the wind blew it down after only a few weeks. Records and Minutes of the Sheffield Football Club FCR 7.

8   *Athletic News* 18 April, 5 September 1883.

9   *Football Field* 27 September 1884.

10 *Athletic News* 29 December 1885.

11 As at the Aston Villa *v* Preston cup-tie in January 1888. *Athletic News* 17 January 1888. See also *Sheffield Daily Telegraph* 31 January 1888 and *Blackburn Standard* 25 March 1882.

12 Even at the Crystal Palace, home of the F.A. Cup Final from 1894 until 1914, there was little deep terracing. Most of the crowd stood on huge earthen mounds and as contemporary photographs clearly indicate, many people at the back could only have seen the ball when it was twenty feet in the air. These mounds could become slippery and dangerous after rain as in 1913. *The Times* 21 April 1913. However, as William Pickford remarked, the Palace 'was more than a venue for a football match; it took on the character of a pic-nic. Long before the game happy parties sat in groups, under the trees, munching sandwiches, and generations of football folk met there to renew acquaintance.' W. Pickford, *A Few Recollections of Sport* (n.d.) p. 65.

13 For Everton see P.M. Young, *Football on Merseyside* (1963) and *Athletic News* 1 August 1892, 19 January, 18 September 1893. By 1909 Everton had acquired a double-decker stand and had replaced the earth mounds with concrete terracing. *Athletic News* 9 August 1909. For West Bromwich Albion see P. Morris, (1965) op.cit. pp. 34–5.

14 *Athletic News* 10 April 1888, 21 August 1899.

15 See Figure 5 : 1. The first crowd of 50,000 ever to watch a match in Britain was probably the one which came together at Celtic Park Glasgow in 1896 to see Scotland beat England 2–1. The first gate of 50,000 at a league match in England was probably at the Aston Villa-Sheffield United match in 1900 which was essentially a championship decider. The match was drawn 1–1 and Villa won the title. *Athletic News*, 5 March 1900.

16 H. MacFarlane, 'Football of Yesterday and Today; a Comparison', *The Monthly Review*, vol. 25, October 1906, p. 129.

17 *Athletic News* 3 February 1896, 13 January 1908.

18 *Pall Mall Gazette* 20 April 1896.

19 *Football Players' Magazine*, vol. II no. 7, February 1913.

20 See H. MacFarlane op.cit. *Gamages Football Annual* for 1909–10 claimed that six millions had watched First Division matches alone in 1908–9.

With a total of 380 matches that was an average crowd of 16,000.

21 *Birmingham Daily Gazette* 28 June 1899.

22 *Sheffield Daily Telegraph* 27 October 1891. The band was a 'leather strap connecting the grinder's stones to the pulleys of the driving shafts from which they got their power'. When thrown off, it meant that the machine stopped; S. Pollard (Introduction), *The Sheffield Outrages* (Reprinted Adams and Dart Social Documents Series, 1971) p. xviii. There was enough Monday football to suggest that the practice of some groups of workmen in taking Mondays off, Saint Monday, was a long time declining. For another example of a big crowd on a Monday see the report of the Aston Villa *v* Notts. County match in the *Dart* 9 November 1883.

23 The figures were taken from *Athletic News* 20 January 1908.

24 P.M. Young (1960) op.cit. pp. 18–19.

25 Records and Minutes of the Sheffield Football Club FCR 7.

26 For a fuller discussion of the role of the press in the growth of the game see chapter six.

27 The exclusive Sheffield Club placed the following advertisement in the *Sheffield Daily Telegraph* 25 February 1865. 'FOOTBALL-SHEFFIELD v LINCOLN. The members of the Sheffield Football Club are respectfully informed that the above Match will take place on SATURDAY next, at Newhall Cricket Grounds kick-off at Two o'clock. Members may obtain tickets for themselves and friends on application to Messrs. LOXLEY BROTHERS, Fargate. The players will DINE together at the BLACK SWAN HOTEL immediately after the Match, and will be glad to see as many Members and Friends as can conveniently be present.'

28 *Sheffield Daily Telegraph* 13 December 1873.

29 *Wolverhampton Evening Star* 15 February 1884 quoted in P.M. Young (1959) op.cit. p. 32.

30 *Athletic News* 14 October 1889. For further examples see *Sheffield Daily Telegraph* 2 December 1876, *Blackburn Times* 19 October 1878, 1 March 1879, 31 March 1883. *Athletic News* 29 September 1880, 7 September 1881 etc.

31 See R. Hoggart, *The Uses of Literacy* (1957) p. 120 and Asa Briggs; *Victorian Cities* (1968 edn) pp. 15–16. The advantages of the tram were significant. Sheffield Wednesday moved to a new ground three miles from the city centre in 1899 but electric trams made the journey for 1d. *Athletic News* 18 September 1899.

32 *Athletic News* 19 April 1879. See also chapter seven.

33 *Athletic News* 31 August 1891.

34 Ibid. 1 February, 22 March 1882. We do not, of course, know how many of the passengers actually went to the match, but it is difficult to think of many reasons why people would want to go to Huddersfield.

35 *Athletic News* 29 March 1882, 23 January 1884.

36 Ibid. 30 March 1886, *West Bromwich Free Press* 3 April 1886. There were similar complaints in Sheffield in 1890 that 8/6 was too much for working men to pay for a trip to the capital and back: 5/6 was considered the most they could afford. *Sheffield Daily Telegraph*, 12, 19 March 1890.

37 A. Gibson and W. Pickford, vol. IV op.cit. pp. 41–2. *C.B. Fry's Magazine*, vol. III, no. 13, April 1905, p. 39.

38 *Athletic News* 23 November 1891.

39 He alleged that the railway company lost £500 and the meat pie purveyors

were left with a mountain of unsold stock. Ten years later it was still known as Pie Saturday in Bolton. *C.B. Fry's Magazine*, vol. 1, no. 2, May 1911, p. 215.

40   *Athletic News* 3 February 1896. 170 'specials' went from Lancashire to London for the Cup Final of 1914. Burnley and Liverpool were the teams. P.M. Young (1963) op.cit. p. 100.

41   By this time, of course, the cinema, football pools and greyhound racing had joined drink and tobacco as competitors for the expenditure although it is not clear how stiff the competition was. B.S. Rowntree, *The Human Needs of Labour* (1937) pp. 126–7.

42   *Men without Work* (Cambridge 1938) p. 99. I wonder if many stood outside the ground during the time in which the game was in progress and followed its fortunes by the roars of the crowd? On smaller grounds they might be let in free at half time. Some clubs in the 1930s, notably Sheffield United, wanted to charge unemployed men half price but the Management Committee of the Football League refused. C.E. Sutcliffe *et al.*, (1938) op.cit. pp. 37–8.

43   *Glasgow Herald* 7 September 1908. The Scottish F.A. made donations amounting to £500 to various unemployed funds thus 'recognising some responsibility to the working class which provides the great bulk of the supporters'. *Athletic News* 27 January 1908.

44   *Athletic News* 21 August 1893. Sunderland won the League championship in that year.

45   Ibid. 20 November 1893.

46   A letter to the *Blackburn Standard* in December 1884 had said that 6d to see the Rovers was too much in a period of poor trade.

47   On the impact of trade depression on football club attendances it is as well to remember the case of Woolwich Arsenal discussed in chapter two although that club's situation was probably unique. Booth's class A was 'the lowest class of occasional labourers, loafers, semi-criminals and street sellers' while class B consisted of the very poor whose earnings were casual. For more details see C. Booth, *Life and Labour of the People* (1889) vol. I pp. 33–61.

48   *Blackburn Times* 1 March, 29 November 1879.

49   *Athletic News* 29 September 1880, *Darwen News* 19 April 1879, 2 October 1880, 7, 14 October 1882, 6 October 1883.

50   *Sheffield Daily Telegraph* 1, 8 March 1879, 13 March 1880. Wednesday charged 6d to get in and a further 6d to enter the enclosure for their New Year match with the strong Scottish side Vale of Leven in 1880. *Sheffield Daily Telegraph* 3 January 1880.

51   *Athletic News* 10 October 1883, *Saturday Night* 24 March 1883.

52   *Football Field* 20, 27 September, 25 October, 8 November 1884.

53   *Blackburn Standard* 18 September 1886, *Athletic News* 9 February 1886.

54   *Athletic News* 22 November 1887. *Sheffield Daily Telegraph* 1 October 1887.

55   *Derby Express* 27, 28 January 1888.

56   Behind the goal seems to have been a favourite spot for spectators at least as early as 1883. *Saturday Night* 27 January 1883.

57   *Athletic News* 14 March 1883.

58   Ibid. 1 February 1882, 3 May 1887, *Preston Herald* 11 May 1887. In each case the Press thought that the gate was less than might have been expected but welcomed the absence of overcrowding. Aston Villa charged £1

for the best seats in what was normally the press box, 10/- for three other rows and 5/- for the remainder of their grandstand seats for the famous cup match with Preston North End in January 1888. *Birmingham Daily Gazette* 9 January 1888.

59 *Athletic News* 25 January 1887, *Preston Herald* 26 January 1887.

60 Football League Management Committee Minutes 28 March 1890. The Lancashire League, composed of the reserve sides of Football League clubs and small town sides made up of amateurs and part-time professionals fixed its minimum entry charge at 4d in 1892. *Athletic News* 23 May 1892.

61 *Athletic News* 1 May 1899. £1 was the price of some seats at the Scotland-England match in 1900. *Athletic News* 12 March 1900.

62 For some additional thoughts on the sporting press see chapter six. We do know that a young school teacher working in Nottingham and Woolwich in the 1890s would generally find sixpence to watch the local team on Saturday afternoons. Ironically he became a research assistant for the Webbs during the years 1899–1903 when they were working on their history of English local government. It did not prevent him from continuing to watch league football. F.H. Spencer (1938) op.cit. pp. 161, 180, 216.

63 *Athletic News* 3 March 1877. On the social heterogeneity of the Sheffield Football Association, as opposed to the Sheffield Club see below p. 227.

64 *Preston Herald* 5 December 1883.

65 *Sheffield Daily Telegraph* 31 January 1888. The match referred to was an F.A. cup-tie between Preston North End and Sheffield Wednesday. It sounds as though on that ground at least, for an important match, there was some class mixing outside the privileged pavilion or grandstand.

66 *Athletic News* 3 November 1890.

67 *Athletic News* 20 October 1880.

68 *Saturday Night* 27 January 1883. See also *Preston Herald* 18 November 1885.

69 *Blackburn Standard* 8 March 1884.

70 *Sheffield Daily Telegraph* 27 February 1884.

71 *Blackburn Standard* 25 March 1882. This was out of a crowd of over 10,000, the largest ever at Darwen up to that time. *Preston Herald* 22 March 1882. According to a Sheffield newspaper 'ladies always turned up in some numbers for matches at Bramall Lane' in the 1870s, *Sheffield Daily Telegraph* 17 March 1873.

72 *Preston Herald* 23 January 1884. And for a match *v* Bolton Wanderers in November 1885 there were 'many ladies' on the reserved portion of the stand. *Preston Herald* 18 November 1885.

73 *Preston Herald* 15 April 1885.

74 *Athletic News* 22 November 1887, 13 February 1899.

75 B.O. Corbett *et al.*, *Football* (1907) p. 19. A. Gibson and W. Pickford, vol. IV op.cit. p. 43.

76 See for example *Athletic News* 23 December 1889 'the British working man—grimed by recent toil—there was no time for a wash or a "snack"'. See also *Athletic News* 28 December 1896.

77 *Preston Herald* 23 January 1884.

78 Although we should not forget the 'infuriated beings in petticoats' at Great Lever in 1884. See below p. 162.

79 *Athletic News* 9 February 1886.

80 *Athletic News* 20 January 1885.

81 *Athletic News* 6 January 1890.
82 *Sheffield Daily Telegraph* 17 October 1893.
83 *Athletic News* 13 April 1886.
84 B.O. Corbett, *et al.* (1907) op.cit. pp. 18–20.
85 *Sunderland Football Echo* 21 November 1908.
86 *Preston Herald* 8 March 1887.
87 *Glasgow Herald* 7 July 1902.
88 3,295 paid 6d and 57,814 paid 1/-.
89 It is interesting, though difficult, to compare the occupations of those involved in the Ibrox disaster of 1902 with similar catastrophes at Bolton in 1945 and Ibrox again in 1971. Unfortunately, this cannot be done from the press because they failed to list occupations in any comprehensive way. It is probable, however, that the death certificates of the 33 killed at Bolton and the 66 at Ibrox will be made available although both samples are small. One interesting area of comparison already opened up concerns the ages of those people who attended. Of the 160 Ibrox casualties in 1902 for whom ages were listed 90, or 56 per cent, were in their twenties. They were men whose youth and early manhood had been spent at a time when football was already popular and when both playing and watching were expanding activities. There was only one schoolboy and 22 other teenagers (15 per cent). At Ibrox in 1971, on the other hand, of 89 people involved for whom ages were given 46 were in the range 8–19 (52 per cent) including 12 schoolboys and 25 were in their twenties (28 per cent). I'm not sure what this reflects except perhaps the increased affluence of youth in the 1970s compared with the 1900s. It cost 6/- or 30p to get into that part of Ibrox in 1971 and boys under 14 almost certainly paid less. *Glasgow Herald* 5 January, 4 March 1971, *Scotsman* 4 January, 17 February 1971.
90 On the other hand the London contingent of the 1890 Cup Final was described as 'nearly all young men, and a great majority seem to be football players themselves, and wear the badges of their respective clubs'. They were also of 'superior social standing' to the working men from Sheffield who were there to support Wednesday. *All the Year Round* 3rd Series no. 69, 26 April 1890 p. 394.
91 *Pastime* 7 April 1886. *C.B. Fry's Magazine*, New Series, vol. 1 no. 1, April 1911.
92 *Glasgow Herald* 7 September 1908.
93 G.B. Pollock Hodsell in *C.B. Fry's Magazine* vol. VI no. 31, October 1906, p. 90. *The Times* 21 April 1913.
94 *Athletic News* 5 March 1884, *Nottingham Daily Guardian* 3 March 1884.
95 See for example *Pastime* 7 April 1886 and *Athletic News* 9 January 1893 which described two ladies 'freely bedecked' in Sunderland's colours before a league match at Preston. For uninitiated readers, if there are any, those were red and white. Death cards were also popular. 'In Loving Memory of Everton who died whilst fighting for the English Cup against Sheffield United at Goodison Park on 10 January 1896.'

> Boldly to the fray they went
> But got beaten to their sorrow;
> They were put to sleep, by a better team,
> And the funeral's tomorrow.'

George R. Sims (ed.), *Living London* (1901) vol. I, p. 296.

96 *Barnsley Independent* 16 April 1910.

97 *Pastime* 2 October 1895.

98 *Barnsley Independent* 30 April 1910.

99 *Pastime* 25 March 1891; *Manchester Guardian* 23 March 1891. One man played a concertina throughout the Small Heath-Stoke City cup-tie in 1899. The thoughts of adjacent spectators were not recorded. *Athletic News* 13 February 1899.

100 *Preston Herald* 9 March 1887.

101 *Sheffield Daily Telegraph* 13 February 1882. Such wild spontaneity was doubtless prompted by the fact that this was Sheffield's first victory over Glasgow. Examples could be multiplied and for another see *Athletic News* 2 April 1884.

102 *Sheffield Daily Telegraph* 26 April 1915.

103 *Sheffield Daily Telegraph* 5 March 1888. He concluded that excitement was all right but no excuse for excess. It is fairly clear what three of the names mean but what about 'Setpot'?

104 See for example *Athletic News* 4 April 1883, 17 April 1899.

105 A. Gibson and W. Pickford, vol. I op.cit. pp. 106–7, 109, 115, 123. G. Green (1953) op.cit. p. 172. A Referees Association was formed in 1893–4 to help organise and qualify these important officials and the F.A. set up their own referees committee in 1899. Neutral linesmen for important professional matches were the rule from 1898–9. But on changing laws see chapter seven.

106 *Blackburn Standard* 14 May 1881.

107 *Manchester Guardian* 1 November 1883.

108 *Pastime* 13 February 1895. *Association Football Handbook* 1895–6, p. 2. As early as 1892 League clubs were requested to put up a notice asking 'Spectators and players ... to assist in keeping order at all matches ... and to prevent any demonstration of feeling against the referee, visiting team, or players.' N.L. Jackson (1900) op.cit. p. 123. The notice continued, 'a breach of any of the above may cause the ground to be closed for football purposes for a period, thus causing great disappointment to all well wishers of the game, and bringing disgrace and great monetary loss to the club'.

109 *Manchester Guardian* 24 February 1890. And the match was a local 'derby'.

110 *Athletic News* 2 October 1893. Once again such examples could be multiplied and undoubtedly help to account for the F.A's concern with the training of referees. For others instances see *Manchester Guardian* 5 January 1891, *Sheffield Daily Telegraph* 8 April 1895, *Wolverhampton Express and Star* 30 September 1895, *Athletic News* 23 March 1896, *Morning Post* 12 February 1906.

111 *Preston Herald* 12 January 1884. Preston won the match 2–0.

112 See *Athletic News Football Annual* 1908–9.

113 *Athletic News* 16 June 1890.

114 *Football Players' Magazine*, vol. II, no. 7, February 1913. For other criticisms of the league list of referees see *Athletic News* 17 January 1910.

115 *Athletic News* 23 April 1884.

116 *Athletic News* 28 September 1891.

117 *Athletic News* 2 June 1885. Later that year there was more trouble after a match between Walsall Town and Aston Villa with the carriages of Villa supporters being stoned. For a description see *Sunday Chronicle* 25 October 1885 and *Birmingham Daily Post* 19 October 1885. The match

was abandoned with four minutes to go and Villa leading 5–0. The anger of the crowd appeared to be directed at two Villa players who had formerly been with Walsall Swifts.

118   *Athletic News* 9 March 1886; *West Bromwich Free Press.* 13 March 1886.

119   See *Birmingham Daily Post* 11 May 1885; *Preston Herald* 13 May 1885; *Athletic News* 12 May 1885 and *Birmingham Daily Gazette* 11 May 1885. *Saturday Night*, the Birmingham sports paper, published a description of the assault circled by a black border. According to the *Birmingham Daily Gazette* 14 May 1885 there were actually no policemen on the Villa ground.

120   *Athletic News* 27 March 1893.

121   *Athletic News* 10 January 1888. *Birmingham Daily Gazette* 9, 16 January 1888. The club later claimed that the failure to provide mounted policemen was not their fault. The West Bromwich police superintendent in charge of the operation said he did not like them and consequently did not bring any with him. For other examples see the *Athletic News* 23 March, 6 April, 5 October 1896, 3 April 1899. See also the *Manchester Guardian* 3 February 1913, for an account of the overcrowding which eventually led to the abandonment of the Manchester City-Sunderland cup-tie. The F.A. fined City £500 and ordered the match to be replayed at Sunderland.

122   *Birmingham Daily Mail* 10 January 1888. Even at the Wembley Cup Final in 1923 when something like twice the capacity got into the ground, there was little disorder.

123   C. Francis, op.cit. pp. 150–4.

124   *Manchester Guardian* 12 February 1896.

125   *Glasgow Herald* 19, 20, 23, 26 April 1909. Several letters to the paper blamed the police for the worst of the fighting. Most of the rioters were alleged to have been boys or youths in the 16–20 age group.

126   *Athletic News* 20 October 1890, 29 February 1892. The mounted police-men had been on duty at a Salvation Army procession in the town. Preparing for a cup match with Sunderland in 1903, Aston Villa ordered 70 policemen and six dozen stewards, the stewards to be chosen by each director 'submitting half a dozen names of good workmen'. Aston Villa F.C. Directors' Meetings Minutes 29 January 1903.

127   *Athletic News* 9 January 1893. It is not clear who provided the soldiers.

128   *Athletic News* 27 March 1893.

129   *Athletic News* 20 February 1893.

130   *Athletic News* 23 March 1896.

131   *Athletic News* 17 April 1899.

CHAPTER SIX
DRINK, GAMBLING AND THE SPORTING PRESS

THERE is no doubt that the drink trade was closely involved with both amateur and professional football from a very early stage in the game's development. In chapter two we drew attention to the role of the publican and the public house in providing crucial facilities such as fields to play on, rooms to change and dine in, and even an early results service. Public houses both spawned and supported many small clubs. With the coming of professionalism we noted the frequency with which brewers and publicans featured among club shareholders and directors and the number of players who were placed in public houses. It was clear money was to be made for some. As early as 1883 a Blackburn publican complained that football was causing the trade losses save to the few 'football' houses.[1] The *Licensed Victuallers' Sportsman* put the point in its issue of 8 December 1888:

football worship is, indeed carried to excess, and the chief players are looked upon as heroes, and the return from a win becomes a veritable triumphant progress, and lucky is the hotel giving shelter to a visiting team. It is besieged by those wishing to get a nearer glimpse of the favourites of the hour, the consequence being that the house does a roaring trade.

But what fascinated some contemporaries was not whether some brewers took a close enough interest in the game to put money in a club nor whether some public houses thrived on their football connections. The real issue for those concerned with the state of the nation's workers was how had the rise of this new pastime affected the old one of drinking? Had the growth of football both as a game for players and as a mass spectator sport led to a decreased amount of drinking by working men or not?

So far as opinion can be discovered and analysed, the views of those inside the game expressed few doubts. The *Athletic News*, for example, saw football as an important weapon in the fight for sobriety. 'It tides a man over that most dangerous part of the week-end afternoon when he does not know what to do with himself, and so goes and gets drunk, or would do but for football'.[2] At Aston Villa's annual general meeting in 1905 the club president was applauded when he said that football had a 'marked tendency' to produce sobriety among the working classes.[3] Even N.L. Jackson, by no means an uncritical admirer of the professional game, agreed that there were some men who 'if there were no football, would spend their Saturday afternoons in a public house. Well, these are . . . kept outside for an hour or two if they play or go to look on'.[4]

Moreover, it was not merely people inside football who subscribed to these notions. As early as 1881 Sir Watkin Wynne M.P. had accompanied his presentation of the Welsh Challenge Cup to the Druids F.C. of Ruabon by remarking that 'much had been said of the English spending their time on drinking, but these kind of sports kept young men from so spending and wasting their time, for, after playing a good game of football, he thought they would be more glad to go to bed than to visit the public house'.[5] The lay secretary of the Sunderland branch of the Church of England Temperance Society said he wanted to buy some shares in Sunderland F.C. 'It would be a serious blow to the work of temperance in Sunderland if the great counter-attraction of the Saturday afternoon matches was to be discontinued.'[6] The Chief Constable of Liverpool, Captain J.W. Nott Bower, agreed that increased means of recreation in general and football in particular was one of the factors which had led to a diminution of drunkenness in that city in the 1890s. During evidence given to the Royal Commission on the Liquor Licensing Laws he said:

The working man who would formerly have left his work after being paid on Saturday and gone home in a leisurely manner, with a number of his friends would have stayed at the first public house he came to, stood a drink round, gone on to the next house, and then one of the friends would have stood a drink round, and so on, until they had had a great deal more than was good for them. I think that now when there is a match on the Everton or Liverpool grounds, a great number of working men, the instant they get paid, rush off home as quickly as they can, get a wash and a change, leave their wages with their wives, and are off to see the football, and I think that has led to a great decrease in drunkenness.

He emphasised that although there were many public houses in the vicinity of the Anfield and Goodison Park grounds 'the football matches have not led to drunkenness in those public houses'.[7] Similarly the Chief Constable of Middlesbrough reported in 1909 that there was less drunkenness in the town when Middlesbrough were playing at home than on those Saturdays when they were out of town.[8] A Lancashire football enthusiast had made a similar point twenty years before: when the team played at home, it was a rush to get home and to the match especially when the kick off was at 2 p.m. or 2.15 p.m. in the November-January days. But when the local team was away then the working man would still dally at the pub. The action of the Church Temperance Society in the diocese of Liverpool in circularising all magistrates in the diocese protesting at the granting of occasional licenses for the sale of intoxicants at football matches in Lancashire does, however, suggest that drink could be obtained on some grounds.[9]

Outside the temperance press the arguments linking drink and drunkenness with professional football do not seem to have had much of an airing.[10] But Guy Thorne, in an article entitled 'Sport and Drink', published in 1906, was unequivocally combative. 'After a big football match the hotels were always crowded, packed so closely that it was difficult for a latecomer to enter. . . . Drunkenness was very common.' Not only was this bad for the athlete concerned but

the hero corrupts innumerable valets. . . . A Blue Book of statistics of crime for 1904 [shows] that drunkenness is greatest in the great football centres of the North and of Wales. . . . Decent people no longer care to attend football matches. . . . A new class of spectators has been created, men who care little or nothing for the sport itself, but who use a match as a mere opportunity and an excuse for drinking. . . . If you go into the cheaper parts of the field at any big match . . . you'll see that every other man has a bottle of spirits in his jacket pocket, which he drinks at half-time. . . . Saturday afternoon matches are a curse to the home. It is not the few pence that the husbands spend for admission . . . but it is the drinking that follows, often protracted till late at night.[11]

It is not difficult to point up the weaknesses of the allegations. The 'great football centres' were the greatest centres of populations. In absolute terms and perhaps even per capita, on the basis of the old adage about the quickest way out of Manchester, you would expect to find more drunkenness there. Football probably had little to do with it. Moreover, the idea that a new class of spectators had been created whose sole reason for attending a match was to drink seems highly unlikely. And every other man with a bottle of spirits in his pocket? On the other hand those people who believed that football had reduced drunkenness might well have been guilty of a little wishful thinking or over-optimism.

It was more often the tap room activities of the players which provoked a critical response from the public. Poor results were often explained by dark hints that players had been spending too much time at the bar. Thus the Darwen president in 1892 directly attributed a succession of heavy defeats to the effects of drink and appealed to club members not to treat the players.[12] In 1899 the chairman of Woolwich Arsenal issued a similar request to the followers of that club.[13] Several members of the Aston Villa side were accused of over-indulgence during the Christmas and New Year celebrations in 1891.[14] Moreover, their erratic perform-ances in 1892–3 were alleged to be largely the result of drinking among the players. The temptation to drink was clearly a problem for some players. The wife of Tom Brandon, the Blackburn Rovers and England international, asked for a separation order in the Blackburn magistrates court, alleging that her husband drank and assaulted her. 'He was well known to be fond of drink and had been up before the Rovers' committee for it. He could not see the football sometimes he was so bad.' Brandon had apparently been keeping a pub for fourteen months. On behalf of the Rovers it was said that Brandon was 'far from always drunk' and that Mrs Brandon also found drink tempting.[15] As we saw in chapter four, drink was associated with some tragic cases and it is not surprising that some clubs, Bristol Eastville Rovers for example, went so far as to stipulate that all their players must be total abstainers.[16]

It seems likely that some working people attended football matches on Saturday afternoons who might otherwise have gone to public houses. They may still have done so when the local team were away from home. On the other hand, football may have helped them to break the habit. But it is all very speculative. A.E. Dingle has shown that beer consumption appears to have reached a peak in the 1870s and then declined to a lesser peak around 1898–1901. He has also shown that expenditure on drink as a percentage of total consumer expenditure on goods and services at current prices fell from a peak of over 15 per cent in 1876 to 12–13 per cent from the 1880s to the end of the century after which it continued downwards to the outbreak of war.[17] He suggests that two major economic changes were at work. In the first place, from the 1880s the range of commodities coming within the reach of the working-class pocket had been considerably extended both in variety and price. Second, drink consumption per head rose when an increase in real wages came in response to rising money wages as in the mid-1870s and around 1900. But when real wages rose as a result of falling prices, as they did between 1880 and 1895 then the level of drink consumption stagnated. Clearly professional football was a competitor with drink in this field and in order to spend regularly on that less might have been spent on drink and therefore less drinking done. The relationship between drinking or drunkenness and the growth of football is always likely to be an imprecisely defined one. It was rarely, if ever, going to be a case of one or the other. The whole ritual of 'going to a match' might well involve having a drink at some stage. In general it seems safe to say that football, along with several other factors, did make some contribution to a decline in drunkenness in some places but that neither the optimism of those who saw football as itself producing a large decrease in the consumption of drink, nor the pessimism of those who felt that football led to increased drinking, were justified.

So long as there have been men there has probably been gambling.[18] Certainly it is difficult to think of any of the sports and pastimes of nineteenth-century England which was carried on without gambling being present in some form. Even the Oxford and Cambridge boat race produced a mass of wagering on the result, although, as one editorial observed in 1873, 'everybody is cheerful, including even the makers of losing bets, for everybody knows that the race has been in the hands of gentlemen, and that the result is above suspicion'.[19] That was the great anxiety about betting. It led to corruption. In order to make money by betting participants were prepared to sell races and fix matches: it happened in horse racing, prize fighting and pedestrianism in particular. It was, of course, the ruination of true sport. As we saw earlier the ex-public school, university-trained, professional and commercial members of the middle classes who dominated the Football Association were determined to keep their game pure. That meant excluding professionals and gambling. By 1885 it was clear that the former could not be eliminated without serious dislocation to the structure of the game and the F.A.'s control of it. But gambling was always to be opposed in our period although, in the end, like professionalism and Topsy, it just 'growed'.

Sir Frederick Wall was greatly surprised to discover that odds had been quoted by bookmakers on the first F.A. Cup Final in 1872 when a team largely composed of public school old boys met a team of army officers from the Royal Engineers.[20] By 1877 the *Manchester Guardian* claimed that the 'objectionable practice' of betting was a feature of local matches and was frequently indulged in by both players and umpires.[21] The *Athletic News* agreed that betting on the results of matches did take place

but it cannot possibly assume the character of gambling. There being only two sides or parties to the contest long odds cannot possibly be obtained unless people are foolish enough to desire to back a hopelessly inferior team . . . thus the bookmaker's occupation is gone, or rather it can never come, so far as football is concerned. The betting cannot consequently assume any more objectionable form than the members of a club or team backing this club or team to win; and this, we submit, is perfectly legitimate betting.[22]

This might appear slightly complacent not to say naive, but the football coupon was not invented in the 1870s. In that decade betting, like the game itself, was not taken too seriously although one ought to be careful as the reporter on the *Darwen News* emphasised following a match between the locals and the men from Turton just down the road. 'Their goalkeeper did pretty well, but we should recommend him to cease his contention with the spectators and keep his money in his pocket.' Turton was becoming well known for betting and if they saw their money disappearing they might be tempted into rashness.[23]

In so far as one is able to collect evidence on such betting on football matches as there was in the 1880s it seems to have been mostly confined to the grounds before and during the games. It was apparently commonplace enough at matches in Sheffield through the 1880s if the comments of the local newspapers are an accurate guide. Even as late as 1891 the football correspondent of the *Sheffield Independent*, describing the scene before the Wednesday—United local derby, wrote: 'the "pencillers" were busy before the match commenced, and I should not like to pro-phesy how many "thick 'uns" they dropped over the contest, but, if their faces after the match were any criterion, they had "copt it hot" and the "punters" had been having a merry time of it.'[24] In the following year, when the F.A. Council was trying to outlaw all betting on football, the chairman of Blackburn Rovers strongly opposed the idea and said that although he agreed that 'open and noisy betting on the field' should be put down 'Sheffield was the only place in which this was practised'.[25] It is not clear how different Sheffield really was from other places.[26] Ten years earlier the A.G.M. of the Birmingham Football Association had heard its chairman say that the 'betting nuisance' was the greatest evil with which they had to contend.[27] It appears to have been a persistent evil because, in 1887, when two local teams, Aston Villa and West Bromwich Albion, met in the F.A. Cup Final, some large bets were being made at half-time (no goals had been scored in the first half and one local newspaper claimed that 'many working men staked whole week's wages' on the result.[28] One just cannot find corroborative evidence for this sort of report and, in any event, a special occasion like a cup final was always likely to persuade people who did not bet regularly to have a little flutter. It was all part of the excitement of the day particularly if it was your home-town team or someone you knew was actually going to London for the match.[29] The chairman of Blackburn Rovers believed that the Anti-Gambling League's claims about football field betting were exaggerated and that more money changed hands in one London club in one week than in all of a season's matches.[30] By 1899 the *Athletic News* was arguing that football was singularly free from betting and that a bookmaker was not to be seen at a Cup Final 'nowadays'.[31] C.E.B. Russell was probably closer to the truth when he wrote in 1905: 'there may be a trivial wager, the price of a cigar, or a drink, but betting, in the sense in which one speaks of the man who bets on horses, is fortunately almost absent from the football field'.[32] By the time he wrote those words however, another form of betting on football matches was beginning to spread, especially in the north and midlands, namely the football coupon.

The idea of asking interested parties to forecast the results of several given matches for a small stake and in the hope of winning a big prize seems to have originated within the sporting press. The *Football Field* of Bolton, for example, was offering its readers 22/6 if they could pick the winners of all the first round matches in the Lancashire Cup in 1886. *The Lantern*, of St. Helens, and *Football*, of Wolverhampton, offered respectively a guinea for forecasting the correct results of seven rugby and seven association matches and 10/- for guessing the results and goals scored in four local soccer matches.[33] The *Athletic News* offered a prize of £5 to anyone selecting the winners of all the matches in the first round of the F.A. Cup in 1890. Later in that season the paper was also offering £5 for correctly predicting the result and actual score of four stipulated matches and from November 1891, it began a regular weekly-prize competition. Four guineas were awarded for 'an absolutely correct guess of the results and scores in six matches' with a consolation prize of two guineas to the best effort should no one manage to obtain an all correct result. There was no entry fee and if there was no outright winner then the four guineas would be added to the following week's prize until a total of twenty guineas was reached.[34] With the formation of leagues and the coming of regular Saturday fixtures which were not disrupted by cup-ties, bookmakers began to issue their own lists of matches. The earliest references the author has been able to find date from 1889 and the second season of the Football League. The following advertisement had appeared in the *Athletic News* on 18 February, 'English Cup—£2. 2s. given for having

four winners in Third Round. Send list and six penny stamps by
March 2nd—BROOK, Rose Cottage, Dewsbury'. Later that year,
the fully-fledged coupon had arrived as is shown by the advertise-
ment which Astley, a Blackburn bookmaker, placed in the *Athletic
News* of 16 December 1889. 'Weekly One Penny—The
"Universal" Football Programme and Prize Coupon, £12 for a
penny. May be had wholesale and retail from the following agents.'
There followed a list of names and addresses in Accrington,
Bolton, Burnley, Birmingham, Heywood, Liverpool, Manchester,
Newton Heath, Preston, Stoke and Wolverhampton. A list of
the matches, drawn from the Football, Lancashire and Midland
Leagues, was then given. The list cost $1\frac{1}{2}$d per copy although you
were urged to save money and buy six for $6\frac{1}{2}$d and a dozen for $1/0\frac{1}{2}$d.
The following week a further notice announced that the £12
prize had been shared by two people, £37 was now available to
be won, and the number of matches on the coupon had increased
to 13.[35]

It is not clear how fast this new form of betting on football
matches grew in the 1890s. One northern newspaper (unnamed)
was alleged to have made £70,000 per year out of its coupon
system.[36] However, in 1901 the Anti-Gambling League brought
several actions against football coupon organisers and the method
was declared illegal.[37] It seems that it was the collection of stake
money which infringed the Betting Houses Act of 1853. Newspapers could continue with their competitions but no separate
entrance fee, other than the price of the paper, could be charged.
They also had to beware of being accused of promoting a lottery
which was also illegal.[38] Some bookmakers and competition
proprietors, in an effort to avoid the rigours of the English legal
system, or at least the searching eye of the anti-Gambling League,
set themselves up in Holland, relying on a postal trade entirely
or the post plus a distribution system of agents.[39]

Nevertheless, there seems to have been a considerable expansion in football-coupon betting, based on the issuing of coupons
by bookmakers, in the first decade of the twentieth century.[40]
Coupons were given out in bundles to the agents generally on a
Wednesday.[41] Most of the agents had a clutch of regular customers.
It is not clear whether any of the agents did well enough to make
a living at the job. It is more likely that some workmen earned
useful sums on the side by collecting the coupons from their
fellows. The completed slips, together with the money staked,
were usually collected on Saturdays before kick-off time. Paying
out was then a Monday morning ritual with Wednesdays generally

regarded as the last day for settling up. Robertson in his study of the Liverpool district, collected coupons from 42 different agents for the matches played on Saturday 9 March 1907. One of these is reproduced in Figure 6.1. Nine were collected in Liverpool itself, ten in Garston, five each from Bootle, Birkenhead, St. Helens and Seaforth and three from Rock Ferry. These 42 agents actually

Figure 6.1

HEARTS	Saturday March 9 1907

Home Team	Visiting Team
No. 1	No. 2
CRYSTAL PALACE	v EVERTON
STOCKPORT C.	v NOTTS FOREST
BRISTOL CITY	v MANCHESTER CITY
WEST BROM. A.	v NOTTS COUNTY
BARNSLEY	v WOOLWICH. A.
SHEFFIELD WED'Y	v LIVERPOOL
STOKE	v BIRMINGHAM
PORTSMOUTH	v TOTTENHAM H.
BLACKBURN R.	v SUNDERLAND

NAME...........................STAKE ....

ODDS	MATCHES		ODDS	MATCHES
4 to 1	111	1 denotes Home Team	7 to 1	1111
5 to 1	112		8 to 1	1112
7 to 1	122	2 denotes Visiting Team	10 to 1	1122
8 to 1	11X		12 to 1	111X
8 to 1	222		16 to 1	112X
10 to 1	12X	X denotes draw	20 to 1	1222
14 to 1	22X		25 to 1	2222
14 to 1	1XX		25 to 1	122X
20 to 1	2XX		25 to 1	11XX
25 to 1	XXX		25 to 1	222X
LONG ODDS				
10 to 1 Any Five Winners of Above			33 to 1	12XX
16 to 1 Any Six Winners ,,			33 to 1	22XX
33 to 1 Any Seven Winners ,,			50 to 1	1XXX
50 to 1 Any Eight Winners ,,			50 to 1	2XXX
100 to 1 Any Nine Winners ,,			66 to 1	XXXX

6 to 1 any Correct Score
8 to 1 Top Score on Coupon

RULES

All matches not played on the date mentioned, or matches not played to a finish, ALL BETS STAND, until the Game is officially decided, except Cup Ties. All Commissions must be on printed forms, no plain paper received. All Claims must be made not later than Wednesday following matches.[43]

FIGURE 6.2 *Football coupons distributed and collected, Liverpool district 1907*

	White			Blue			Yellow		
		Out	In		Out	In		Out	In
LIVERPOOL									
Hearts		5000	2000	Royal	5000	2000	Weather	3000	2000
Finlay		7500	5600						
Half-Time		2500	1800						
Rees		1000	600						
Meister		3000	1000						
Final		10000	6000						
Crossing		2000	1000						
GARSTON									
				Hearts	2000	1000	H.H.H.	3000	2000
Corn		2500	1000	Crash	2000	1000	Try Again	2000	1000
Play Up		1000	500	Hurrah	5000	3000			
Down-hearted		3000	2000	Old Firm	1500	1000			
BOOTLE									
				Goal	3000	1000			
Outside		2000	1000						
				Cross Bar	2000	1000			
				Foot	3000	2000			
							Nash	3000	1000
SEAFORTH									
				Off	2000	1000	Banns	4000	2000
BIRKENHEAD									
				Tower	2000	1000			
							Lamb	7000	5000
				Captain	5000	4000			
							Tally Ho	4000	2500
ROCK FERRY							Spion Kop	3000	2000
							Shout	3000	2000
				Weather	3000	2000			
							Head In	3000	2000
ST. HELENS									
				Song Song	5000	2000	Arthur		
							Grim	2000	1000
Notes		3000	2000				Royal	2500	1300
Game		3000	2000				Pretty Iris	4000	3000
Finish		3000	2000				Towers	2000	1000

Source: A.J. Robertson op.cit. p. 83. White, Blue and Yellow stand for the three different bookmakers.

worked for three bookmakers, the coupons collected being divided up between them in the ratio 15, 14 and 13. Although there were three separate bookmakers involved, the choice of teams, odds offered, style and printing were identical which suggested to Robertson that the workings of the free market were probably being interfered with. Robertson also claimed that the group operated elsewhere in Lancashire and Yorkshire. A 'considerable' staff was employed in Liverpool sorting and classifying the coupons. In an attempt to give an estimate of the amount of business undertaken, Robertson took a statement from the 42 agents he saw 'of the number of coupons handed to them weekly to distribute and the average number which are returned to them with stakes by their clients on Saturday morning'. Figure 6.2 fills in the details. A total of 136,500 coupons were issued for that particular week and 79,800 taken in with money. Robertson claimed that these figures did not represent half the output in the districts in question and that it was probable that at least 250,000 coupons were on the market every week in the Liverpool and St. Helens districts alone with perhaps three firms receiving 140,000 monetary deposits. As the minimum stake received was 1/- he suggested that an estimated weekly income of between £8–10,000 was probably a conservative one. 'I have been informed by several workmen that 2/6 is very commonly wagered on a football match [sic] by a man earning not more than 25/- to 30/- per week.'[42]

The expansion of football-coupon betting stimulated the growth of two related phenomena. One was an opposition movement which aimed at sponsoring legislation to make such activities illegal. The other was the football tipster. The press had been suggesting who might win and why for many years, but the private tipster appears to have been a product of the early twentieth century.[44] By 1914 a modicum of sophistication had been reached in the form of 'The Incomparable Football Forecasting System' by W.J. Duckworth.

There are several systems for Football Forecasting, but the only possible and most profitable system is, by what is known as the law of averages. This means that you must get the averages of the teams for the last four weeks. My system had been fully tested . . . (and) is a great aid to competitors, different to the many, so-called forecasting systems which are generally difficult to understand and unworkable.

What had to be done was to obtain the results of the last four matches.

Note the clubs successful in all four, put them to win home or away. Any team with three wins out of four, to win if playing at home, or a draw if away. A team which has obtained ... four points out of eight, to win only if at home, and a team with less than 50 per cent to draw. Of course in the event of teams meeting with the same average out of the last four matches, choice of ground should be taken into consideration.

This was obviously a crude attempt to measure the current form of individual clubs. Needless to say we do not know anything about Mr Duckworth's clients, if he had any.[45]

Opposition, although periodically coming from the football authorities themselves, was mainly orchestrated by the Anti-Gambling League.[46] It was the committee of the York branch, doubtless dominated by Rowntree, which in 1905 produced the collection of essays which he edited entitled, *Betting and Gambling : A National Evil*. Most of the essays were polemical and alarmist in tone.[47] The League wanted a change in the law so that all competitions in which there was a material element of chance were made illegal. In addition they wanted prizes offered by publications to be limited to an aggregate value of £5.[48] But they had to wait until 1920 until the appropriate legislation was passed having failed to get through the Ready Money Football Betting Bill of 1914.[49]

So how can an assessment be made of the impact of betting on football or indeed football on betting? Betting might have stimulated interest in football and *vice versa*. It may be that many people who did not play the game nor watch it nevertheless had a weekly gamble. That is a well known fact about today's pools but we do not have any evidence for the pre-1915 era. Why did working men gamble on the pools? Some people told John Hilton why they thought they did it in the 1930s.[50] Not many mentioned that brains were needed for such a skilful task. But there were a few who, while emphasising that the hope was to win some money, obviously gained a certain amount of satisfaction out of the exercise of skill and judgement. How far they were deceiving themselves is, of course, another matter. It should be quickly emphasised that for the Edwardian years we have no John Hilton. Perhaps fewer pools gamblers would claim to be exercising a skill than those who habitually bet on horses.[51] Were there more variables to be considered on the race track? Was there more to read? Was it simply that there was racing nearly every week-day, on all but ten days of the year in 1907, for example? Stakes on the pools were small and prizes much smaller than they were to become in the 1930s. Betting on the new pools, even when the odds were fixed (in both senses of that word), might just provide a quicker way out of Manchester than drink, or at the least, a little more of the necessary to purchase that commodity.

Writing even a short and mainly descriptive piece about the history of the football press is very difficult. It is clear that there is an important symbiotic relationship between the expansion of the game, both amateur and professional, and both the growth of a specialised press and the spread of football coverage in the general newspapers although the exact nature of such a relationship is difficult to establish. By 1915 the football press is enormous! One cannot hope to have done more than sample it spasmodically and produce impressions whose greatest impact will be to make the social scientist blanch. Nonetheless such a start might prompt someone to undertake a study, not of football papers merely, but the sporting press as a whole or even an examination of sport in newspapers.

The first specialist sporting paper in England appears to have been *Bell's Life in London and Sporting Chronicle* which began in 1820. It was a weekly and dealt mainly with field sports such as hunting, shooting and fishing, together with athletics and the prize ring. It cost 5d before the removal of the taxes on knowledge in the 1850s and was apparently aimed at the 'fancy', that landed fringe who played and gambled hard largely because they had nothing else to do.[52] The paper was published from London and was very much southern England, not to say capital city, orientated. It was joined by the *Field* in 1852, a paper with similar interests and a similar, if slightly more refined, readership.

The 1860s and 1870s saw a considerable expansion of much cheaper sporting papers. Their concentration appears to have been on the clerical and artisan market although little is known about the actual readers. The papers tended to specialise in horse-racing results and information. They mixed reports and descriptions with views, gossip, and analysis, all aimed at selecting winners on whom their readers doubtless hoped to make a few bob. The *Sporting Life* was probably the first of this genre in 1859. It was published from London twice a week and by 1881 claimed a circulation of 100,000.[53] The *Sporting Life* was followed

by the *Sporting Gazette* (1862) and the *Sporting Opinion*, first
published in 1864. The *Sportsman* and the *Sporting Times* both
first saw the light of day in 1865 while the *Sporting Clipper* followed in 1872.[54] These were all London papers with very much a
man-about-town flavour. They celebrated the leisured, moneyed
life around the drama, music hall and race track.[55] It was the
world of the late nineteenth century equivalent of the young
Regency bloods who obtained their excitement and experience
from the professional performances of actresses and jockeys.

By the 1870s, the provinces, that vast area of the country
outside London, had several sporting papers of their own. It
is difficult to discover which was actually the first but it was
probably the small-scale *Sporting Chronicle and Prophetic Bell*
which was first published in Manchester in 1871. The next year
saw the *Midland Sporting News* brought out in Birmingham and
the *Athletic News* first appeared in Manchester in 1875. None of
these papers, save the *Athletic News*, devoted much space to
association football although the *Sportsman* was to do so later and
the *Field* certainly reported the major southern matches, particularly once the F.A. Cup had begun in 1871–2. There had been
an attempt to run a weekly football paper in London in 1873–4
but it had failed due to insufficient support.[56] The *Athletic News*
was from the beginning, a rather different proposition to all the
rest because it eschewed all materials on horse racing.[57] Its aim
was to disseminate 'all the current news' relating to a wide variety
of sports 'tending to promote Physical Education'.[58] Its columns
rapidly concentrated on cricket, athletics and cycling in summer
and association football and rugby in the winter.

The *Athletic News* was first published on Saturdays and cost
2d. So far as football was concerned

we will give every facility ... for all information relating to clubs and their matches in Lancashire, Yorkshire, Cheshire, Staffordshire and the northern and midland counties generally. Full and carefully written reports about leading contests
in the north will appear in each issue, and, as before, we propose publishing weekly all the fixtures to be played on the Saturday of the date of publication, and also
for the forthcoming week. We shall ... be happy to give all lists of teams down
to play in the various matches, with full information about the places of meeting,
the dressing rooms, times, and any arrangements that may be of the slightest
use to any individual player.[59]

The paper also declared its intention to comment on the rules
and the style of play and, of course, to publish as many match
results as could be obtained.[60] By 1879 the paper was running a
regular football notes and gossip column during the season put

together by 'On the Ball', and it sported a separate 'Scotch Football Notes' by Jonathan Oldbuck.[61] Its match reports and results service was already as comprehensive as befitted a paper which, in the autumn of 1880, could be bought, by then every Wednesday morning, in Barnsley, Beverley, Birmingham, Blackburn, Bolton, Bradford, Burslem, Bury, Cheadle Hulme, Chester, Crewe, Derby, Dewsbury, Edinburgh, Fleetwood, Glasgow, Halifax, Hanley, Haslingden, Huddersfield, Keighley, Leeds, Leicester and Liverpool as well as Manchester.[62] A typical edition of the paper in May 1879 contains a front page 'En Passant' of jokes, axioms, stories and short news items. On page two was published a list of athletics fixtures, the names and addresses of club secretaries, and a section entitled 'Athletic Notes' which included reports of meetings and comments on performances. At this stage the paper regularly contained an editorial on some leading sporting issue of the day and was still featuring a 'Town Talk' social miscellany with the emphasis on the theatre. Oxford and Cambridge boating, bicycling, cricket fixtures, notes, scores and reports, together with a column on billiards and a back page of advertisements mainly concerned with sports goods or forthcoming events completed the paper.

The first editor of the paper was a young man named Thomas Robert Sutton, the son of 'a well-known buyer and seller of books in Manchester' who stayed in the editorial chair until his death in 1895. He had been a rugby football player but was a founder of Manchester Rangers association club and actually played for Lancashire against Staffordshire in 1886.[63] He had first contributed to a journal called the *Athlete*. Unfortunately no more details of his life and background are known. J.A.H. Catton, who edited the paper in the 1920s and had earlier written regularly under the name of 'Tityrus', first wrote for the *Athletic News* in 1886 as 'Ubique'. He had been bound apprentice as a journalist to the *Preston Herald* in 1875 and apparently went to school with the 'Blackburn Hargreaves' which would make him an old boy of Malvern.[64] The style of the paper, by the late 1880s and early 1890s at least, and in particular its match reports, certainly suggests they were put together by men of some literary aspiration who had drunk fairly deeply of the Greek classics and Shakespeare whom they were particularly fond of quoting. 'Ubique' thus began his report of the Nottingham local derby in 1890.

The fierce partisans of each side rubbed their shoulders together, and as I looked round the parallelogram the words of Hecate, in *Macbeth*, were brought vividly to mind:

> Black spirits and white,
> Red spirits and grey,
> Mingle, mingle, mingle,
> You that mingle may.[65]

They were keen to avoid repetition and the too frequent use of common or garden words although the notion that parallelogram would do for field or ground seems to be taking it a bit far. But then, they were rather fond of that too, and without, so far as one can judge, any (or much!) intentional irony. This was how 'Gideon Grump' began his report on the League match between Sunderland and Aston Villa in the issue of 12 January 1891.

A match quotha! I call it a fraud, a villanous fraud, perpetrated upon 5000 innocent people who went to Newcastle-road on Saturday afternoon to see the return League fixture between Sunderland and Aston Villa, in the fond, but as events proved, vain hope that they would enjoy a football treat. They had some ground for the faith that was in them, for had not the 'Villa' drawn with Sunderland away, and had they not also defeated North End in a pseudo League match? I am now quite of opinion with a leather-lunged, raucous-voiced Wearsider among the spectators on Saturday, that the draw at Perry Barr was 'aal wrang', and that Sunderland ought to have won that match, as, indeed, they ought to win all their matches. There have been some football forces at Newcastle-road during the present season, such as when Renton, Cowlairs, and the Vale of Leven were here. But I cannot recall a single instance since last September where any club, let alone a league club, were as utterly pulverised as Aston Villa were on Saturday. The elemental conditions were, on the whole, favourable. 'Tomato-red the sunlight glowed.' But perhaps I had better dismount from my ethereal Pegasus and descend to the firm earth of plain practical prose.

And all that because Villa lost 5–1 and did not make much of a game of it.

The reports of the major matches tended not to waste too much space on a blow-by-blow account of the proceedings. Comment on teamwork and the play of individuals was preferred. And they had plenty of time and space to do this with match reports of up to 1500 words (perhaps more for a major Cup game or international) being allowed and the paper not due to go to press until Sunday evening from the mid-1880s on. We do not know who read these reports. At 2d a week it is not very likely that many artisans bought it, although many more probably read it in clubs or pubs. However, from 13 September 1887 it was a penny paper and that enabled it to exploit the growing popularity of the game which the coming of regular weekly league football from 1888 both indicated and promoted. It appeared on Mondays from Christmas 1888. There was a hint in the paper that it was selling about 25,000 copies in 1883.[66] Mitchell's *Press Guide* of 1888 quotes a figure of 20,000 which had risen to 50,000 in the 1891 edition. The 1893 issue of the guide claims a figure of 80,000 a week and by that time the paper itself was claiming a weekly sale during the football season of 128,000.[67] By the autumn of 1896 the paper was drooling over a claim that 180,000 copies per week were leaving its Manchester offices.[68] As we saw earlier the paper had dropped its subtitle 'a weekly journal of amateur sports' by 1888 and in spite of its beginnings as a propagandist for physical education it smoothly adapted to the coming of professionalism in football in the mid-1880s, so much so that it was without doubt the country's leading football weekly in the last decade of the nineteenth century and the first fifteen years of the twentieth.

In fact, the paper became closely associated with the professional game, in part through the activities of one man, John James Bentley. Bentley was born in Turton, Lancs., in 1860, the son of the local grocer and church organist. He grew up in the take-off period for association football in Lancashire in the 1870s and played for the Turton club soon after its formation in 1872, becoming club captain by the 1881-2 season. He also acted as secretary and treasurer and represented the club on the Lancashire F.A. Although he had several jobs, including one of clerk to the Bolton School Board, he began to contribute match reports to the *Bolton Evening News*, the *Football Field* and finally the *Athletic News* whose staff he joined some time in the 1880s. He wrote under the *nom de plume* of the 'Free Critic'. He became editor of the paper in 1892 and kept the chair until 1900. Meanwhile in February 1885 he had become Secretary of Bolton Wanderers, a Lancashire F.A. committee member in the next year and an F.A. Councillor two years after that in 1888. In 1893 he succeeded William McGregor as President of the Football League, a post he held until 1910 so that from 1893 to 1900 he was both editor of the paper and President of the League. It is hardly surprising that the paper became so firmly committed to the professional game. Bentley became chairman of Manchester United in 1908.[69]

The *Athletic News* was unique in terms of its geographical coverage of matches and its widespread distribution, especially, as we have seen, in the midlands and north. But by the 1880s regular Saturday evening sports papers, largely devoted to publishing results and reports of the afternoon's football matches, began to appear in those same areas served by the *Athletic News*.[70] It is impossible to make a comprehensive list of such papers because there is no source from which it could be done. Some of the papers do not even appear to have left behind any copies. One of the first was in Birmingham. Called simply but effectively *Saturday Night*, it first appeared in the hands of the paper boys at seven o'clock on 30 September 1882. Buyers were treated to four large pages for $\frac{1}{2}$d. Its progenitors claimed that it had

long been apparent that a cheap Saturday night newspaper containing matter of a lighter and more varied character than that usually to be found in the columns of the 'ordinary' evening journals, would meet with a ready sale within the large circle of persons who are interested in the progress of athletic sports, such as cricket, football, cross-country running, and events on the track.

Moreover, the 'jaded workman' and the 'leisure-seeking business-man' wanted a journal of 'homely and amusing tendency'.[71] *Saturday Night* claimed that it was the 'very first paper ever established for the special purpose of giving the results of athletic events on the day of their occurrence'.[72] By November it was pushing out a second edition at 8 p.m. and was proclaiming a bigger circulation than any paper in the midland counties save for the two Birmingham dailies, the *Post* and *Mail*. It boasted 12,000 copies sold in January 1883 and 15,000 only two weeks later.[73] With the coming of professionalism and the league system the paper tended to concentrate more and more on the professional and semi-professional clubs and by 1891 was claiming 21,000 copies sold every Saturday night in the football season.[74]

Other towns were not very far behind Birmingham. Blackburn, for example, from the beginning of season 1883–4, had its *Saturday Football Journal* on sale from seven o'clock at 1d containing accounts of 'all important and other matches, interesting notes, conundrums etc.', and just down the road in Bolton, the Tillotsons began publishing their *Football Field and Sports Telegram* with dateline Bolton 7.30 p.m. in 1884.[75] In Sheffield, a special football edition of the *Evening Star* was published at 7.15 p.m. from September 1886.[76] Derby had a similar production at least from 1888 and by 1889 the *Blackburn Evening Express* was publishing four Saturday football editions: the Primrose at 5.40 p.m., Special at 6.30 p.m., Extra Special at 7.0 p.m. and Last Football at 7.45 p.m.[77] The technical basis for the frenetic expansion of the sporting evening paper was the telegraph and later the telephone and, inside the newspaper machine shop, the web-fed rotary presses and from the 1880s, the linotype machines in the composing room.[78] By 1905 6,000 copies a minute of the London *Football Star* were turned out on Saturday afternoons and instead of a troop of cyclists pedalling furiously from each of the various London grounds with their match reports, a staff of specially trained clerks is engaged for Saturday afternoons, each [with] his ear glued to a telephone for the greater part of an hour. Each man writes down the report of one match only, and each strip of paper as he writes is taken off to the composing room . . . [where] a whole page of seven columns, say 12,000 words, is now frequently set up in thirty minutes.[79]

By the 1890s few towns of any size in England were without their football special. It was as much a part of the cultural scene as the gas lamp and the fish and chip shop. (See Table 6.1.)

Sport in general and football in particular had also become

TABLE 6.1 Football specials, 1880–1915

Name of Paper	Town	1880s	1890s	1900s
Saturday Night	Birmingham	✓	✓	
Football Pink 'Un	Birmingham		✓	✓
Football Field	Bolton	✓	✓	✓
Blackburn Evening Express ⎫		✓		
Saturday Football Journal ⎬	Blackburn	✓		✓
Football Argus	Bradford			✓
Football Express	Derby			✓
Football Express	Exeter		✓	
Football Chronicle	Grantham		✓	
Football Telegraph	Grimsby		✓	✓
Football Telegraph	Kettering		✓	✓
Football Evening News	London		✓	✓
Football Sun	London		✓	✓
Evening Star	London			✓
Football Leader then Football Mail	Newcastle		✓	✓
Football Special	Newcastle			✓
Football Post	Newport			✓
Football Echo	Northampton		✓	✓
Football Post ⎫	Nottingham		✓	✓
Football News ⎬			✓	✓
Football Herald	Plymouth		✓	✓
Football Mail	Portsmouth			
Football Chronicle	Reading		✓	✓
Evening Star Football Edition ⎫			✓	✓
Football Echo ⎬	Sheffield			✓
Football & Cricket World ⎪			✓	✓
Football & Sports Special ⎭			✓	
Football Echo & Sports Gazette	Southampton			✓
Football Standard	Southport			✓
Football Gazette & Telegraph	South Shields			✓
Football Echo	Stockport			✓
Football Echo	Sunderland			✓
Football Mail	West Hartlepool			
Football Express	Weymouth			

Source: Willings Press Guide 1890–1910

part of the regular features of both the daily and weekly press by the 1880s. The 'Football Notes' in the *Blackburn Standard* was first compiled at the beginning of the 1880–1 season.[80] It usually consisted of brief comment and detail about the previous week's matches with some prognostication about the weeks to come. The *Darwen News* started a football column by 'Throw In' later in the same season; no doubt not uninfluenced by their East Lancashire neighbours.[81] The *Sheffield Daily Telegraph* was running a Sports and Pastimes column in their Saturday Supplement also by the beginning of 1881. In the midlands, the *Birmingham Daily Mail* began printing the results of Saturday games in its late Saturday editions in 1883 and by 1888 it was including match reports as well.[82] The *Sunday Chronicle*, owned by Edward Hulton, published from Manchester and circulating largely in the midlands and the north, claimed from its inception as a penny paper in 1885 that it would contain the results of all Saturday football matches.[83] The *Weekly Despatch* had a regular 'Sporting Notes' column in the early 1880s although it was boxing and the turf rather than football which received the most coverage.[84] The *Manchester Guardian* was reporting the more prominent matches from the mid-1870s.[85] By 1880 the paper was reviewing the prospects for the coming season and a regular Thursday 'Football Notes' column appears to have been started at some time during the 1881–2 season. By the end of the decade two columns of results and reports on a Monday was a common feature, especially following important cup or international days.[86] Even *The Times*, which through the 1870s largely concentrated on public schools football and the international matches in which it was mainly ex-public school players who took part, had begun to notice the more important matches played by provincial clubs by the end of that decade although it did not provide full reports of league matches on a regular basis before 1915.[87]

A more systematic study of three London-based Sunday newspapers shows a similar growth in the interest and space given over to the game in the 1880s to that which we have just impressionistically charted.[88] *Lloyds'* apparently published its first football report in 1874. By 1878 it had 39 reports which amounted to 41 per cent of the total sports coverage. One recent study suggests that by the mid-1880s, and even before in *Lloyds'*, football was clearly the major sporting interest for readers of *Lloyds'* and the *Weekly Times*.[89] The following table showing the growth of football match coverage has been taken from V.S. Berridge vol. 2, p. 159.

There was never any doubt in the minds of both newspaper

TABLE 6.2 Association and Rugby football reports in *Reynold's News,*
Lloyds' Weekly News and *Weekly Times*

	Reynold's		*Lloyds'*		*Weekly Times*	
Date	A	R	A	R	A	R
1874	—	—	1	—	—	—
1878	—	—	38	1	—	—
1882	10	3	18	5	3	—
1886	25	8	34	8	33	3
A = Association	R = Rugby					

proprietors and editors that racing results and tips sold news-papers. Football coverage probably helped too. Moreover, the publicity given to the game by all sections of the press was in part a stimulus to growth and popularity, part a recognition of its news value and an indicator of its importance.[90] Not even our ubiquitous social scientist with his multiplicity of concepts and technical sophistication can be more precise than that. By the middle of Edward VII's reign the *Athletic News* was providing 500-word reports on every match played in the two divisions of the Football League and of all games in the Southern League. Without being a highbrow sports paper, it attempted to combine a wide and detailed coverage with intelligent and informed critical commentary. It was the leading football weekly of the day. It was publishing action photographs by January 1911. The rest of the specialist football press was much less thought-provoking and ranged from the rapidly produced first results sheets on a Saturday night to papers like *Football Chat*, a weekly that was as much concerned with making money out of football competitions as providing its readers with both knowledge, opinion and amusement.[91] No newspaper could ignore professional football by 1915. But the football press remains a mystery in several respects. We know comparatively little about who owned it and who wrote for it. We do not know much more about who read it. It would be fascinating to have some detailed knowledge to compare, for example, the socio-occupational background of *Football Chat* readers with that of *Athletic News* readers. But the evidence is never going to materialise.

Notes

1   *Blackburn Times* 14 April 1883.
2   *Athletic News* 2 October 1899.

3   Aston Villa F.C. Directors' Meetings Minutes 23 June 1905; *Birmingham Daily Post* 24 June 1905. Two years later he expanded his ideas on this subject by remarking that the excitement at football matches was so intense that there was no time or desire to get drunk. *Birmingham Daily Post* 22 June 1907. It is not at all clear how refreshments were obtained on the grounds, although there was apparently a 'drinking saloon' at Aston Villa's Perry Barr ground in 1885. *Athletic Star* 9 November 1885.

4   *Pall Mall Gazette* 23 March 1889.

5   *Athletic News* 22 June 1881. Interesting that he should speak of the English in Wales.

6   *Sunderland Herald* 14 July 1896, *Athletic News* 20 July 1896. It was claimed by this paper that local workmen were keeping better time since the growth of the club. The temperance leader, however, was unhappy about the players taking pubs. *Sunderland Herald* 15 July 1896.

7   Royal Commission on the Liquor Licensing Laws PP. 1898 XXXVI 26310, 26311. It is not certain how he knew that all the men left their wages with their wives. It would be interesting to learn how widespread a practice that was. See also W.R. Cockcroft, 'The Liverpool Police Force 1836–1902' in S.P. Bell (ed.), *Victorian Lancashire* (1974) p. 159. The Chief Constable of Dundee gave similar evidence to Capt. Nott Bower. PP. 1898 XXXVII 44343.

8   *Athletic News* 8 February 1909.

9   *The Lantern* 22 November 1889. See also *Athletic News* 23 January 1893, *Manchester Guardian* 23 December 1896.

10   For temperance assaults see, for example, the article by the Rev. W.W. Beveridge condemning the close connections which, he alleged, the trade had with Scottish clubs and the Scottish F.A. in the *Temperance Record* 15 June 1899. He subsequently made the same points in an essay on Scottish football in N.L. Jackson (1900) op.cit. p. 241.

11   *C.B. Fry's Magazine*, vol. V, no. 27, June 1906 pp. 196–8.

12   *Athletic News* 18 January 1892.

13   *Athletic News* 19 June 1899.

14   *Athletic News* 11 January 1892. *Birmingham Daily Mail* 30 January 1893, *Birmingham Daily Gazette* 25 February 1893. One of the Villa committee agreed that police had been called to the house of one of the players at 3 a.m. on a Saturday morning before an away match with Notts. County. But he pointed out that Villa had won that one 5–4. And, of course, not all the incidents made the newspapers. Aston Villa supporters might have been a little put out if they had been told that several players were drunk on the evening of 26 December 1903 in the hotel at Droitwich where they were underoging special training. On the other hand, the club won two matches in the following week and the directors felt a caution and a reprimand sufficient. Three more players were severely cautioned for a similar offence in the following November. Aston Villa F.C. Directors' Meetings Minutes 31 December 1903, 7 January, 24 November 1904.

15   *Blackburn Times* 6 June 1896. The separation order was granted, the player being ordered to pay 12/6 per week maintenance.

16   *Athletic News* 10 April 1899.

17   A.E. Dingle, 'Drink and Working-Class Living Standards in Britain 1870–1914', *Economic History Review* 2nd series vol. XXV no. 4 November 1972 pp. 609, 612. Working men probably spent a larger proportion of

their income on drink than other classes so that the figures are slightly lower than they should be.

18   On the subject in general see, for example, J. Halliday and P. Fuller (eds) *The Psychology of Gambling* (1974); C. L'Estrange Ewen, *Lotteries and Sweepstakes* (1932).

19   *Sheffield Daily Telegraph* 31 March 1873.

20   Sir F. Wall, op.cit. p. 171. The Royal Engineers were 7–4 favourites but they lost.

21   *Manchester Guardian* 26 November 1877.

22   *Athletic News* 1 December 1877.

23   *Darwen News* 9 March 1878.

24   *Sheffield Independent* 17 November 1891. A rare enough event no doubt.

25   *Athletic News* 30 May 1892. Asked by a Sheffield representative how he could tell whether it was Sheffielders or the visitors who were doing the betting he replied, 'do you think it's possible to mistake the voice of a man who comes from Sheffield?' Eventually it was agreed that prohibition ought to apply to players and officials betting on those matches in which they were engaged.

26   There was an energetic anti-gambling magistrate in the town during the 1880s and 1890s named Edwin Richmond who was associated with an organisation called the Social Questions League. He persuaded the city council to pass a resolution instructing the chief librarian to blot out all betting news (presumably mostly in connection with horse racing) contained in those newspapers taken by Sheffield Free Libraries. For just over a year he ran a small newspaper called *The Hammer*.

27   *Athletic News* 21 June 1882.

28   *Birmingham Daily Gazette* 4 April 1887.

29   A Manchester bookmaker offered £25 for giving the correct half time and final scores in the Cup Final of 1890, *Athletic News* 17 March 1890. The first issue of *Sporting Luck*, 'the best racing tips in England,' was published that week and it also offered £25 for giving the Cup Final score. I doubt if many people got it right: it was Blackburn Rovers 6 Sheffield Wednesday 1. *Sporting Luck* 21 March 1890.

30   *Blackburn Weekly Standard and Express* 2 March 1895.

31   *Athletic News* 31 July 1899.

32   C.E.B. Russell (1913 edn) op.cit. p. 156.

33   *Football Field* 20 November 1886. *The Lantern* 6 September 1889, 3 January 1890. *Football* 8 October 1895.

34   *Athletic News* 13 January, 14 April 1890, 2 November 1891. The paper also ran a competition which asked entrants to name those four clubs which would fill the places created by the proposed extension of the Football League. Over 9000 entries were received. *Athletic News* 21 April, 5 May 1890. A few months earlier, Northwich Victoria, doubtless in an attempt to stimulate interest in the competition, said they would give a £5 note to 'the person naming the finalists, result and goals scored' by each team in the Cheshire Cup Final. *Athletic News* 18 February 1889. For the evolving *Athletic News* competition see also issues dated 29 August 1892, 20 January, 31 August, 21 September 1896, 2, 23 January 1899. By this last date the prize for twelve correct results was £400 with £300 for the next best effort.

35   *Athletic News* 23 December 1889.

36   A.J. Robertson, 'Football Betting' in *Transactions of the Liverpool Economic*

and Statistical Society 1906–7, p. 74. Much of what follows is based on material from this paper which concentrated on a detailed study of Liverpool and district.

37   See *Manchester Guardian* 23 January; 2, 8 March; 1 May; 5 June; 7 November; 12 December 1901. See Appendix I for the kind of coupon betting being offered by specialist newspapers.

38   Some newspapers attempted to get round this in ingenious ways. One method was to emphasise the element of skill involved in the competition. One newspaper insisted that entrants accompanied their selections by a football essay. Robertson quotes the following example (on p. 75).

G. Oldham of Manchester Street, Long Eaton, Nottingham named four of the winning and drawing clubs, and also gave the correct scores in three matches. His essay was as follows: 'West Bromwich Albion should beat Derby County, as I consider their backs much superior.' This estimate of the play proved accurate and to Mr. Oldham has been awarded the prize of £10.

We shall return to the question of skill below.

39   In the autumn of 1909 Aston Villa prosecuted three men who were distributing coupons outside Villa Park. They were employed by a turf accountant with an address in Flushing. One man was fined £1 plus costs or fourteen days and two others 5/- plus costs or seven days. To the bookmaker this must have seemed cheap at half the price. *Athletic News* 4 October 1909. See also *Half Time* 11 December 1907 for sellers at Leicester.

40   Robertson thought that 1904 was the first year in which it appeared and Birkenhead the place although this seems doubtful. The 1902 House of Lords Select Committee on Betting had heard from the interim Chief Constable of Glasgow that it had been begun there by a Mr McCreedie in 1899. According to an article in the *Edinburgh Evening News and Despatch* 28 February 1965 and quoted by R. Miller 'Gambling and the British Working Class 1870–1914' unpublished thesis University of Edinburgh M.A. 1974, p. 50, a Mr Robert Spittal, an apprentice cooper, began a pool there in 1902 when he was only 20. Clients had to forecast the scores in six Scottish football matches. The coupons were printed in his own house and he sold them for 2d each. They had to be returned by Wednesday. The prize was two guineas at first but as business boomed a weekly prize of £70 was offered. 5,600 coupons, by now threepence, had to be sold to break even. He employed assistants to go round other breweries and maintained the business part-time until 1923.

41   Most of what follows is based on Robertson, especially pp. 81–5.

42   See particularly p. 85. He also believed that the firms in question were doing a large postal business with London. On the geographical spread of the trade the secretary of the York branch of the Anti-Gambling League wrote to Robertson saying that he had been informed 'by a competent authority in Sunderland that 30,000 coupons were issued in the shipyards every week, and £2500 in connection with them changed hands weekly. I know a bookmaker in Edinburgh, and not in a very large way either, who stated 'that he had an average of 1,000 bets a week on football, and he stated it was on the increase with all bookmakers'. Similarly the annual report of the Chief Constable of Leeds in 1906 described the existence of

an organised system of gambling in many of the factories and workshops of the city, conducted in the form of betting on the results of football matches. In some cases the principles in this business are employees in the works. In other cases employees act only as agents for betting men outside the premises. There is reason to believe that this practice has obtained enormous proportions.

43   Figure 6 : 1 is reproduced from Robertson, op.cit. p. 78. The names in the left hand column of each bookmaker's list refer to the codename of the agent. Most adopted this method of identification. Other names included Downhearted, Arthur Grim, Spion Kop, Weather, Goal and Try Again. Ibid. p. 81. Robertson also claimed the odds were hardly generous.

44   Though form guides were being published in the 1890s. See for example 'Invaluable to Couponites' (1899) and the *Weekly Football Star* which began in Birmingham in 1894.

45   W.J. Duckworth, *The Incomparable Football Forecasting System* (1914). Duckworth hailed from Padiham in Lancashire. For one of the more absurd efforts see 'The Excelsior System' undated leaflet probably about 1910 set out in Appendix II, and for other experts see Robertson, op.cit. p. 76.

46   The football authorities were worried least betting men should persuade players to try to fix matches. For one attempt to bribe a team via an international player which ended in farcical disaster for the tempter see *Birmingham Gazette* 12 December 1913, 17, 18 February 1914. See also J.W. Horsley, *How Criminals are Made and Prevented* (1913). Canon Horsley was especially worried about football coupon betting among soldiers and sailors (p. 171).

47   See, for example, those by the League's National Secretary, John Hawke, and J. Ramsay MacDonald.

48   B.S. Rowntree (ed.) op.cit. p. 163.

49   P.P. 343 X 1914 and also Report and Proceedings 57 VIII 1920. The Anti-Gambling League was directly opposed by the National Sporting League whose aim was primarily to resist anti-gambling legislation. One Liverpool football coupon in 1905 had a footnote to the effect that 'Gentlemen whose names are on the Parliamentary or Municipal Voting Registers are requested to sign the appended form for the purpose of having their names placed on the register of the National Sporting League for Electioneering purposes.' A.J. Robertson, op.cit. p. 86.

50   See John Hilton (ed.), *Why I go in for the Pools* (1936) especially pp. 21–64. By 1951 49.5 per cent of all households in England and 53.3 per cent of all working class households did the pools. B.S. Rowntree and G.R. Lavers, *English Life and Leisure : A social study* (1951) p. 136. Of course football sweeps on the scores of local matches were probably common, especially in workplaces, by the 1890s. In order to win you had to draw the team who scored most goals in a Saturday match. Later it would be first to reach 21. *Athletic News* 27 January 1908. A.J. Robertson, op.cit. p. 73.

51   What worried Canon Horsley was that lads could be persuaded that they knew nothing about horse racing 'but one cannot persuade them that they are equally ignorant concerning football for they are not'. J.W. Horsley, op.cit. p. 175.

52   A.J. Lee, *The Origins of the Popular Press 1855–1914* (1976) p. 71. By the late nineteenth century the 'fancy' had been replaced by a certain kind of Tory who, like John Corlett, the proprietor of the *Sporting Times*, probably

'abominated Mr. Gladstone, revered Lord Beaconsfield ... detested Cobden and Free Trade ... was a believer in the House of Lords, and distrusted John Burns: read the lessons in the Church of Sutton Valence each Sunday, and looked upon the Derby as a semi-sacred institution'. J.B. Booth, *Sporting Times* (1938) pp. 19–20.

53   See Deacon's *Newspaper Handbook* for that year. It became a daily in 1883 and took over *Bell's Life* in 1886. According to one writer the *Sporting Life* was much in demand as a sports promoter, fixing up many of the great contests in boxing, billiards and coursing, holding the stakes and appointing referees. See H. Simonis, *The Street of Luck* (1917), pp. 121–3.

54   For the *Sporting Times* see J.B. Booth, *Old Pink 'Un Days* (1924) and his *Sporting Times* (1938). The paper was described in 1865 as 'A Chronicle of Racing, Literature, Art and the Drama' and cost 2d.

55   John Corlett was allegedly the first man to call a certain kind of lady a tart. J.B. Booth (1924) op.cit. p. 20.

56   See *Goal:* 'The Chronicle of Football' especially issues of 22 November 1873 and 25 April 1874.

57   Its owner, Edward Hulton, could afford to do this, of course, as he had the *Sporting Chronicle* in his stable for that purpose. Hulton had been born in Manchester in 1838 and was later apprenticed to a printer. Eventually he worked as a compositor on the *Manchester Guardian*. He was keen on horse racing himself and opened a small book on the side. He then obtained the financial assistance of a Manchester cotton merchant, E.O. Bleackley and with a capital of between £100 and £500 bought a little printing plant in a cellar in Spear Street, Manchester. On it he produced his own racing paper early in 1871, edited by himself under the soubriquet. 'Kettledrum'. At first it was printed on one side only of a single sheet and circulated, at 1d, to subscribers in public houses and sporting clubs. Known locally as the 'Tissue' it was actually called the *Prophetic Bell*. It was enlarged and renamed the *Manchester Sporting Chronicle and Prophetic Bell* in February 1873 and two months later became simply the *Sporting Chronicle*. It was out of the profits made by this paper that the *Athletic News* was born. Hulton later founded the *Sunday Chronicle* (1885) and when his son sold the business to Allied Newspapers Ltd, in 1923 it brought in £6,000,000. See the obituary of Hulton in *Manchester City News* 2 April 1904, *Financial Times* 23 February 1905, *Banyan* (The Official Organ of the National Bookmakers' Protection Association) vol. 16 no. 4, October 1953, pp. 57–60. *Sporting Mirror* vol. II, August 1881-January 1882, pp. 201–2.

58   *Sporting Chronicle*, 17 August 1875.

59   This was still probably an important task in the mid-1870s although it was quickly taken over by more specifically local newspapers. For example, the *Birmingham Daily Gazette* was publishing teams for the afternoon in local leagues in their Saturday morning edition by the 1890s.

60   *Athletic News* 23 September 1876.

61   *Athletic News* 8 October 1879.

62   See *Athletic News* 14 January, 11 August, 1 September 1880.

63   This close, 'inside', connection with the game was to be continued, particularly by the editorship of J.J. Bentley, the President of the Football League. *Athletic News* 22 July 1895. F. Boase, *Modern English Biography* vol. III (1907; 1965 edn) p. 838.

64   See his *Wickets and Goals* (1926) op.cit. pp. 135, 137, 165.

65 *Athletic News* 29 December 1890.
66 *Athletic News* 12 December 1883. F.H. Spencer when a pupil teacher in Swindon in the late 1880s said that he read the *Athletic News*. F.H. Spencer (1938) op.cit. p. 85.
67 *Athletic News* 28 August 1893. Mitchell's *Press Guide* (1888) p. 215 (1891) p. 248.
68 *Athletic News* 2 November 1896. It increased its size from eight pages to twelve at this time but was back to eight pages for the 1898–9 season.
69 See his obituary notice by James Catton in *Athletic News* 3 September 1918.
70 In the early 1880s some newspapers would write the match results on sheets of paper and display them in the office windows. See W. Pickford, *A Few Recollections of Sport* (n.d.) p. 13. Pickford sometimes had the task of compiling them for the *Bolton Evening News*.
71 *Birmingham Weekly News* 23 September 1882. This paper was incorporated with *Saturday Night* in September 1882 although its own beginnings earlier in that year had been very different. It had started life as a penny weekly aimed at 'the intelligent artisans and working men of Birmingham' supporting 'advanced Liberalism' and in particular, the extension of the franchise and the rights of the working classes 'to a special representative in the House of Commons'. *Birmingham Weekly News* 13 May 1882.
72 *Saturday Night* 7 October 1882.
73 *Saturday Night* 27 January, 10 February 1883.
74 D.D. Molyneux, op.cit. p. 105. When Aston Villa won the F.A. Cup in 1887 the paper sold a record 24,000 copies and in 1892, when the Villa were beaten finalists, over 33,000 copies.
75 *Blackburn Times* 29 September 1883. The author has not been able to trace any copies of the Blackburn paper nor has he seen any issues of the *Football Field* before 1886. The regular format of the *Football Field* seems to have involved commenting critically on the matches played on the previous Saturday, with much local context and colour, while devoting the middle two pages to the day's results and reports. It was a very 'chatty' paper, studded with brief paragraphs of the 'tit-bits' type. The *Blackburn Standard* had published a special Saturday afternoon edition on 25 March 1882 at 4.45 p.m. as a single sheet, 16″ × 8″, reporting the Cup Final defeat of the Rovers.
76 *Sheffield Independent* 23 September 1886.
77 *Blackburn Standard* 21 September 1889.
78 For the telegraph see J.L. Kieve, *The Electric Telegraph* (Newton Abbot, 1973). See also A.J. Lee, op.cit. pp. 54–63.

It is probable that never in the history of evening football papers has the result of a match played at a considerable distance been published so quickly as was that of the Wolverhampton Wanderers *v* Wednesday match in the *Sheffield Evening Telegraph* on Saturday. Through the kindness of the manager of the National Telephone Company arrangements were made by which the result of the match was sent by telephone from Wolverhampton. The match finished at six minutes to five, and at two minutes to the hour the result was received in the office. At five o'clock the machines were running, and a minute or two later the papers were being eagerly bought up in the street.

Sheffield Daily Telegraph 4 March 1889. As late as 1884 carrier pigeons were used to bring the result of Aston Villa's home matches to a tobacconist's shop in the Birmingham city centre. *Saturday Night* 15 November 1884.

79   A. Gibson and W. Pickford, vol. II op.cit. pp. 25–8. See also G.G. Armstrong, *Memories* (1944) p. 59. Armstrong worked on the *North Eastern Gazette* in Middlesbrough in the 1890s. 'Saturday was the busiest afternoon, due to sports news, and a reporter used to come in and take copy over the telephone. We had to make tables of results as we went along—half-time scores first, and full-time scores afterwards.'

80   *Blackburn Standard* 2 October 1880.

81   *Darwen News* 15 January 1881.

82   D.D. Molyneux, op.cit. p. 110.

83   The *Athletic News* 16 February 1886 contained an advertisement which pointed out to readers that the *Sunday Chronicle* had contained reports of 148 matches in its last Sunday edition although at the height of the 1885–6 season, on 1 and 22 November respectively, it gave the results and brief reports of only 74 and 78 matches, still twice as many as in *Reynold's Newspaper* and *Lloyds' Weekly Newspaper* as we see below. The Sunday *Referee*, another penny paper, was also very sport conscious and was reporting the more important fixtures as early as 1877. See for example, issue of 2 December 1877.

84   *Weekly Despatch* 21 January, 4 March 1883.

85   See for example its report of London *v* Sheffield, 3 January 1876 and the considerable space it gave to the England-Scotland match of that season. *Manchester Guardian* 6 March 1876.

86   *Manchester Guardian* 10 September 1880, January 28, 4, 11 March 1889. By 1913 the paper was reporting football quite extensively with a Friday preview and Monday results and reports. Rugby Union, however, received even more space. See, for example, *Manchester Guardian* 3, 6, 10, 13, 17, 20, 24, 27 January 1913.

87   Nor did it employ a specialist football correspondent. When it did turn its attention to football, knowledge of European history was useful. Discussing professionals in general and those of Newcastle United in particular, the writer compared them in 1911 'with the regiment of German condottiere who were in the pay of the Polish Commonwealth during the long struggle with the Cossacks of the Ukraine and were caught and surrounded by a vastly superior force led by Honelnetzi the Cossack hutman'. They were given the choice between annihilation or transference (at an increased rate of pay) to Honelnetzi's army; and they chose death, rather than break their agreement with Poland, which had six months more to run. All this to show that though they be mercenaries, professionals would play just as hard for any team. *The Times* 22 April 1911.

88   See V.S. Berridge, 'Popular Journalism and Working-Class Attitudes 1854–86: A Study of *Reynold's Newspaper, Lloyds' Weekly Newspaper* and the *Weekly Times*,' 2 vols. unpublished thesis University of London Ph.D. 1976, esp. vol. I, pp. 141–52.

89   *Reynold's* sports coverage was not dominated by football to the same extent. It only began to publish a separate football column in the 1890s.

90   Of course, the relationship between the game and the press had its ups and downs. Newton Heath F.C. brought a libel action against the *Birmingham Daily Gazette* in 1894 because one of the paper's reporters had accused

them of brutality in a match against West Bromwich Albion. He had concluded his match report by nothing that 'next week Newton Heath have
to meet Burnley, and if they both play in their ordinary style it will perhaps
create an extra run of business for the undertakers'. For an hilarious account
of the hearing see *Manchester Guardian* 2 March 1894. The jury found for
the plaintiffs with one farthing's damages. Three Celtic players refused
to take the field against Hibernians in December 1896 unless reporters
who had severely criticised their play of the week before were removed
from the ground. The club refused and suspended the players. *Manchester
Guardian* 4 December 1896.

91   As the editor of the *Football Chat* somewhat complacently assured his
readers in 1900 'no space will be found for long wearying reports of uninteresting events. The readers who ask for longer reports of this, that, and
the other must please look to a morning or evening newspaper'. *Football
Chat* 10 March 1900.

SKILI

£100 0 0

Prize will be given to the Competitor or divided amo▮

Failing which the £100 will be equally divided amo▮

*SHEET No. .—COMPETITION FOR MATCHES PLAYED SATURDAY, SEPTEMBER 2, 1899.

N.B.—Each of the Numbers given under this Line represents One Coupon.

SELECTED MATCHES.		1	2	3	4	5	6	7	8	9	10	11	12	13	14	15	16	17	18	19	20	21	22	23	24
1	*versus*																								
2																									
1	*versus*																								
2																									
1	*versus*																								
2																									
1	*versus*																								
2																									
1	*versus*																								
2																									
1	*versus*																								
2																									
1	*versus*																								
2																									
1	*versus*																								
2																									
1	*versus*																								
2																									
1	*versus*																								
2																									
1	*versus*																								
2																									
1	*versus*																								
2																									

HERE SELECT YOUR MATCHES

FREE VOTES		No. OF VOTES	NAME	CLUB	ADDRESS
	PLAYER				
	TRAINER				
	GROUNDSMAN				

WRITE PLAINLY AND WITH INK

(If this be not filled up the Prize Money will not be paid)

I send in the above series of Coupons as a Competitor for the Prize ｜advertised herein, and subject to any and all conditions set forth in the Rules｜and Regulations

Name _____

Address _____

I enclose stamps value _____

"   Postal Orders value _____ numbered _____

RULES AND REGULATIONS

1.—Above will be found a series of 24 Coupons and a column for the matches selected by the Competitor.

2.—ELIGIBLE CLUBS.—Competitors may select any 12 matches played on Saturday, September 2nd, 1899, in which any Club belonging to any of the undermentioned Leagues is engaged : English League (1st and 2nd Divisions), Scottish League (1st and 2nd Divisions), Irish League, Lancashire League, Midland League, Southern League (1st and 2nd Divisions), and both sections Northern Union (Rugby) Senior Competition. Both teams in a match need not be members of one of these Leagues but *one* Team must be.

3.—Select any 12 matches from the Eligible Teams and write their names distinctly in *ink* opposite the figures 1 and 2 in the column marked "Selected Matches". Each Club will then be numbered 1 or 2. All the Competitor has to do is to repeat the number of the Club he selects to win in space provided; if a draw is intended put X. N.B.—The Coupons must not be cut. Send in this sheet, Page 2, entire, to The Manager, 'Football Competitions," Skill Limited, 174 Fleet Street, London, E.C.

4.—Send Page 2 complete, retain Page 3 filled in duplicate only.

*Please number your Sheets consecutively.

OMPETITION

e Competitors who on <u>One Coupon</u> shall give <u>12 Correct Results.</u>

20 Competitors who send in the greatest number of Coupons.

£100 0 0

DUPLICATE SHEET No.

.—COMPETITION FOR MATCHES PLAYED SATURDAY, SEPTEMBER 2, 1899.

N.B.—Each of the Numbers given under this Line represents One Coupon.

SELECTED MATCHES.		1	2	3	4	5	6	7	8	9	10	11	12	13	14	15	16	17	18	19	20	21	22	23	24
1	versus																								
2																									
1	versus																								
2																									
1	versus																								
2																									
1	versus																								
2																									
1	versus																								
2																									
1	versus																								
2																									
1	versus																								
2																									
1	versus																								
2																									
1	versus																								
2																									
1	versus																								
2																									
1	versus																								
2																									
1	versus																								
2																									

		No. OF VOTES	NAME	CLUB	ADDRESS
REE OTES	PLAYER				
	TRAINER				
	GROUNDSMAN				

5.—Enclose one penny stamp for every Coupon used, and where more than 12 Coupons are sent Postal Orders must be used and the full name and address of sender must be written on back. The exact sum must in all cases be sent, as the Proprietors will not notify deficiencies or return excesses. No alterations, scratchings or erasures are permitted. Coupons received without full name and address are disqualified and remittance is forfeited.

6.—Claims for Prize must be made in writing so as to reach us by midday on Tuesday following the dates that the matches are fixed to be played, and the number of sheet and winning coupon number therein must be plainly stated.

7.—In the event of all the matches selected not being played on dates given, the Proprietors reserve to themselves the right to award or retain the whole or any part of any prize and to deal with all subscriptions received in a manner they deem most equitable.

8.—Coupons must reach the Office by latest nine a.m. Thursday after the date of this issue. If the envelope bears Wednesday's post mark date it will be received up till Thursday five p.m. If although bearing the Wednesday's post-mark the letter is not delivered in due course of post, but is delayed, no matter from what cause, it will not be examined.

9.—Persons filling up the first eight numbered Coupons must fill in one free vote. Also fill in one free vote for every additional eight Coupons filled. Thus, a person filling up the sheet and remitting to us Postal Note for 2s. must fill in three votes, which may be given all to one man or one to each of the three different men, whoever his favourite may be, the result being that, according to the number of votes received by either the Groundsman, the Trainer, or the Player, they will each receive a Cash Bonus from us, and thus the Competitor can materially help his friends.

10.—Any number of these sheets may be filled in, provided the requisite amount of money is sent with them, and the rules and regulations observed.

11.—The Proprietors will publish a list of the winning Competitors in No. 3 of "FOOTBALL COMPETITIONS," September 7th, 1899. "FOOTBALL COMPETITIONS" No. 2 will be published on Thursday, August 31st.

12.—A claim for a Scrutiny must be received at the office not later than Monday following publication of winning Competitors, by registered letter, and must contain a fee of 21s., accompanied by Page 3, which should be the exact copy of the Competition. Should the complaint be considered frivolous, the guinea will be forfeited. Letters demanding a Scrutiny must be addressed to "The Manager 'FOOTBALL COMPETITIONS,' " and the word Scrutiny must be written in the corner of the envelope. The Proprietors will send in writing to the Competitor the result of the Scrutiny.

13.—Payment of Prizes will be made by Post by Cheque from the Head Office of the Proprietors of the paper "SKILL LIMITED" at the Competitor's risk, but the Proprietors claim the right in their discretion to ask for the personal appearance of a Competitor before making a payment.

14.—In the event of no Scrutiny being demanded in accordance with Rule 12, Cheques in payment of Prize or Prizes won will be posted according to Rule 13 on Tuesday following publication of winners' names.

any Football Ground where gate-money is charged.

ootball Competitions", 174 Fleet Street, London, E.C., and a supply will be forwarded to you post free.

APPENDIX II
The "Excelsior" System

'You select a Professional Football Team, and back it to draw every week, the fixed odds for a Draw being 3 to 1 against, a glance at the League Tables at the end of a Season will show that every team averages a Draw about every fourth or fifth game, now what you have to do is to back it two weeks with an even stake, then double it on the third, like the following, we will suppose you are backing Portsmouth, the first week you put on 2/6 or what you can afford.

```
                  2/6 to Draw  Portsmouth loses
Second Week   —   „    —       —      „    —
Third Week    5/– to Draw  —          „    —
Fourth Week   —   „    —     Portsmouth Draws at 3 to 1
                             You get back        £1 – 0 – 0
                             Investments substracted 15 – 0
                                                   ————
                             Winning Balance       5 – 0
```

Undated leaflet c. 1910.

CHAPTER SEVEN
THE GAME

ANY book about association football which does not have at least a short chapter on the game itself is open to the criticism that it is Hamlet without the Prince. What did spectators see when they went to matches? How did the players play? How did these matters change over the four decades or so after 1870? Inevitably, any such chapter must be largely concerned with the professional elite of clubs and players. Some notice must be taken of amateur players. At least into the early 1900s the best amateur players, notably those brought together in the Corinthians football club, regularly competed with the cream of the professionals and it would be a distortion if no account at all was taken of them. But in general it was the professionals who gave the most skilful performances of the game and attracted both the largest crowds and the most detailed critical comment. It was their demonstration of the arts and crafts of the game which was most likely to produce changes in the laws governing the way in which it was conducted.

A man attending the first F.A. Cup Final on the Oval cricket ground in London in March 1872 between the Wanderers and the Royal Engineers would probably have been a gentleman. Certainly the twenty-two players and the officials were. He would have seen a field with flags marking the boundaries and a tape eight feet above the ground stretching between two flimsy looking goalposts twenty-four feet apart. There were no other markings on the pitch. Most of the players probably wore long trousers and fancy caps in addition to their team shirts and rather formidable looking boots. The game probably started late.

As to the play itself, dribbling with the ball by individuals past opponents was its central feature. Individual players hung on to the ball as long as they could and other members of their team backed them up in the hope of gaining possession when the man on the ball lost it. 'Rushes' down the field by one side or the other probably provided some of the game's more exciting moments. Passing, or combination, was not yet in vogue although by the following year the Royal Engineers were noted for it. They did not use the new method in this game, however, or if they did, it did not help them much because they lost 1–0.[1] Most players were attackers and both sides played with a goalkeeper, two backs, one half-back and seven forwards. The long kicking of the backs, selected for their strength and solidity rather than their ball skill or speed, would also have been prominent, as would the heavy shoulder charging by all players. There was little heading. The goalkeepers, when called upon, did a lot of punching out and kicking rather than catching. The main reason for that was that they could be charged over even when not in possession of the ball. Indeed an unsubtle but fiendishly effective tactic was for one attacker to charge the goalkeeper to the ground while another tried to steer the ball between the posts. Many goals were scored from 'scrimmages' following such incidents or from individual efforts like the one which resulted in Lord Kinnaird scoring for the Wanderers in their 2–1 Cup Final victory over Oxford University in 1873. *Bell's Life* described how

Kinnaird got the ball to himself at the lower side of the play and brought it toward the Oxford goal in such splendid style that, despite the strenuous exertions of some of the fastest of the Oxonians to overhaul him, he eluded their efforts and the goalkeeper's (who should have charged him instead of remaining at home) also.[2]

When the ball went out of play on either side of the pitch it was thrown in one-handed and at right angles to the playing area, by whichever player from either side reached it first. Free kicks for handling the ball or for foul play were very few as were appeals by the players to the two umpires and referee although that was the accepted method of drawing the attention of those officials to a particular incident.[3] The spectacle was vigorous and robust in the main although some of the dribblers were very good.

By the middle of the 1880s, the passing game had taken over. Most sides were now trying to make progress towards goal by passing the ball among themselves, sideways and forwards. This new 'combination' was a particular feature of the play of half-backs and forward players. The Scots—particularly in the form of the Queen's Park Club—the Sheffield Club and the Royal Engineers appear to have pioneered the passing game in the 1870s although precision in such matters is clearly impossible. Passing seems to have been first introduced into Lancashire by visiting Scots teams in the late 1870s.[4] When Queen's Park visited Aston Villa in 1881 they worked as one man

every player being in his place at the right moment. The backs and half-backs played splendidly. . . . The forwards are splendid lot, their dribbling being close and good and the passing wonderfully accurate, while no trace of selfishness was visible in any one of them.[5]

When Blackburn Rovers visited Sunderland for the first time in November 1880,

it seemed quite clear to critical spectators that not only were well learned rules observed by those who possessed themselves of the ball, but also by the other players, who appeared to keep certain positions in relation to those in possession. The result of this was that a pass rarely failed, and the player who passed never risked losing the ball by having to look for another to whom to send it. Their long passing straight from wing to wing was greatly admired.[6]

By 1885 Preston North End was admired for the 'machine like method in working the ball along the ground' whereas their opponents from Bolton did 'their work in rushes'.[7]

Nor was it merely short distance passing. The long crossfield pass and the thrust down the wing before crossing the ball into the goal mouth had also been widely taken up by the middle years of the 1880s.[8] The backs were still long kickers standing on little ceremony. As a reporter at the Aston Villa—Queen's Park game in 1881 noticed, 'for the next few minutes, some good kicking between the back division of either side was witnessed'.[9] The ferocious charging of the early period had probably diminished somewhat although one claim that charging had practically been abolished in the north seems rather premature.[10] The goalkeeper remained vulnerable to assault and battery. When Aston Villa defeated the Corinthians 4–1 in 1886, the second Villa goal was described in the following way by a local paper. 'The ball was soon transferred to Corinthian quarters, a fine tussle ending by Archie (Hunter) sending a grand one through the posts, while Allen grassed the goalkeeper in a most efficient, unceremonious manner.'[11] The goalkeeper could now use his hands to play the ball anywhere on the field and perhaps that was some consolation. There was more heading in the game. Dribbling had not, of course, disappeared; it was now merely an important characteristic of the association game rather than its basic method.

With the emergence of combination, a new playing formation was born. As we saw earlier when looking at the game in the 1870s, most players were forwards. In the late 1870s some teams had begun to strengthen their defence and midfield by withdrawing two forward players into a literally 'half-back' position. It is impossible again to be certain about which clubs were the innovators. Turton may have been one of the first. By the early 1880s Queen's Park (Glasgow) and Old Westminsters were experimenting with three half-backs and they were soon joined by many other leading elevens. The impact of the new formation can be gauged by the sour comment of the English reporter who complained, after his side had lost to Scotland in 1884, that the Scots had played three half-backs which had 'checked all dribbling and scientific play'.[12] In effect it meant the introduction of the centre half-back, who played between the two wing half-backs and had a part-defensive, part-attacking role. The new style of play appears to have been taken up quickly by most leading sides, presumably because it worked. In practice the change involved the defending side, when close to their own goal, setting their wing half-backs to mark the opposition's wing forwards with the full backs attending to the inside forwards. As play moved upfield, the full-backs would watch the wingers while the half-backs kept in touch with the opposing inside men. The Cup Final of 1884 was probably the last major fixture in which both teams played two half-backs and six forwards. The arrival of the third half-back was the last important change in the structure of the team until the 1930s when the centre-half was withdrawn to play between the two full-backs so becoming literally a 'third back'.[13]

There had been few changes in the laws of the game by the mid-1880s but the stiffening of competition, especially in the growing number of cup matches, may have led to more appealing from the players to the umpires over foul play, offside and whether the ball had actually passed between the posts.[14] This did more than any other single factor to undermine the idea that control of the game by two umpires, one appointed by each side, with a referee to decide on knotty points, was sufficient. By the middle of this decade the clear tendency was for the neutral referee to take more power. Even in 1879, those two local rivals, Blackburn Rovers and Darwen, between whom not much love was lost, agreed to play without umpires, appointing a neutral referee instead. 'The result was one of the most friendly games Rovers and Darwen have ever played.'[15] Incidents like the one which took place during a league match between Sunderland and Blackburn Rovers in November 1890 only served to underline the need for change. During the game the Sunderland players claimed a corner kick.

The officials were discussing the claim, *play meanwhile proceeding*, [my italics] when one of the Rovers kicked the ball against the Blackburn Umpire (with such force as to knock him down) and it rebounded through the kicker's goal. After some discussion and much heated argument, the referee properly allowed the goal to Sunderland.[16]

The growth in competitive play, both cup and league, made the referee as objective arbiter, divorced from direct connection with the competing clubs, essential.

By the mid-1880s, then, association football had more or less reached its twentieth-century form. Matches generally kicked off at the time previously announced, teams rarely failed to turn up or field their full strength. It is true that the London Cup Final of 1887 had to be postponed even though both teams, the Casuals and Old Westminsters were stripped and ready for action. There was no ball and a wait of one and a half hours, and presumably an exhaustive search of the Sydenham district, failed to produce one.[17] But that could be put down to southern amateur eccentricity. The professionals from Birmingham and points north were better prepared.

If our imaginary spectator, who saw the Cup Final of 1872, went to one of the first league matches of the season in September 1902 he might well have remarked on the changes which had taken place over the three decades. The neutral referee as sole judge of the proceedings had been established since 1891. The umpires were now linesmen largely concentrating on offside and indicating to the referee when the ball was out of play and to which side the throw-in should be given. The referee had been giving free kicks for foul play without appeal since 1889–90. Perhaps the most significant change after the emergence of the referee as the crucial controller of events on the field was the institution of the penalty kick. This was a free kick at goal from a spot twelve yards away with only the goalkeeper of the opposing side between the kicker and the goal. It was awarded for certain acts of deliberate foul play committed by defenders in an area twelve yards from the goal line and stretching from one side of the field to the other.[18] Penalty area markings took their present form in season 1902–3.

Goalkeepers now received some protection from physical attack: from 1893–4 they could only be charged when playing the ball or obstructing an opponent. Their privilege of using their hands was restricted to the penalty area in 1912. The following year the distance which opponents had to be from the ball at a free-kick was increased from six yards to ten.[19] Our watcher would no doubt have noticed the goal nets, first used in 1891, and the neater dress of the players with shinpads no longer outside the stockings.[20] Their sartorial improvements included shorter shorts, short enough, indeed, to offend some Football Association proprieties. At the annual meeting in 1904 a new rule was passed setting out that knickerbockers worn by players should be long enough to cover the knees.

This rule, though introduced for excellent reasons, it being the practice of many players to wear extremely abbreviated 'pants' to the discredit of the game, went a little too far, and though several clubs were fined for not seeing it enforced, it was in the next year relaxed so that knickerbockers need only 'reach to' the knees.[21]

What was the game itself like to watch by 1902? How had it changed from the mid-1880s? It is very difficult to be precise about these questions. It was almost certainly faster in 1902 with the professionals of the leading clubs benefiting from full-time training. However, although important, speed does not seem to have been as important before 1914 as it was to become later in the twentieth century. Quick, firm tackling and the heavy shoulder charge were still prominent. Professionals in particular had become especially good at heading with continued practice improving both timing and accuracy. Goals were scored most often from close range after a wing forward had outflanked the defence and centred the ball to a colleague, or following a sharp through pass by a half-back or inside forward, leaving perhaps the centre-forward with a clear run in on goal. Although passing was by now the foundation of the game, the individual dribbler remained a common and popular feature, especially among wing and inside forwards. The centre-half was perhaps the key member of the team. As Gibson and Pickford note in 1906 'a centre-half of the best type has a special license to roam, to move out of his place to follow where danger threatens, whether it be defending in his own goalmouth or pressing home the attack in the vicinity of his adversaries' goal'. He was a skilled, constructive player and not the relatively undistinguished defender he was to become in the 1930s.[22]

There are hints that not all was well with the game. We noted in chapter four the criticism of the ball-skills of individual players. *The Times* correspondent felt that professional backs and half-backs were all right but the forwards were 'a poor ineffectual lot' who passed too much and missed the influence of the ex-public school dribbler. The game was 'in a groove and utterly unprogressive'.[23] There are also hints that some leading professional clubs could play defensively when it suited them: continually kicking the ball out of play was a favourite if rather crude method of wasting time. Towards the end of the 1896 Cup Final, the Sheffield Wednesday captain and centre-half dropped back to cover the goal and withdrew the inside left to half-back in an attempt to protect a 2–1 lead. It worked.[24] But in general attacking strategies were the order of the day. This was especially the case when teams had that extra injection of confidence which playing at home brought them and apparently brings still. Home crowds also liked the game to be taken to the opposition. But, attacking or defending, combination was king. Of course, some players found great difficulty in giving up the ball to a better placed colleague unless absolutely forced by circumstances but it is doubtful if even many amateurs in 1902 would have replied to the criticism that they were dribbling too much and persistently failing to transfer the ball to unmarked teammates as the Hon. Alfred Lyttleton did to W. Mosforth during the English-Scotland match of 1877, 'I am playing purely for my own pleasure, Sir!'[25]

Which of the leading clubs gave spectators the most pleasure— after their own home town team, of course? Inevitably it was the more successful sides who proved the greatest attractions and who drew the largest crowds when they travelled away from home. It is probably useful to divide the period into two at 1888, the year in which the Football League began its first season. Before the League it was the F.A. Cup competition which offered some indication of who the strongest teams were and until 1882, as we saw in earlier chapters, that competition was dominated by amateur teams from the south of England. Public school old boy teams, notably the Old Carthusians and the Old Etonians together with Oxford University and the Royal Engineers were the elite of a relatively small body of clubs. As we saw in chapter two the most successful club of all was the Wanderers whose players had all attended the leading public schools. They won the F.A. Cup in 1872, 1873, 1876, 1877 and 1878. The club clearly did much to stimulate interest in football in the south but rarely played any matches outside London.

If the south produced the strongest teams of the 1870s the north and midlands took over in the 1880s and two clubs in particular stand out. It is difficult to imagine any follower of the game by 1885 not at some point discussing the merits of Blackburn Rovers and Preston North End. Neither side could be said to have had working-class origins. The Rovers had been founded in 1874 by sons of local businessmen, some of whom had been to school together. But the club rapidly built a reputation for itself in the town and surrounding east Lancashire area and by the end of the 1870s was not averse to persuading good players from other teams to turn out for it. Rovers were among the earliest English teams to recruit Scotsmen and the reward was three successive F.A. Cup victories in 1884, 1885 and 1886.[26] The club had grown from a membership of around 150 in 1879–80 to one of 700 in 1881–2.[27]

The rise of Preston North End was even more rapid. It began life as a cricket club, played a species of rugby football from 1869 and did not change over to association until 1880–1. As late as September 1882 it was beaten 13–2 by Blackburn Rovers and the club's proficiency can be gauged by the fact of other crushing defeats at the feet of Darwen, 14–1 in October 1880 and Blackburn Rovers again, 16–0, in March 1881.[28] The club improved considerably in 1882–3, losing only 7 out of 35 matches, but it was the importation of Scots 'professors' after that which made them the strongest team in the country for the rest of the 1880s. Between the season 1883–4 and February 1889 Preston played 366 matches, won 294 drew 35 and lost only 37, scoring 1502 goals and conceding 385. In 1887–8 the club had a winning streak of 44 consecutive games and were only beaten 7 times out of 69 matches.[29] The club won the first league championship in 1888–9 without losing a match and the F.A. Cup in the same year without conceding a goal. As we saw earlier it was their accurate passing which did most to set them apart from their contemporaries, together with the fact that they had better players, at least half a dozen of whom had learned the game in Scotland. They had been signed up before the legalisation of professionalism by Major William Sudell, a major in the Volunteers, who had been chairman of the club committee since 1874. He was the manager of a Preston cotton mill.[30] North End were known as the 'Invincibles' and attracted large crowds at most grounds which they visited.

After 1888 and most notably in the league championship it was the big city clubs which were increasingly dominant. The F.A. Cup remained a more open competition because of its one match knock-out structure. Although leading teams such as Aston Villa and West Bromwich Albion figured frequently as semi-finalists, finalists, and winners, sixteen different clubs managed to have their names engraved on the three different trophies which were played for as the F.A. Cup between 1893 and 1915.[31]

Winning the Football League title was a different matter. This competition required consistent form and ability over a season of at first 22 matches and later 26, 30, 34 and from 1905, 38 matches. Preston won the first two championships and Everton the next but the 1890s were dominated by two clubs very much as the 1880s had been: Aston Villa and Sunderland. Sunderland were known as the team of all the talents presumably because they appeared to have all the skills and so few weaknesses. Again they were a team dominated by Scotsmen, brought together

by an ex-schoolmaster, Tom Watson, who became one of the
first team managers although his official title was club secretary.
He later built another powerful side at Liverpool. Sunderland
were champions in 1892, 1893 and 1895 and again in 1902 and
1913. Moreover, they were highly placed in several other years.
Aston Villa, with one of the club's first players as secretary and
a committee and later board of directors dominated by F.W.
Rinder, a Birmingham architect, did even better. Villa won the
championship in 1894, 1896 and 1897, when they also won the
F.A. Cup, 1899, 1900 and 1910. Six other clubs, Blackburn Rovers,
Liverpool, Manchester United, Newcastle United, Sheffield
United and Sheffield Wednesday shared twelve championships
between them. These were the teams on which the national
press continually focused attention. These were the sides everyone
wanted to see and beat.

The list not only emphasises the urban character of the professional game but the strength of the big city clubs. The census
of 1911 listed 97 urban districts with populations exceeding 50,000
and these included the homes of all the clubs in the two divisions
of the Football League save Glossop and Gainsborough Trinity.
Not surprisingly both of these clubs were in the vicious circle of
failure on the field, poor support at the gate and financial
difficulty.[32]

If Villa and Sunderland had been the *crème de la crème* of the
1890s, the 1900s saw the rise of Manchester United and, in
particular, Newcastle United. Manchester, as we saw in chapter
two, arose from the ashes of Newton Heath's bankruptcy of 1902
under the chairmanship of a local brewer. The club won the
League in 1908 and 1911, the F.A. Cup in 1909 and moved to
a splendid new ground at Old Trafford in 1909. United were
quick to snap up some of the best players from Manchester City
after they had been forbidden to play for that club any more
following financial irregularities in 1906. But Newcastle United
was the most successful club of the Edwardian years, building
up a reputation for studious progressive football based upon the
short pass.[33] Newcastle were league champions in 1905, 1907
and 1909 and reached five F.A. Cup Finals, in 1905, 1906, 1908,
1910 and 1911, winning only in 1910. Apparently cup finals at
the Crystal Palace produced a loss of nerve.

These then were the most successful sides of the period with
several others not far behind. They were the ones who consistently
drew the largest crowds at Bolton or Bury, Southampton or
Swindon, Millwall or Middlesbrough. These were the clubs which,

after the local heroes, were probably the subjects of most of the football conversations in the street or public house, at home or at work. But in emphasising the domination of the professional elite mention must be made of the most popular amateur team of these years, the Corinthians.

The Corinthians were formed in 1882 by N.L. Jackson, sporting journalist and honorary assistant Secretary to the F.A. England had suffered a series of defeats by Scotland in their annual meetings which Jackson put down to the better teamwork of the Scots. If the best players in England could be brought together to play matches against good opposition on a regular basis, then they too might achieve the understanding which the Scotsmen clearly showed. The club was based in London and limited to fifty members. Although there was neither entry fee nor subscription unwritten law confined election to ex-public schoolboys or members of a university.[34] The club played only friendly matches, remaining aloof from all cup-ties. It did, however, develop a distinctive style of play with five forwards attacking in a line with long sweeping passes, usually into space, for a colleague to run on to. Their northern and Scottish tours at Christmas and Easter were particularly popular. Not only did everyone love a lord, but they loved an amateur too, especially when he was a gentleman who was quite capable of giving the professionals a good run for their money. In December 1884, for example, the Corinthians played six games in six days in Lancashire, demolishing Blackburn Rovers, the F.A. Cup holders, in the first match by 8–1.[35] They did even better in April 1885 beating Blackburn Rovers again, Blackpool and Preston, drawing with Derby County and only losing 1–0 to Aston Villa, all in the space of six days.[36] Around the turn of the century they regularly took on the previous year's F.A. Cup winners in a match played for the Sheriff of London's shield, all proceeds going to charity. The club often produced astonishing results, like the one in 1904 when, after being two goals down, they slaughtered Bury 10–3.[37] The club also undertook European and Empire tours.

There is no doubt that the public schools and the ancient universities were turning out some good players, certainly throughout the 1880s and 1890s. In both 1894 and 1895 the Corinthians provided all the eleven players for England against Wales and during the whole of the club's existence 33 per cent of the places in England teams against Scotland were filled by Corinthians.[38] Whether they were that much better than the professionals must remain doubtful: their supporters believed their play to be more intelligent and spontaneous than the paid players. G.O. Smith, an Old Carthusian and one of the finest centre-forwards of the pre-1915 era playing nineteen times for England between 1893–1901, told Edward Grayson that the Corinthians of his day never trained, 'and I can safely say that the need of it was never felt. We were all fit and I think could have played on for more than one and a half hours without being any the worse.'[39] But this began to be a serious drawback as the professional trained harder and the game, as a result, grew faster, if not necessarily more skilful. That fact, together with the temporary withdrawal of some leading amateurs from the F.A., including most of the Corinthians, in 1907 probably ensured that its period of serious competition with the full-timers was over.[40]

It is very difficult to discuss objectively, or indeed to offer much in the way of evidence about which players, by their presence on the field, added substantial numbers to the gate. It would be easy to produce a list but not very valuable. Moreover, contemporary descriptions of leading players do not always help. They are largely uncritical and shot through with the kind of hero-worship that many people undoubtedly felt towards the prominent players of their own team in particular, whom they might see once a fortnight from September to April. As an example of hyperbole the following idealised portrait of G.O. Smith, the Corinthian and England centre-forward who was quoted above, takes some beating.

He opposed subtlety to force. . . . He knew that football is a manly game, calling for qualities of pluck, grit and endurance, and when he got hurt—as all men do— he never whined or grumbled. He took his courage in both hands, and never funked the biggest back that ever bore down on him. If not exactly a sprinter few men could run faster with the ball at their toe, and one wondered where he acquired the power that sent the ball whipping into the net like a shot from a gun. To see him walk quietly onto the field with his hands in his pockets, and watch the fine lines of an intellectual face, one wondered why the student ventured into the arena of football. But watch him on the ball with opposing professionals— may be the best in the land—in full cry after him, and you saw a veritable king amongst athletes.[41]

Gibson and Pickford's is an excellent book in many ways but the above passage probably reveals more about them than it does about the play of G.O. Smith. On the other hand Smith was an exceptional player. C.B. Fry, for example, wrote later that 'he was the cleverest centre-forward I saw between 1888 and 1903'.[42] All we can hope to do here is to select four players who appear to have provoked widespread admiration and between them spanned the whole of our period. Both press and public elevated them into 'stars': Archie Hunter, Steve Bloomer, Ernest Needham and Billy Meredith.

Archie Hunter was a Scot from Ayrshire and had learned his football there. He took a clerical job in Birmingham in the late 1870s. He began to play with Aston Villa and was one of the key factors in the success of that club both inside Birmingham and further afield. He was a renowned dribbler and a fine shot and, according to Gibson and Pickford again, 'hundreds of new adherents came each week to watch a forward the like of whom had never been seen in Birmingham games'. They also relate how the club once hired a special train in order to get Hunter to Nottingham in time for a match.[43] He did not play for Scotland because, during his time, the Scots were not selecting Anglos. He was clearly an outstanding centre-forward apparently with some so-called modern skills, like shielding the ball from an opponent. 'The way in which, when apparently circumvented, he would turn round and keep the man off with his hindquarters while he adroitly put the ball back to a colleague, used to mystify everyone.' His coaching had a good deal to do with Villa's rise to prominence. He finished playing after having what was described as an epileptic fit at Everton in January 1890.[44] Unfortunately, he contracted tuberculosis and died at the age of 35 in 1894. The club erected a memorial stone in Witton Cemetery, Birmingham, which still stands.

Steve Bloomer first played for Derby County in 1892 and after a brief sojourn in Middlesbrough played his last league game for Derby County in 1914. In between he scored 352 goals in the league and eight goals in ten appearances for England against Scotland, most of them, according to Ivan Sharpe who played with him in the Derby County team in 1911–12, by sudden, first-time shooting.[45] Bloomer was an unpredictable but highly successful individualist, difficult to play with and, again according to Sharpe, not slow to criticise his team mates if they did not fulfil his expectations. He was small and pale, indeed he did not look the part of a professional footballer at all which made him all the more attractive to press and public. He was quick and accurate though not a great dribbler or especially tricky on the ball. But he was the finest goalscorer of his generation. After he stopped playing he went coaching in Europe and was interned in Germany during the First World War.

The one wing half-back who always played well against Bloomer was Ernest Needham of Sheffield United and England. He was only 5′5″ but he was quick, had plenty of stamina, tackled well and passed skilfully. He was especially good at persistently harassing the man with the ball. He played for England sixteen times and when, in coronation year 1902, the *Sheffield Independent* published a series of biographies under the general title of 'Who's Who in Sheffield' Needham was amongst them. He said he was hoping to become a landed proprietor when he finally finished with football. He was one of the few players of the period to write a book about the game although sadly, from the historian's point of view, it said very little about his own experiences as a player.

Billy Meredith we have already met in chapter four but it is difficult to omit such a fine, goal-scoring winger and one who played at the highest level for so long. He first played the first-class game in 1894 and did not finally call it a day until 1924 after 857 league appearances for Manchester City and Manchester United. In all he played 1568 matches including 51 for Wales and scored 470 goals.[46] Thin, pale and spindly legged, he was, as we saw earlier, an activist in the Players' Union and by no means an easy man for the football bosses to confront. But he undoubtedly brought in a gaggle of extra sixpences wherever he turned out. What an autobiography he might have written! Football is a simple game which must in part at least explain its world-wide popularity in the twentieth century. Players may be fitter and faster now but the virtues possessed by players like Hunter, Needham, Bloomer and Meredith were the ones all good players must have: good balance, accurate passing, judgement in all matters and, in particular, the knack of finding an empty space for yourself when you do not have the ball.

Notes

1   On the Royal Engineers as one of the earliest English clubs to adopt 'passing on' see R.M. Ruck, 'R.E. football in the Early Seventies', *Royal Engineers Journal* NS vol. 42 (1928) pp. 636–43.

2   *Bell's Life* 5 April 1873.

3   'Umpires should always give their decision immediately a claim is made and it should be understood that when either or both of the Umpires hold up their stick, umbrella, or arm . . . that they decide in favour of the claim-ants.' *The National Football Calendar* (1881) p. 3. This was an official Football Association publication edited by C.W. Alcock and N.L. Jackson.

4   *Athletic News* 2 April 1879. An article in the *Athletic News* of 11 January 1887 looking back on the game as it was played in Lancashire in the previous decade claimed that it was all dribbling and little or no passing. Darwen were one of the first local sides to adopt passing and their match with Turton in March 1878 was very much a dribbling versus passing struggle.

5   *Birmingham Daily Mail* 21 October 1881.

6   *Sunderland Daily Herald* 14 November 1880.

7   *Athletic News* 6 October 1885. See also *The Sportsman* 1 April 1889 which

compared unfavourably the individual rushes and long kicks of the Wolves with the short passes and combined attacks of Preston in the Cup Final of that year.

8   According to the *Athletic News* 26 March 1879, the one thing which the Old Etonians learned from Darwen during their three cup meetings of that year was the 'crossing game.'

9   *Birmingham Daily Mail* 21 October 1881.

10 *Athletic News* 15 November 1887.

11 *Birmingham Daily Times* 21 December 1886.

12 *Athletic News* 19 March 1884.

13 That was in England. More adventurous realignments were going on abroad but their full impact on what by then had become a world-wide game was not felt until after 1945.

14 See, for example, the report of the Preston North End *v* Blackburn Olympic match in the *Athletic News* 26 January 1886.

15 *Athletic News* 12 November 1879.

16 N.L. Jackson (ed.), *The Association Football Handbook* 1894–5, p. 89.

17 Ibid. p. 87.

18 The controversy over the introduction of the penalty kick is discussed in more detail in chapter eight.

19 The only major alteration in the law after that was the offside changes in 1925.

20 As late as 1897 a photograph of the England team who played Scotland shows that not all the players wore shorts of the same colour.

21 A. Gibson and W. Pickford, vol. I op.cit. pp. 131–2. According to Ivan Sharpe, Charlie Roberts wore short shorts and this, together with his activities on behalf of the Players' Union led to him playing fewer games for England than his ability merited. See I. Sharpe, *40 Years in Football* (1952) p. 102.

22 A. Gibson and W. Pickford, vol. II op.cit. p. 61.

23 *The Times*, 16 November 1910. See the almost identical criticisms of the play in that year's Cup Final. *The Times* 25 April 1910.

24 E. Grayson, *Corinthians and Cricketers* (1955) p. 113. See also *The Times* report of the Aston Villa—Sunderland Cup Final of 1913. *The Times* 21 April 1913.

25 *Sheffield Daily Telegraph* 6 April 1903. Mosforth was reminiscing about his early football career in a special interview on the Monday following the playing of the England—Scotland match at Sheffield. In fact he said that the incident happened during England's game against Wales in 1879 but he must have been mistaken as he only played with Lyttleton for England in the match against Scotland in 1877. It was Lyttleton's only international appearance.

26 There were three Scotsmen in the victorious eleven of 1884. Rovers also won the cup in 1890 and 1891.

27 *Athletic News* 4 May 1881, *Blackburn Standard* 13 May 1882.

28 *Athletic News* 13 October 1880, 30 March 1881, *Preston Herald* 9 September 1882.

29 *Preston Herald* 6 February 1889.

30 Unfortunately he was sentenced to three years imprisonment for embezzling his firm's funds in 1895. Counsel suggested that his expenditure on the club and in particular the hospitality lavished on visiting teams and officials had caused him to yield to temptation. He later emigrated to South Africa.

Preston Herald 13 April 1895, *Pastime* 17 April 1895, *Athletic News* 13 September 1909.

31 The F.A. Cup had been stolen from a Birmingham shop window in 1895 and its successor was presented to Lord Kinnaird in 1910 to mark his 21 years as F.A. President.

32 Census of England and Wales 1911, General Report with Appendices Cd. 8491 (1917) pp. 39–40. In 1911–12 Glossop finished eighteenth out of twenty in Division II, eighteenth again in 1912–13, seventeenth in 1913–14 and bottom in 1914–15, after which the club left the league. Gainsborough Trinity failed to secure re-election to the league in 1911–12 and joined the lesser Midland League. The only towns in England with a population of 50,000 or more which do not seem to have had professional football teams in 1911 were Bournemouth, Dudley, Eastbourne, Great Yarmouth, Gloucester, Ipswich, Stockton-on-Tees and Tynemouth. Big city domination, especially of the First Division continued after the war. One scholar estimated that the average population of districts containing a First Division club in 1937–8 was 337,000: only 253,000 for a Second Division club, 228,000 for a club in the southern section of the Third Division and only 95,000 for the Third Division North. L.N. Harding, 'Some business aspects of association football and county cricket in England: a study of certain aspects of the organisation of games dependent upon gate receipts'. Unpublished manuscript, British Library of Political and Economic Science RX 23074. See also the 'ex-director of an important professional club' who thought, in 1911, that no town with less than 250,000 population could run a first-class professional club, supporting an earlier comment by the Chairman of Aston Villa. *Athletic News* 11 March 1907, 6 November 1911.

33 See, for example, E. Grayson, op.cit. pp. 135–7 and I. Sharpe, op.cit. p. 102.

34 B.O. Corbett, *Annals of the Corinthians* (1906) pp. vi, 6.

35 *Athletic News* 17 December 1884. What is not usually mentioned is that they also lost 7–0 to Bolton Wanderers and 3–1 to Preston.

36 *Athletic News* 14 April 1885.

37 E. Grayson, op.cit. pp. 137–9.

38 B.O. Corbett, op.cit p. 12, E. Brayson, op.cit. p. 28.

39 E. Grayson, op.cit. p. 31.

40 On the formation of the Amateur Football Association see chapter eight. There was something of a resurgence of the Corinthians in the 1920s and for a time they even entered the F.A. Cup. But relative lack of leisure and full-time training meant that it was going to be an increasingly rare individual talent which could compete on equal terms with the professionals. See also F.N.J. Creek, *A History of the Corinthian Football Club* (1933).

41 He may have had an intellectual face but he only got a third class in History at Oxford. E. Grayson, op.cit. p. 96. The quotation comes from A. Gibson and W. Pickford, vol. I op.cit. p. 166.

42 E. Grayson, op.cit. p. 5.

43 A. Gibson and W. Pickford, vol. II op.cit. pp. 55–6.

44 Ibid. He managed a public house for a few years and was an unsuccessful Villa committee member, *Birmingham Daily Mail* 6 January 1890, 30 January 1893.

45 Ivan Sharpe, op.cit. p. 22.

46 *Manchester Guardian* 21 April 1958, *Western Mail* 21 April 1958.

CHAPTER EIGHT
FOOTBALL AND THE WORKERS

In the last quarter of the nineteenth century and in the years up to the outbreak of war in 1914, playing and watching association football became a widespread activity among working people, particularly men and boys. By the end of the period it had become one of those cultural manifestations which not only help sociologists to distinguish one group from another in society but assist members of the group itself to locate themselves. It had become one of those things which working men did. This chapter will try to describe a set of attitudes to the game in general and its professional sector in particular which appear to be those to which most working men subscribed if interested in the game at all.

It is a common enough complaint among historians who write about the attitudes of working people that these are difficult to discover. Working men, for example, did not leave behind them the relatively rich documentary materials which some members of the middle classes have bequeathed to later generations and this is particularly true if the subject being investigated is outside the industrial and political mainstreams. In order, therefore, to reconstruct some of the ideas and perceptions of working men we have to view them through the sometimes narrow and often misty lens of what middle-class observers thought and felt and said about them. Moreover, it is important to notice how middle and working-class attitudes differed, and to see what changes, if any, can be identified over our period. Therefore a considerable part of this chapter will be concerned with describing a set of attitudes which will be crudely characterised as 'middle class'. In fact, that section of middle-class opinion which viewed the development of association football with approval will be discussed first. An attempt will then be made to suggest the ways in which working people thought and felt about football: this will involve a consideration of the portion of middle-class opinion which looked on the game's development with some anxiety. There does seem to have been some shift in the balance of middle-class attitudes to the game in the period 1870–1915 and that shift will be explored in the third section of the chapter. Finally I shall attempt to say something about the possible relationship between the growth of association football and that philosopher's stone, 'working-class consciousness'.

Middle-class attitudes to sport in general and association football in particular were encapsulated in the notion of 'playing the game'. We noted earlier, in the first chapter, the part which games played in the reform of the public schools in the early years of the nineteenth century. The cult of manliness particularly was appropriately expressed through the vehicle of team games, an area where individualism could flourish and yet be controlled by the idea of serving the group. By the second half of Victoria's reign the sportsmanship ethic received widespread public acceptance in middle-class circles. What were the major tenets of this ethic? First, playing for the side and not for self. Being modest and generous in victory and staunch and cheerful in defeat. Playing the game for the game's sake: there might be physical and moral benefits but there should be no other rewards and certainly not prizes or money. No player should ever intentionally break the rules or stoop to underhand tactics. Hard but fair knocks should be taken and given courageously and with good temper. In the public schools from the mid-century on, the relationship between the playing of games and the formulation of character in the individual was thought to be close. Indeed, that belief was a major justification for playing games. These ideas are delightfully expressed in two verses, which may seem hackneyed today. 'Vitai Lampada' was written by Sir Henry Newbolt in 1898:

> There's a breathless hush in the Close tonight
> Ten to make and the match to win—
> A bumping pitch and a blinding light,
> An hour to play and the last man in.
> And its not for the sake of a ribboned coat,
> Or the selfish hope of a season's fame,
> But his Captain's hand on his shoulder smote—
> Play up! Play up! and play the game!

The second verse showed how the schoolboy experience was vital in rallying the ranks to fight for the Empire.

> The sand of the desert is sodden red—
> Red with the wreck of a square that broke;
> The Gatling's jammed and the Colonel dead,
> And the regiment blind with dust and smoke;
> The river of death has brimmed its banks,
> And England's far, and Honour a name;
> But the voice of a schoolboy rallies the ranks:
> Play up! play up! and play the game!'

'Alumnus Football' was composed a good deal later by an American, Grant Rice:

> For when the One Great Scorer comes
> To write against your name
> He marks—not that you won or lost—
> but how you played the game.[1]

'He marks not that you won or lost—but how you played the game.' N.L. Jackson, a leading proponent of gentleman amateurism, player, referee, Football Association councillor, founder of the Corinthians F.C. and sporting journalist (although he vigorously criticised the professional player, as we saw earlier, he did not seem to think that paid journalism infringed amateur canons)[2] was clear how association football should be played by gentlemen. Moreover, if his advice was followed, then the moral benefits were certain.

Every allowance should be made by players for the difficulties which beset a referee, and his decisions, even though apparently improper, should be accepted and obeyed without the slightest demur. Silence should be the general rule, and no voice but that of the captains should be heard in any team.

Players should never lose their tempers. If they get the worst of a charge, or of a tussle for the ball, let them admire the skill which has beaten them and let them try to profit by the lesson. The game should be played for enjoyment, which should be the first consideration; the result should be a secondary one.

Be absolutely unselfish. Play only for your side, and never keep the ball when you ought to pass it to a more favoured player. No captain should retain a selfish player in his team, no matter how good he may be, for he values the applause of the spectators more than the interests of his side; he sets a bad example to his club-mates, and he generally demoralises the team.

Hanging about on the verge of offside amounted to 'sneaking.'[3]

The idea that association football, and rugby football too, of course, might be an exceptionally good vessel for fostering the kind of attitudes encompassed by the sportsmanship ethic was particularly prominent at the beginning of our period, especially in educational and religious circles but not confined to them. H.H. Almond, headmaster of Loretto, in an article published in the *Nineteenth Century* in 1893, regarded football of both codes played for its own sake or as 'a means of testing the manly prowess of representative teams of schools, colleges, clubs, villages, or other communities . . . productive of scarcely anything but good to representative players or to the immensely greater number who aspire to be such'. Once foul play was eliminated the game would be 'an education in that spirit of chivalry, fairness and good temper'.[4] A letter from 'Clericus' in the *Glasgow Herald* of 18

June 1894 observed that 'football justly deserves to be the popular game; it has in it all the elements for the development of physical strength and agility, swiftness of foot, self control, courage and manliness'. Lord Rosebery, when presenting the F.A. Cup in 1897, said he was sure the game helped to bring out those 'splendid characteristics of the British race—stamina and indomitable pluck'.[5] Some grandiose claims were made, perhaps none more so than that published by a Sheffield sports paper, the *Football World* as it welcomed the new season in 1895:

an eminent German military authority . . . recently offered the opinion that it [football] satisfies a craving which renders conscription unnecessary in this country. It does not make trained soldiers of our young men, it is true, but it enhances in them the spirit of pluck, opposition, competition, never-know-when-they-are-beaten, never-say-die, play up Wednesday or United kind of feeling, which tends to the greatness of our national character. Long live football![6]

If football brought in its train clear moral benefits: if it helped to make men plucky, good tempered and unselfish, it could also, hopefully, improve their physical health as well. At the fifth annual general meeting of the Lancashire Football Association in 1883, James Kerr, of Church, a vice-president of the Association and managing partner in a local dye-works, said that

it was perfectly clear to anyone who worked much amongst those who took an interest in athletic affairs that football had certainly developed the physique of the youth of Lancashire to a remarkable degree. He was certain from experience that there are finer legs and finer chests at the present moment than there were eight or ten years ago. There were a great many thousands of young fellows in Lancashire now capable of enduring an amount of fatigue and exertion that they could not have gone through eight or ten years ago . . . they might be the best spinners and the best weavers in the world, and the best printers or merchants, but if they had not bone and muscle to enable them to take a sufficient interest in it decadence would not be far off. A man must have more than mere commercial ability and the power of producing cheaper than their neighbours. This country had obtained success in the world because of the hard knocks we were able to give and to receive, and those of our forefathers had generally come out the best who were able to give the hardest knocks. He was not an advocate for hard knocks . . . but when it was necessary they ought to be in a position to strike straight from the shoulder.

He completed his peroration by emphasising that there were about two and a half thousand young men in the prime of life belonging to clubs in membership with the Association 'and they might depend upon it that amongst them they would find a capacity to do a higher average of work than among any other 2,500 young men in Lancashire'.[7]

Such a splendidly optimistic view was not confined merely to
the physical benefits of playing. Even watching others play could
be physically advantageous. H.H. Almond, again, urged that
those ex-players now engaged in sedentary occupations ought
to take spare-time exercise.

But it must ... be remembered that a large part of the spectators (at football
matches) are manual labourers. They do not want exercise on Saturday afternoons, but they want rest, the open air, and some excitement which stirs their
blood. They get all this from the big football matches. The roads in the neighbourhood of Manchester and Blackburn would not be crowded with eager pedestrians
if the football matches ceased; but the public houses, and reading-rooms, and
young men's institutes and indoor 'shows' of various kinds would be more
crowded and stuffier.

He agreed that it was often said that 'the falling nation spectates;
the nation at its prime does things for itself ... but the spectacles
which cause people to do good and wholesome things must be
carefully separated from those which have no such influence'.[8]

So football improved character and helped develop muscle
and good circulation. Moreover, that did not exhaust its social
advantages in middle-class eyes. As we saw in chapter six there
was a body of opinion which felt that the game inhibited the spread
of drunkenness. Less specifically, but perhaps even more crucially
from the middle-class point of view, it was a rational recreation
which provided working men with something to do, even if it
was only watching twenty-two hirelings kick an inflated piece of
leather about. The fear regularly surfaced that they might have
been worse employed even than drinking:

is it not wonderful that 60,000 men of like passions with yourself, stronger passions very likely, and certainly less schooled, should quickly assemble round a
plot of ground, wait patiently for a considerable time, watch an exciting match
in which they are intensely interested, and as soon as it is over quietly disperse?
... Or could you wish for proof more striking of the good sense, good humour,
and strong self-control of your own countrymen? ... Whenever I see such a
crowd my heart goes wholly out to that Lord Derby who could cry 'Lord, what
am I that I should govern such a nation!' And I muse on what might happen if
they gave their passions play?[9]

It was all very reassuring.

F.E. Smith, who, as Lord Birkenhead, was later to become
adept at conjuring up revolutionary spectres with which to frighten
the electorate, asked the same question fourteen years later and
came up with much the same answer.

What would the devotees of athletics do if their present amusements were abolished? The policeman, the police magistrate, the social worker, the minister of

religion, the public schoolmaster and the University don would each, in the sphere of his own duties, contemplate such a prospect with dismay. Is it to be supposed, for instance, that the seething mass of humanity which streams every Saturday at mid-day out of the factories and workshops of our great towns would ever saunter in peace and contentment through museums and picture galleries, or sit enraptured listening to classical concerts . . . ' or 'spend his leisure studying botany or horticulture. . . . The poorer classes in this country have not got the tastes which superior people or a Royal Commission would choose for them' and were cricket and football abolished, it would bring 'upon the masses nothing but misery, depression, sloth, indiscipline, and disorder'.[1]

But if sport generally and association football in particular helped to keep the workers off the streets by giving them something to take their minds off whatever it was they would have been on otherwise, it was also felt to be an experience in which all classes could join. Sport could provide the cement which would fill the dangerous gaps between the classes and wedge them tight in a relationship based in part on common excitements and shared pleasures. As early as 1877 some people were saying how nice it was to have football teams which were socially heterogeneous. At the dinner and presentation following the first Sheffield Football Association Cup Final, the Association's President, J.C. Shaw, said he was glad that the Sheffield team 'was a mixed one of gentlemen, the middle classes, and working men. Such meetings broke down prejudice, and had a beneficial effect in cementing good feeling between all classes'.[11] But if sport was something which the highest, the lowest, and all those in between could share a concern for in the relatively stable communities of the industrial north and midlands, the same was not true of London.

The work of Stedman Jones has demonstrated that the 1880s was a period of some crisis for the English capital, or at least that many middle-class spokesmen thought it was. Since the 1870s the feeling had been growing that in London, far from coming closer together, the classes had been growing further apart. Those who had demonstrated over the issue of unemployment in 1886 appeared to be the advance guard, if not of the Revolution, then of a period of some social unrest and disorder.[12] Frederick Gale both monitored the feeling and suggested one way in which class relationships might be improved in 1887.

There never was a period in our national history when it was of more importance to unite all classes in promotion of our old English sports than now. We have "lost touch" so to say, between rich and poor.

Sport had become more extensive but more expensive and the poor had been left out.

In the rougher days there were wakes and fairs, bull-baiting, cock-fighting, cudgelling, village green cricket and country races which were open to rich and poor, and all to be seen for nothing . . . .

Some employers were providing facilities for cricket and football but they were a minority.

The discontinuance of the [prize] ring has one drawback, which is that it has severed the tie between the roughs and the gentlemen. The roughs hate a cad, but they were always civil to gentlemen because they knew that they spent their money . . . . I know for a fact that it only wants a kind word in season to convert the rougher element into a very effective self-regulated police for order and good manners . . . those who are a little below in the world appreciate sympathy without patronage.[13]

The timing of that piece is probably the most interesting thing about it. Of course, the expansion of playing and watching, especially in the two major team games of association football and cricket, which continued throughout the 1890s, cannot merely be put down to the working out of such social motives. It was more complicated than that. But sport was something that all classes could share, though perhaps at different levels of commitment and experience. The pessimism of propertied London was a good deal diminished by the end of the next decade. *The Times* leading article which appeared on the Monday morning after the Cup Final of 1899 is worth quoting in full for the way in which it neatly encapsulates the penumbra of favourable middle-class attitudes to association football which we have been discussing. But summarising briefly, it begins by saying that the match was an important event in its own right: that games were schools of discipline for all who played and watched. The good order and temper of the spectators was noted, even in crowded and trying circumstances. 'The self-reliance of the individual football player and the cohesiveness of the team are of almost as much value in the battles of life' as in football.

It is, indeed, in athletic games, and in the increased hold which they have obtained upon all classes of the community, but especially upon the industrial classes, that the best remedy is to be found for conditions which tend to crowd workers into cities, and to deprive them of some of the requirements of sound physical development.

Football was particularly useful for muscle and chest capacity development. Cecil Rhodes, a spectator at the match, must have been aware that he was in the presence of the raw material of Empire both on the field and on the terraces.[14] The fact that each

political party had sent its leader showed that 'whatever may be
our divisions for political purposes, all Englishmen meet upon
common ground for the furtherance of every pursuit which can
add to the manliness of the people, or to the available strength
and resources of the country'. Such optimism seems to have been
widely shared in middle-class circles before the shocks of the
Boer War prompted a gloomier reappraisal.[15]

So football was good for the physique, it helped to build character, it perhaps led to a diminution in drinking, it brought the
classes together. Devotees also said that it was more scientific
than formerly and that was very important in an age of science
and apparently unending material progress. What commentators
meant when they described the game as more scientific was that
brain had become allied to brawn, that the most violent excesses
of charging and hacking had been removed, that 'combination'
or the passing game had replaced the old individual rushes and
dribbles whilst leaving scope for individual skill and judgement.[16]

This short discussion of middle-class attitudes favourable
to the emergence of association football as a game widely played
and watched in late Victorian England should not be finished
without drawing the attention of the reader to the undoubted
fact that many middle-class men, who had or had not played football, simply approved of it because they enjoyed watching it.
Dr. E.S. Morley, brother of the Liberal M.P., John Morley,
and chairman of Blackburn Rovers made the point neatly in 1882.

He had been asked . . . what he could see in football. . . . The fact was somewhat
after that given by the old lady when asked why she had a drop of gin and water
at night . . ., 'Some folks takes it 'cause it does 'em good; but I takes it 'cause
I likes it.'[17]

Working-class attitudes to football are much more difficult
to uncover. In order to explore the attitudes of working people,
therefore, it is necessary to examine that area of middle-class
opinion doubtful about the virtuous impact that sport in general
and professional football in particular was having on society.
Even before the crisis over the legalisation of professionals critical
voices were heard deploring what were thought to be deteriorating
standards of conduct by clubs and players. Major Francis Marindin, the President of the Football Association, giving judgement
on a complaint by one team against another in a Bolton Charity
cup-tie of 1882, said that he

looked back with much regret to the time—not above ten or twelve years ago—

when many matches were played without umpires at all . . . and very few, comparatively, with a referee . . . the rivalry was every bit as keen and play as hard as it is now [but] disputes as to the result of a match were unheard of.

He thought that money and betting were at the root of it.[18]

The coming of professional players gave such criticism a sharper focus and a clearer target. As we saw in chapter three, opponents of professional football players used a variety of arguments which basically boiled down to five: that professionals made into a job of work what should have been a sport; that professionalism destroyed amateurism because no amateur could compete with the best professionals who trained and practised together regularly and a gentleman could not receive pay for playing and remain a gentleman. Third, that professionals would lead to big-town domination and undermine those local rivalries on which the game had thrived. Fourth, that professionalism meant an over-emphasis on winning, probably at any cost because the livelihood of the professional depended upon it, and, finally, that the football professional was no 'professor' in the true sense: he had no teaching role and therefore had too much free time on his hands.[19]

By the 1890s, after ten years or so of professionalism in football and the considerable increase in the numbers of both players and spectators, critics of the game felt that some of their fears, at least, had been justified. In particular they doubted whether the sportsmanship ethic really thrived among the largely working-class football crowd. First of all they were so clearly partisan. They wanted their own side to win. They were supporters.[20] They did not see the other side. They did not even applaud its skill and courage nor give it any credit at all. It was merely a sacrificial lamb on which the home team could practise ritual slaughter. These views were particularly well expressed in two articles written for *C.B. Fry's Magazine*, one in 1906, the other, entitled 'The Case Against Professional Football', in 1913. The earlier writer pointed out that 'there is no real local interest to excuse the partisan frenzy of the mob, since the players come from all over the kingdom, and many change their clubs each season'. Moreover, 'how can the Saturday's match be a mental recreation to those who have been thinking, reading, and talking of football all the week?'[21] W.H.C., in 1913, provided a more detailed description and indictment.

A home player will be bowled over, by fair means or foul (that is entirely beside the point) and the crowd will immediately shout on behalf of the culprit 'Turn 'm off,' and should the injured (apparently) player retaliate later in the game, the referee will probably find it his duty to administer a caution, while the crowd will yell at the victim with all its 20,000 might 'Serve 'im right.'

... A magnificently fought out game ending in a goalless draw will leave the crowd sullen and morose; they will wend their way from the ground with black looks, cursing the bad luck of the home side. An undeserved victory for their own team will leave no regrets as to the result. ... There is no sportsmanship in a football crowd. ... Partisanship has dulled its idea of sport and warped its moral sense. It cannot enjoy a game that has been won by the visiting team. A referee is good or bad (with adjectives), according to the manner in which his decisions affect the home side. ...

Out-of-form home players are abused because 'the football crowd is the most fickle body on earth. It lives and thrives on success. Defeat disheartens it, and rather than watch its club get defeated it will stay away'.[22] An Aston Villa supporter who went to watch Small Heath play Bury in 1896 was disgusted by the repeated cheers of Small Heath supporters as each telegram was received announcing the downfall of Villa in the cup at Derby.[23]

If working-class crowds were reluctant to appreciate both sides, so the professional football players themselves also failed to reach the standards of sportsmanship expected by ex-public school men. As a writer in the *Badminton Magazine* pointed out in 1896,

the artisan differs from the public-school man in two important points: he plays to win at all costs, and, from the nature of his associations, he steps onto the football field in better training ... his strong desire to win ... leads him to play up to the rules [and] to indulge in dodges and tricks which the public school man is apt to consider dishonourable, while it is difficult for him to realise that you can be defeated with honour.[24]

Is this the voice of class prejudice? Were the characteristics of the working-class football crowd outlined above drawn from sources so opposed to the professional game that they reveal much about those expressing the opinions but little about the subject on which those opinions were expressed? The answer to both questions might be an unqualified affirmative if it were not for the fact that sources on the whole well-disposed towards professional football and usually prepared to defend it against all comers supported the view that spectators at football matches were only interested in their own side winning and were often roughly critical if things did not go well. The *Athletic News*, for example, as has been shown, was a very strong supporter of the professional game more or less from 1885. Nonetheless it could say, in 1899, that most of the 74,000 crowd at the Cup

Final were 'considerably interested in one team winning for they shouted or kept silent just as fortune favoured or otherwise the efforts of their chosen players'.[25] Similarly the *Birmingham Daily Mail's* football correspondent, at the beginning of season 1892–3, felt the need to make a plea for 'courteous and impartial treatment for all teams. . . . If people could but bring themselves to go to matches free from prejudice, prepared to impartially cheer any deserving piece of play and to applaud, both winners and losers . . . how intensely delightful would the game be.'[26] An article by the former English international wing forward, Billy Bassett, came to largely similar conclusions. 'The crowd in the mass are not experts on football. They go to a match . . . to see a stern fight between keen rivals, and if their chosen side happens to win I don't know that they care very much beyond that. To them victory covers a great multitude of sins or weaknesses.'[27] Finally Sheffield United published a list of 'Dont's' [sic] for spectators in their match programme on 26 October 1907.

Don't think because you are on the stand you have a right to shout instructions to the players. They know what to do without any assistance from you.

Don't boo at the referee because he gives a decision which *you* think wrong. He has his opinion as to what happened, and his opinion is surely worth as much as yours.

Don't commence shouting 'send him off' if one of the opposing team happens to commit a foul on one of your pet players. Would you shout the same thing if the positions were reversed, and one of your own side had committed the offence?

Don't make yourself a nuisance to those around you by continual bellowing at the top of your voice, it gets on people's nerves and takes away a lot of the enjoyment of the game, besides making yourself look ridiculous.

Don't snap your neighbour's nose off because he thinks differently to you. You have come to see your side win, and he has perhaps come to see the other.

Don't get excited and bad tempered when you argue about this player or that. It does no good in the end, and only breeds bad feeling, and spoils your enjoyment of the game.[28]

If crowds did not appear to have imbibed the sportsmanship ethic, the behaviour on the field of the professional player also left something to be desired. It is possible that there had been an increase in intentional foul play since the mid-1880s, especially by defenders close to their own goal.[29] As early as 1873 a free kick had been awarded for deliberate hand ball and in 1881 referees were empowered to award a goal if the ball was prevented from passing between the posts by a defender other than the goal-keeper handling it. This did not work very well and the penalty kick was introduced in 1891. An area was marked off immediately in front of the goal within which, should the referee decide an intentional infringement of the laws had taken place, a free kick should be awarded from which a goal could be directly scored. Only the goalkeeper of the defending side could attempt to prevent the kick from scoring. This provoked some opposition from within the ranks of middle-class amateur football players and commentators. C.B. Fry summed up some of their feelings. 'It is a standing insult to sportsmen to have to play under a rule which assumes that players intend to trip, hack, and push their opponents and to behave like cads of the most unscrupulous kidney.' Gentlemen did not deliberately commit fouls. More shrewdly he noted in 1911 that

in football a curious conventional morality has grown up under which it is regarded as legitimate to play against the rules and the referee as well as against the opposing team, and to play on the principle that as there is a penalty for cheating it is permissible to cheat at the risk of a penalty . . . in football it is widely acknowledged that if both sides agree to cheat, cheating is fair.[30]

It is difficult to know how far this new morality extended to the mass of organised football below the professional elite and was encouraged both by imitating professionals and playing under the same rules. Conduct on the field in Lancashire, for instance, appears to have deteriorated if you take as an indicator the number of cases dealt with by the local Football Association's Disciplinary Committee. The figures rise rapidly through the 1890s to the outbreak of war.[31] But the numbers of players, clubs, and leagues was also increasing. This is yet another area where precision is impossible. However, any foul play was disagreeable in the eyes of the professional and administrative middle classes brought up on the sportsmanship ethic.[32] It does not seem an exaggeration to conclude that football does not appear to have been played or watched by working men with that devotion to the ideals of sportsmanship which middle-class people would have liked and which, as we have seen, was one of their hopes for the influence of the game.

But the support given by the working man to his town team could have by-products which middle-class people might appreciate. Professional and semi-professional teams seem to have developed first in those towns in Lancashire and the midlands which were industrial and urban but relatively settled. By the

1860s and 1870s their most rapid period of industrial and population growth was over. Moreover, as P.F. Clarke has pointed out, these clusters of towns had risen together during the Industrial Revolution and achieved political status together. They were used to doing things together and this may well have facilitated the spread of the association game.[33] In such circumstances it would not be surprising to find a growing identification with place emerging among both middle and working classes. Football can be seen both to contribute to this and to benefit from it. It benefits from it in that if there already exists this sense of identification with place then any organisation which takes the name of the town has a good chance of attracting support particularly if it is competing with similar institutions in other places and especially if it succeeds in such competition. But the football team can also contribute to the intensity or diffusion of this local consciousness and particularly among working people. Nor does this happen only among those working people who regularly watch its matches. Regular matches, local newspaper coverage, conversations with people who do watch, all these help to buttress notions of being from Bolton or Blackburn, Bury or Sheffield, Nottingham or Derby.[34]

This sense of local belonging seems to have been particularly strongly manifested on those occasions when a final or a semi-final was reached or a cup was won. On such days the whole town turned out in a popular celebration reminiscent of the antics of smaller communities at fair time. There are plenty of examples of this from the early 1880s onwards, and well before 1900 it had become certainly customary and almost a social cliché. There is only space here to illustrate the point with one newspaperman's account of the welcome given to Blackburn Rovers when they arrived back in Blackburn after winning the F.A. Cup in 1884.

Between six and seven o'clock people could be seen flocking to the station from every direction. Station-road, Canal street, and Church street, quickly became filled with thousands of persons all anxious to get a glimpse of the members of the club which had brought such honour to the town. The space of ground in front of the station was kept clear by two large forces of police, though with great difficulty . . . the tremendous crowd frequently attempted to break into the reserved part, but they were repelled in a justifiable manner by the truncheons of the officers. . . . (Then) the players issued from the station surrounded by a number of ardent admirers and . . . took their places in a large wagonette drawn by six handsome greys. The procession then began to move. At the head, in a commodious vehicle drawn by four horses was the Borough Band, playing lively airs. Then followed the carriage containing the team, all standing, in the centre being Jimmy Brown, the captain, holding the cup on high so that everybody could see it. The ball with which the match was played was also carried aloft, being attached to the end of a pole whilst the blue and white colours of the club waved from each corner of the vehicle. Next came a wagonette in which were the members of the committee, and they were followed by members and players of the Olympic Club. . . . Along the route they frequently sang 'Our Jack's come home to-day'. Following these were the Park Road team in a wagonette . . . and one . . . with some of the butchers of the town on it. The Livesey Brass Band was also present, and played some inspiriting tunes. As the procession entered the throng tremendous cheering began, and was continued along the whole route. Some idea of the number of persons may be gathered when it is stated that Station-road, Church-street, King William-street, up to Sudell Cross, were all densely packed, and great care had to be taken that people were not pushed under the wheels of the carriages. At the corner of Station-road and Church-street brilliant illuminations, by various coloured lime lights, were produced, the effect being grand, and rockets were sent in the air as fast as they could be lighted. This was more or less the case in all the principal thoroughfares. . . . Turning round Richmond Terrace, the procession proceeded along Victoria-street, past the Market, into Church-street, and up Penny-street. Mr Boyle's shop had been splendidly adorned for the occasion. . . . The triumphal march was continued along Birley-street and Eanam, the Rovers being enthusiastically received everywhere. On reaching the White Bull a stop was made, and the procession broke up. . . . Jimmy Brown's and Joe Lofthouse's were visited, and finally Mac's was reached. . . . Here the festive occasion was celebrated in right royal style until late. We are sorry to state that since the match, Hugh McIntyre has been very unwell, and he is yet confined to his bed.[35]

Working people could be helped to feel that they belonged to a community by the activities of the local football team and their attachment to that team. It seems reasonable to suppose that such identities and loyalties might have inhibited the emergence of other kinds of loyalties which could have attracted all working people as working people. These are complex issues. Clearly, working people developed over time a whole series of loyalties. There were many different groups to which they might see themselves as belonging. Football seems to have helped further a kind of local consciousness although it may have had no positive results outside the fact that supporting Bolton Wanderers reminded you that 'you were a Bolton lad and not one of them Bury lot'.

Still in pursuit of that holy grail of what working people thought and felt, about football in this case, it is instructive to examine the attitudes and positions taken up by the various socialist groups in the late Victorian and Edwardian periods. How did they respond to the phenomenon of mass spectator sports in general and association football in particular? Did they feel that the role of games in society merited their attention? If so, does that attention throw any light on the attitudes of working people?

The Social Democratic Federation's London-based journal,

Justice, does not seem to have taken much notice of sport or football, save for one very heavy-handed satirical piece under the heading of 'Topical Tattle' in 1899.[36] However, it is clear that S.D.F. members did play the game. Some attempt appears to have been made to form an S.D.F. football team in 1896 and occasional matches were played such as the one in March 1898 when the *Clarion* was defeated by 5–0.[37] Moreover, some local branches obviously ran very successful sides, none more so than in Northampton. Its football club was formed at the beginning of December 1896 and in 1897–8 won the Junior League competition run by the Northampton Town Football Association.[38]

The *Clarion* was much more interested in sport than *Justice*. It ran a general sporting gossip column by 'Muff' every week, from the start of the paper in 1891. This is probably not surprising when Robert Blatchford's journalistic experience on the *Sunday Chronicle* is recalled. That newspaper had devoted a considerable amount of space to sport from its inception in 1885. Muff wrote short comments on actual football matches and the general sporting scene in an affectionate avuncular style. Here is a sample from February 1892.

The Rev. Mr. Johnnie Horner Baxter is a bloke thats always prophesying when and how this little globe of ours is going to take the knock. So far not one of his 'special morning wires' have come off. If the Rev. Johnnie would only try his hand at tipping winners of football matches he might be a little more successful than he is in his own cheerful and peculiar line. But I'm not quite sure. Very likely he would have sent last week—all other touts did—Preston North End as the 'paddock snip' for the Lancashire Cup stakes, and have gone a floperina on the result. You can't be too careful when you prophesy before-hand—its very risky business.[39]

They were inclined to lack seriousness of purpose at the *Clarion*.

No one could accuse the I.L.P. of that. Bruce Glasier noted around the turn of the century that 'cycling, football, and other forms of personal recreation have cost us the zealous services of many admirable propagandists'.[40] In March 1904 the *Labour Leader* went so far as to publish an article entitled 'Is Football Anti-Social?' What is interesting about it is not that the writer, 'Gavroche', thought it was, but that in general his views about football were very like some of those middle-class critics of the game whose opinions we looked at earlier. The article deserves lengthy quotation.

You may think that the football craze is a foolish infatuation, a form of madness, a sign of national intellectual decadence; you may think these things, but, if you value the goodwill of your fellow workmen do not so much as whisper them above your breath. . . . For the football enthusiast—and he is the mass of the male population—brooks no depreciation of his recreative hobby.

The article went on to say that sport was all right as an exercise for mind and body

but when it comes to sport syndicated, trustified, and professionalised, that is a different thing: when it comes to troupes of trained athletes performing for hire before excited spectators, whose only exercise is the exercise of lung power, that is not sport, nor exercise, nor recreation—it is a spectacle, and a debasing spectacle at that; and when it comes to absorbing, from year's end to year's end, the minds of the great mass of the workers, rendering them mentally incapable of understanding their own needs and rights, and the common duties of citizenship, then it becomes a menace to all democratic and social progress. . . . We are in danger of producing a race of workers who can only obey their masters and think football. This is the material out of which slaves are made; the material which gives us shouting Jingoes, ignorant electors, and craven blacklegs.

He went on to make the obvious comparison with Imperial Rome describing modern football as a 'gladiatorial show with the death scenes left out'.[41] It was humiliating that 'every Saturday afternoon during the winter months more working-class money is spent upon football than would fight every constituency in the country, and man the House of Commons with the representatives of Labour'. He ended by writing that he would rather have been defeated at the Glasgow Chartist demonstration of 1838 than stand with the modern proletariat at a football match. So football made the work for socialism more difficult, at least for the I.L.P.[42]

A more interesting position was taken up by a London socialist weekly, the *Willesden Call* in the months before the outbreak of war in 1914. All socialists should take an interest in whatever interests the workers. Those members of the middle classes who criticised workers' pastimes were merely trying to damage the workers' self-image.[43] The *Fabian News* meanwhile took issue with those who said that the excitement which working people sought in football matches was only about combat and winning. 'Close observation shows not only that games produce many beautiful movements, but also that the spectators are conscious of and delight in the beauty that they see.' The paper went on to advocate trade union sports clubs along the lines of the S.D.P. in Germany and noted that

in the extension of the welfare of the employee idea lies a very real danger to labour, and it is amazing that Mr. Belloc has not seen that in the capturing of the social life of the workers is one of the most potent weapons of the servile state . . . the fellowship of the cricket and football field will bear precious fruit on sterner fields of industrial warfare.[44]

Out of this veritable cornucopia of opinion what kind of conclusion can we come to about working-class attitudes to football before 1915? There is no doubt that a lot of young men played and watched and enjoyed it and that a lot of older men had played and still watched and took pleasure from it. It is more than likely that a substantial number who neither played nor watched talked about it as though they did or had. The coercive effect of football conversation should not be underestimated. By 1915 football, on all its various levels, was a sizeable minority interest. The competitive element seems to have been important: it was not playing for the game's sake which stimulated the plethora of cups and leagues which dominated the structure of the game by the end of our period. Perhaps betting was important too. The working-class spectator identified with a team and through that team with a place. He liked to win and did not have much patience with honourable defeat. The aspiration to become a professional footballer must have been fairly widespread among working-class boys and youths. It offered, at least for a time, a way out of working for a perhaps not very good living. Although relatively few achieved a career in professional football, many more must have tried and failed. S.G. Hobson said that sport appealed to revolutionaries because it was fair. Perhaps part of its appeal to working men lay in the role of chance or luck. When the *Clarion* said that no footballer ever believed that his team had been beaten by a better one, the caricature was one of those which serves merely to underline the essential truth of the statement. People who 'got on' in life were lucky: people who did not, were not. And in any event, next Saturday was another game. It seems that so far as association football was concerned, working people had rejected both the attitudes of a substantial section of the socialists, and much of what the southern-orientated professional and administrative middle classes would have prescribed.

It was partly a realisation of this fact which stimulated a subtle shift in the balance of middle-class attitudes to football in the early years of the twentieth century. Some of the game's critics have appeared earlier in this chapter and their increasing vocality after 1900 was doubtless prompted by a variety of experiences. But the defeats of the Boer War, the revelations of the poor physical condition of so many of the recruits and the growing anxiety about Germany, were probably the most important for the timing of the reappraisal. Lord Milner, for example, feared 'that the British people, sheltered for so many years from keen competition in trade or war, had developed the bad habit of approaching their work as if it were a game, often sacrificing work altogether for the pleasures of sport'.[45] In January 1902 *The Times* published Kipling's famous panegyric on a decadent nation 'The Islanders', in which he criticised a country that spent so much time and energy on sport and yet refused to master the arts of warfare, stigmatising all classes who contented their souls 'with the flannelled fools at the wicket or the muddied oafs at the goals'. It was a cry taken up by people from such diverse backgrounds as C.B. Fry, John Burns and Robert Blatchford.[46] Those social imperialists from Rosebery and Haldane to Hewins, Wells and the Webbs who had joined in the 'quest for national efficiency' frequently referred in their campaign to the dangers of substituting sport for more serious pursuits. Arthur Shadwell, comparing the industrial efficiency of Britain, Germany and the United States, concluded that

we are a nation at play. Work is a nuisance, an evil necessity to be shirked and hurried over as quickly and easily as possible in order that we may get away to the real business of life—the golf course, the bridge table, the cricket and football field or some other of the thousand amusements which occupy our minds, and for which no trouble is too great.[47]

Even the *Athletic News* mirrored the concern of its betters to some extent when alluding to the question of replayed cup-ties which were to be decided on mid-week afternoons. 'Those of us interested in football are anxious that football should interfere with work as little as possible.'[48] Some employers were prepared to get tough. Two Bolton cotton mills prosecuted twenty-five of their workmen at the local borough court in February 1908 for absenting themselves from work when Bolton Wanderers played Notts County in a cup replay. Some 329 men had failed to turn up for work at one of the mills. Twenty-two men had been willing to work but could not do so due to the absence of the others. The employers said that they did not wish to be vindictive and if the defendants were prepared to pay 7/- including 2/- costs they would withdraw the summons and there would be no conviction. Eighteen agreed but five did not and they were convicted and fined 5/- each and ordered to pay 5/- damages.[49] Aston Villa even opposed the proposed extension of the Football League on the grounds that it would necessitate more mid-week matches and would therefore tempt working men away from their proper concerns.[50]

And, of course, if football interfered with work, neither it nor the general passion for sport had done much to improve the nation's physique.[51] This was underlined by the poor physical quality of recruits for the army and the three volumes of reports, evidence and appendices of the Inter-Departmental Committee on Physical Deterioration of 1904. It mattered little that the Committee stressed that the health and physique of army recruits did not accurately reflect the physical state of the population as a whole whose standards were probably being slowly but steadily raised. All those interested from social imperialists to race degenerationists concentrated on the shocking revelations about the recruits and drew the appropriate conclusions.[52] Even some professional footballers were caught up in the whirlwind of concern. J.L. Jones, captain of Tottenham, contributed the volume on association football to Pearson's 'Popular One Shilling Handbooks of Sports and Pastimes' series. He emphasised that spectating was all right, but young men who did not play lacked manliness. More players would mean an improved physical condition for the youth of England.[53] Perhaps the extent to which attitudes among influential sections of middle-class opinion had changed is best illustrated by *The Times*. We noted earlier the eulogistic editorial of 1899 after the Cup Final of that year when football was manly, physically beneficial and conducive to social harmony. Compare that with the much more sour note that entered the paper's report of the 1907 Final which consisted of 'professional football of the commonplace type; there was much pace, the kicking was hard, the ball was much in the air, and fouls were plentiful'.[54] For the political classes times had changed. Germany threatened: the Empire was in danger. Sport and games had to be less passionately embraced and more vigorous physical training on the best Prussian or Swedish lines taken up. It was a period in which some people became quite high on social Darwinism and eugenics.

But this change of balance was not a complete change of view and, in any event, it does not appear to have retarded the continued expansion of organised sport. Whatever indicators are used they seem to confirm that fact. Association football was finally given the establishment's stamp of approval at the Cup Final of 1914 when the King attended for the first time and presented the Cup to the captain of the winning team.[55] Clearly as there was no monolithic middle class, so there was no monolithic middle-class attitude to football. A particular attitude to the playing of all games, but especially team games and especially football and cricket grew up in the public schools in the second half of the nineteenth century and became diffused in the wider society, notably in middle-class circles. Ex-public school boys and ex-university men took the games to either their former homes or the communities whence they had gone to live and work. They hoped that their enjoyment of playing would rub off on people from the lower classes whom they met and that they too would accept the ideas of sportsmanship and fair play that were thought to be not only essential to all games-playing but useful rules of conduct for life itself. The coming of professionalism in the 1880s was a blow to this aspiration and an articulate and influential group of southern players, ex-players, journalists and officials centred on London, though with isolated outposts elsewhere, continued to campaign against professionalism and spectatorism right up to the First World War.[56]

But in the midlands and the north, where professionalism grew strong and waxed fat, the doctors and solicitors, schoolteachers and manufacturers, grocers and brewers who manned the committees and, from the 1890s with the coming of limited liability, the boards of directors of the more successful clubs, took a somewhat different attitude. They believed professionalism should be controlled: they believed that the players were servants and that the directors were the masters, as in any other trade, though as we saw in chapter two, in other respects they rarely ran the clubs like any other trade. They also believed that there was nothing wrong in playing to win and that southern criticism of their ways and attitude was part of a wider contempt which the south in general and London in particular held for regional and especially northern life. Such rivalries within the middle classes helped to harden attitudes to watching and playing that had started out not outstandingly distinct.

These directors and committeemen of the professional and semi-professional clubs acted out of a variety of motives as we saw in chapter two. Local prestige—remember Arnold Bennett's Denry Machin, *The Card* was published in 1911—even Ramsay MacDonald, hoping to become M.P. for Leicester in 1905, was told that he might collect quite a few votes if he 'did something' for the local football team. He did not![57] Identification with the town or community where they made their living, love of the game (many had been players in their youth), a belief in the efficacy of football as a force for social harmony, all these motives might be present in a single individual. Or none! Some middle-class people got involved because they thought it helped to keep workers out of the pubs; others because they were brewers and thought it helped to attract them in. Some thought there was money to be made out of it. As dividends were limited to 5 per cent and making a profit seemed as difficult for some clubs as their centre-forward passing through the eye of a needle, a good many must have been disappointed. But if you could obtain a stand building contract or a match-day catering franchise, then every little helped. And the prestige might be worth something if your team did not lose too often.

We have seen how much more difficult it is to capture direct evidence about working-class perceptions of the game. They do seem, on the whole, to have been supporters of a side rather than lovers of the game for its own sake.[58] Again, football may have contributed to the growth of local or community consciousness, may have assisted in helping working people identify with the town where they lived, and may itself have benefited from the growth of such feelings. It probably made life a little sweeter for those who enjoyed playing and watching, at least when they won. Some employers claimed that a successful football team was good for productivity and that output always rose on the Monday after a victory. The return of Saint Monday with a new look.[59] If association football did stimulate a more aware localism, building on those pre-existing local loyalties which historians seem to agree were characteristic of working people in this period, it also helped to break down such loyalties by providing an experience, a topic of conversation even, which, assisted by increasingly extensive press coverage, was almost nationwide by 1915. Working people do not appear to have accepted the notions about what games playing and football should have meant as subscribed to by middle-class opinion nor by some socialists. Football may have contributed to an easing of class tensions and a diminution of a consciousness of class on the part of working men, while encouraging the idea among working men that they were a part of a group with similar experiences and interests which were not shared by the bulk of another group, the middle classes. As the numbers both playing and watching association football grew, the great majority came to be working people. Moreover, the game came to be judged, especially in middle-class eyes, increasingly by the activities surrounding its professional elite section. As this happened, the newer public schools and, increasingly, the grammar schools, turned away from association football and took up the still wholly amateur Rugby Union.[60]

Notes

1   The National Physical Recreation Society was also formed by

men of all politics ... to put within the reach of the masses the privileges and enjoyments which have done so much to form the character of the English public schoolboy. . . . The strict discipline, observance of rules, and the love of fair play were very good training for the more serious business of life, and had a great deal to do with the formation of character.

Baily's Magazine of Sports and Pastimes, vol. 47, March 1887, p. 166. On Sportsmanship see also the booklet of instructions issued by the Council of the British Olympic Association to each member of the British team before setting out for the Paris games in 1924. A Sportsman, it said, plays the game for the game's sake. Plays for his side and not for himself. Is a good winner and a good loser i.e. modest in victory and generous in defeat. Accepts all decisions in a proper spirit. Is chivalrous towards a defeated opponent. Is unselfish and is always ready to help others to become proficient. As a spectator applauds good play on both sides. Never interferes with referees or judges no matter what the decision. Reprinted in H.J. Savage, *Games and Sports in British Schools and Universities* (New York, 1927) pp. 21–2. Baron Pierre de Coubertin was so impressed by English notions of games and games playing and by the widespread mythology surrounding the ancient Greek games that he was stimulated into reviving the Olympic idea. On the reality of athletics in ancient Greece see M.I. Finley and H.W. Pleket, *The Olympic Games: The First Thousand Years* (1976) esp. pp. 70–3, 121, 132. See also E. Weber, 'Pierre de Coubertin and the introduction of organised sport in France' in *Journal of Contemporary History*, vol. 5 no. 2, 1970. Even some Germans were captivated. See for example R. Kirchner, *Fair Play: The Games of Merrie England* (English ed. 1928).

2   Although most football administrators were unpaid voluntary workers, substantial material rewards were not unknown. Charles Crump, President of the Birmingham F.A. 1875–1923, F.A. Councillor 1883–1923 and Vice-President from 1886, received an illuminated address together with a tea and coffee service after Stafford Road, the team he had helped to found and still played for, won the Wednesbury Charity Cup in 1880. Four years later the Birmingham F.A. recognised his work by another illuminated address, a piano, and a suite of dining room furniture. In 1897 he received a third illuminated address together with £200 from the Birmingham F.A. Finally in 1920, when 80 years old, he qualified for a fourth illuminated address and a cheque for £1255 according to the *Birmingham Daily Post* but $4000 according to the *Birmingham Daily Mail*. *Birmingham Daily Post* 16 April 1923, *Birmingham Daily Mail* 16 April 1923.

3   N.L. Jackson (1900) op.cit. pp. 192, 203.

4   *The Nineteenth Century*, vol. 34, December 1893 pp. 899–911.

5   *The Times* 12 April 1897. One could multiply such illustrations. See, for example *The Argonaut* no. 1, 1 January 1874, pp. 21–3 and the *Preston Herald* 9 March 1889 which quoted an article from *Baily's Magazine of Sports and Pastimes* to the effect that

the fathers of modern football have reason to be thankful that they have offered to thousands of the younger working men . . . a harmless relaxation. It is one which will not only tend to give them honest and hearty enjoyment, but cannot fail at the same time to inculcate lessons, calculated to influence their daily life and to their moral advantage.

Nottingham Forest F.C. met weekly to discuss football from a moral point of view in 1879. *Athletic News* 10 December 1879.

6 *Football World* 9 September 1895. For a similar comment see *Athletic News* 24 January 1889.

7 *Preston Herald* 30 May 1883. A few weeks earlier another Lancashire newspaper, commenting on the fact that the amateur working men players of Blackburn Olympic had gone to Blackpool for special training before both the semi-final and final of the F.A. Cup, warned that 'such a break in the ordinary routine of work is likely to upset the business habits of the individual members who may be so highly favoured, and what is still worse, to lead to some degree of unpleasantness between employers and employed'. *Darwen News* 5 May 1883. On the value of sports getting the worker out into the open air see the same paper 1 March 1884. For further examples of similar arguments see the *Nottingham Daily Guardian* 17 December 1883, quoting a *Spectator* article, and the *Preston Herald* 3 December 1887.

8 H.H. Almond, 'Football as a Moral Agent' in *Nineteenth Century*, vol. 34, December 1893. J.R. Fleming in an article on rugby football in the *Badminton Magazine of Sports and Pastimes*, vol. III, 1896 pp. 563–4 made the same point as did F.E. Smith in a piece entitled 'The Vogue of Games: Is it worth it?' *The New Fry's Magazine*, vol. I no. 1, April 1911 pp. 3–4.

9 W.J. Lias, 'The Future of Rugby Football', *Badminton Magazine of Sports and Pastimes*, vol. 5, 1897, pp. 605–6. Note the almost identical sentiments of Mr G. Kynoch, the Birmingham manufacturer and President of Aston Villa when proposing the toast 'Our Team' at the club's annual general meeting in 1883. *Birmingham Daily Gazette* 22 May 1883.

10 F.E. Smith, op.cit. p. 3. Surely there is a note of contempt here?

11 Patrick Joyce has suggested that sport was playing this role in the East Lancashire cotton towns as early as the 1860s. See his unpublished Oxford D. Phil. Thesis, 'Popular Toryism in Lancashire 1860–90' (1975), pp. 338–40. *Sheffield Daily Telegraph* 12 March 1887. The *Athletic News* had boasted in 1880 that it was well known that

at this very moment some of our greatest football players feast, in international times, between commercial magnates, who worship them because they are the possessors and interpreters of a species of science which brings glory to their country and honour to their club.

Athletic News 13 October 1880. The paper later pointed out that so far as horse racing was concerned, the classes did not fraternise on the track because they had separate stands and enclosures. *Athletic News* 19 January 1881. Professionalism complicated this relationship: see chapters three and four above.

12 See G.S. Jones, *Outcast London* (Oxford, 1971) esp. Part III.

13 *Baily's Magazine*, vol. 37, 1881 p. 330 and vol. 47, 1887 pp. 165, 167, 169.

14 When he founded the Rhodes Scholarships at Oxford, he listed as qualifications not only 'literary and scholastic' achievements' but also 'fondness for and success in, manly outdoor sports such as cricket, football and the like'. J.R. de S. Honey, op.cit. p. 210.

15 *The Times* 17 April 1899. The *Athletic News* of the same day thought that the Cup Final gave people a chance to visit the 'Heart of the Empire' who would not otherwise have the opportunity. When Barnsley reached the Cup Final in 1910 the local paper gave a list of the important sights of London which

a first-time visitor should not miss. *Barnsley Independent* 16 April 1910.
For the value of football as a sport of all classes see M. Shearman, *Athletics
and Football* (1887 edn), p. 369. Similarly 'Creston' (N.L. Jackson) in an
article entitled 'Football', *Fortnightly Review*, vol. 55 N.S. 1894 p. 38—
'We are withall strong supporters of that good fellowship which makes
all classes equal in the cricket or football field. It has done a great deal for
the country and the people.'

16 On the game being more scientific see, for example, *Blackburn Standard*
16 October 1880, *Badminton Magazine of Sports and Pastimes* August-
December 1895 p. 485, *Pastime* 10 March 1886, *Preston Herald* 30 March
1887. *All the Year Round* 3rd Series No. 69 26 April 1890, p. 393, and for
more detail see chapter seven.

17 *Blackburn Standard* 27 May 1882.

18 *Blackburn Standard* 29 April 1882. The number of such protests dealt
with by the Lancashire F.A. had gone up from 3 in season 1879–80 to
17 in 1882–3. Lancashire Football Association Minute Books. Marindin
was from an old Huguenot family and had been educated at Eton. He was
a Major in the Royal Engineers and had fought in the Crimea. He was
Brigade Major of the School of Engineering at Chatham from 1869 to
1874 and played an active part in the football club. He was later appointed
Chief Inspecting Officer of Railways at the Board of Trade. He was F.A.
President from 1874 until 1890.

19 It should be remembered that the professional clubs being criticised were
themselves largely run by middle-class committee-men. See chapter two.

20 Dr. Morley of Blackburn Rovers had been accused of being partisan in
1882 and he agreed that he liked to see his team win. However, he rejected
the charge that he had 'no eyes for the excellencies of their opponents and
had no good wishes for them when they succeeded'. *Darwen News* 27
May 1882. Similarly the Sheffield *Football World* saw nothing wrong with
supporting.

We believe in backing up the local teams heartily, and we do not believe
in the wishy-washy talk about no partisanship. . . . While treating opposing
teams with scrupulously sportsmanlike fairness, we shall do our best to
encourage our own side to win. [To be] deeply interested in a side . . . is
the only healthy state of feeling respecting exciting sports. Give the other
man the fairest of fair play but go in for winning.

Football World 9 September 1895.

21 *C.B. Fry's Magazine* vol. VI no. 31, October 1906, pp. 90–1. *The Times*
believed that the chief 'motives' of the football crowd were (i) gregarious
instinct, (ii) the 'natural and rather praiseworthy wish to make a joyous
hullabaloo,' (iii) the feeling that their 'coppers' have purchased the players,
(iv) the desire for a topic of subsequent conversation over a pint, (v) petty
betting and (vi) 'the holiday-maker's lust for taking exercise by proxy'.
The Times 16 November 1910.

22 *Fry's Magazine of Sport*, vol. XX no. 2, November 1913 pp. 201–3. For
further discussions of spectator partisanship see *Sheffield Daily Telegraph*
17 November 1891:

good play is only appreciated when it is part of the programme of the
favourite team. . . . A good shot which fails is hailed with a derisive storm
of booing and sarcastic rejoinders in those quarters where the partisans

of Wednesday are . . . when the shot comes from United: but a chorus of approving shouts hail the attempt when it is made by one of their own team.

See also C.B. Fry in *Badminton Magazine*, vol. I 1895, p. 485; 'Creston' in *Fortnightly Review* no. 5 vol. 55, N.S. 1894, p. 33; E. Ensor 'The Football Madness' in *Contemporary Review* vol. 74, 1898, p. 758; H. Graves, 'A Philosophy of Sport' in *Contemporary Review*, vol. 78, 1900, pp. 877–93; *Pastime* 16 January, 13 February 1895; An Old Player, 'Football: The Game and the Business' in *The World's Work*, vol. I, December 1902, p. 79; R. Mellors, *In and About Nottinghamshire* (1908) p. 439.

23   *Birmingham Daily Mail* 3 February 1896.
24   *Badminton Magazine*, vol. III, 1896 p. 560. See also *Pastime* 13 February 1895.
25   *Athletic News* 17 April 1899.
26   *Birmingham Daily Mail* 5 September 1892. These exhortations were apparently repeated three years later.

It is a certain fact that many thousands go to Perry Barr, not so much to see football, as to see the Villa win. . . . Ninety out of every hundred of the spectators who patronise the Villa ground (. . . I do not write specifically of (the Villa) but of all clubs and their supporters), would rather see the Villa win in a scrambling second-rate game than they would see them beaten by a narrow majority in a scientific and finely contested struggle.

Quoted in *Pastime* 18 September 1895.

27   *Sunderland Football Echo* 4 January 1908. John Lewis, founder of Blackburn Rovers, leading referee and long-time F.A. Councillor claimed that there were 'few instances nowadays of crowds applauding visitors. . . . Everybody now seems to want to be on the winning side, caring little for the reason of the game or its beauties.' *Athletic News* 23 March 1908.
28   I owe this reference to Michael Morris.
29   There was, of course, general agreement that the heavy charging which had earlier been a feature of the game had much diminished. See, for example, Gibson and Pickford, vol. I op.cit. pp. 211–12, *How to Play Football* (Manchester, 1891) p. 3, and chapter seven.
30   *C.B. Fry's Magazine*, vol. II no. 8, November 1911 pp. 126–27. The Corinthians, on a tour of South Africa, felt so strongly about the penalty kick that when one was awarded against them their goalkeeper left his goal. They had no wish to prevent the other side from fairly scoring. Similarly when the Corinthians were awarded a penalty their kicker deliberately shot wide of the goal. *Amateur Football*, vol. 1 no. 1, 31 October 1907 p 7.
31   C.E. Sutcliffe and F. Hargreaves, *History of the Lancashire Football Association 1878–1928* (Blackburn, 1928) pp. 22, 105. The number of cases increased from 481 per year in 1907–8 to 600 per year in 1914–15, by which time there were 50 leagues as opposed to 35 in 1907–8 and 178 clubs as against 203 in the earlier period.
32   Note the controversy following the Cup Final of 1913 when the F.A. suspended the Sunderland centre-half and the Aston Villa centre-forward though neither had been sent off in the game. The F.A. also suspended the referee. Most newspapers agreed that there had been much rough play in the match with the correspondent of the *Manchester Despatch* labelling it 'the dirtiest final for many a year past'. *Birmingham Daily Mail* 21 April

1913, *Birmingham Daily Post* 21 April 1913, *The Times* 21 April 1913, *Sunderland Daily Echo* 21 April 1913.

33 Discussing the possibilities of professionalism in London one paper concluded that it was 'hardly possible . . . in a region as destitute of local partisanship that more than one or two first rate teams . . . would retain the popular favour'. *Pastime* 13 May 1891. P.F. Clarke, *Lancashire and the New Liberalism* (1971) p. 27.

34 We have seen something of local press coverage in chapter six. It could give the local team massive publicity if it was doing well. The *Preston Herald*, for example, devoted a whole page of seven columns to pre-match coverage of the F.A. Cup Final of 1888 in which Preston North End played West Bromwich Albion. *Preston Herald* 24 March 1888.

35 *Preston Herald* 2 April 1884. For another example see *Blackburn Times* 7 April 1883.

36 *Justice* 28 October 1899.

37 See *Justice* 14 November 1896, 12 March 1898, 13 November 1897. In this issue the club actually advertised for players who must have been in the S.D.F. for at least three months in order to be eligible.

38 *Justice* 16 January 1897, *Northampton Socialist* June 1898. It may be that the players were drawn from all socialist groups in the town. Having said that, football could be used to buttress hostile feelings which already existed, in particular between the S.D.F. and the I.L.P. in some places. In Southampton, for example, the two groups disagreed over the parliamentary candidacy of J.R. MacDonald in 1895 and 1896. 'The bad feeling prevalent between us and the local members of the I.L.P. has broken out afresh. They have challenged us to a football match on Good Friday. Some of our old warhorses are in training, and a list of the killed and wounded will be sent next week.' *Justice* 4 April 1896.

39 *Clarion* 13 February 1892. Clarion members probably played a lot of football too. They certainly formed clubs and advertised for matches often enough. See, for example, *Glasgow Commonweal* June 1896.

40 See S. Pierson, *Marxism and the Origins of British Socialism* (Ithaca, 1973), p. 250. On the other hand Brougham Villiers in his book, *The Socialist Movement in England* (1908) pp. 172–3, thought that in the workshops of Lancashire and Yorkshire towns on Monday mornings, the discussions were about the latest I.L.P. meeting after the topic of Saturday's football match had been exhausted. But note the anxious tone of the compiler of the 'Birmingham Notes' in the *Workmen's Times* 12 September 1890. 'Now that the football season has commenced it is to be hoped that Birmingham and all trade unionists will not allow the national pastime to in any way interfere with their duties to the various trade organisations.'

41 W.T. Stead made the same point in *The Revival in the West* (1904) p. 14. 'Gavroche' was William Stewart, the first biographer of Keir Hardie. I owe this reference to Fred Reid.

42 This article provoked a reply from South Wales which said that football was fine, it was professionalism that was the cancer. Football brought together people who might otherwise not meet and socialists whom the writer knew liked it. Capitalist and worker were equal on the football field. *Labour Leader* 19 March, 2 April 1904. The chairman of Handsworth I.L.P. thought that the working class 'would rather have sport than hard thinking'. Quoted by M.D. Blanch, 'Nation, Empire and the Birmingham

Working Class 1899–1914', unpublished thesis, University of Birmingham Ph.D. 1975, p. 87. S.G. Hobson in his autobiography, *Pilgrim to the Left* (1938) p. 46, said that he wrote an athletics column in the *Labour Leader* under the pen name 'Olympian' but dropped it when he found himself so christened at I.L.P. meetings. 'I was not minded to begin serious work with the reputation of a sporting journalist. But I missed some fun.' Later in the same book, attempting to illustrate the proposition that all revolutionaries are human, Hobson wrote that the revolutionary 'cannot keep away from games—football, cricket, athletics. I have met him at Kennington Oval, and watched his eyes glisten at Old Trafford. . . . ' He then described his attendance at a meeting of revolutionaries in Chicago which, after long discussions about oppression and injustice, got onto boxing, cricket, and finally football. 'The reason for the revolutionists' love of games is . . . they are nearly as possible absolutely fair.' pp. 273–4. Herbert Spencer might have agreed with Gavroche. In a letter to Beatrice Webb dated 25 February 1890 he wrote: 'Your reference to Socialism as putting down games (Query, would not the games rather put down Socialism . . .)' Karl Kautsky also felt that British workpeople spent too much effort on 'foot-ball [sic], boxing, horse-racing and opportunities for gambling'. Such activities moved them deepest and to them they devoted 'their entire leisure time, their individual powers, and their material means'. K. Kautsky, *The Social Revolution* (1916 edn) p. 102. The lectures were given in 1902. For an English socialist's agreement see T. Barclay, *Memoirs and Medleys: The Autobiography of a Bottle-Washer* (Leicester, 1934) pp. 56, 59, 63. I. Maisky, watching football in Burnley in 1913, also thought it a pity that English workmen did not put the passion which they had for football into politics. He seemed to think that those seated around him in the stand at Burnley were working people. See I. Maisky, *Journey Into the Past* (1962) pp. 208–9.

43   *Willesden Call* February-July 1914.
44   *Fabian News*, vol. XXIV no. 8, July 1913. The article ended: 'sport will furnish a valuable factor in the new synthesis of society by providing organisations cutting across other associations and assisting in the sweetening process of intermingling of various sections of society.' *The Servile State* (1912) by Hilaire Belloc was written 'to maintain the thesis that industrial society as we know it will tend towards the re-establishment of slavery'. The Birmingham and District Works Football Association, with many prominent local employers among its list of vice-presidents, was formed in 1906. S.W. Clives, *The Centenary Book of Birmingham County Football Association* (Birmingham, 1975) p. 89.
45   C. Headlam (ed.), *The Milner Papers: South Africa*, vol. II (1933) p. 233.
46   R. Kipling, *The Five Nations* (1903) p. 135. *C.B. Fry's Magazine*, vol. IV, October 1905-March 1906 pp. 361–2. Fry himself ran a series of articles entitled 'The Blot on British Games' which he identified as the fact 'that not one of our games, or popular sports, has in any degree a martial character; not one of them—beyond the improvement in physique which they effect . . . is of any military value.' He believed that rifle shooting ought to be a national sport like cricket and football. For Blatchford, see the *New Fry's Magazine*, vol. I, no. 1, April 1911, pp. 11–15, 'Universal Military Training and the National Physique'. John Burns thought that 'football has been carried too far' in J.B. Atkins (ed.), *National Physical Training: An Open Debate* (1904), p. 67. For a contemporary criticism of the cult of athletics in the

public schools see the essay by L. Ford in C. Cookson (ed.), *Essays on Secondary Education* (Oxford, 1898), pp. 284–305.

47 Arthur Shadwell, *Industrial Efficiency* (2 vols. 1906) vol. II p. 454 and G.R. Searle, *The Quest for National Efficiency* (1971), p. 42.

48 *Athletic News* 15 February 1909. Attendance at eight such replays in January 1908 had totalled 116,000. *Athletic News* 20 January 1908.

49 *Bolton Evening News* 13, 20 February 1908. Public warnings had been issued by the Director-General of Ordnance Factories at the Woolwich Arsenal in 1895 threatening serious action should workmen continue to absent themselves on the occasion of local football matches. *Pastime* 4 December 1895. Bristol Corporation decided in 1909 that any future approach by unemployed men engaged on relief works to be allowed time off to see a Saturday afternoon football match would result in immediate dismissal. *Athletic News* 8 February 1909.

50 *Birmingham Daily Post* 24 June 1905.

51 See some of the contributions to J.B. Atkins (1904) op.cit. especially those by E.J. Broadfield and the Rev. E. Roper, pp. 146, 150, who both believed that football and cricket could never replace 'systematic physical training'.

52 G.R. Searle, op.cit. p.61. See also Inter-Departmental Committee on Physical Deterioration PP. XXXII (Cdl.2175 Cdl.2210 Cd.2186) (3 vols. 1904). G.F. Shee, 'The Deterioration in the National Physique', *Nineteenth Century*, vol. LIII, May 1903. E.B. Iwan-Muller 'The Cult of the Unfit' *Fortnightly Review*, vol. 86, August 1909 pp. 207–22.

53 J.H. Jones, *Association Football* (1904) p. 18.

54 *The Times* 22 April 1907. Repeated in 1913 *The Times* 21 April 1913.

55 This got the game into the Court Circular. *The Times* 27 April 1914. The Prince of Wales (later Edward VII) had been patron of the F.A. but that was one thing: associating overtly with the professional side of the game quite another.

56 Some of them led a breakaway Amateur Football Association in 1907 although they returned to the fold in 1914. The ostensible issue was the Football Association's determination that all local football associations should admit to membership professional clubs in their area. The F.A.'s of London, Middlesex and Surrey were militantly opposed. They saw themselves as the David of pure amateurism standing up to the Goliath of professionalism and business football. They denied that it was a 'class movement' but its list of vice-presidents was dominated by old boys of the soccer-playing public schools and there were very few affiliated clubs or associations north of Suffolk. See *Amateur Football Association Annual* 1907–8.

57 See B. Sachs, *J. Ramsay MacDonald* (Albuquerque, 1952) p. 15. He did win the election. For a cynical appraisal of the importance, for local politicians, of keeping in with the constituency football team, especially in its more successful moments, see *Pastime* 20 April 1892. See also J.R. Clynes, *Memoirs 1924–1937* (1937) p. 30, who recalled kicking off for Manchester United in his first general election campaign in 1906. The Chairman of Middlesbrough tried, disastrously, to use football to influence politics in December 1910. Middlesbrough were due to play Sunderland in a local 'derby' match just before the second general election of 1910 in which Colonel Gibson Poole was the Conservative candidate. An attempt by the Middlesbrough club's secretary to persuade the Sunderland team, through

their captain, to let the 'Boro' win and hopefully increase their chairman's chances at the polls ended in an F.A. inquiry and the suspension of both the secretary and Colonel Poole from all football management. *The Times* 17, 18 January, 30 May 1911. *North Eastern Daily Gazette* 5 December 1910. Ironically 'Boro' won the match 1–0 and the Liberal candidate the election by 3745 votes.

58   Some were no doubt both. Information on actual supporters' clubs in this period is sparse indeed although Lincoln City had a 'Working Men's Committee' in 1901 which had raised £90 for club funds, banked the ground and built and paid for a covered stand. *Lincolnshire Echo* 2 March 1901. Northampton, Norwich, Croydon Common, Exeter and Watford, all of the Southern League, apparently had active supporters' clubs before 1915 and a federation was formed in 1913 whose first aim was to promote 'Sportsmanship and Goodfellowship in connection with the game of football . . .' *Football Players' Magazine*, vol. II no. 9, April 1913.

59   The author has not been able to discover any attempt by employers in Britain to quantify such increases in production. However, A. Texeira has claimed that 'in weeks that Corinthians (the most popular team in Sao Paulo) win, production in Sao Paulo rises 12.3 per cent. In weeks in which they lose, the number of accidents at work increases by 15.3 per cent.' *Realidade Ano* 11 no. 15, July 1967 quoted by J. Lever, 'Soccer as a Brazilian Way of Life' in G.P. Stone (ed.), *Games, Sport and Power* (New Brunswick, 1972) pp. 139–40.

60   It is difficult to document this before the war. Radley, for example, changed from association to rugby during 1914. *The Radleian* nos. 395, 398, 28 February, 1 July 1914. See also A.K. Boyd, *The History of Radley College 1847–1947* (Oxford, 1948). The new warden appears to have been behind the change. According to the games master at Rossall, rugby took the place of soccer there because the high winds and extreme cold of Rossall in winter made the kicking game difficult to play properly. S.P.B. Mais, *All the Days of My Life* (1937) p. 59. Most public schools played the rugby game anyway and if J.A. Hobson's view of why sport was encouraged at his grammar school in the 1870s—in order to bring the boys into the company of more socially reputable people on the basis of equality—can be more widely applied, then the adoption of rugby by many grammar schools should not surprise us. But this is an area worth spending an M.A. thesis investigating. J.A. Hobson, *Confessions of an Economic Heretic* (1938) pp. 31–2.

CHAPTER NINE
IN CONCLUSION

THOSE critics of the professional game who had been active, if ineffective, before 1914 were given a further opportunity to assail it by the outbreak of war in that year. The first suggestions that the game should be abandoned for the duration were made as early as August.[1] But it was the need to recruit a new army to support the shattered remnants of the B.E.F. and the obvious fact, by the end of October, that the war would not be over by Christmas which provoked a campaign, both inside and outside Parliament, most notably in the columns of *The Times*, to end the national scandal which the continuance of Cup and League professional football was thought by many people to constitute. The historian A.F. Pollard made most of the critics' major points in a letter published in *The Times* on November 7.

Some of us who are debarred from enlisting by age or other disqualification feel shy of urging on others a duty to which we are not ourselves liable. But we need feel no compunction in saying what we think of courses which act as deterrents to duty: and we view with indignation and alarm the persistence of Association football clubs in doing their best for the enemy.

We must, of course, discriminate. Football is an excellent thing, even in time of war. Armies and navies can only be maintained so long as the community fulfils its function of producing means for their support; and healthy recreation is essential for efficient production. A man may be doing his duty in other fields than the front. But there is no excuse for diverting from the front thousands of athletes in order to feast the eyes of crowds of inactive spectators, who are either unfit to fight or else unfit to be fought for. .... Every club that employs a professional football player is bribing a needed recruit to refrain from enlistment, and every spectator who pays his gate money is contributing so much towards a German victory.[2]

Needless to say there were many individuals in the Football Association who were very sympathetic to such views. Following a meeting between F.A. officials and representatives of the War Office, the F.A. issued an appeal to all players and spectators who were single men to come forward and join the colours. It was agreed to use the Saturday afternoon league match as a recruiting opportunity and it was the failure of this crude instrument which produced the outrage and near hysteria of the following weeks.[3]

The plan was that prominent men should make a recruiting speech during the half-time interval. Ideally a military band should be in attendance and at the end of the game those men who had volunteered would march behind it to the nearest recruiting station. But as *The Times* Monday morning headline proclaimed, 'One recruit at Arsenal match', the scheme was far from successful. The speech by Colonel Burn M.P. at the Chelsea ground failed to produce even one recruit while at Nottingham Forest the reserve battalion of the Robin Hood Rifles marched around the ground at half-time 'and were received with great enthusiasm but unfortunately that was the only result achieved'. Other attempts fared little better.[4] *The Times* contrasted association football's failure with the distinguished performance of cricket, rugby union and rowing clubs. Several letters to the paper blamed the professional element. Money was at the root of it. The game must be stopped in order to ensure that some young men took the war seriously.[5]

In Parliament Mr Bridgeman wanted the railway companies to charge football excursionists double and put the money into a fund for the prosecution of the war. Another Conservative M.P. suggested a tax on all those spectators at football matches who were not in uniform. A lofty editorial in *The Times* followed, largely mirroring Pollard's arguments. The paper stressed its opposition to compulsion. It felt confident that public opinion would soon be strong enough without it. It was a national scandal that professional football players 'in the prime of manhood,' should be bribed away from their country's service by club managers.

British sports and British games have done our race a service which other nations have emulated too late and freely acknowledge on the field today. Except, however, in this one solitary instance of professional football, they have long since fallen into their proper places as a pastime and a training, not as a business or a trade.[6]

The response of the football authorities to all this was hurt but firm. No one could doubt the patriotism of either the Football Association or the Football and Southern Leagues. There were genuine differences of opinion between individuals in all the organisations as to how far, for example, continued play would boost morale on the home front, or hamper recruitment for France. But the two leagues did have an additional anxiety. All their member clubs had signed contracts to pay the wages of their players at least until the end of April 1915. If the game should stop what would happen to those liabilities? On the other hand, attendances at matches were falling and receipts correspondingly declining. This had been clear since the end of September when the Football League had carried out a detailed survey comparing the receipts so far taken in 1914–15 with the previous three seasons. The Saturday gate for First Division matches had dropped from an average of £735 in 1913–14 to £414. The average mid-week gate had fallen from £511 to £291. Moreover, average receipts from season tickets had dropped from £907 to £440. The Second Division showed a similar picture.[7]

The League's response to this financial emergency was to reduce players' wages on a scale of from 15 per cent from the best paid to 5 per cent from the lowest paid. The money was to be collected by the League and used to pay the wages of players whose clubs were in financial straits. In addition, each club was to pay its visitors 10 per cent of the match receipts.

These financial considerations probably inhibited a strong reply from the League. But the Football Association did not share the same problems and it was that body which almost certainly sponsored the special article which appeared in *The Times* on 28 November 1914 defending football's contribution to the war effort. The article claimed that football had provided something close to 100,000 recruits already, far in excess of any other branch of sport. Professional players with the leading clubs were undergoing military drill on certain days of the week and miniature rifle ranges had been erected on many grounds.[8] Emphasis was laid on the fact that there were only about 5,000 professionals all told and 2,000 were already serving in the armed forces. Only about 600 unmarried men who depended on the game for their livelihood had not volunteered. This compared with around two million who were eligible in the country as a whole. It did not seem fair to single out those 600 for special vituperation. Moreover, attendances at matches had halved. Most clubs would be glad to stop if it was not for the problem of the players' contracts. It was quite wrong to suggest that the clubs had not encouraged recruiting. On the same page a list of leading clubs was given together with some detail about the volunteers which they had provided. West Bromwich Albion, for example, had formed a special company attached to the Fifth South Staffordshire Territorials. Although it had been raised principally from among their supporters eight of the club's players had enlisted. The same day *The Times* published a letter from the Secretary of the Hertfordshire F.A. who was also an F.A. Councillor. It made much the same points as the article and said that the controversy was due to panic. The chairman of Arsenal pointed out that it was unreasonable to expect young men to sign on after a football match before consulting relatives and friends and he reiterated an argument to which defenders of the game had increasing recourse: why were the crowds at football matches declining if it was not due to large-scale volunteering?[9] A meeting of London clubs hit back harder still when they offered to close their grounds simultaneously with the closing of 'racecourses, golf links, theatres, music-halls, picture palaces and kindred entertainments'. The *Athletic News* agreed.

> The whole agitation is nothing less than an attempt by the classes to stop the recreation on one day in the week of the masses. . . . What do they care for the poor man's sport?
> The poor are giving their lives for this country in thousands. In many cases they have nothing else. . . . There are those who could bear arms, but who have to stay at home and work for the Army's requirements, and the country's needs. These should, according to a small clique of virulent snobs, be deprived of the one distraction that they have had for over thirty years.[10]

The *Athletic News* sometimes found ingenious ways of defending the professional player. In November 1914, for example, the paper pointed out that association football players did not have the physiques of the rugby men. Association football was a game of skill in which the short and light played an important part. There was a vast difference between men capable of playing football for ninety minutes and attaining the rigid physical standards necessary for military duty.[11]

December 1914 really saw the end of the public controversy although the pressure on the football authorities to stop play remained. The War Office undoubtedly made their views known at every opportunity. The Council of the Newspaper Proprietors Federation, representing London dailies, resolved not to publish more than the bare results of football matches, save in the specialist sporting press.[12]

Weeklies such as the *News of the World* and the *Sunday Chronicle* remained unmoved by this outburst of patriotism. The former continued its five columns of football on page two and the latter wrote in an editorial that there was no need to forego football and acted accordingly. A Sheffield newspaper columnist said that it was a disgrace to the city that United had won the F.A. Cup at such a time. It was significant that the newspaper in question did not disassociate itself from those views nor publish an editorial on the cup final which before the war it certainly would have done. But the paper did not discontinue its detailed football reporting either, with a whole page recording the activities of all the local sides every Monday.[13] On the other hand there was no public celebration when United arrived back with the cup. In spite of the lack of publicity, however, about two thousand people met the train. Pressures of this kind, together with falling attendances and associated financial problems, the increasing difficulty of keeping up team strengths and the perils of travelling on a wartime railway, all in the context of a struggle whose end was by no means in sight decided the football authorities not to continue after the end of the 1914–15 season.

Professional football's severest patriotic critics were probably not completely satisfied that the game and all those connected with it were really doing their share in the prosecution of the war until they read of the attack of the First Battalion the 18th London Regiment at Loos in 1915 led by men kicking a football. The hopes which many middle-class people had for the game before 1914 must have appeared, temporarily at least, to have been justified.[14] As Lord Derby said after he had presented the F.A. Cup and medals in 1915, 'the clubs and their supporters had seen the cup played for, and it was now the duty of everyone to join with each other and play a sterner game for England'.[15]

Association football was refined and organised by the educated classes. It was they who worked out a body of rules and set up an organisation, the Football Association, by whose efforts those rules quickly came to be widely accepted. The educated elite dominated the Football Association throughout the period of this study. Most leading clubs, both before and after the acceptance of paid players in 1885, were run by members of the professional or employing groups. But the many clubs below this elite may well have been run by working men for working men. Moreover, it was working men who formed the bulk of players and spectators particularly from 1880 on. In that sense, association football became a working-class game.

It was also the educated classes who developed and articulated an ethical code governing the way in which games in general, including association football, should be played. This can be summarised under the heading of sportsmanship and the notion of 'playing the game'. Although it was adopted by a games-playing elite with a largely middle-class social background, it was in essence based on aristocratic notions of chivalry as a look at

N.L. Jackson's novel prescription for football players, set out on p. 224, clearly indicates.

It is one thing to set down a code of conduct: it is another to have its detailed provisions observed. Even before 1885, knock-out cup competitions had produced numerous complaints about the results of matches and how those results had been arrived at. After 1885 the conduct of some professional players fell a good way short of the sportsmanship ideal. The referee was given increased powers: intentional infringements of the law became an increasingly accepted part of the game. Neither did the predominantly working-class crowd which watched the games manifest signs that they had imbibed the sportsmanship ethic. Winning was all, or almost all, and the opposition were there to satisfy the craving for success.

Professionalism undoubtedly brought technical improvements in the way the game was played. Moreover, in some respects they were improvements which could be filtered down to the host of minor clubs outside the paid elite by emulation. But in so far as the chivalric ideal was well and truly not attained, something was lost in the process. The Sheffield *Football World* probably had the right idea: give the other side the fairest of fair play but go in for winning. The predominantly working-class football crowd found the former very difficult to do. Watching their team lose at home was rather like going to the melodrama and seeing the villain get the girl in the end.

But it would be a mistake to dismiss the intensity of feeling which the football spectator might experience in the course of a match. Even if winning was all, the colour, excitement and dramatic quality of the play were all part of a fortnightly ritual which was both predictable and unpredictable at the same time. And if the worst came to the worst it could always be put down to bad luck. An opponent might even provoke grudging appreciation if he was skilful or powerful enough.

The widespread experience which working men had of playing and watching association football probably aided the formation of a more general consciousness of class. On the other hand, in so far as support for a team emphasised community, it probably encouraged the fragmentation of class feeling though it can hardly be considered as important in this respect as jobs, wages, housing and general expectations of life. It certainly enhanced the quality of life for those working men and boys whose interest it so captured that most other matters were relegated to second place and a long way back at that. It was an interest whose strength meant, for example, that there was 'no contest' in Sunderland in 1890 when the Prince and Princess of Wales visited the town on the same day as Blackburn Rovers. The Royal couple were actually just down the road at Seaham Harbour where 2,000 turned out. Twenty thousand went to the match.[16] Association football was a pastime but more than a pastime, something to enjoy even if the moral benefits which middle-class propagandists had hoped the game would bring did not quite materialise.

Apart from the paid player very few people made much money out of professional football, least of all the club director. Being on the board might produce lucrative contracts: it might impress other businessmen who had trade to offer. But with dividends restricted to 5 per cent men like Houlding, who obviously was keen to make his patronage of Everton financially beneficial, were always going to be few and far between. Football club directors had a variety of motives for wanting to be directors but branching out into a new and profitable line was not one of them.

By 1915 they had their reward in their role in supporting a common cultural form. No towns and few villages were without their football team. Although public interest would wax and wane according to size and success the local football team was as much a part of local life as church or chapel, factory or political party. It could command loyalties as fiercely partisan as any of them. To play for it was an achievement of few but an aspiration of many. Merely watching its matches brought a new kind of solidarity and sociability.

Notes

1 Football League Management Committee Minutes 7 September 1914, *Athletic News* 31 August 1914.
2 Kitchener had made his appeal for 300,000 volunteers at the end of October. Pollard was supported, among others, by Robert Bridges, the Poet Laureate. *The Times* 7, 19 November 1914.
3 *The Times* 19 November 1914.
4 *The Times* 23 November 1914. Colonel Burn M.P. was quoted as saying at Chelsea, where it was estimated that about one third of a crowd of around 15,000 were in khaki,

I want you to understand that I am a sportsman as well as a soldier, I believe in football. I believe in your games being carried on as usual. I have come here to ask if there is any young man who has no encumbrances to join the forces. I don't say come I say 'Come, for God's sake. You are wanted.' I have given my son. He enlisted at the start of the war. He is now dead.

5   *The Times* 24, 26 November 1914. One suggestion was for compulsory service for all bachelors between the ages of 19 and 38. It was also at this time that the idea of a footballer's battalion was taken up although it had been suggested by F.N. Charrington in a letter to the *Morning Post* in August, *Athletic News* 31 August 1914.

6   *The Times* 25 November 1914. A further editorial two days later suggested a regimental football competition based on the county towns to replace the league.

7   The circular letter was dated 30 September 1914. The average Saturday gate for Second Division clubs fell from £306 in 1913–14 to £176. It is interesting that the only two clubs in either division to have improved their average match receipts were Bradford and Arsenal: the former had just been promoted to the First Division and the latter were only in the second season at their new north London ground.

8   Like the one at Tottenham which was opened by Baden Powell. In a letter to the Tottenham directors he wrote, after eulogising the value of football—he was, after all, an Old Carthusian—that war was a man's game 'full of honour and adventure for those with guts in them. The chance may not come again. Come on, my lads, and lend a hand. We can do our football when we have done the war'. *Daily News* 5 October 1914.

9   *The Times* 28, 29 November 1914 Forty players from 11 Football League Clubs, and a total of 4,765 Lancashire football players volunteered. C.E. Sutcliffe and F. Hargreaves (Blackburn, 1928) p. 144.

10   *The Times* 1 December 1914. *Athletic News* 7 December 1914. Horse racing was abandoned from May 1915 but a limited number of days racing was allowed in 1917 and 1918. See W. Vamplew op.cit. pp. 62–8.

11   *Athletic News* 30 November 1914. 738 clubs replied to an F.A. questionnaire that over 8,000 of their players had enlisted but the Colonel-in-Chief of a footballer's battalion was disappointed that only 122 professionals out of a possible 1800 whom he claimed were eligible had come forward in the early months of 1915. *The Times* 2 December, 1914, 30 March 1915.

12   *The Times* 28 November 1914. This was probably less of a sacrifice for *The Times* than most of the other papers. *News of the World* 29 November, 6, 13, 20, 27 December 1914. *Sunday Chronicle* 29 November 1914.

13   *Sheffield Daily Telegraph* 2, 29 March, 26 April 1915.

14   P. Fussell, *The Great War and Modern Memory* (1975) p. 27. Fussell also quotes the example of Captain W.P. Nevill of the 8th East Surreys who organised a platoon competition at the Somme in 1916 with a prize for the first platoon to kick its football up to the German front line.

15   *Sheffield Daily Telegraph* 26 April 1915.

16   *Athletic News* 3 November 1890. The *Birmingham Daily Mail* of 16 February 1893 recognised football's hold over the local population.

No apology need be offered for making the Aston Villa Football Club the subject of a leading article just now. Even if the Home Rule Bill is on everybody's tongue it is not the exclusive subject of discussion. All those who take an interest in football—and in Birmingham they are legion—are as much exercised about the prospects of the Aston Villa as they are about the future of Ireland.

SELECT BIBLIOGRAPHY

PRIMARY SOURCES

1. *Manuscript Sources*

Aston Villa F.C. Directors' Meetings Minutes 1896–1905
    Annual General Meeting Minutes 1896–1915
                Aston Villa F.C.,
                Villa Park, Birmingham.
Birmingham and District Football Association Minutes and Reports 1885–1914
Derby County F.C. Committee Meetings Minutes 1890–1893
    Directors' Meetings Minutes 1898–1902
                Derby County F.C.,
                Baseball Ground, Derby.
Football Association Committee and Council Minutes 1886–1915
                Football Association,
                Lancaster Gate, London.
Football League Management Committee Minutes 1888–1915
                Football League,
                Lytham St. Annes.
Football Players' Union Committee Minutes 1907–1913
                Professional Footballers'
                Association Offices,
                Manchester.
Lancashire Football Association Minutes 1878–1915
                Lancashire F.A., Blackburn.
Shareholders' and Directors' Lists: Returns to the Registrar of Companies
                Public Record Office,
                Companies House.
Sheffield F.C. Members' Lists 1858, 1859, 1867–1881, 1881–1923
    Minutes 1858, 1860, 1864–9, 1881–1950
    and other items in Sheffield Collection, Sheffield City Library.

2. *Printed Sources*

(a) Contemporary Books, Pamphlets and Articles

C.W. Alcock, 'Association Football', *English Illustrated Magazine*, 1890–91
F.G. Aflalo (ed.), *The Cost of Sport* (1899)
H.H. Almond, 'Football as a Moral Agent', *The Nineteenth Century*, vol. 34, December 1893
An Old Player, 'Football: The Game and the Business', *The World's Work*, vol. 1, December 1902
Anon, 'Are we an Athletic People?', *New Review*, vol. 16, 1897
Anon, *Famous Football Clubs* (1898–9)

Anon, *Football. Described by Giants of the Game* (1904)

Anon, *How to Play Football* (Manchester 1891)

Anon, 'Some Tendencies of Modern Sport', *Quarterly Review*, vol. 199, 1904

Anon, 'Sport and Decadence', *Quarterly Review*, vol. 211, 1909

J.B. Atkins (ed.), *National Physical Training: An Open Debate* (1904)

G.A. Auden (ed.), *Handbook for Birmingham* (1913)

Sir R. Baden-Powell, *Scouting for Boys* (1908)

M.G. Barnett, *Young Delinquents* (1913)

J. Baron, *Blackburn Rovers: The Blackburn Weekly Telegraph's Handy History* (Blackburn, 1906)

Beaton's Football Book (1865)

Blackburn Rovers, *Bazaar Handbook* (Blackburn, 1895)

F. Boase, *Modern English Biography*, 6 vols. (1965 reprint of 1897 edn)

Bristol and District Football League, *Handbook* (Bristol 1892)

H.R. Brown (ed.), *Football Who's Who* (1907)

J. Cameron, *Association Football* (1909)

J.A.H. Catton, *The Real Football* (1900)

C. Cookson (ed.), *Essays on Secondary Education* (Oxford, 1898)

B.O. Corbett, *Annals of the Corinthians* (1906)

B.O. Corbett *et al.*, *Football* (1907)

'Creston', 'Football', *Fortnightly Review*, N.S. vol. 55, 1894

W.H. Davenport, *Secret of Success* (1879)

W.T. Dixon, *History of Turton Football Club and Carnival Sports Handbook* (Turton, 1909)

W.J. Duckworth, *The Incomparable Football Forecasting System* (1914)

C. Edwardes, 'The New Football Mania', *The Nineteenth Century*, vol. 32, 1892.

E. Ensor, 'The Football Madness', *Contemporary Review*, vol. 74, 1898

Famous Football Clubs, (Nottingham 1898)

J.R. Fleming, 'Rugby Football', *Badminton Magazine of Sports and Pastimes* vol. III, 1896

A. Freeman, *Boy Life and Labour* (1914)

Rev. C.F. Garbett (ed.), *The Work of a Great Parish* (1915)

A. Gibson and W. Pickford, *Association Football and the Men Who Made It*, 4 vols. (1906)

J. Goodall, *Association Football* (1898)

W.G. Grace, *'W.G'.: Cricket Reminiscences and Personal Recollections* (1899)

J.W. Horsley, *How Criminals Are Made and Prevented* (1913)

E.B. Iwan-Muller, 'The Cult of the Unfit', *Fortnightly Review*, vol. 86, August 1909

N.L. Jackson, *Association Football* (1900)

N.L. Jackson (ed.), *The Association Football Handbook*, (1894-5)

J.H. Jones, *Association Football*, (1904)

T. Keates, *History of the Everton Football Club 1878-9—1928-9* (Liverpool 1929)

R. Kipling, *The Five Nations*, (1903)

W.J. Lias, 'The future of Rugby Football', *Badminton Magazine of Sports and Pastimes*, vol. 5, 1897

B. Meakin, *Model Factories and Villages* (1905)

R. Mellors, *In and About Nottinghamshire* (1908)

E. Needham, *Association Football* (1900)

P. Newman, *The Boy's Club in theory and practice* (1900)
A. Paterson, *Across the Bridges* (1911)
Rev. H.S. Pelham, *The Training of a Working Boy* (1914)
A.W. Pullin ('Old Ebor'), *Talks with old English Cricketers* (1900)
S.J. Reid, *Sir Richard Tangye* (1908)
A.J. Robertson, 'Football Betting' *Transactions* of the Liverpool Economic and Statistical Society, 1906–7
B.S. Rowntree (ed.), *Betting and Gambling : A National Evil* (1905)
C.E.B. Russell, *Lads' Clubs: Their History, Organisation and Management* (1908, 1932 edn)
C.E.B. Russell, *Manchester Boys: Sketches of Manchester Lads at Work and Play* (1913 edn)
A. Shadwell, *Industrial Efficiency*, 2 vols. (1906)
M. Shearman, *Athletics and Football* (1887)
G.F. Shee, 'The Deterioration In the National Physique', *The Nineteenth Century*, vol. LIII, May 1903
G.R. Sims, *Living London* (1901)
F.E. Smith, 'The Vogue of Games: Is it worth it?', *The New Fry's Magazine*, vol. I no. 1, April 1911
G.R. Stead, *The Reds* (1899)
Joseph Strutt, *The Sports and Pastimes of the People of England* (1903 edn)
R.J. Sturdee, 'The Ethics of Football', *Westminster Review*, vol. 159, 1903
'Tityrus', *The Rise of the Leaguers from 1863–1897: A History of the Football League* (Manchester, 1897)
E.J. Urwick (ed.), *Studies of Boy Life in Our Cities* (1904)
B. Villiers, *The Socialist Movement in England* (1908)
A. Williams, *Life in a Railway Factory* (1915)

(b)   Parliamentary Papers

Education Department Special Report on 'The Organisation of Games out of School for the Children attending Public Elementary Schools in the large industrial centres as voluntarily undertaken by the Teachers' PP 1898 XXIV
Inter-Departmental Committee on Physical Deterioration PP 1904 XXXII
Royal Commission on the Liquor Licensing Laws PP 1898 XXXVI
Royal Commission on Public Schools and Colleges PP 1864 XX

(c)   Newspapers and Periodicals

All the Year Round
Amateur Football
Amateur Football Association Annual, 1907–8
Association Football Handbook
Athletic News
Athletic News Football Annual, 1890–1914
Athletic Star
Badminton Magazine of Sports and Pastimes, 1895–1914
Baily's Monthly Magazine of Sports and Pastimes, 1860–88
Barnsley Independent
Bell's Life in London and Sporting Chronicle

Birmingham Daily Gazette
Birmingham Daily Mail
Birmingham Daily Post
Birmingham Daily Times
Blackburn Standard
Blackburn Standard and Weekly Express
Blackburn Times
Bolton Evening News
Boy's Own Book, 1859
Bradford Daily Telegraph
Clarion
Crewe Chronicle
Cricket
Cricket and Football Times
Daily Mail
Daily News
Dart (Birmingham)
Darwen News
Derby Daily Telegraph
Derby Express
Fabian News
The Field
Film
Football (London)
Football (Wolverhampton)
Football Annual, 1873–99
Football Argus (Bradford)
Football Chat (London)
Football Field (Bolton)
Football Players' Magazine
Football World (Sheffield)
C.B. Fry's Magazine
Gamages Football Annual, 1909–10 1913–14
Glasgow Herald
Half-time (Leicester)
Justice
Kinematograph and Lantern Weekly
Labour Leader
Lancashire Evening Express
The Lantern (St Helens)
Manchester Despatch
Manchester Guardian
Midland Athlete
Monthly Review
National Football Calendar, 1881
Newcastle Daily Chronicle
News of the World
North Eastern Daily Gazette
Nottingham Daily Guardian
Pall Mall Gazette
Pastime

Preston Herald
Referee
St James's Gazette
Saturday Night (Birmingham)
Sheffield Daily Telegraph
Sheffield Independent
Sport and Play
Sporting Chronicle
Sporting Luck
Sporting Mirror
The Sportsman
Sunday Chronicle
Sunderland Daily Herald
Sunderland Football Echo
Sunderland Herald
The Times
Weekly Despatch
Weekly Football Star
West Bromwich Free Press
Willesden Call
Windsor Magazine
Wolverhampton Evening Star
Wolverhampton Express and Star
Woolwich Gazette and Plumstead Times

(d)   Local Directories

E.R. Kelly (ed.), *Post Office Directory of Sheffield with the Neighbouring Towns and Villages* (1865)
Mellville & Co., *Commercial Directory of Sheffield, Rotherham and the Neighbourhood* (1859)
Ryder's Annual, *The Wednesbury Red Book and Directory* (1910)
F. White & Co., *General and Commercial Directory and Topography of the Borough of Sheffield and Official Guide* (1871–2)
W. White, *Directory of the Boroughs of Sheffield, Doncaster and Chesterfield* (1868)
W. White, *General Directory and Topography of the Borough of Sheffield and all the Towns, Townships, Parishes and Villages within the distance of more than twelve miles round Sheffield* (1864)
W.M. White, *General Directory of the Town, Borough and Parish of Sheffield* (1860)

SECONDARY SOURCES

(a)   Books

A. Appleton, *Hotbed of Soccer* (1960)
G.G. Armstrong, *Memories* (1944)
P.C. Bailey, *Leisure and Class in Victorian England: rational recreation and the contest for control 1830–1885* (1978)
P. Banburn, *Shipbuilders of the Thames and Medway* (1971)

T. Barclay, *Memories and Medleys: The Autobiography of a Bottle-Washer* (Leicester, 1934)

M.A. Bienefeld, *Working Hours in British Industry* (1972)

A.H. Birch (ed.), *Small Town Politics* (1959)

R. Bowen, *Cricket: A History* (1970)

A.K. Boyd, *The History of Radley College 1847–1947* (Oxford, 1948)

A. Briggs, 'Mass Entertainment: The Origin of a Modern Industry', 29th Joseph Fisher Lecture in Commerce, University of Adelaide (1960)

A. Briggs, *Victorian Cities* (1968 edn)

J.A.H. Catton, *Wickets and Goals* (1926)

F.N.J. Creek, *A History of the Corinthian Football Club* (1933)

H. Cunningham, *The Volunteer Force* (1975)

B. Dobbs, *Edwardians at Play: Sport 1890–1914* (1973)

E. Dunning (ed.), *The Sociology of Sport: A Selection of Readings* (1971)

H.J. Dyos and M. Wolff (eds), *The Victorian City, Images and Reality* 2 vols. (1973)

C. L'Estrange Ewen, *Lotteries and Sweepstakes* (1932)

A.H. Fabian and G. Green (eds), *Association Football*, 4 vols. (1960)

M.I. Finley and H.W. Pleket, *The Olympic Games: The First Thousand Years* (1976)

C. Francis, *History of the Blackburn Rovers Football Club 1875–1925* (Blackburn, 1925)

P. Fussell, *The Great War and Modern Memory* (1975)

Sir H. Gordon, *Background of Cricket* (1939)

E. Grayson, *Corinthians and Cricketers* (1955)

G. Green, *History of the Football Association* (1953)

G. Green, *The Official History of the F.A. Cup* (1949)

A. Guttmann, *From Ritual to Record* (New York, 1978)

J. Halliday and P. Fuller (eds), *The Psychology of Gambling* (1974)

B. Harrison, *Drink and the Victorians* (1971)

J. Hilton (ed.), *Why I go in for the Pools* (1936)

S.G. Hobson, *Pilgrim to the Left* (1938)

R. Hoggart, *The Uses of Literacy* (1957)

J.R. de S. Honey, *Tom Brown's Universe* (1977)

J. Huizinga, *Homo Ludens* (1970 ed.)

E.H. Hunt, *Regional Wage Variations in Britain 1850–1914* (1973)

N.L. Jackson, *Sporting Days and Sporting Ways* (1932)

F. Johnston (ed.), *The Football Encyclopaedia* (1934)

B. Joy, *Forward Arsenal!* (1952)

R. Kirchner, *Fair Play: The Games of Merrie England* (1928)

A.J. Lee, *The Origins of the Popular Press 1855–1914* (1976)

J. Lowerson and J. Myerscough, *Time to Spare in Victorian England* (Brighton, 1971 and Hassocks, 1977)

E.C. Mack, *Public Schools and British Opinion 1760–1860* (1938)

E.C. Mack and W.H.G. Armytage, *The Life of Thomas Hughes* (1952)

S.P.B. Mais, *All the Days of My Life* (1937)

I. Maisky, *Journey Into the Past* (1962)

R. W. Malcolmson, *Popular Recreations in English Society 1700–1850* (Cambridge, 1973)

M. Marples, *History of Football* (1954)

M.R. Marrus (ed.), *The Emergence of Leisure* (New York, 1974)

P.C. McIntosh, *Physical Education in England Since 1800* (1968 edn)

P.C. McIntosh, *Sport in Society* (1968)

H.E. Meller, *Leisure and the Changing City 1870–1914* (1976)

P. Morris, *Aston Villa: The History of a great football club, 1874–1960* (1960)

P. Morris, *West Bromwich Albion, Soccer in the Black Country, 1879–1965* (1965)

D. Newsome, *Godliness and Good Learning* (1961)

J. Osborne (ed.), *Saltley College Centenary 1850–1950* (1950)

S. Parker, *The Sociology of Leisure* (1976)

W. Pickford, *A Few Recollections of Sport* (n.d.)

S. Pierson, *Marxism and the Origins of British Socialism* (Ithaca, 1973)

S. Rogerson, *Wilfred Rhodes* (1960)

G. Routh, *Occupations and Pay in Great Britain 1906–1960* (Cambridge, 1965)

B.S. Rowntree and G.R. Lavers, *English Life and Leisure: A Social Study*, (1951)

B. Sachs, *J. Ramsay MacDonald* (Albuquerque, 1952)

H.J. Savage, *Games and Sports in British Schools and Universities* (New York, 1927)

G.R. Searle, *The Quest for National Efficiency* (1971)

I. Sharpe, *40 Years in Football* (1952)

R.A. Sparling, *The Romance of The Wednesday* (Sheffield, 1976)

F.H. Spencer, *An Inspector's Testament* (1938)

G. Stedman Jones, *Outcast London* (Oxford, 1971)

C.E. Sutcliffe, J.A. Brierley and F. Howarth, *The Story of the Football League 1888–1938* (Preston, 1938)

C.E. Sutcliffe and F. Hargreaves, *History of the Lancashire Football Association 1878–1928* (Blackburn, 1928)

P. Thompson, *The Edwardians: The Remaking of British Society* (1975)

W. Vamplew, *The Turf: A Social and Economic History of Horse Racing* (1976)

C.A. Vince, *History of the Corporation of Birmingham* 4 vols. (1923)

D.Q. Voigt, *American Baseball: From Gentleman's Sport to the Commissioner System* (Norman, 1966)

Sir F. Wall, *Fifty Years of Football* (1935)

J. Walvin, *The People's Game* (1975)

S. Yeo, *Religion and Voluntary Organisations in Crisis* (1976)

P.M. Young, *A History of British Football* (1968)

P.M. Young, *Bolton Wanderers* (1961)

P.M. Young, *Football in Sheffield* (1962)

P.M. Young, *Football on Merseyside* (1963)

P.M. Young, *Manchester United* (1960)

(b)   Articles

T.W. Bamford, 'Public Schools and Social Class 1801–1850', *British Journal of Sociology*, XII no. 3, September 1961

R.W. Coles, 'Football as a Surrogate Religion?' in M. Hill (ed.), *A Sociological Yearbook of Religion in Britain*, no. 6 (1975)

A.E. Dingle, 'Drink and Working-Class Living Standards in Britain 1870–1914', *Economic History Review*, vol. XXV no. 4, November 1972

E. Dunning, 'Industrialisation and the Incipient Modernisation of Football', *Stadion*, vol. I no. 1, 1975

E. Dunning, 'The Development of Modern Football' in E. Dunning (ed.), *The Sociology of Sport : A Selection of Readings* (1971)

S. Edgell and D. Jary, 'Football: a Sociological eulogy' in M. Smith, S. Parker and C. Smith (eds), *Leisure and Society in Britain* (1973)

J.S. Hurt, 'Drill, discipline and the elementary school ethos' in P. McCann (ed.), *Popular Education and Socialization in the Nineteenth Century* (1977)

J.H.S. Kent, 'The Role of Religion in the Cultural Structure of the late Victorian City' Royal Historical Society *Transactions*, 5th series, 23 (1973)

C.P. Korr, 'West Ham United Football Club and the Beginnings of Professional Football in East London, 1895–1914', *Journal of Contemporary History*, vol. 13 no. 2, April 1978

C. Lasch, 'The Corruption of Sports', *New York Review of Books* 28 April 1977

W.F. Mandle, 'Games People Played: Cricket and Football in England and Victoria in the late nineteenth century', *Historical Studies* (Melbourne) vol. 15 no. 60, April 1973

W.F. Mandle, 'The Professional Cricketer in England in the nineteenth century', *Labour History* 23, November 1972

J. Myerscough, 'The recent history of the use of leisure time' in Ian Appleton (ed.), *Leisure Research and Policy* (1974)

D.A. Reid, 'The Decline of Saint Monday 1766–1876' *Past and Present*, 71, May 1976

R.M. Ruck, 'R.E. football in the Early Seventies' in *Royal Engineers Journal*, N.S. vol. 42, 1928

G. Stedman Jones, 'Working-Class Culture and Working-Class Politics in London 1870–1900: Notes on the remaking of a working-class' in *Journal of Social History*, vol. 7 no. 4, Summer 1974

Norman Vance, 'The Ideal of Manliness' in B. Simon and I. Bradley (eds), *The Victorian Public School* (1975)

Eugen Weber, 'Pierre de Coubertin and the introduction of organised sport in France' in *Journal of Contemporary History*, vol. 5 no. 2, 1970

(c)   Theses

V.S. Berridge, 'Popular Journalism and Working-Class Attitudes 1854–1886: A Study of *Reynold's Newspaper, Lloyds' Weekly Newspaper* and the *Weekly Times*', 2 vols, University of London Ph.D. 1976

M.D. Blanch, 'Nation, Empire and the Birmingham Working Class 1894–1914', University of Birmingham Ph.D. 1975

R. Day, 'The Motivation of Some Football Club Directors: An Aspect of the Social History of Association Football 1890–1914', University of Warwick M.A. 1976

M.H. Elsworth, 'The Provision for Physical Recreation in Bolton in the Nineteenth Century', Dissertation, Diploma in Advanced Study in Education, University of Manchester 1971–72.

H.R. Harrington, 'Muscular Christianity: the study of the Development of a Victorian Idea', University of Stanford Ph.D. 1971

R.J. Holt, 'Aspects of the Social History of Sports in France 1870–1914', University of Oxford D.Phil 1977

P. Joyce, 'Popular Toryism in Lancashire 1860–1890', University of Oxford D.Phil 1975

R.W. Malcolmson, 'Popular Recreations in English Society 1700–1850', University of Warwick Ph.D. 1970

A. Metcalfe, 'Working Class 'Free-Time': Its Development and Limitation', University of Wisconsin M.A. 1968

R. Miller, 'Gambling and the British Working Class 1870–1914', University of Edinburgh M.A. 1974

I. Moir, 'Association Football: The Evolution of the Laws of the Game', University of Birmingham M.A. 1972

D.D. Molyneux, 'The Development of Physical Recreation in the Birmingham District from 1871–1892, University of Birmingham M.A. 1957

R. Rees, 'The Development of Physical Recreation in Liverpool During the Nineteenth Century', University of Liverpool M.A. 1968

K.G. Sheard, 'Rugby Football: A Study in Developmental Sociology', University of Leicester M.Phil. 1972

M. Tozer, 'The Development and Role of Physical Education at Uppingham School 1850–1914', University of Leicester M.Ed. 1974

D.G. Wilkinson, 'Association Football in Brighton before 1920', University of Sussex M.A. 1971

INDEX